SCHOOL ADMINISTRATOR'S ENCYCLOPEDIA

Also by the Authors

Educator's Lifetime Library of Stories, Quotes, Anecdotes, Wit and Humor

Encyclopedia of School Letters

Handbook of Discovery Techniques in Elementary School Teaching

One-Hundred-One (101) Pupil/Parent/Teacher Situations and How to Handle Them

The New Psychology of Classroom Discipline and Control

Personalized Behavioral Modification: Practical Techniques for Elementary Educators

SCHOOL ADMINISTRATOR'S ENCYCLOPEDIA

P. Susan Mamchak
and
Steven R. Mamchak

PARKER PUBLISHING COMPANY, INC.
West Nyack, New York

©1982, *by*

PARKER PUBLISHING COMPANY, INC.
West Nyack, N.Y.

Library of Congress Cataloging in Publication Data

Mamchak, P. Susan,
  School administrator's encyclopedia.

  Bibliography: p.
  1. School management and organization—United
States—Dictionaries   I. Mamchak, Steven R.
II. Title.
LB2801.2.A2M35   371.2'00973   81-22492
ISBN 0-13-792390-2   AACR2

Printed in the United States of America

ABOUT THE AUTHORS

P. Susan Mamchak has been involved in all aspects of education from substitute teacher to school disciplinarian. She is currently engaged in educational research and serving as director of S&S Research Associates. She has done extensive public speaking in education and has conducted numerous workshops for educators. Steven R. Mamchak is an educator with 20 years experience in the field. In that time, he has done everything from working with remedial and "disaffected" students to extensive public relations work for the school, to hosting a radio program about the educational scene. The Mamchaks have devoted their lives to education. They are the authors of six popular books on education, including the best-selling *Encyclopedia of School Letters*. *Authors' address:* S&S Research Associates, 28 Riverview Dr., Tinton Falls, New Jersey 07724.

HOW THIS BOOK WILL AID
THE SCHOOL ADMINISTRATOR

Our business is knowledge. As educators and educational leaders, we are intimately involved with that subject, taking on our shoulders the responsibility for disseminating information to students and faculty; for maintaining the quality of instruction within our schools; and for dealing with the thousands of everyday details involved in efficiently running a modern school, each requiring highly specialized and precise knowledge.

We are all aware of how much there is to do and to know. When it comes to education, it sometimes seems as if there are not enough hours in the day to handle the exacting pressures of school administration, let alone to keep abreast of constantly changing laws, regulations, new programs, and new philosophies.

Ours is a profession where knowledge proliferates at an astronomical rate. Each day brings more ideas, more demands upon our abilities as educators, and more for us to know. It is little wonder, therefore, that we often feel inundated by the sheer volume of the knowledge and the tasks before us.

Yet, as we all know, we must be familiar with the intricacies of our profession and keep up with the latest developments if we are to remain in the forefront of education as an active and involved educational leader, which is, after all, our number one priority.

Wouldn't it be wonderful, therefore, if there were somewhere we could go to find the exact knowledge we required on a myriad of educational topics affecting our daily lives; a single source, rather than a confusing array of references from which we could gain specific insights that would help us to effectively deal with those problems and situations arising in our daily educational activities and that affect us all; a single source that would contain the most accurate, incisive and up-to-date definitions, observations, laws, references, and commentary on educational topics that are a vital part of every administrator's existence.

It was precisely with this idea in mind that *School Administrator's Encyclopedia* was conceived and compiled. Within the pages of this book, you will find close to *500 topics* directly related to all phases of education in general and your position in particular. From ABILITY GROUPING to ZONING BOARD, these topics are as real and vital as today's classrooms, and under each heading you will find an accurate, contemporary definition whenever necessary in order to assure complete understanding, followed by an encyclopedic-type entry that investigates the topic, provides invaluable and accurate information, and is geared to help you in dealing effectively with that topic—knowledge that has helped others as it will help you.

Would you be interested in knowing the legalities of formulating a dress code? Do you need to know more about federal or state aid? Are you looking for insights into reducing vandalism or violence in your school? Could you or someone on your staff profit from knowing the latest ideas and practices on teacher observation, parental liability, the handling of personnel records, or psychological testing? You'll find all of these topics, plus many, many more fully covered within the following pages.

Here you will find those topics that directly relate to your position as an administrator; topics such as BOARD OF EDUCATION, CENTRAL STAFF, COMMISSIONER OF EDUCATION, PRINCIPAL, SUPERINTENDENT OF SCHOOLS, VICE-PRINCIPAL, and more.

You will find listings that give direct insight into the learning situations that occur in your school. Here, among others, you will find COMPETENCY-BASED PROGRAMS, INDIVIDUALIZATION, INTERDISCIPLINARY APPROACHES, REMEDIAL INSTRUCTION, and VOCATIONAL PROGRAMS.

There are headings of vital importance to the administrator in today's legalistic society; topics that will help you function within the current statutes of educational and civil law. Just a few of the listings are ACCEPTANCE OF CONTRACTS, CIVIL RIGHTS, CONTRIBUTORY NEGLIGENCE, FUNDAMENTAL INTEREST THEORY, SAFE PLACE STATUTES, SUSPENSION, and TENURE.

You will find those topics which, while definitely a part of the educational scene, lie outside of the academic aspect of school life. BACK-TO-SCHOOL NIGHT, DANCE, EXTRACURRICULAR ACTIVITIES, LEASE OF SCHOOL PROPERTY, and TRIPS are just a few.

You will be provided invaluable insights into the administrator's dealings with the community and general public. Among the many topics listed are AMERICAN EDUCATION WEEK, GRADUATION, HONOR ROLL, NEWSLETTER, P.T.A., and VOLUNTEERS.

You'll discover a plethora of headings that deal with effectively processing and educating our students. Look for ABSENTEEISM, CHILD ABUSE, GIFTED STUDENTS, LEARNING DISABILITIES, MAINSTREAMING, and UNDERACHIEVERS, to name just a few.

You'll gain new insights into the administrator's part in the disbursement of educational funds. BANK ACCOUNTS, BIDS, SCHOOL FUNDS, FEDERAL AID, and *PER DIEM* are only some of the topics listed.

You'll examine topics that have to do with the functioning of the physical plant of the school. Here you will find AIDES, CALENDAR, CHAIRPERSONS, EARLY CHILDHOOD PROGRAMS, FIRE DRILL, OPEN CLASSROOMS, SUBSTITUTE TEACHER, and TRANSPORTATION, among others.

You'll find topics dealing with those necessities that allow a school to function as an ordered environment. Among the myriad of listed topics you will find DRESS CODES, IN-SCHOOL SUSPENSION, HOMEWORK, OPENING PROCEDURES, SAFETY, SMOKING, and TARDINESS.

You will even find listings that involve the administrator's relationship to the faculty and the evaluation of the teaching staff. Just a few are ACCOUNTABILITY, DISMISSAL PROCEDURES (SCHOOL), DUE PROCESS, LEAVE OF ABSENCE, MORAL TURPITUDE, and OBSERVATION.

Moreover, following each entry you will find a section labeled *See Also*. Here you will find, already cross-referenced for you, those other topics in the book that relate or have application to the entry you just finished. Add to this two appendices dividing the topics in this book into educational subject areas for quick reference and supplying a complete bibliography for further study, and you have that single source of information to aid you in your administrative duties each and every day.

Thousands of hours of exhaustive research and exacting work went into the preparation of *School Administrator's Encyclopedia*. It is a book you will want to keep on your desk, ready for immediate use. Thoroughly researched and compiled with the school administrator in mind, this book offers a plethora of facts, references, insights, and innovative observations on the widest range of educational topics that are the sum and substance of our professional lives. It is a book *you will use,* today, tomorrow and throughout the entire school year.

P. Susan Mamchak

Steven R. Mamchak

ACKNOWLEDGEMENTS

It is with deep gratitude that we acknowledge the following individuals who so generously gave of their precious time, considerable talents and professional expertise to aid us in our research, provide invaluable information or review the materials in this book.

Mr. Vern Achtermann, *National Assessment of Educational Progress*
Mr. Roger Alcore, *Coordinator of Career Education*
Mr. Robert C. Andringa, *Executive Director, Education Commission of the States*
Mr. Clair Bailey, *Guidance Counselor*
Dr. Frederick W. Ball, *Assistant Superintendent of Schools*
Dr. E. Allan Bartholomew, *Assistant Superintendent of Schools*
Dr. Tina Bernstein, *State Department of Education*
Ms. Claudia Bepko, *School Social Worker*
Mr. Jack Bordolino, *State Director of UniServ*
Mr. Larry Boresen, *Career Education Coordinator*
Mrs. Kathleen H. Brazas, *Teacher of English*
Mr. Henry Bretzfield, *Chief, Publications Branch Office of Public Affairs, U.S. Department of Education*
Mr. Morey Burger, *Supervising Librarian*
Mrs. Wanda Burke, *Administration Secretary*
Mr. Walter Curry, *Teacher of Industrial Arts*
Mrs. Barbara Dean, *Reading Specialist*
Ms. Kay Deturo, *Credit Union Manager*
Ms. Lenore F. Farrah, *County Educational Services*
Mr. William Freeman, *Principal Librarian, Municipal Government Information Center*
Mrs. Helen Frisco, *Administration Secretary*
Mr. Lawrence M. Fuchs, Esq., *Attorney at Law*
Mrs. Roberta H. Gauvreau, *Teacher of Art*
Mr. Frederick Gernsbeck, *Vice-Principal*
Mrs. Marcia Giger, *Teacher of English*
Dr. William Gillcrist, *Assistant Superintendent of Schools*
Mrs. Barbara Goldstein, *Director of Community Services*
Mr. Charles Goodhart, *Teacher Association President*

Mrs. John Hall, *Vice-Principal*

Ms. Allyn Heck, *Commissioner of Registration and Superintendent of Elections*

Dr. Barbara Holstein, *School Psychologist*

Mr. George Jarrach, *Township Coordinator of Federal and State Programs*

Mrs. Beverley Kelly, *Supervisor of Instruction*

Mrs. Ann Kirshner, *Curriculum Coordinator*

Miss Rosemary Knawa, *Department Chairperson*

Mr. Donald Kurz, *Guidance Counselor*

Mrs. Lois M. LaSalle, *Teacher of Special Education*

Mrs. Betty Lazur, *School Secretary*

Mrs. Helen Lee, *Division of Youth and Family Services*

Detective Salvatore Maccioli, *Police Juvenile Officer*

Mr. William Mack, *Principal Probation Officer, Juvenile Court*

Mr. Wayne H. Martin, *Director of Public Information, Education Commission of the States*

Mr. Bud Messner, *N.J.E.A. UniServ Officer*

Mrs. Evelyn Nachtman, *Supervisor of Instruction*

Mr. John Najar, *Principal*

Mr. Fred Oser, *Head of Research and Principal Librarian*

Mr. John Pietrowicz, *UniServ Coordinator in Charge of Field Services*

Mrs. Mickey Roehrig, *Administration Secretary*

Mrs. Virginia Schaller, *Administration Secretary*

Dr. Bernhard W. Schneider, *Superintendent of Schools*

Dr. Marshall Silver, M.D., *Doctor of Medicine*

Mr. Louis Sodano, *Township Commissioner*

Mrs. Victoria Taylor, *Principal*

Mrs. Edith Tuffiash, R.N., *School Nurse*

Dr. Leonard B. Williams, *Professor of Education, Coordinator of Teacher Training*

Mrs. Joan Wyman, *Administration Secretary*

Mrs. Rosemary Zimmerman, *Document Librarian*

TABLE OF CONTENTS

P

Q

R

S

SCHOOL ADMINISTRATOR'S ENCYCLOPEDIA

A

ABILITY GROUPING

Ability grouping refers to the grouping of students, either on a school-wide basis or within an individual class, on the basis of some perceived and/or measured ability.

Obviously, there must be some established criteria for the placement of students within groups. Traditionally, these criteria have included the student's performance on standardized tests, the student's performance on teacher-made tests, and teacher judgment of the student's ability. Of these three, teacher judgment has traditionally carried the most weight, since it is assumed that the teacher is in the best position to evaluate the overall performance of the student.

When engaged in ability grouping, it is best to take into account both the mental ability of the student and his or her evidence of scholastic achievement. If standardized ability tests are used, one must take into account that these tests are an indication of the various factors being tested and do not necessarily reflect innate intelligence.

Moreover, in ability grouping one may only group for the single factor one is seeking. For instance, a child in an advanced group in math may, of necessity, need placement in a medium- or low-ability group in language arts. High ability in one subject area should not be misinterpreted to mean a similar high ability in all subjects.

See Also: ABILITY LEVELS: ACHIEVEMENT; APTITUDE; REMEDIAL INSTRUCTION.

ABILITY LEVELS

Ability levels is a general term used to describe various stages of ability in learning, such as beginning, intermediate, advanced, etc.

Many schools have traditionally used the intellectual capacity of the learner as a basis for instruction

21

within a class or group. A difficulty arises, however, when we enter the field of how these ability levels are determined. For many years, standardized intelligence tests were used to determine ability levels, and the results used for ability grouping. Within the past several years, however, there have been a number of legal decisions *(Hobson v. Hansen, 408 F.2d 175, 1969; Diana v. State Board of Education, Civil #C-70 37 RFR, California, 1970; Moses v. Washington Parish School Board, 456 F.2d 1285, 1972)* which indicate that IQ tests cannot be the single factor used in determining ability levels for ability grouping. Moreover, if standardized intelligence tests are used, special care should be taken that they are not discriminatory to children who, for example, speak a language other than English as their primary tongue. Indeed, the argument has been proposed that these intelligence tests often fail to measure the ability of children who come from various racial, cultural or even disadvantaged backgrounds, since most of the tests contain questions which represent the standards and values of white, middle-class society.

Consequently, common sense must prevail in determining the ability levels of students, and all factors which contribute to the child's level of ability must be weighed and considered.

See Also: ABILITY GROUPING; ACHIEVEMENT; APTITUDE; CULTURE; DISCRIMINATION; INTELLIGENCE TESTING; LEARNING DISABILITIES; UNDERACHIEVERS.

ABSENCE

Absence, as applied to education, means the failure of a pupil or an educator to be present in school or class during the time when the school or class is normally in session.

In setting policy on absence, it behooves the educator to strictly define the term. For example, if a student is present for the last ten minutes of a class only, is he or she to be marked present or absent for that class? If a student is absent at the beginning of the school day but comes to school later in the day, at what point does the student's tardiness become an absence? The answers to such questions should be set forth plainly in the school absence policy.

There are many types of student absence: *legal absence* is a legitimate absence under existing laws of city, state or federal codes (e.g., legal holidays). *Illegal absence* falls into two categories: (A) *illegal detention,* in which the parents willfully participate in the child's absence, and (B) *truancy,* in which the parents do not willfully participate in the child's absence. *Excused absence* is a legitimate absence under the rules of the school or system. *Unexcused absence* occurs when a student is absent without an excuse that is acceptable, either under the school rules or the legal codes. *Aggregate absence* is the total absence in proportion to the total time of the session, either for an individual or on a district-wide basis. (e.g., After how many absences must a student be required to repeat a course?)

Likewise, there are many types of teacher absences: *personal illness,* sometimes called *sick days,* are those days (usually 10 per school year, cumulative to 90 or above at the discretion of the local school board) allocated to a teacher for personal illness. Usually, a doctor's certificate is required if the absence extends beyond three consecutive school days. After a teacher's personal illness days have been used, a deduction from salary is usually imposed for each further absence at a rate established by the local board. *Illness or death in the family* is a cause for absence and may be charged against personal illness days. Usually, three days are allotted for this excused absence. "Family" has been defined as mother, father, sister, brother, husband, wife, son, daughter, mother-in-law, father-in-law, maternal and paternal grandparents, and any others living within the immediate household. *Personal days,* usually three per school year, are those days allotted for a teacher to be absent for personal reasons such as conducting personal business, religious observances, etc. A teacher may or may not be required to disclose the reason for a personal day and personal days may or may not be cumulative, at the discretion of the local school board. *Professional days* are those days granted by the local school board for a teacher to be absent

in order to engage in some professional activity that takes place during normal school hours (e.g., workshop, professional association meeting, etc.). These absences are not charged either to the teacher's sick days or personal days. *Aggregate absence* is the total absence in proportion to the total time of session, either individually or district-wide. The aggregate absence of a teacher may be used as the basis for disciplinary action.

See Also: ABSENTEEISM; ATTENDANCE; COMPULSORY EDUCATION; CUTTING; DISMISSAL OF PERSONNEL; LEAVE OF ABSENCE; MONTHLY REPORTS; TRUANCY; YEAR-END REPORT.

ABSENTEEISM

Absenteeism is the continued absence or repeated absences, over a period of time, by an individual or group of individuals.

Since federal and state aid is dependent upon the numbers of students physically present in the school on a day-to-day basis, absenteeism among students can present a financial as well as an academic difficulty. A high degree of absenteeism on the part of an individual, whether student or teacher, can be considered grounds for administrative action. A student continually absent without cause, for instance, can be held accountable and may face disciplinary action, either within school or even before juvenile authorities. The continued absenteeism on the part of a staff member can constitute grounds for punitive action, possibly including dismissal.

A high degree of absenteeism on the part of an individual or group of individuals is generally thought to be reflective of a problem or difficulty which inspires the action. The causes may be many and varied, from the feeling of a lack of a relevant curriculum and poor institutional practices, to economic hardship within a family; from peer pressure to a form of political action or protest. Whatever the cause, it becomes the responsibility of the school and its administration to deal with it.

In working for solutions to an absenteeism problem, remember that one must first look for the underlying causes of the absenteeism and then work toward alleviating, or at least lessening, the impact of those causes. Quite often this becomes a team effort, requiring the interaction of many branches of the school structure.

See Also: ABSENCE; ASP; ATTENDANCE: CHILD STUDY TEAM; COMPULSORY EDUCATION; FAMILY SERVICES; JUVENILE DELIQUENCY; TRUANCY.

ACADEMICALLY TALENTED

Academically talented is a term used to describe either a student or a group of students who, through observed and/or tested ability, have the capacity to benefit from enriched academic experiences.

The term academically talented is generally applied to children of above-average learning ability, but whose potential is less than that of "gifted" children. As with ability grouping and ability levels, a difficulty often arises when we begin to determine who shall classify as "academically talented." Quite often, there may be outside pressures from the home to have a child so classified, but it falls within the province of the school to make that determination. Observed ability, as gleaned from previous academic records, observed behavior and teacher recommendation seems the most solid basis, and if tests are used, the school must take particular care to see that these tests do not discriminate against the students, as we detailed earlier under ABILITY LEVELS.

In setting up a program for academically talented children, it should be remembered that the words "talented" and "gifted" are not interchangeable. "Talented" denotes high motivation, usually evidenced by high grades and/or high to medium ability, and the very fact that a child evidences such qualities does not mean that a subject naturally "comes easy" to him or her. Academically talented children may not have the intuitive grasp of a subject as manifested by gifted children, but they perform well.

See Also: ABILITY GROUPING; ABILITY LEVELS; ACCELERATION; ENRICHMENT; GIFTED STUDENTS.

ACADEMIC FREEDOM

Academic freedom is a philosophy that teachers have the right to teach and students have the right to learn without being impeded, or experiencing restriction or censorship of what is being taught, and that both teachers and students have the right to exercise free thought without arbitrary restraint.

The principle of academic freedom may also be extended to include an educator's right to advocate his or her personal viewpoint regarding the practices and policies of the school or school district. Further, proponents of academic freedom argue that a teacher has the right to air controversial issues in the classroom, whenever he or she judges that the issue is appropriate to the maturity and intellectual level of the students and the curriculum.

The principle of academic freedom has been upheld on all jurisdictional levels including the Supreme Court. The Supreme Court has stated that academic freedom is "of transcendent value to all of us and not merely to the teachers concerned. That freedom is therefore a special concern of the First Amendment, which does not tolerate laws that cast a pall of orthodoxy over the classroom. *(Keyishian v. Board of Regents,* 385 U.S. 589)" Further, in the case of *Sweezy v. New Hampshire* (354 U.S. 234), Justice Felix Frankfurter enumerated the essentials of academic freedom as applied to universities. Finally, in the case of *Albaum v.*

Carey, 283 F.Supp. 3, U.S. Dist. Ct. N.Y. 1968), it was determined that "the considerations which militate in favor of academic freedom—our historical commitment to free speech for all, the peculiar importance of academic inquiry to the progress of society in an atmosphere of open inquiry, feeling always free to challenge and improve established ideas— are relevant to elementary and secondary schools as well as to institutions of higher learning."

Problems concerning academic freedom periodically arise in our nation's schools. Most often this conflict arises around the teaching of controversial issues. An individual or group of individuals may feel particular concern over a teacher's political, moral or theological views, as expressed in reading lists, subject content, classroom lectures, etc. While these disputes are never easy to ejudicate, opening full lines of communication between community action groups and the school is always the first step.

It must be remembered that teachers and administrators have guaranteed to them, under law, certain constitutional rights, including protection from arbitrary, capricious or discriminatory actions or dismissals on the part of the local board; freedom of association; freedom to lead their lives in privacy; freedom from undue restrictions on their personal appearance; freedom of speech outside the school environment; freedom of speech within the classroom; freedom of religion and the right to have due process. Consequently, no school board may enact rules or laws which violate these rights. The principle of academic freedom, however, cannot be used as a defense against breaking a law. A teacher may not, for instance, incite a class to riot (a clear violation of law) and claim protection from prosecution under the principle of academic freedom.

See Also: ADVISORY COUNCILS; CENSORSHIP; CHRISTIAN SCIENTISTS; CIVIL RIGHTS; COMMUNICATION; CONSTITUTIONAL RIGHTS; DEMONSTRATIONS; DISCRIMINATION; DRESS CODES; DUE PROCESS: FIFTH AMENDMENT GUARANTEES; FIRST AMENDMENT GUARANTEES; FOURTEENTH AMENDMENT GUARANTEES; FOURTH AMENDMENT GUARANTEES; FREE SPEECH; HEARINGS; JEHOVAH'S WITNESSES; OATHS; PETITIONS: POLITICS AND THE SCHOOL; PRIVACY; RIGHTS AND RESPONSIBILITIES; SELF-INCRIMINATION; UNIONS.

ACADEMIC PROGRAM

The **academic program** of a school is that series of academic courses and/or experiences which aim at the accomplishment of specified instructional goals over a stated period of time.

Courses such as English, History, Foreign Languages, Mathematics, and Science are usually considered to be part of the academic program of the school. The academic program is that part of the total educational program which is composed of subject matter that transmits knowledge of the past and present, in order that the learner can apply it to his or her own experiences.

There are many guidelines and models for setting an academic program. Two of the more viable are PPBS (Planning-Programming-Budgeting System) and DEPS (Data-Based Educational Planning Systems). While there are many differences in these models, their basic similarity is the philosophy that, in setting an academic program, one starts with the goals or outcome one wishes to achieve and then sets up a program that will implement desired outcomes.

The academic program of a school must be so constituted that upon its completion, a student will have attained sufficient knowledge, skills, values, etc., which will enable him or her to perform adequately or better in his or her personal and professional life.

See Also: ACCOUNTABILITY; BASICS; CHILD-CENTERED; COMPETENCY-BASED PROGRAMS; COURSE; COURSE OF STUDY; CURRICULUM DEVELOPMENT; EARLY CHILDHOOD PROGRAMS; ELECTIVES; ENRICHMENT; EXTRACURRICULAR ACTIVITIES; FIELD TRIPS; GOALS AND OBJECTIVES; GRADUATION REQUIREMENTS; INTERDISCIPLINARY APPROACHES; MINI-COURSES; VOCATIONAL PROGRAMS; WORK-STUDY PROGRAMS.

ACCELERATION

As applied to education, **acceleration** may apply to any process whereby a student progresses through school at a quicker rate than an average student in the same school.

One common method of acceleration which has been used for many years is that of "skipping" a grade. For example, a child in the second grade may be promoted directly to the fourth, entirely bypassing the third grade because it is believed to be warranted by the child's academic ability. If this method is considered, it should be remembered that the child's degree of social maturity must also be taken into account.

A second type of acceleration is that in which the educational program is expanded to provide advanced learning experiences, which pupils may undertake when they are prepared to do so, without regard to grade levels. In this type, a child in a fourth grade class could be doing ninth grade work in math if his or her talents so warrant.

See Also: ACADEMICALLY TALENTED; ACHIEVEMENT; APTITUDE; CURRICULUM DEVELOPMENT; ENRICHMENT; GIFTED STUDENTS; GRADES; INDIVIDUALIZATION; PROMOTION; UNGRADED.

ACCEPTANCE OF CONTRACTS

Acceptance of contract may be oral, but it usually consists in formally signing a document that attests that the individual has accepted the terms of the contract. As applied to education, it should be made clear

that when an educator signs a contract, there usually will be a clause in it that binds the educator to the rules and regulations of the state and local school boards. Consequently, should an educator then violate any of those rules or regulations, he or she may be in breach of contract. This can and has been used as grounds for dismissal.

Since formally accepting a contract binds an individual to the terms of the contract, it behooves each individual to carefully read and understand all the terms within it. This is particularly true for an administrator, who must often sign contracts for goods or services to be obtained from outside the school.

Once a contract has been signed, it is considered a binding legal document; the failure of either party to comply with the terms of the contract is grounds for legal action.

See Also: AUTHORITY, BOARD; BOARD OF EDUCATION; CIVIL RIGHTS; CONSTITUTIONAL RIGHTS; CONTRACTS; EQUAL EMPLOYMENT OPPORTUNITIES; NON-RENEWAL OF CONTRACT; OATHS; POLITICS AND THE SCHOOL; RENEWAL OF CONTRACT; VENDORS.

ACCEPTANCE OF DONATIONS

Acceptance of donations is the acceptance by a school official, or the school board, of a donation of a tangible asset to the school or school system.

In accepting donations, an administrator must ask him- or herself if the donation is of such nature that could be construed as an attempt to exert undue influence, either upon the school's administrator or the faculty members. A donation, for example, of a set of encyclopedia to be used in a classroom may be perfectly fine and acceptable. If, however, the person making the donation is the parent of a child who is failing, and has spoken to the teacher and/or administrator about how anxious he or she is that the child be promoted, then the donation is questionable, as it might be construed as a bribe.

The school board must likewise be wary of donations of property. Should the donation of property come, for example, from someone who provides contracted services or supplies to the school system, or from someone who would benefit from the donation by having other of his or her properties increase in value, then the donation is a questionable one and will, most likely, be politely declined by the school board.

If the donation is acceptable, however, the acceptance should be a formal one. The acceptance should be acknowledged in a formal letter signed by the administrator, the superintendent of schools, or the board president. This is also an opportunity for favorable public relations, including, but not limited to, mention in a newsletter, article in the local press, or even media coverage.

See Also: ACKNOWLEDGEMENT; APPRECIATION, LETTER OF; GIFTS; NEWS COVERAGE; NEWSLETTER; NEWS RELEASES; P.T.A.; SPECIAL INTEREST GROUPS.

ACCESSORY

In legal terms, an **accessory** is anyone who, after an illegal act has been committed, aids the perpetrator of the crime in escaping just punishment for the commission of the act.

As applied to education, an administrator might leave him- or herself opens to the charge of being an accessory after the fact if he or she should try to cover up an illegal act that has been committed within the school. For example, if a teacher struck a child and caused serious bodily injury to the child and the administrator tried to cover up the incident by concocting a story that the child fell on the stairs, then that administrator is an accessory after the fact and may be held legally accountable.

Of course, the above example is a far-fetched one meant for emphasis only, but in any situation with any tinge of illegality to it, honesty is not only the best policy for the administrator, it is the *only* policy.

See Also: BATTERY; BURGLARY; JUVENILE DELINQUENCY; NEGLIGENCE; THEFT; TRUANCY.

ACCESS RIGHTS

An **access right** is an owner's vested right to passage over adjoining public property in order to enter and leave his or her own land.

The only way this term applies to education is if the access right of an individual should happen to fall within school property. If this is the case, a problem may arise with students either blocking the access (either intentionally by congregating there, or unintentionally by leaving athletic equipment in the access way, for example) or using the access to congregate on private property and causing a disturbance to the owner. Quite often, this can lead to some anger on the part of the property owner, particularly if it is raining and he or she can't get to his or her property without getting out of the car to move the track hurdles that have been left in the access way. At the very least, this is poor public relations.

If a school has grounds that include an access right to adjoining property, the students should be made aware of the school's responsibility to keep the access way clear and should be admonished to avoid trespassing on private property. Supervision in order to insure compliance would also be welcome.

See Also: EASEMENT; GROUNDS; INSURANCE; LIABILITY; ZONING BOARD.

ACCIDENTS

In schools, **accidents** are fairly common occurrences. In most cases, accidents are minor, with injuries of the scraped knee variety being the rule rather than the exception. However, there will inevitably be some accidents which are far more serious, resulting in broken bones or even life-threatening situations. Naturally, the school authorities will do everything in their power to make the physical plant as safe a place as possible. They will see to it that safety hazards are eliminated and that there is adequate supervision. Even so, it is inevitable that accidents will occur.

When they do, it is wise to follow a two-step procedure: first, aid the victim; and second, prepare a written report of the accident. The first part would seem to be common sense; if a child has fallen and is writhing in pain, the school nurse is going to be called and/or first aid administered. The difficulty arises, however, when the accident is minor (such as the scraped knee we mentioned earlier). In such a case, the child's supervisor may feel inclined to let it go because it is so minor. This is not a wise procedure, however, since a possible infection might set in, and the parent might legitimately ask why his or her child did not receive attention in order to prevent this further complication. The best rule, therefore, is to insist that every accident victim, no matter how minor, be seen by the school nurse immediately.

Next, every accident should be reported in writing. Such a report might include the name of the child and the person supervising the child, the nature of the accident, exactly how the accident occurred, the nurse's report of the nature and treatment of the injuries, the time of occurrence and treatment, and any explanatory material the teacher in charge or witnesses to the accident may be able to provide.

It might also be wise to establish a procedure whereby the child's parents or someone designated by them is informed of the accident, and will take responsibility for the child if the accident is of such a nature that the child must leave school.

See Also: BUS AND BUS DRIVERS; CHRISTIAN SCIENTISTS; DAMAGES; FIELD TRIPS; FIRST AID; FORESEEABILITY; HEALTH; *IN LOCO PARENTIS;* INSURANCE; LIABILITY; NEGLIGENCE; NURSE, PARENTAL LIABILITY; PERMISSION SLIPS; PHYSICAL EDUCATION; PLAYGROUND; RECESS; SAFE PLACE STATUTES; SAFETY; SAVE-HARMLESS STATUTES; SPORTS: STUDENT INFORMATION; SUPPLIES AND EQUIPMENT; X-RAY REPORT.

ACCOUNTABILITY

Accountability is a general term for the belief and theory that both school systems and/or individual educators may be held liable for the degree of improvement or achievement of pupils.

Accountability is an extremely hot issue among educators. Proponents argue that educators bear the responsibility for educating every child to the best of that child's ability and that, consequently, that child's achievement can legitimately be used as an indication of whether or not educators are fulfilling that responsibility. Opponents often argue that there are too many variables, not the least of which is the individual degree of motivation and the home situation, for a single educator to be held responsible for the success or failure of an individual student.

In a sense, there has always been accountability in education, since a teacher is accountable to his or her supervisor for adequately performing his or her functions, and observation and evaluation have always been a part of school life.

The theory of accountability focuses on holding schools and individual educators responsible for the students' learning. There are a number of reasons why accountability has come to the forefront. Some of these reasons are the poor academic showing of disadvantaged children, the greater stress to evaluate results in federally subsidized programs, the general movement to make schools more responsive to the communities in which they exist, and the increasing concern of the public over rising school costs and exactly what they are getting for their money.

Whatever the causes, many school systems have set up systems of accountability. In order for a system of accountability to be viable, there should be at least four component parts: first, outcome goals must be established. Next, educators must specifically spell out the means and methods by which they hope to attain these goals. Third, there must be some method of supervision and evaluation in order to determine that these stated means and methods are being used. Finally, there must be a report which correlates and assesses the performance of students to the original goal and the means and methods employed.

There are a number of management systems which handle the academic program in order to insure a high level of accountability as outlined above. Two such methods commonly used are PPBS (Planning-Programming-Budgeting System) and DEPS (Data-Based Educational Planning System), both of which are tested and proven programs currently being used throughout the nation.

See Also: BASICS; CURRICULUM DEVELOPMENT; EVALUATION; GOALS AND OBJECTIVES; INDIVIDUALIZATION; INSTRUCTION; OBSERVATION; PERCENTAGE OF PROMOTION; REPORT CARDS; RIGHTS AND RESPONSIBILITIES; SUPERVISION (STAFF).

ACCREDITATION

Accreditation is a process whereby an educational institution is accorded recognition that the institution has met certain minimum standards of educational quality.

Standards for accreditation are fairly consistent within the United States. Based upon the basic principles and goals of public education, they are accepted by the general consent of the institutions who agree to abide by them. Accrediting associations usually establish standards very clearly, and schools initiate curricula that facilitate these standards.

Accreditation of public schools within the United States is issued through six main agencies, after a process which includes a team evaluation and report. This process may take several days and may involve personal interviews, as well as the study of written data and reports.

These six agencies for accreditation are the Middle States Association of Colleges and Secondary Schools founded in 1887; the New England Association of Colleges and Secondary Schools founded in 1885; the North Central Association of Colleges and Secondary Schools founded in 1895; the North West Association of Secondary and Higher Schools founded in 1917; the Southern Association of Colleges and Schools founded in 1895; and the Western Association of Schools and Colleges founded in 1924.

The process of accreditation is generally repeated every ten years.

See Also: ACADEMIC PROGRAM; ADULT EDUCATION; CERTIFICATION; COMPETENCY-BASED PROGRAMS; COURSE OF STUDY; CURRICULUM DEVELOPMENT; EARLY CHILDHOOD PROGRAMS; ELEMENTARY SCHOOLS; EVALUATION; INSTRUCTION; MIDDLE SCHOOL; PRIVATE AND PAROCHIAL SCHOOLS; SUMMER SCHOOL; U. S. DEPARTMENT OF EDUCATION; VOCATIONAL PROGRAMS; WORK-STUDY PROGRAMS; YEAR-END REPORT.

ACHIEVEMENT

Achievement is the progress that a learner makes in learning, often measured either by standardized and/or teacher-made tests. Achievement can be used as a criterion for homogeneously grouping a class or grade, and it may also serve as an entrance criterion for programs for the gifted and talented. Moreover, it is one of the more common criteria used in acceleration. Achievement is also a major criterion in assessing the academic program and meeting the requirements of any system of accountability.

There are a number of ways to measure achievement, but by far the most common is the standardized achievement test. Some educators believe that they should be given in the early part of each school year, while others believe that they should be given twice a year; once in the fall and once in the spring. Careful choosing of the test or tests to be used should incorporate two standards: first, the educational philosophy of the school as it compares with the goals of the testing program, and second, the similarities in the school's curriculum and the items in the test.

There are many standardized commercial achievement tests available to the schools. Some of the more common are the California Achievement Tests for grades 1-12, Cooperative General Achievement Tests for grade 12, Cooperative Sequential Test of Educational Progress for grades 4-12, Coordinated Scales of Attainment for grades 1-8, Essential High School Content for grades 9-12, Iowa Test of Basic Skills for grades 3-9, Iowa Test of Educational Development for grades 9-12, Metropolitan Achievement Test for grades 1-9, SRA Achievement Series for grades 2-9, and Stanford Achievement Test for grades 2-9.

Some educators believe that teacher-made tests are even more effective in measuring achievement. They feel that this type of test, which is given with greater frequency than the standardized variety, helps determine the instructional level of students and provides teachers with the ability to change that level; since they measure progress and growth during instruction, they determine the need for remedial work and its effectiveness; they motivate the pupil's interest in a subject, activity or task at hand; and they maintain continuity in the pupil's experience through effective grouping, which results from appraisals of pupil progress all along the way.

See Also: ABILITY GROUPING; ABILITY LEVELS; APTITUDE; EVALUATION; LEARNING DISABILITIES; PROMOTION; REMEDIAL INSTRUCTION; RETENTION OF STUDENTS; UNDERACHIEVERS.

ACKNOWLEDGEMENT

Acknowledgement is an act of recognition and/or an expression of thanks or appreciation for something that has been done by another.

While it is not strictly necessary,

acknowledging the ideas, services, help, and cooperation of others is an excellent method of building a good working rapport. For an administrator especially, a simple acknowledgement can often be the basis of good morale within a school by showing the faculty that the administrator both appreciates and understands their efforts.

A typical letter of acknowledgement might run something like this:

Dear Mrs. Thomas,

I just finished reading the note you left for me. May I say that I think your idea is outstanding.

We have been looking for a solution to the study hall problem for some time, and it looks as if you have provided us with the answer. Your suggestions are not only sensible, but also perfectly within the realm of realization.

Please set up an appointment with me so that I may thank you personally and further discuss your excellent idea.

Thank you for sharing your thoughts with me.

Sincerely,

Consideration of this type on the part of an administrator is long remembered and definitely aids in establishing an atmosphere which insures the smooth functioning of the school.

See Also: ACCEPTANCE OF DONATIONS; ADDRESSES (SPEECHES); APPRECIATION, LETTER OF; COMMUNICATION; EMPLOYEE RELATIONS; GIFTS; NEWS COVERAGE; NEWSLETTER; NEWS RELEASES.

ACTIVITIES

Activities are those programs or learning situations in which children are engaged as a means to attaining an educational goal.

The various activity programs offered in school are highly effective in motivating students. They help students master specific skills. They provide motivation by allowing association with students having common interests. They help students build pride, not only in themselves but in others. Projects undertaken by these groups quite often lead members into problems involving the use of mathematics, oral and written communications, and many other school subjects.

An activity such as the Student Council, for example, provides a plethora of benefits for students. Not only is it a very real exercise in citizenship training and preparation for life in a democracy, but this activity group may perform functions such as acting as advisors to the principal, publishing a student handbook, aiding at graduation ceremonies, running certain school functions, and many other worthwhile and genuinely useful activities. Consequently, these activities are real learning situations and are definitely of educational value.

Activity programs in a school also have a carry-over effect in terms of community relations. The accomplishments of students in learning algebra or interpreting literature are essentially intellectual in nature. A display of paintings by members of the Art Club, a production of a musical comedy by the Drama Club, a fund-raising drive by the Student Council, however, are very tangible realities that a community can perceive and appreciate. These activities, therefore, are quite often signals to the community that the school is functioning and producing. A perceived attitude of this nature finds carry-over in passed school budgets and increased community support.

Therefore, activity programs in the school have a very real value, in both educational and practical terms.

See Also: AMERICAN EDUCATION WEEK; ART; ASSEMBLY PROGRAM; BACK-TO-SCHOOL NIGHT; BAND; CALENDAR; CLUBS; DANCE; ENRICHMENT; EXTRACURRICULAR ACTIVITIES; FIELD TRIPS; GRADUATION; MOVIES; MUSIC; NATIONAL HONOR SOCIETY; NEWS COVERAGE; NEWSLETTER; NEWS RELEASES; OPEN HOUSE; PHYSICAL EDUCATION; PLAYGROUND; POLITICS AND THE SCHOOL; PROM; P.T.A.; SPORTS; STUDENT COUNCIL (STUDENT GOVERNMENT); STUDENT INFORMATION; TRIPS.

ADDRESSES (SPEECHES)

Educators and administrators particularly are being constantly asked to **address** groups. From a formal speech before a professional organization to an informal welcoming address at a school function, the administrator must often prepare and deliver addresses on a variety of subjects.

One of the best ways to prepare an effective address is to follow a speaker's formula called P*R*E-*P*A*R*E. Each letter stands for one block in the foundation of a good speech.

P *Pinpoint your topic. Narrow down the scope of your speech until you are talking about a specific area which you can cover thoroughly in your allotted time.

R *Research your subject. It is best not to trust your memory. Do some research until you are completely conversant in your topic.

E *Examples help to clarify points of the speech. Make certain that the examples you use are appropriate and understood by everyone in the audience, and avoid "inside" jokes which might be misunderstood by anyone listening.

P *Practice for presentation and poise. Any actor will tell you that the best "spontaneous" speeches are those that have been thoroughly rehearsed. If possible, record the speech and listen to your delivery. Practicing before a mirror is also helpful.

A *Analyze your audience. Whether your delivery will be formal or informal, relaxed or highly professional, humorous or strictly serious will depend on the composition of the audience and the nature of the affair. Suit the speech to the audience.

R *Relax and enjoy yourself. In most cases, the audience wants you to succeed. If you can appear relaxed and enjoy yourself, so will the audience.

E *Enthusiasm is the key to success. If you are enthusiastic about what you are saying and believe in what you have to say, you will build a lasting, positive impression in the minds of your audience.

When an administrator gives a public address, it is a great chance to build positive public and community relations. Following the formula outlined above will help you construct and deliver a memorable speech.

See Also: AMERICAN EDUCATION WEEK; ASSEMBLY PROGRAM; BACK-TO-SCHOOL NIGHT; COMMUNICATION; CONVENTION; DEPARTMENTAL MEETINGS; FACULTY MEETINGS; GRADUATION; HEARINGS; NEWS COVERAGE; OPEN HOUSE; P.T.A.; PUBLIC ADDRESS SYSTEM; RETIREMENT; WORKSHOPS AND INSERVICE.

ADDRESS (RESIDENCE)

Address (residence) is the listing of an individual's actual place of abode.

For a variety of obvious reasons, not the least of which are contact in emergency situations and verification of eligibility to attend the institution, the correct addresses or actual places of abode of students and faculty are necessary. These are usually gathered during the first several days of each school year and kept within the files of the school.

School systems have a variety of forms and methods of obtaining the addresses of students and teachers, and if a child should move during the school year, there is usually no problem, as a child's records will be forwarded to the new school upon request. Many times, however, a problem arises when a child moves to a new address within the same system. A new location may require attendance at another school within the township. Parents may not be

---

NAME: _____ DATE: _____

SCHOOL: _____ GRADE: _____

NAME OF PARENT OR GUARDIAN: _____

OLD ADDRESS:_____

_____

NEW ADDRESS:_____

_____

DATE OF MOVE: _____

OLD TELEPHONE NUMBER: _____ NEW NUMBER: _____

PRESENT ASSIGNED BUS STOP, IF ANY: _____

THIS FORM IS TO BE FILLED OUT AND PRESENTED TO THE GUIDANCE OFFICE UPON STUDENT'S CHANGE OF ADDRESS.

aware of this, and a certain amount of confusion may ensue. Therefore, many schools require that every child who is moving, even within the same district, fill out a change of address form. A typical form of this nature is shown on the bottom of page 35.

Similarly, a form of this nature should also be available for any faculty member who changes address during a school year.

See Also: BUILDINGS; BUSING; GROUNDS; INSURANCE; NON-RESIDENTS, ADMISSION OF; RESIDENCE; STUDENT INFORMATION; TAXES; TRANSFERS; TRANSPORTATION; TRESPASSER.

ADMINISTRATOR

In education, the **administrator** is any person who is responsible for the instructional, operational or organizational systems of the institution at any level.

An educational administrator may be known by a number of titles such as superintendent of schools, principal, vice-principal, etc. The duties and purview of each office will vary from system to system, depending on a number of factors, not the least of which is the philosophy of the school board or an administrator's immediate superior. For instance, in one school, discipline may be the responsibility of the vice-principal because the principal believes that he or she should deal primarily with the academic or business aspects of school life; while in another school, the principal may wish to handle all discipline cases personally, assigning the vice-principal duties of a purely administrative nature. Quite often, one can find the above examples in two schools within the same district.

While duties may vary, every effective administrator shares certain basic characteristics: they help define the roles of each member of their group; they delineate, through patterns of organization, ways of getting the job done; they help establish a relationship of mutual trust between themselves and the group. Basically, an administrator is an educational leader.

While fiction and certain past practices have frequently painted the administrator as an autocratic, unyielding individual, current thinking on the role of the administrator places great emphasis on the methods he or she uses to accomplish his or her purposes. Especially today, administrators must be mindful of interpersonal relationships and public relations. Certainly, the administrator still has the final word, but asking for the advice and counsel of the community and faculty, treating all individuals with courtesy and consideration, and taking a personal interest in the lives of the staff can only bring benefits in increased morale and productivity.

See Also: ACCOUNTABILITY; ADVISORY COUNCILS; AUTHORITY, BOARD; AUTHORITY, EXPRESSED AND IMPLIED; BUDGET; CENTRAL STAFF; CHIEF STATE SCHOOL OFFI-

CIAL; CODE OF ETHICS; COUNTY SU-PERINTENDENT; DISCIPLINE; EM-PLOYEE RELATIONS; EVALUATION; FORESEEABILITY; GRIEVANCES; *IN LOCO PARENTIS*; INTERVIEW; LIAI-SON; MINISTERIAL ACTS; MONTHLY REPORTS; OBSERVATION; PRINCI-PAL; PROFESSIONAL ASSOCIATIONS FOR SCHOOL ADMINISTRATORS; QUALIFICATIONS; SUPERINTEN-DENT OF SCHOOLS; SUPERVISION (STAFF); SUPERVISION (STUDENTS); VICE-PRINCIPAL; YEAR-END REPORT.

ADULT EDUCATION

Adult education is the term generally applied to a wide variety of educational activities offered to adults within a community by the public school system of that community.

A valid and accredited adult education program consists of three components. First is community organization, based upon the belief that there is a need within the community for the program. A survey of community needs and interests should be conducted, and the community should be sufficiently informed of the availability of the program. Second is curriculum; an accredited program should consist of three main areas which are Language Arts, Arithmetic and Computation, and General Knowledge. Third is classroom procedures; certified teachers must be used in all academic classes. Local expertise may be used in any area of general knowledge. Material used

should be of adult interest and level, and should be motivational in nature.

A thorough adult education curriculum might include courses on history and civics, both for Americans and for the foreign-born; arts and crafts; music, art and drama; recreation and physical education; industrial arts and technical courses; safety education; health education; home and family relationships; English literature and English for the foreign-born; community understanding; leadership training; programs for senior citizens; gardening and agriculture; home economics; media; teacher in-service training; and foreign languages.

Funding for an adult education program may come through local taxes, federal or state vocational aid, state aid, or from fees and tuition.

See Also: ACADEMIC PROGRAM; AP-PLICATION; ART; BASICS; BUDGET; BUILDINGS; COMMUNICATION; CONTRACTS; COURSE OF STUDY; CULTURE; CURRICULUM DEVELOP-MENT; DIPLOMA; DROP-OUTS; EVAL-UATION; FEES; FINANCE; HOME ECONOMICS; INDUSTRIAL ARTS; LANGUAGE ARTS; MATHEMATICS; MUSIC; NEWS RELEASES; PHYSICAL EDUCATION; READING; SCHEDULE; VOLUNTEERS.

ADVISORY COUNCILS

An **Advisory Council** is a group that is set up to study particular problems relating to curriculum, finance, personnel policies, textbook and other teaching materials, and other problems which may arise within a school district.

An advisory council is generally not an action group, but rather a group which offers suggestions or recommendations to an individual or group within a school system.

There are several types of advisory councils with which the school administrator should be familiar. Some of the more common are: the *Building Advisory Council,* which advises the principal on matters pertaining to the school building; a *Citizen's Advisory Council,* composed of members of the community, usually at the invitation of the school official, which may offer suggestions on a wide variety of educational concerns within a community; a *Curriculum Advisory Council,* which helps to delineate future areas of concern or need within the curriculum, but does not review present curriculum; the *District Advisory Council,* which operates under the auspices of the district administrator, who directs the council's efforts toward the study of a specific task within the district and passes on its recommendations to an action committee; a *Joint Professional-Citizen's Advisory Council,* which is composed of professional educators and concerned citizens to investigate matters of concern to both or either, and reports to the official at the level of their purview; and the *Personnel Advisory Council,* which studies problems that arise with personnel policies within a building or district.

In forming an Advisory Council,

care should be taken to direct the council toward its specific responsibilities, and members should be reminded that their task is to advise and recommend, not to take action.

See Also: BOARD OF EDUCATION; BUDGET; CENTRAL STAFF; CHAIRPERSONS; COMMITTEE; CONSULTANTS; EMPLOYEE RELATIONS; FACT FINDING; FACULTY; LIAISON; P.T.A.; RECOMMENDATION; SPECIAL INTEREST GROUPS.

AFFIRMATIVE ACTION

Affirmative Action is a legal tenet which states that adults and children deserve to be treated with fairness and must have maximum opportunities for realizing their potential regardless of sex, race, creed, or national origin. The term also applies to various programs initiated in order to implement this philosophy. It is part of the national Civil Rights concern in America.

Affirmative Action has been formally expressed in the Civil Rights Act of 1964, Title 7 (74 Stat. 86) and Title 9 of The Educational Amendments of 1972 (PL 92-318) which have a primary emphasis on sex considerations. Regulations delineate how institutions may provide equal educational and employment opportunities for both sexes. Institutions were required to undertake self-studies in order to identify policies that were improper or illegal, and to indicate how these policies would be changed. They were then required to keep records to show how these changes were implemented.

These laws were the first that required both positive Affirmative Action to prevent sex bias and also remedial action to overcome the effects of that bias. The law further required educational institutions to designate an employee to act as an Affirmative Action Officer, whose duties are to maintain Affirmative Action principles and to investigate complaints. Violations of Affirmative Action may be adjudicated in the courts, and a finding against the institution may result in the loss of federal funds.

Affirmative Action provides for equal admission, equal student treatment, both in courses and in extracurricular activities, including athletics; and equal employment and promotion.

Recently, the decision in the case of *United Steel Workers of America, AFL-CIO v. Brian F. Weber, et al.* (NLRB) 126 U.S. App DC 255, 377 F.2d. 140) affirmed the right of labor organizations to negotiate Affirmative Action provisions in contracts with employers, including specific goals, timetables and quotas. The National Education Association has hailed this as a landmark decision that has great application to education.

See Also: ATHLETICS, SEX DISCRIMINATION IN; CIVIL RIGHTS; CLUBS; DISCRIMINATION; EMPLOYEE RELATIONS; EQUAL EMPLOYMENT OPPORTUNITIES; ETHNIC MINORITIES; FOURTEENTH AMENDMENT GUARANTEES; GRIEVANCES; PHYSICAL EDUCATION; SEXISM; SPECIAL INTEREST GROUPS; SPORTS.

AGE LEVELS

Age levels refer to those stages of development in physical and mental growth, from birth through maturity.

According to Jean Piaget, a recognized expert in the field, a human being goes through four stages of development. The first stage is called the *sensorimotor stage,* which runs from birth to about age two. In this stage, the child has no language skills, but is in touch with his environment and investigates the world around him or her. The second stage is called the *preoperational stage,* which runs from around age two to approximately age seven. In this stage, language develops and the child begins to recognize symbols and to differentiate between them. This is the stage during which most children enter school. During the latter part of this stage, they have the ability to learn the alphabet, count, etc. The third stage is called the *stage of concrete operations,* which lasts from about age seven to approximately age eleven. In this stage, a child can hold and retain (conserve) such qualities as mass, number, weight, volume, surfaces, etc. These operations are still concrete, without the ability to go into abstract ideas. The final stage is called the *stage of formal operations,* which Piaget claims starts around the age of eleven or twelve and continues to death. In this stage, the child becomes fully capable of abstract operations and thinking. From approximately eleven to fourteen, the child begins to deduce from hypotheses and can operate on facts not directly related to his or her personal experience. Above age fourteen, the individual can take pieces of hypotheses and form an entirely new concept.

In terms of public education, a knowledge of the functions of age levels is important to administrators and teachers. This knowledge will be used in formulating curriculum, school discipline, class management, and many other areas of school life.

See Also: CHILD-CENTERED; COUNSELING; CURRICULUM DEVELOPMENT; DISCIPLINE; EARLY CHILDHOOD PROGRAMS; FORESEEABILITY; INDIVIDUALIZATION; KINDERGARTEN; LIBRARY AND MEDIA CENTER; PHYSICAL EDUCATION; PSYCHOLOGICAL STUDIES; READINESS; STUDENT INFORMATION.

AGENT

Agent is a legal term used to designate any person who acts on the behalf of another. An agent has the power to bind the person he or she represents, as long as the agent does not exceed the scope of his or her authority.

As applied to education, much concern has been expressed as to whether an administrator or a teacher acts as an agent of the school system. If, for instance, a teacher were to commit an act in school which was illegal or led to the physical injury of a student, could the board of education be held legally responsible since the teacher was acting as an agent of the board? In the courts, the line of distinction for agent liability seems to be whether or not the person has exceeded the scope of his or her authority. In our example, if the teacher was acting within the scope of authority as delineated by the board, then the board may be held liable. If he or she was not and had exceeded the scope of that authority, then the board may not be held liable.

Therefore, it behooves every school system to clearly define the scope of authority of every agent.

See Also: AIDES: AUTHORITY, BOARD; AUTHORITY, EXPRESSED AND IMPLIED; AUTHORITY, TEACHER; BOARD OF EDUCATION; BUS AND BUS DRIVERS; DAMAGES; IMPUTED NEGLIGENCE; LIABILITY; NEGLIGENCE; REASONABLE AND PRUDENT; STUDENT TEACHER; SUBSTITUTE TEACHER.

AIDES

The word **aide** is sometimes loosely defined. The term has been applied to everyone, from students who act as workers in the main office of the school or in the school library, to adults who perform tasks such as lunchroom supervision or tutoring students in specific areas.

Aides should receive training for the tasks they are to perform and their performance should be evaluated. Particularly for teacher aides, these individuals must meet the standards of care that a teacher would be expected to evidence in similar circumstances. Also, teacher aides must be certified if they are to handle instruction. An aide must be instructed in the methods of supervision and safety, therefore, and should an aide fail to meet these standards, he or she may be held personally liable. Should an aide perform a liable act, the question arises as to whether or not the teacher and administrator are equally liable. In most cases, if the aide were given proper instruction, the teacher or administrator would not be held liable, but if they knew or should have known that the aide was not capable of performing the assignment and ignored this fact, then they would be guilty of negligence and both could be held liable.

It is important, therefore, that the aides used in school are screened and trained, and their performance regularly evaluated. Indeed, it has been held that the administrator and teacher have a duty to supervise the aide and make certain that the aide is properly carrying out the assigned duty.

See Also: AGENT; AUXILIARY PERSONNEL; AUXILIARY SERVICES; CAFETERIA; CLERICAL SERVICES; EVALUATION; EXTRACURRICULAR DUTIES; FIELD TRIPS; LIABILITY; NEGLIGENCE; RECESS; SPECIAL SERVICES; SUPERVISION (STAFF); VOLUNTEERS.

AMERICAN ASSOCIATION OF SCHOOL ADMINISTRATORS (AASA)

The **American Association of School Administrators (AASA)** is a professional organization dedicated to the improvement and advancement of public education, particularly through upgrading the quality of educational administrators and strengthening the capabilities and resources of the superintendent of schools.

The AASA is extremely active in American education. Their avowed purpose is to suggest procedures; identify resources; stimulate action programs by which technical information, professional help and guidelines may be used by superintendents and principals, along with their faculties, boards and communities, to work out solutions to their own problems. Over the years, the AASA has conducted studies on in-service training, the relationship of principals to their assistants, and testing programs, to name just a few. They have also constructed the twelve imperatives for education, enumerated ten priorities for publicity, and delineated reasons for teacher dissatisfaction and militancy.

The AASA has its own publications and holds an annual convention. Inquiries may be addressed to:

American Association of School Administrators
1801 North Moore Street
Arlington, VA 22209
Telephone: (703) 528-0700

See Also: PROFESSIONAL ASSOCIA-
TIONS FOR SCHOOL ADMINISTRA-
TORS.

AMERICAN COUNCIL ON EDUCATION (ACE)

The **American Council on Education (ACE)** is a professional organization. It is the principal coordinating organization in American higher education.

The stated aims of the American Council on Education are: (1) to serve the higher education community as observer, spokesman and coordinator; (2) to act as an information clearing house, especially in federal relations; (3) to act as a catalyst, research center and publisher.

The ACE has been extremely active in American education. Some of their contributions have been the standardization of cumulative record folders and official reports to accrediting associations; they have also been active in creating alliances throughout the educational spectrum. They also take an active part in reviewing presidential appointees to the Department of Education.

For further information, address inquiries to:

American Council on Education

1 Dupont Circle

Washington, DC 20036

(202) 833-4700

See Also: PROFESSIONAL ASSOCIA-
TIONS FOR SCHOOL ADMINISTRA-
TORS; PROFESSIONAL ASSOCIA-
TIONS FOR TEACHERS.

AMERICAN EDUCATION WEEK

American Education Week is a week set aside for a national observance in support of American education in general and the schools in particular.

American Education Week was started in 1921, under the joint sponsorship of the American Legion and the National Education Association. The National Congress of Parents and Teachers and the U.S. Office of Education (U.S. Department of Education) later lent their support and sponsorship as well.

Nationally, many types of observances and programs are planned in the schools. These may include such items as an Open House in which the community is invited to tour the school and even sit in on classes and/or special programs featuring students. If a program is to be presented in the school, it should be remembered that those programs featuring large numbers of students are far more effective public relations vehicles than single performers or adult speakers.

American Education Week is an excellent opportunity to build favorable community relations. Quite often, joint committees of educators and community members may be formed in order to establish programs and procedures for the week. These may include programs outside the school building that encourage community support of the schools. Displays in local store windows, poster campaigns, an exhibit in a local museum or even in the shopping center, on the history of education or the local history of the school system, are all very effective in promoting both the ideals of American Education Week and the good job being done in the schools themselves.

Each year, the national sponsoring organizations proclaim a theme for American Education Week such as "Schools—Your Investment in America." Wherever possible, this theme should be incorporated into the planned activities for the week.

See Also: ASSEMBLY PROGRAM; BACK-TO-SCHOOL NIGHT; BAND; CALENDAR; CLUBS; COMMUNICATIONS; CULTURE; EXTRACURRICULAR ACTIVITIES; MEDIA; MUSIC; NEWS COVERAGE; NEWSLETTER; NEWS RELEASES; OPEN HOUSE; PHYSICAL EDUCATION; SPECIAL INTEREST GROUPS.

AMERICAN FEDERATION OF TEACHERS

The **American Federation of Teachers** is an organization of teachers affiliated with the AFL-CIO.

Founded in 1916 by John Dewey, the organization was slow in growing. Affiliated from its inception with the labor movement, it was quickly labeled as a "teacher's union." There immediately existed a rivalry between the AFT and the National Education Association (NEA). Throughout the years, both organizations have striven to be the official spokesmen for teachers within various districts. The AFT has significantly grown in membership over the years, from 75,000 members in 1962, to 250,000 members in 1970, to over 475,000 members today.

There were three major turning points in the history of the AFT. In 1944, the local in Cicero, Illinois signed a collective bargaining agreement with the Board of Education, one of the first of its kind in the nation. In 1947, the Buffalo Teacher's Federation struck for higher salaries. At that time, the AFT had a "no strike" policy, but they backed this local none the less. In 1960, the showdown which had been brewing between the AFT and the NEA came to a head in New York City when the local union, the United Federation of Teachers, headed by Albert Shanker, struck and the AFT, rather than the NEA, became their official spokesman.

There is little doubt that the AFT has had a profound effect upon the professional lives of teachers throughout the nation. The AFT may be credited with three major changes in American education. First, a larger proportion of teachers are politically knowledgeable and active than previously. Second, the nature of collective bargaining has fundamentally changed the way in which resources used for education are allocated. Third, a subtle shift in authority relationships within a school district and in the way schools are viewed by people on the outside has taken place.

The militancy of the AFT has caused the NEA to undergo some subtle changes. For instance, in the ten-year period from 1946 through 1965, there were only 22 teachers' strikes nationwide, while in the 1969-1970 school year alone, there were over 180 such strikes and the increase continues, year after year. This has caused the NEA to adopt a strike policy that went from a totally non-strike position to one of aiding local associations so engaged.

It has been speculated that it is within the realm of possibility that eventually the NEA and the AFT may merge into a national teacher's organization.

See Also: ARBITRATION; COLLECTIVE BARGAINING; CONTRACTS; EMPLOYEE RELATIONS; JOB ACTION; NATIONAL EDUCATION ASSOCIATION; NEGOTIATIONS; POLITICS AND THE SCHOOL; REPRESENTATION; STRIKES; UNIONS; UNISERV.

APPRECIATION, LETTER OF

A **Letter of Appreciation** is any note or letter written to acknowledge the writer's appreciation for a service rendered.

Letters of appreciation help to establish a viable rapport which can be of help in all future dealings. A letter of appreciation should be sincere, relatively short and indicate the reason for appreciation.

An example of a typical letter of appreciation is on the bottom of this page.

The letter of appreciation should be sent soon after the service has been rendered.

See Also: ACCEPTANCE OF DONATIONS; ACKNOWLEDGEMENT; COMMUNICATION; EMPLOYEE RELATIONS; GIFTS.

APPLICATION

An **Application** is a written document prepared by an applicant

---

Dear Mr. Tanner,

Thank you so much for allowing our student drama classes to visit your school and perform for your primary grades. From the comments I have received, it is evident everyone profited from the experience.

We'd like you to know how much we appreciate your continued cooperation. Your graciousness in allowing us to visit your school has been so helpful that it has become part of our drama curriculum. Your kindness is deeply appreciated by all concerned.

If there is any way in which we may reciprocate, please feel free to call upon us.

Sincerely,

seeking a job or position, which outlines the position sought and provides information on the qualifications of the applicant.

There are many jobs within a school system, and hiring for these positions is done by the school board upon recommendation from a central staff administrator, usually the superintendent of schools. Applicants for a position are usually required to fill out an application, upon appraisal of which an interview is granted and a subsequent recommendation about hiring made.

A good application provides the reviewing official with sufficient information about the applicant's qualifications that the official may make decisions as to further procedures. Obviously, the questions on an application will differ slightly depending on the position sought. An application for the position of a chief custodian, for example, may ask if the applicant holds a "Black Seal" license, while an application for a teaching position would require information on proper teaching certification.

Every application should ask for the name, address, telephone number, position being sought, and qualifications for the position of the applicant. An application might also require information on education, past experiences, and special qualifications for the position. It may require a listing of recommendations from qualified individuals as to the applicant's ability to perform.

It must be remembered, however, that there are certain questions that have been asked on applications in the past, which may no longer be asked legally. As concern for civil rights grew in our nation, many past practices were reevaluated and found wanting. As far as applications are concerned, an applicant *may not be required* to identify his or her race, ethnic background, national origin, marital status or religious belief. Only that information which is pertinent to the performance of the job may be required.

See Also: ADDRESS (RESIDENCE); AFFIRMATIVE ACTION; CERTIFICATION; CIVIL RIGHTS; CONSTITUTIONAL RIGHTS; CONTRACTS; DISCRIMINATION; EQUAL EMPLOYMENT OPPORTUNITIES; ETHNIC MINORITIES; FOURTEENTH AMENDMENT GUARANTEES; INTERVIEW; OFFERS OF CONTRACT AND RECRUITING; QUALIFICATIONS; RECOMMENDATION; REFERENCES; SEXISM.

APTITUDE

Aptitude is a general term used to describe a variety of characteristics and abilities of an individual that would seem to indicate a general ability to achieve a mastery or a proficiency within a given area.

Since aptitude is basically the potential to master a specific series of skills, many school systems are anxious to discover the aptitude of pupils prior to placement within a particular program. To do this, they have resorted to aptitude tests, sometimes called specific intelligence tests. These tests attempt to measure an individual's aptitude and forecast the probability of future success.

There are a number of aptitude tests ranging from the Differential Aptitude Test, which is a wide-range battery covering verbal, numerical and abstract skills, to the Perdue Pegboard, which tests manual dexterity, to the Algebra Aptitude Test, which acts as a specific predictor of success in algebra.

A good aptitude test attempts to measure an individual's potential, apart from those abilities derived from specific training. Quite often, the word "aptitude" has been used interchangeably with "readiness," and aptitude tests have been paralleled to intelligence testing. The same problem that arose with intelligence testing and the imputing of ability levels have applied to aptitude testing as well.

While the results of aptitude tests are less significant for class analysis and the setting of school norms, they do play a valuable part in assisting students in the making of decisions, usually academic or vocational in nature, prior to their participation in a particular program.

See Also: ACHIEVEMENT; CHILD-CEN-TERED; COURSE OF STUDY; DIAG-NOSIS; EVALUATION; GUIDANCE; INDIVIDUALIZATION; INTEL-LIGENCE TESTING; PSYCHOLOGI-CAL STUDIES; READINESS; STU-DENT INFORMATION.

ARBITRATION

Arbitration is a process sometimes used in negotiations whereby both parties, having failed to reach agreement, will submit the dispute to an impartial third party, either an individual or a panel, who studies all sides of the dispute and recommends a course of action.

Most collective bargaining contracts call for arbitration as the final step in grievance procedures. Arbitration has more often become a part of negotiations between teacher's associations and boards of education. A point of contention is often whether the arbitration should be binding or non-binding. If both parties are bound to accept the decision of the arbitrator, the process is called binding arbitration. There has been reluctance on the part of parties in negotiations to be bound by a third party's decisions, however, and many times the arbitration process becomes little more than another opinion to be added to the negotiation fires.

Arbitration may be compulsory, as when a government agency compels the disputing parties to submit their differences to an outside party; or it may be voluntary, when it takes place by mutual consent of the parties involved.

See Also: COLLECTIVE BARGAINING; CONTRACTS; EMPLOYEE RELA-

TIONS; FACT FINDING; GRIEVANCES; HEARINGS; IMPASSE; MEDIATION AND MEDIATOR; NEGOTIATIONS; REPRESENTATION.

ART

Art is that subject area covering the knowledge and skill relative to mankind's esthetic experience with objects or artifacts.

Art in the public schools has a twofold purpose. It should provide an opportunity for students, using various media, to gain a freedom of expression without limitation, and it should be used to develop an appreciation within the child for the beauty inherent in our culture and the world around us. A consensus on the subject would seem to indicate that the art program in grades K-6 should contain a great many hands-on experiences in arts and crafts; art in grades 7-8 should provide exploratory experiences, including some art history and appreciation; and art in grades 9-12 should center around specific areas of art interest, with these courses usually offered as electives.

Children's art has also been used for diagnostic purposes. A child's art has been linked to his or her self-concept and is also a form of self-expression. Consequently, art can be used as a diagnostic tool and as a therapeutic device. For example, J. H. DiLeo, E. Kramer and R. H. Silverman, all recognized experts in the field of the interpretation of children's art, have proven that careful observation and the use of children's art can

significantly aid educators, psychiatrists, psychologists, social workers, etc., in understanding and guiding children in their developmental growth and progress.

This growing concept of the use of art is well worth the attention of the administrator, guidance personnel, and special service teams.

See Also: ACTIVITIES; CHILD STUDY TEAM; CLUBS; COURSE OF STUDY; CULTURE; ELECTIVES; ENRICHMENT; KINDERGARTEN; PSYCHOLOGICAL STUDIES; SPECIAL SERVICES; YEARBOOK.

ASP (ALTERNATE SCHOOL PROGRAM)

An **Alternate School Program** refers to any program whereby students continue their education outside the boundaries of the traditional classroom setup.

With the call for accountability, educators are examining many methods of reaching all sections of that infamous bell-shaped curve that has traditionally been applied to students. In this search, it has been found that the traditional classroom, while still functioning well for a majority of students, is not necessarily the perfect learning environment for all students. Consequently, alternate programs for learning have been investigated and developed.

These programs range from university-affiliated schools for the exceptional student, to work-study programs for economically motivated students, to in-school suspension programs for students who would normally have had their education interrupted, to drop-out programs specifically geared to allowing for continued education after the student is no longer formally enrolled in the school.

There are many nationally validated alternate school programs which administrators may investigate if they so desire.

See Also: ACADEMIC PROGRAM; CAREER EDUCATION; COUNSELING; DROP-OUTS; ENRICHMENT; IN-SCHOOL SUSPENSION; UNGRADED; VOCATIONAL PROGRAMS; WORK-STUDY PROGRAMS; YEAR-ROUND SCHOOLS.

ASSAULT

Assault is the threat made with the apparent intention of doing bodily harm to another.

It should be noted that an essential element of assault is the real or apparent ability, on the part of the person making the threat, to do bodily harm to another. Mere words do not constitute assault, but must be combined with a perceived ability on the part of the offender to make such an assault. Consequently, a second grader who informs his or her teacher that he or she is going to "beat up" the adult cannot be construed as being guilty of an assault. Basically, a person is assaulted when he or she is placed in fear for his or her own personal safety.

Moreover, the threat must be immediate. That is, a threat to "get" a teacher after school is not technically an assault, because the threat of harm is not immediate. This is a threat, however, and the student is liable to punishment within the school for making it.

Within any school situation, it is inevitable that we will find students who assault other students. When a complaint of assault is voiced by anyone, whether a student or a member of the faculty or staff, it must be investigated. Every educator should understand that it is their duty to prevent an assault or battery where it is reasonably foreseeable.

See Also: AUTHORITY, TEACHER; BATTERY; FORESEEABILITY; LIABILITY; MALICE; MENTAL DISTRESS; REASONABLE AND PRUDENT; SAFE PLACE STATUTES; SELF-DEFENSE; SUPERVISION (STUDENTS); VIOLENCE.

ASSEMBLY PROGRAM

Assembly programs in the school serve many purposes. First, they inform students with programs such as orientation to the school or a presentation on governmental issues or drug prevention. Second, they educate students by exposing them to new ideas and new ways of thinking, during such programs as panel discussions and debates. Third, they entertain with talent shows, dramatic and musical presentations, etc. Finally, they provide recognition to students who have achieved honors in any of the many aspects of school life through awards assemblies.

Assemblies are generally considered to be valid educational experiences, and many advocates suggest that the school hold at least one assembly per week whenever possible. Except in special circumstances, the length of an assembly program should be between 45 minutes and one hour. It is also generally believed that the last period of the day should be reserved only for assemblies of the "pep rally" nature.

Assembly programs can be developed in many ways. Individual classes or grades within a school may be asked to prepare a program. Various clubs and extracurricular activities may be invited to participate. A school-wide program may be developed around a central theme such as an observance of American Education Week. An outside assembly source such as a noted speaker or a prepared assembly program by an industry or professional entertainment group may be presented. Finally, there are always groups within the community who are willing and will welcome the chance to provide an assembly program.

In the administration of an assembly, the key word is planning. Not only must the program be carefully planned, but the movement of students and the control of their behavior must also be well-planned. There must be procedures for students to enter and leave the auditorium, for seating arrangements, and for adequate supervision. There should also be a plan to handle assembly disruptions, such as a room to which students who disrupt may be taken, where they will be able to hear the assembly but not directly participate in it. Finally, some thought must be given as to who will run the assembly. Traditionally, it has been the principal or faculty member in charge, but lately, greater emphasis has been placed on having students who have been adequately trained in making introductions, giving announcements, etc., continue the assembly process.

Assemblies may also be viewed as public relations vehicles. There is great appeal for parents, particularly when their children are participating in an assembly program. Prominent members of the community, when asked to participate in assembly programs in the capacity of administering oaths, presenting awards, etc., are quite often impressed and carry back to the community a higher esteem for the schools. An administrator should also be aware that many assemblies make excellent news coverage for local papers, and this type of favorable publicity can only benefit the school's image in the community.

See Also: ACADEMIC PROGRAM; ACTIVITIES; ADDRESSES (SPEECHES); CHILD-CENTERED; CLUBS; COMMUNICATION; CULTURE; EXTRACURRICULAR ACTIVITIES; MOVIES; NEWS COVERAGE; NEWSLETTER; NEWS RELEASES; SAFETY; SCHEDULE; STUDENT COUNCIL (STUDENT GOVERNMENT).

ASSIGNMENTS

An **assignment** is an oral or written document, formal or informal in nature, which prescribes an action or service on the part of the assignee.

In education, this assignment may deal with either teachers or students. In the case of students, the grade level to which a student is assigned is at the discretion of the local school board. The criteria for assignment are age, ability, training, and intelligence. The parents have no grounds to object if the board has ruled using these criteria. Also, assignment to special classes is also permissible by the board. Parents cannot refuse this assignment without being guilty of failing to allow the child to attend school. Finally, the specific school to which a child is assigned is within the purview of the board. The nearest school to the child's residence is not automatically the school that the child will attend. The board may send any student to any school within the district for any reason, and can be assured that, provided no civil, state or federal laws have been violated, their decision will be upheld. There have been exceptions for cases of special need, however, and parents may request a hearing on their child's assignment. The parents, however, must have good educational or legal reasons for their actions. Individual cases have been brought to the courts which have reversed board rulings, but it is to be understood that *the policy has always been upheld,* and that reversals have only been based on an *individual* student's welfare.

The assignment of teachers is one of the hardest jobs faced by an administrator. The criteria for teacher assignment should include an individual teacher's qualifications, temperament and his or her desires. Assignments should never be used as a reward or punishment. In a nationwide study, however, it was determined that, for the most part, new teachers and those teachers who have become labeled as "troublemakers" are given poor assignments, teachers with a degree of longevity got harder assignments, and those teachers who were the conformers got the best assignments.

In assigning teachers, one must also remember that a teacher who has done a superlative job with "A" classes or in a fifth grade classroom may not have the temperament to handle remedial classes or a second or seventh grade classroom.

There are also special circumstances that should be taken into account when assigning teachers. There should be periodic questioning of the faculty, in order to determine who wishes to change and who does not. Changes in the health, family and education of an individual teacher should also be considered. In addition, the age, nearness to retirement and the individual's prestige among the faculty or community may call for some special assignments. If there is one key principle of making assignments, it is this: Consent means content.

ATHLETICS

See: SPORTS.

ATHLETICS, SEX DISCRIMINATION IN

Sex discrimination in athletics
is the exclusion of a person from any
aspect of an athletic program because
of the person's sex. Further, it means
any disparity between existing athletic
programs in equipment, coaching,
time, and/or money allocated, or any
other allocations because of sex
considerations.

Under Title 9 of the Educational
Amendments of 1972, no public
school or school receiving public
funds may show sex bias in any aspect
of its academic program. It was further stated that this includes athletics.
Due to several test cases such as *Reed
v. Nebraska School Activities Association* (341 F. Supp. 258, 262 [U.S.
Dist. Ct: NE, 1972]) and *Brendon v.
Independent School District Number
742* (342 F. Supp. 1224 [U.S. Dist.
Ct: MN, 1972]), the courts suggested
what a school could do to eliminate

sex discrimination. They suggested
that individualized tryouts should be
used as the basis for determining
which students are eligible to compete
on teams, a comparable girl's team be
established, and/or the boy's team be
eliminated.

Cases in which sex discrimination is easily proven involve participation in non-contact sports such as
golf, tennis, cross-country, and ski-
ing. However, since Title 9 makes the
distinction that while competitive and
contact sports can be sex-segregated
and unequal aggregate expenditures
are permitted, there are cases that
arise which are not so clearly defined.
The main basis for sex discrimination
in contact sports has been the safety of
the female athlete. In extreme cases
such as football and boxing, such
discrimination has never been, nor is
it likely to be, tested. The gray areas
are those competitive and/or contact
sports such as basketball, hockey,
soccer, and even wrestling, where
physical characteristics are not the
only, or even the main, requirement
for success. Athletes and coaches
seem to concur that determination,
intelligence, sensory perception, and
constant practice are more pertinent
keys to success. The courts will look
closely at the facts on a case-by-case
basis, if necessary, to insure that denial of participation to a female comes
from other factors than her sex.

Finally, the courts have been,
and will probably continue to be,
open to the timetable problems that
schools are having in complying with
all aspects of this problem. They can

and will demand, however, that a program be investigated and carried out within a reasonable time.

See Also: ACTIVITIES; AFFIRMATIVE ACTION; CIVIL RIGHTS; CLUBS; DISCRIMINATION; EXTRACURRICULAR ACTIVITIES; FUNDS, SCHOOL; HEARINGS; PHYSICAL EDUCATION; SAFETY; SEXISM; SPORTS; SUPPLIES AND EQUIPMENT.

ATTENDANCE

Attendance, as applied to education, refers to the number of students physically present in the school building or under school auspices during any given time.

It has long been recognized that a prerequisite to teaching students is that the students be present in order to be taught. With the advent of compulsory education laws, states were granted the power to compel student attendance. In most cases, children were required to attend school regularly between the ages of 7 and 16. Historically, attendance regulations arose in order to protect children from harsh child labor practices and as a means of facilitating the integration of immigrants into the mainstream of American life.

There have been many challenges to various states' compulsory attendance laws. For the most part, the state has been upheld in these cases. In the case of *Wisconsin v.*

Yoder (406 U.S. 205 [1972],) however, the United States Supreme Court ruled the state's interest in compulsory education "is by no means absolute to the exclusion or subordination of all other interests." This was a case on religious grounds, where the parents wished their child to terminate her education prior to age 16 for religious reasons. The courts ruled in favor of the parents, but only in this particular case. Minimum literacy is still held to be a compelling state interest.

While compulsory attendance regulations will probably continue to be challenged in the courts, the trend seems to be that the courts will only make decisions on a case-by-case basis.

Attendance records are a very necessary part of school life. Since much federal and state aid is dependent on the day-to-day attendance of pupils, the taking of proper attendance is imperative. Procedures for taking and recording attendance should be an established part of every school's operation. Many school districts employ an attendance officer in order to follow up on cases of chronic non-attendance.

See Also: ABSENCE; ABSENTEEISM; AUTHORITY, BOARD; AUTHORITY, PARENTAL; BASICS; COMPULSORY EDUCATION; FEDERAL AGENCIES; FEDERAL AID; FEDERAL PROGRAMS; MONTHLY REPORTS; PERMANENT RECORDS; STATE AGENCIES; STATE AID; STATE PROGRAMS; TRUANCY; YEAR-END REPORT.

AUDIO-VISUAL MATERIALS

Audio-visual materials are those materials used in instruction to facilitate and promote student growth and understanding that directly stimulates the hearing and/or sight of the pupil.

Audio-visual materials are not only effective in the classroom, but may also be used as part of a school-community relations program. Many audiences, child and adult alike, who may not be reached by written materials, can appreciate the same message when carried by an exhibit, slide presentation or film.

The efficacy of audio-visual materials in the learning process is unchallenged. It should be understood that one key to the proper use of A-V materials is preparation. Time should be set aside to instruct faculty members in the use of the various machines. Some schools prefer to train student aides in the running of these devices, and these aides run them for a teacher who requests a particular machine. In either case, it is a good idea to have a central place where A-V materials are stored and a method whereby these materials are checked out and returned by teachers using them. Many larger schools employ a full-time A-V coordinator whose primary task is to supply, order, maintain, and aid in the functioning of these materials.

Audio-visual materials include radio, TV and/or VTR and VCR, film projectors, filmstrip projectors, slide projectors, opaque projectors, overhead projectors, record players, tape recorders, maps and globes, flannel or felt boards, manipulative devices, movable and permanent chalk boards, posters and charts, and screens. Textbooks are not considered to be part of the A-V materials of a school.

See Also: ABILITY LEVELS; COMMUNICATIONS; COPYRIGHT; INSTRUCTION; LIBRARY AND MEDIA CENTER; MEDIA; MOVIES; MUSIC; SUPPLIES AND EQUIPMENT.

AUTHORITY, BOARD

Board authority is that authority delegated by the states to local school boards or boards of education. The term also refers to those powers expressly reserved for the board.

As a state agency and a quasi-municipal corporation, the school board has certain express and implied rights. Among these rights are the rights to make and adopt reasonable rules regarding the operation of the school; to make and adopt reasonable rules regarding the conduct of students and board employees; to enforce rules of the state and the state board of education; to provide the schools within the district with the materials necessary for instruction; to hire, fire and determine the duties and scope of any school personnel; to enter into binding contracts; and to determine the curriculum of students in accordance with minimum state standards.

Every board has the authority to

require certain courses of study, to adopt certain textbooks and to make reasonable rules regarding instruction, supervision and safety. It should be remembered, however, that this authority may only be exercised when the state has not pre-empted an area, when the exercise of authority is reasonable and not arbitrary, and when the exercise of authority does not violate an individual's contracted or constitutional rights.

Put in basic terms, every local board has the right to manage and control the local schools. This means that a school board may define policy, give direction, list objectives, and do what is necessary to maintain an efficient educational system.

The authority of local boards in specific matters may vary greatly. This includes authority in such matters as the transfers of school personnel, denial of a teacher's increment and other such powers as may come within the board's purview through contractual rights, as a result of collective bargaining.

AUTHORITY, EXPRESS AND IMPLIED

Express authority is where a power to act is given in direct terms. **Implied authority** is where a power to act is given indirectly to reasonable limits.

Express and implied authority may be separated, but there is usually an element of each in the other. While one may give express authority for a person to act, implied authority is also granted, because there may be unstated tasks that must also be accomplished in order to fulfill the original order. An example of this for the administrator would be that he or she has the express authority to control student conduct in the school. Therefore, it is understood (or implied) that the administrator also has the authority to impose and enforce reasonable rules and regulations governing that conduct. The liability is thus removed from a person who has acted under express or implied authority. That person only becomes liable when the bounds of the authority have been overreached. As in the example, there would be no authority, express or implied, for the administrator to lock a student in a closet for an entire school day. The key word in implied authority is "reasonable."

See Also: ASSIGNMENTS; AUTHORITY, BOARD; AUTHORITY, PARENTAL; AUTHORITY, TEACHER; FORESEEABILITY; LIABILITY; MINISTERIAL ACTS; REASONABLE AND PRUDENT; RESERVED POWERS; SUPERVISION (STAFF); SUPERVISION (STUDENTS); TRANSFERS.

AUTHORITY, PARENTAL

Parental authority refers to those rights and powers enjoyed by parents and guardians in regard to the education of their children.

The extent of a parent's authority over school functions and policies is largely restricted to voting for members of the local board of education and the local school budget. Generally, it has been upheld that parents do not have the right to determine who shall teach their children, how subjects shall be taught, what the general curriculum of the school shall be, or what the nature of school rules are or how these rules shall be enforced.

Parents do, however, have certain specific rights and authorities in regard to their children's progress through the educational system, as well as the normal constitutional and civil rights accorded to every citizen. For instance, parents have the right to discuss problems with school personnel and to see their child's records. There have also been rulings that upheld the parents' authority to determine whether or not their children shall participate in certain classes. These have generally been cases in which the parents' objections were reasonably based on constitutional rights, as when participation in a class would have violated the religious principles of parents and child.

The rights and authority of parents have been spelled out through test cases and through the *Federal Family Education Rights and Privacy Act of 1976* (PL93-380 483). Authority is granted to parents to have access, inspection and right of review of any and all official school records, and the schools are required to have the parent's *written* consent before releasing data to any other agency. The single exception is in a case where "an injustice would be done to the student if the record is made available to the

parent or child." However, appeal procedures were also enacted, whereby the parent could appeal, using the child study team for hearings. The child study team *must* hear them. Prior to age 18, these rights and authorities are the purview of the parents, whereas after age 18, they fall to the individual.

Parents also have the authority to demand due process from the schools regarding any action taken involving their children *(Goss v. Lopez,* 1975) (419 U.S. 565), and they have the authority to demand that their children be accorded their constitutional rights *(Wood v. Strictland,* 1975 (416 U.S. 935)).

See Also: CHILD STUDY TEAM; CIVIL RIGHTS; COMPULSORY EDUCATION; CONSTITUTIONAL RIGHTS; DISCIPLINE; DUE PROCESS; EXPULSION OF STUDENTS; HEARINGS; INTELLIGENCE TESTING; MAJORITY, AGE OF; PARENT CONFERENCES; PERMANENT RECORDS; PSYCHOLOGICAL STUDIES; RECOMMENDATIONS; RIGHTS AND RESPONSIBILITIES; SPECIAL SERVICES; STUDENT INFORMATION; VOTING.

AUTHORITY, TEACHER

Teacher authority refers to that authority granted to a teacher in the performance of his or her duties.

The primary task of a teacher is to teach. In order to adequately perform that task, the teacher is granted the authority to make and enforce reasonable rules regarding the conduct of his or her class. This authority comes from the basic principal of *in loco parentis,* which literally means "in place of parents." Under this principle, it is within the authority of the teacher to perform such acts of discipline as would normally be used by a parent with a child.

It has been basically held that teachers in the United States also have the authority to establish their own grading policy, establish a classroom discipline policy, select textbooks, structure the learning activities in a classroom in the way they believe it to be the most effective, and organize classroom time in a manner they feel will be most beneficial to themselves and their students. Teachers also have the right of access to the building of policy.

Teachers do not have the authority to determine those matters and policies that are reserved to the local board such as the class size, the grade level and the ability levels they will teach.

Obviously, teacher authority does not grant the teacher the right to make or enforce any rule or policy; or to perform any action which is in violation of local, state or federal law, or which violates an individual student's constitutional or civil rights.

See Also: ACADEMIC FREEDOM; AGENT; BOOKS; CIVIL RIGHTS; CONSTITUTIONAL RIGHTS; CONTRACTS; DETENTION; DISCIPLINE; EVALUATION; EXAMINATIONS; GRADES; GRIEVANCES; HOMEWORK; *IN LOCO PARENTIS;* INSTRUCTION; PARENT CONFERENCES; REASONABLE AND PRUDENT; REPORT CARDS; RIGHTS AND RESPONSIBILITIES; SAFETY; SUPERVISION, (STUDENTS); SUPPLIES AND EQUIPMENT; TEXTBOOKS.

AUTOMOBILES

The use and parking of **automobiles** may present a real problem for a school, particularly when it is a secondary school, and many students are driving their own or family vehicles to school. In planning a school, therefore, careful consideration must be given to alloting sufficient space for student and faculty parking. Once this area has been established, it has been upheld that it is within a school's rights to make rules regarding automobile use or misuse during the school day. Consequently, specific parking spaces may be assigned, a speed limit while on school property may be established, and rules requiring students to park on school property while they are attending class may be implemented. Moreover, the school may assign penalties for the violations of these rules and regulations.

There should also be a place reserved for visitors' parking with possibly a place reserved for the dropping off and picking up of students by parents. It should also be remembered that when an activity is taking place in school to which a large number of parents or community members have been invited, such as a back-to-school night, there will be a great many automobiles present. In such a case, it would be wise to anticipate the problem, provide people who will direct traffic and parking, and possibly advise local police of the potential difficulty.

See Also: ACCESS RIGHTS; ACCIDENTS; ACTIVITIES; DISMISSAL PROCEDURES (SCHOOL); GROUNDS; INSURANCE; LIABILITY; PARKING; POLICE; SAFETY; STUDENT INFORMATION; TRANSPORTATION.

Auxiliary Personnel

Auxiliary personnel refers to those individuals who act as assistants to members of the school staff including, but not limited to, such persons as teacher aides and paraprofessionals.

Auxiliary personnel may perform a wide variety of useful and very helpful services. For example, auxiliary personnel may assist the professional teacher with such tasks as classroom housekeeping chores, clerical duties such as record keeping and the collecting of notes and forms from home, and even class supervision. Auxiliary personnel might also be used to aid in community relations activities such as organizing displays of student work when teachers may not have the time to do so.

There may arise some difficulties in hiring auxiliary personnel. These individuals, particularly if they are to have direct contact with children,

should be thoroughly screened prior to hiring. Moreover, auxiliary personnel should receive specific training for the task or tasks they are to perform. This is particularly necessary if part of the individual's task will involve the supervision of students. Finally, there should be some mechanism provided whereby the individual's performance is periodically evaluated. This may include observation by an administrator and/or reports from the teacher who is being assisted. These evaluations may then form the basis of recommendations for the continuance or termination of employment.

It must also be noted that, if the auxiliary personnel hold professional certificates, they must be paid commensurately when they perform professional duties.

See Also: AUTHORITY, EXPRESS AND IMPLIED; AUXILIARY SERVICES; BUS AND BUS DRIVERS; CAFETERIA; EMPLOYEE RELATIONS; EQUAL EMPLOYMENT OPPORTUNITIES; IMPUTED NEGLIGENCE; LIABILITY; PLAYGROUND; SUBSTITUTE TEACHER; SUPERVISION (STAFF); SUPERVISION (STUDENTS); VOLUNTEERS.

Auxiliary Services

Auxiliary services is a term used quite often as a classification of financial accounting, which covers those activities of a school or school system that are of a distinctly social nature and may not be classified as instructional.

Every school provides a number of auxiliary services. These services include, but are not limited to, such items as the transportation of students, various lunch programs, playground maintenance, and a host of community activities. It should be noted that an auxiliary service may be required to conform to certain state statutes. For example, in the transportation of students, the state may require certain safety standards, identification markings and liability insurance.

Auxiliary services usually take a large bite out of any school budget, and it has been upheld that community members have the right to know who is performing auxiliary services in their schools.

See Also: ACTIVITIES; AUXILIARY PERSONNEL; BIDS; BUDGET; BUILDINGS; BUS AND BUS DRIVERS; CAFETERIA; COMPUTERS; CONSULTANTS; CONTRACTS; COPYING SERVICES; LIABILITY; POLICE; SAFETY; TRANSPORTATION; VENDORS.

B

BACK-TO-SCHOOL NIGHT

Back-to-School Night is a public relations event in which the parents of the students in a school are invited to come to the school, tour the facilities and meet with various members of the faculty and administration.

Back-to-School Night is known by many names. It is sometimes called "Open House" or even "Parent Familiarity Night." It is an excellent opportunity to establish positive community relations. Since their children have been attending the school regularly, they will have heard a great deal about both the school and its staff. This type of activity affords parents the chance to meet directly with those people who are so much a part of their children's lives.

One excellent idea for a Back-to-School Night is to have the parents run through a miniature school day. This works particularly well in secondary schools where students change classes on a periodic basis. In this technique, parents assemble in a central place, let us say their child's homeroom, are given a copy of their child's schedule, and proceed to follow that schedule with each period being abbreviated. A period is usually five to ten minutes in length and affords the parents the opportunity to meet their child's teacher, have the teacher explain his or her requirements, objectives and procedures for the class, and ask questions if there is time.

The abbreviated periods and the need for the parents to move on to the next class preclude a single teacher's time being monopolized by one parent. Moreover, parents come away with a real taste of what their child's day is like and an impression of what each of their child's teachers requires.

If this technique is used, it should be widely publicized, both by flyers to the home and coverage in the local press. Prior to the event, all students in the school should be required to provide their homeroom teacher with a copy of their schedule to be distributed to parents. On the night itself, there should first be a general gathering of parents where the school administrator explains the night's procedures. Parents then proceed through the "school day." Finally, light refreshments may be served at the conclusion of the program.

This is an excellent activity for American Education Week, and it goes a long way toward building warm and positive community relations.

See Also: ACKNOWLEDGEMENT; ACTIVITIES; ADDRESSES (SPEECHES); BULLETIN; CALENDAR; COMMUNICATION; FACULTY; NEWSLETTER; OPEN HOUSE; P.T.A.; SCHEDULE.

BAND

Band concerts given in schools are generally well-attended, and, at sporting events, a marching band is quite often a highlight of the day's activities. Consequently, a band composed of student musicians not only affords the students an educational and cultural experience but also benefits the school as well in terms of community good will.

While parents and community members do not expect professional quality from a student group, they will be quick to realize if a band, particularly a marching band, is poorly disciplined and poorly prepared. Therefore, every band should be thoroughly rehearsed and practiced before a public performance. Also, appearance is extremely important, and it has been shown that expenditure of public funds for band uniforms is legal in a majority of states. Nor, it should be noted, does requiring a student to wear a band uniform violate that student's right to freedom of expression.

Obviously, there must be criteria established for which students shall be admitted to the band. For educational as well as public relations reasons, the more children who can participate the better, but it would be difficult to justify admitting everyone who applied, even if they were tone deaf or had no recognizable sense of rhythm. It would seem that musical talent, musical aptitude, or a perceived ability to develop these characteristics would be safe criteria for selection. A student may not be kept out of the band because of his or her previous academic or behavioral record.

A band, properly organized, rehearsed and presented, can be a real asset to any school.

See Also: ACADEMIC PROGRAM; ACTIVITIES; APTITUDE; CLUBS; CULTURE; DANCE; DRESS CODES; EXTRACURRICULAR ACTIVITIES; GRADUATION; MEDIA; MUSIC; SUPPLIES AND EQUIPMENT; TRANSPORTATION.

BANK ACCOUNTS

Within a school system, **bank accounts** are maintained by the school board and possibly by individual schools within the system. On the board level (local or district), the chief financial officer is usually responsible for establishing and maintaining the account. Funds from these accounts are used for district-wide expenditures such as salaries, certain auxiliary services, and even for unforeseen expenses. Persons who may draw on these accounts are those individuals who have been officially empowered to do so at the bank, at the discretion of the board of education.

Individual local schools may also maintain bank accounts. Again, these are established and maintained under the auspices of the board of education by a school official designated by them. Individual school bank accounts may be used as petty cash funds, activities funds, and even for general emergency maintenance or vandalism funds. The funds for these local school accounts are generally derived from grants to the local school from the board of education for specified purposes such as vandalism repair, support of school activities, etc.

On whatever level a bank account is established, it is to be understood that the board of education will require strict accounting procedures for all monies deposited and withdrawn.

See Also: AGENT; AUTHORITY, BOARD; BUDGET; CASH; DEBTS; EXPENSES; FINANCE; FUNDS, SCHOOL; PURCHASING; SALARY; SUPPLIES AND EQUIPMENT.

BASICS

Basics are those subjects and/or skills taught in the schools which are essential to the functioning of a literate adult.

There has been a continuing public outcry lately to have the schools return to basics. Much of this outcry has arisen from the publicity centered around cases of individuals who have graduated from public schools with little or no skills in reading, math or other essential areas of knowledge. This interest in "Why Tommy Can't Read" and "Why Mary Can't Add" has sparked a concern that schools, in expanding their curriculums and trying new or innovative methods of instruction, have neglected the teaching of basics to the point where children may not be required to master the essentials.

As this "Back to Basics" movement has gained momentum, there has been an increased demand for programs and evaluations which emphasize narrowly defined skills. Indeed, many local and state school boards have mandated mastery of certain basics as a requirement for graduation from high school. With increasing public pressure and the prevalence of accountability, it seems likely that this trend will continue.

While the exact meaning of basics and exactly what constitutes mastery of basic skills is continually debated, it seems evident that there are some areas in which minimal proficiency is needed, in order for an individual to function in today's society. These areas would seem to include a proficiency in reading, language and communications skills, arithmetic, and work-study habits and techniques. Mastery of certain minimum skills in these areas would seem a *sine qua non* for any advanced program, and sufficient testing in order to verify a student's skill would seem more than warranted.

See Also: ACADEMIC FREEDOM; ACADEMIC PROGRAM; ACCOUNTABILITY; ACHIEVEMENT; COMPETENCY-BASED PROGRAMS; COMPENSATORY EDUCATION; CURRICULUM DEVELOPMENT; GRADUATION REQUIREMENTS; INDIVIDUALIZATION; INSTRUCTION; REMEDIAL INSTRUCTION; WORKSHOPS AND IN-SERVICE.

BATTERY

Battery is the wrongful touching of another's person or clothing as a result of an assault. Battery always includes an assault, but an assault may be made without battery.

An assault is an attack upon a person's mind by the threat of physical harm, while battery is the actual physical harm done to an individual. While the terms "assault" and "battery" are familiar to almost everyone, it should be noted that assault can occur without battery. It is only when actual physical contact has been established that battery has taken place.

It is unfortunately true that battery is an occurrence which one can find in the schools. While it is predominantly students who are battered, there are numerous cases of administrators and teachers who have been battered by students or an outside intruder.

A question often arises as to the liability inherent in an assault and battery. If the perpetrator of the battery is of legal age, then the liability rests with him or her. A difficulty arises in cases where students are battered by other students during the school day. It has been generally held that a teacher or administrator may be liable in situations where students are not properly supervised, or when it was judged to be foreseeable that one student was going to injure another student and nothing was done about it.

It is necessary, however, to understand just what constitutes battery. First, the contact must be *unpermitted*. Consequently, two students who willingly enter into a fight with each other have tacitly granted permission for contact and no battery has taken place. However, if a teacher or administrator failed to stop such a fight, they might be considered liable. Second, it must be *unprivileged*. That is, there are cases in which contact is permitted, as in self-defense. Therefore, the use of force and contact in defending oneself or another committed to one's care, provided that the force used is not disproportionate to the force of the attack, is not battery. Third, there must be *contact*. This contact is usually with the person's physical being, but it has been held that the act of grabbing a person's clothing and ripping off a shirt, let us say, does constitute battery. Finally, the contact must be made in a *rude and angry manner*. Consequently, lightly touching a person's arm to emphasize a point in conversation does not constitute battery, but a shove, push or violent grasping of an arm would constitute battery, if all other elements were present.

Moreover, a person who commits battery assumes liability for anyone else who is injured during the commission. Hence, a student who attacks another student and throws a rock at the victim is liable if the rock misses the intended victim and strikes another student. The perpetrator cannot claim that he or she did not intend harm to *that* individual.

Battery is a very serious occurrence, and school officials and all educators must do whatever they can to prevent it whenever foreseeable, and deal strenuously with offenders when it does occur.

See Also: ASSAULT; CHILD ABUSE; DAMAGES; FORESEEABILITY; LIABILITY; MALICE; SELF-DEFENSE; SUPERVISION (STUDENTS); VIOLENCE.

BIBLE

In the past, many school boards had established rules for daily opening exercises that included a reading from the **Bible.** Through many test cases brought before local and state courts and even the U.S. Supreme Court, it was finally decided that reading from the Bible as part of public school exercises was a violation of First and Fourteenth Amendment guarantees. Consequently, this practice was forbidden in public schools. This ban applies even in

situations where it was argued that anyone who did not wish to participate would be excused from the exercise, and thus the Bible may not be used as part of any exercise in the schools.

The very term "Bible" was defined in order to include any literature of a sacred or religious nature such as the Koran. It was ruled, however, that sections of the Bible or other religious works might be used in school when taught as examples of ethnic literature, and that this would not violate the ruling.

See Also: ACADEMIC FREEDOM; AUTHORITY, PARENTAL; AUTHORITY, TEACHER; CHRISTIAN SCIENTISTS; CIVIL RIGHTS; CONSTITUTIONAL RIGHTS; CULTURE; ETHNIC MINORITIES; FIRST AMENDMENT GUARANTEES; FOURTEENTH AMENDMENT GUARANTEES; JEHOVAH'S WITNESSES; SPECIAL INTEREST GROUPS.

BIDS

A **bid** is an offer, usually written, to perform a service or supply an item for a stated or proposed fee. This offer and statement is usually made in competition with others.

In many cases, there are statutes that require a school board to call for the submission of bids before entering into a contract for services. Where this is true, these statutes must be strictly adhered to or the subsequent contract may be considered void.

Where these statutes are not in effect, the board may award contracts at its own discretion, with or without calling for bids.

If bids are to be called for, then certain procedures should be followed. The bidders must be given sufficient data and time to allow them to prepare their bids for submission. Bids are usually accompanied by a bond. This is done because it may happen that a bidder will fail to enter into contract after the bid has been accepted. In this case, the board is then entitled to the value of the bond, plus any interest, or it is entitled to the amount of the difference between the accepted bid and the next lowest bid. Bidders are allowed to amend or correct their bids prior to the point where the bids are opened.

In accepting bids, the board may reject all the bids unless this is specifically prohibited by statute. If the board is required to accept one of the submitted bids, the law states that it must accept the lowest *responsible* bid. In order to determine if the bidder is "responsible," the board is allowed to take into consideration the bidder's financial responsibility, past practices, etc.

When the contract is formally signed and accepted, it is understood that the regular legal liabilities, penalties and clauses of the contract are binding upon both parties.

See Also: AUTHORITY, BOARD; AUXILIARY SERVICES; CONTRACTS; EXPENSES; PURCHASING; SUPPLIES AND EQUIPMENT; TRANSPORTATION; VENDORS AND VENDING MACHINES.

BILINGUAL EDUCATION

Bilingual Education consists of those programs attempting to overcome the difficulties faced by non- or partially English-speaking individuals in dealing with the educational, social and economic environments of a predominantly English-speaking society.

In the late 1960s and early 1970s a number of test cases were brought before the courts that involved students who were not fluent in English. For example, in 1970, in the case of *Diana v. State Board of Education* (Civil #C - 70 37 RFR [N.D. CA, January, 1970]), a group of Mexican-Americans charged a *de facto* linguistic bias in testing used to determine school placement. In this case, California agreed to use interpreters in order that intelligence testing be given in a child's native language and to review all previous placements.

Subsequent to this and other cases, Congress passed the Emergency School Aid Act of 1972 (ESA), (PL 92-318 Title VII [36 Stat. 235]). Among other things, this act set aside certain funds to aid schools that were engaged in developing programs of bilingual education as well as other educational programs.

Currently, the U.S. Department of Education, Office of Bilingual Education and Minority Language Affairs, supports educational programs for some 300,000 children and a growing number of adults who have one thing in common: English is a second language to them. Their first language may be any one of 70 foreign languages. The programs, all authorized under Title VII of the Elementary and Secondary Education Act (PL 96-374, 1980), stress federal assistance to help states and local school districts improve their capacity to provide special instruction when federal funding is reduced or no longer available. Program funds usually pay salaries of bilingual aides, provide teacher training and purchase bilingual teaching materials.

The Basic Projects Program helps local school districts establish, operate, or improve programs for children who can't speak English well. Demonstration projects develop exemplary approaches to meeting the needs of these children.

Research and Development Programs support research to make bilingual education more effective. Materials Development Projects promote development of instructional and testing materials for bilingual education. Bilingual Eduation Service Centers render technical assistance in the use of testing materials to teachers, parents, and others involved in bilingual education.

Several programs provide fellowships to train teachers to work with children and adults who need help in improving their English. For job-seeking adults who need this help, the Bilingual Vocational Program supports training in specific employment skills.

For further information, contact:

Office of Bilingual Education and Minority Languages Affairs
U.S. Department of Education
Washington, DC 20202
(202) 245-2600

See Also: ABILITY GROUPING; ABILITY LEVELS; ACADEMIC PROGRAM; ACCOUNTABILITY; AFFIRMATIVE ACTION; AIDES; CERTIFICATION; CIVIL RIGHTS; COMPULSORY EDUCATION; CONSTITUTIONAL RIGHTS; COUNSELING; CULTURE; DISCRIMINATION; EQUAL EMPLOYMENT OPPORTUNITIES; ETHNIC MINORITIES; FEDERAL AID; FEDERAL PROGRAMS; INSTRUCTION; LANGUAGE; MIGRANTS; MINORITIES; SPECIAL INTEREST GROUPS; SPECIAL SERVICES; SUPPLEMENTAL EDUCATION; TEACHER AIDE; TEAM TEACHING; TEXTBOOKS; VOCATIONAL PROGRAMS; WORKSHOPS.

BILL OF LADING

A **bill of lading** is written evidence of a contract between a shipper and carrier for the carriage and delivery of goods.

A bill of lading is signed by the carrier or his or her agent. It describes the goods to be carried, the name of the shipper, the terms of the contract of transportation, the place to which the goods are to be sent, and the person to whom or to whose order the goods are to be delivered.

A bill of lading is a contract which describes the terms under which the carrier agrees to transport the goods, it is a document of title, and it is a receipt for the goods.

Particularly important to a school system is the fact that a bill of lading which accompanies ordered supplies, equipment, etc., should be thoroughly checked against the invoice.

See Also: AGENT; CONTRACTS; DEBTS; EXPENSES; PURCHASING; SUPPLIES AND EQUIPMENT; VENDING MACHINES.

BOARD OF EDUCATION

A **Board of Education,** also known as a SCHOOL BOARD, is a group of individuals, usually popularly elected, who serves as an agency that is responsible for conducting the public education system of a locality.

A board of education usually consists of an uneven number of individuals. This generally avoids deadlocked voting. A member of a board of education may be any voter within a school district who is capable and available to serve, as long as it does not represent a conflict of interest. For example, a teacher may not be a member of the board of education for the district in which he or she teaches, as this would make the teacher his or her own boss and present a conflict of interest. As a general guideline, boards of education must reflect a balanced representation of the community they serve.

Power is vested in a board of education only when it acts as a body; individual members have no authority unless it is specifically designated to them by the board acting as a body. A board of education has the authority to examine and set the educational policies and philosophies of the district, providing that these are in accordance with community, state and federal laws. The board of education is also responsible for developing the financing of the local public school system.

A board of education is responsible for the running of the entire school system. The administration of schools within the district, however, is maintained by the superintendent of schools, his or her staff, and various building administrators hired by the board of education. The board of education also enters into negotiations with its employees, particularly teachers, on such items as salary and working conditions. Therefore, a board will try to establish good relations between itself and its employees. It also behooves a board of education to maintain good and positive relations with parents and the community at large. Toward this end, it behooves a board to establish procedures for handling complaints and questions from community members. This helps to delineate an efficient and effective management system that will be appreciated by parents and board employees as well.

See Also: ACCESSORY; ADVISORY COUNCILS; AGENT; AUTHORITY, BOARD; BUDGET; COLLECTIVE BAR-

GAINING; CONFLICT OF INTEREST; CONTRACTS; EMPLOYEE RELATIONS; EQUAL EMPLOYMENT OPPORTUNITIES; HEARINGS; HOSPITALIZATION; INSURANCE; LEAVE OF ABSENCE; LIABILITY; MEET AND CONFER; MONTHLY REPORTS; NEGOTIATIONS; PARLIAMENTARY PROCEDURE; PRIVILEGED COMMUNICATIONS; QUALIFICATIONS; QUORUM; RESERVED POWERS; SALARY; TRANSFERS; TRANSPORTATION; VOTING; YEAR-END REPORT.

district. Therefore, particular care must be taken in the administration of existing bonds.

Since procedures for the issuance of bonds vary from state to state, individual school boards should check thoroughly as to the procedures, bonding limits and attendant legalities to be faced in each situation.

See Also: AUTHORITY, BOARD; BUDGET; DEBTS; TAXES; VOTING.

BONDS

A board of education or school board may take out a **bond** in order to provide funds for the construction of new schools or the renovation of existing schools, etc. Since the issuance of a bond places a financial obligation upon the board of education, and by projection, upon the taxpayers, the issuance of such a bond is usually a matter for a public vote. Once a bond has been approved by the voters of a district, they may not later revoke their approval. Moreover, unless prohibited by specific statutes, a board of education may repeatedly submit a bond issue to the voters.

There are also bonding limits that are established and specified by state law, which set a limit on the amount of indebtedness that any school district may incur through the issuance of bonds. The maximum amount of allowable indebtedness is generally based upon a percentage of taxable property within the school

BOOKS

Schools run on books—all types of books. Textbooks are regularly used in classes as mainstays of the instructional program. Early childhood programs use coloring books with a few words as teaching aids. Federal programs such as *Project Head Start* and *Reading Is Fundamental* place a great emphasis on books and even provide them to schools and children enrolled in these programs. Books have been, are now and will probably continue to be permanent fixtures in all schools.

This is not to say that problems do not arise regarding books in the schools. Although textbooks have been challenged by groups outside the school, the main thrust of opposition seems to be in the area of those books that are or are not a part of the school's library, or are or are not on classwide recommended reading lists.

Many ethnic groups have complained that the books in school libraries do not sufficiently reflect the contributions made to the growth of America by minorities. They contend that a public school library should contain literature that spells out the history, contribution and culture of Blacks, Hispanics, Orientals, and various national heritages such as the Scotch, Polish, Italian, Swedish, etc. Educators have generally responded to this contention by increasing the books on various heritages in school libraries.

Other groups express concern as to the content of the books already present in schools. These groups may object that a book is immoral, subversive or improper for children of school age. These groups may often be well-organized and have community support. These matters are never easy to resolve, and they are quite often the center of a great deal of conflict for a board of education.

It has long been considered educationally sound to establish classroom libraries that contain books on many reading levels and of high interest to students. Many publishing houses and book distributors sponsor student book clubs, in which children are encouraged to buy books within their classrooms. Book Fairs are also popular as fund-raising activities for classes and community groups such as the P.T.A.

See Also: ABILITY LEVELS; ACADEMIC FREEDOM; ACCEPTANCE OF DONATIONS; AUTHORITY, PARENTAL; AUTHORITY, TEACHER; COPYRIGHT; CULTURE; EARLY CHILDHOOD PROGRAMS; ENRICHMENT; ETHNIC MINORITIES; LANGUAGE; LIBRARY AND MEDIA CENTER; MINORITIES; P.T.A.; READINESS; READING; SPECIAL INTEREST GROUPS; VENDORS AND VENDING MACHINES.

BREACH OF CONTRACT

Breach of contract is the failure or refusal by one of the parties to a contract to perform some act that is called for by the contract.

Breach of contract may also occur when performance of the contract is made impossible: for example, if a supplier was to deliver desks to a school, but the factory and warehouse burned down. If the supplier of those desks had them but refused to deliver them, this would also be a breach of contract.

When one party breaches a contract, the other party is freed from the terms of the contract. Consequently, the school board would not be bound to pay for desks that have not been delivered.

Breach of contract may also be reason for one party to sue the other for damages. There would have to have been real financial or personal hardship due to the breach of contract in order for damages to be assessed.

In terms of the professional staff of a school or school district, breach of contract on the part of an employee may serve as the grounds for disciplinary action, including dismissal. For example, were a teacher to improperly leave a school building during the school day (let us hasten to add, for a reason other than illness, family emergency, or other legitimate cause), this might be considered a breach of contract, since by contract the teacher is required to be present except for specific reasons. Consequently, a penalty such as a deduction from the pay check or, in extreme cases, dismissal might legitimately be made by the board under the premise that the teacher was guilty of a breach of contract.

In any case, the advice of the board's attorney should be sought in these matters.

See Also: ACCEPTANCE OF CONTRACTS; AGENT; CONTRACTS; DAMAGES; DEBTS; JUST COMPENSATION; LIABILITY; MISREPRESENTATION.

BUDGET

It is understood that it is impossible for a **budget** to be kept in balance when a great many people make expenditures without authorization to do so. Consequently, the superintendent of schools or the business administrator of the district usually has the task of managing the budget for a school system. To whomever this task falls, it is that person's responsibility to budget and purchase instructional supplies, learning resources and instructional media. Further, he or she should work on matters of improving the instruction and curriculum that may require special financing. These

individuals have the power to make recommendations to the board, who has final authority in these matters.

The budget is the instrument that keeps all the expenditures of the school system in balance in order that a system's total educational plan becomes a reality. There will always be pressure from various segments of the school system for greater expenditures in certain areas, and many times there are good and valid reasons. The total picture, however, should be taken into account and the total educational plan considered before any action is taken on these requests.

To a school administrator, it is a duty to prepare a budget for the individual school and then submit it to the financial officer in charge. Preparation of a school budget is usually done by having the teachers within a school fill out budget requests along pre-established guidelines, submit these to department or grade-level coordinators, and then have the coordinated budgets for grade level or department submitted to the principal. This is then passed on to the member of the central staff who handles the budget.

A building principal should supply department or grade level coordinators, as well as every teacher in the school, with specific directions for preparing individual budgets. Included should be information about the amount of funds allocated, how to list particular items and expenses, the code numbers for various items if such a system is used, and the date by which their budget requests must be submitted to the next level of authority. This date should be well in advance of the date by which the administrator is required to hand in the school-wide budget, as time will invariably be needed for coordination and revision.

See Also: AUTHORITY, BOARD; BANK ACCOUNTS; CONTRACTS; DEBTS; FUNDS, SCHOOL; HEARINGS; INSURANCE; MORATORIUM; PURCHASING; SALARY; SUPPLIES AND EQUIPMENT; TAXES; TRANSPORTATION.

BUILDINGS

A **building** is a fixed construction having walls and a roof, which is intended for use either to store something or to contain individuals. As applied here, building refers not only to schools, but also to all storage sheds, maintenance buildings, administrative office buildings, etc., within a school district.

A major item in any budget is building maintenance. In the normal operations of any building, repairs will have to be made, cleanliness maintained and general appearance considered. While these operations usually fall within the purview of the custodial staff, the funds for them are part of a district budget. Unfortunately, with the rise of vandalism in recent years, there are unexpected expenditures for building maintenance that crop up from such items as windows broken by rocks, lavatory fixtures ruined by students and damage done to walls and classroom facilities during the school day. Consequently, many school districts define a specific area of financial accounting for vandalism repair.

A board of education has the power to construct buildings which they deem necessary to their educational program. They also hold implied power to employ architects to design and facilitate construction. These powers exist, however, only where individual state statutes permit. Quite often, the construction of new school buildings and its attendant cost to the taxpayers is a "hot" issue within a community. Many open hearings and a great deal of positive public relations should be used in these cases.

Buildings may also be used for community relations. For example, the dedication of a new school building is an excellent opportunity to foster community good will. Procedures attendant to the dedication might include an Open House, tours of the school by various community leaders, a general public assembly with teachers on hand to describe the ways in which the new building will benefit the youth of the community, and even a meeting during which the public is encouraged to ask questions of administrators concerning the operation of the new building. The dedication ceremony itself should be a public affair with attendant pomp and circumstance. This is also a natural event for news coverage.

It is also to be remembered that a school is a *public* building. Therefore, it is quite often used for such matters as meetings of local scout troops, community recreation programs and voting during local and national elections. An administrator quite often must work around these public uses of the school.

See Also: BUDGET; CAPACITY; COMMON SCHOOLS; CONSOLIDATION; CUSTODIAL SERVICES; ELEMENTARY SCHOOL; GRAFFITI; GROUNDS; HABITABLE; HIGH SCHOOL; LAVATORIES; LEASE OF SCHOOL PROPERTY; MIDDLE SCHOOL; MONTHLY REPORTS; POLICE; PRIVATE AND PAROCHIAL SCHOOLS; SAFE PLACE STATUTES; SMOKING; SUMMER SCHOOL; TRESPASSER; VANDALISM.

BULLETIN

Bulletins are used quite regularly in the schools. They supply information on upcoming events, summarize meetings, show progress on a continuing program, and are often used in lieu of faculty meetings.

There are several types of bulletins. *The daily bulletin* is a sheet produced daily by the central office in a school, which usually consists of announcements of events and procedures that both teachers and students should be aware of. These items may include the meeting dates for various activities, a reminder of the date when grades are due in the guidance office and even such light matters as congratulations to faculty members on birthdays or other special occasions.

The administrative bulletin, which is usually dated and numbered sequentially throughout the school year, is used for "how to" information. These may be bulletins on how to distribute or collect locker keys, procedures on taking classes to assemblies and schedules for supervision of buses upon dismissal. An administrative bulletin usually covers one topic.

The supervisory bulletin covers explanations and clarifications of topics of interest within the school. These may include the results of a school-wide needs assessment, guidelines for teacher observation and evaluation, or even the citing of a book or article of interest to teachers in particular areas. Like administrative bulletins, these are usually numbered sequentially and limit themselves to a single topic per bulletin. These bulletins may be quite lengthy, however, covering the results of a long period of research.

All bulletins should be clearly written, and their style should be bright and positive. A copy of all bulletins issued throughout the school year should be kept in a central location.

See Also: ACKNOWLEDGEMENT; ACTIVITIES; ASSEMBLY PROGRAM; ASSIGNMENTS; BACK-TO-SCHOOL NIGHT; CALENDAR; CHANGE STRATEGIES; CLOSE OF SCHOOL; COMMUNICATION; FACULTY MEETING; OPEN HOUSE; OPENING PROCEDURES; RECORD KEEPING; SCHEDULE; TRANSPORTATION;

TRIPS; VOTING; WORKSHOPS AND IN-SERVICE.

BURDEN OF PROOF

Burden of proof refers to the duty placed upon an individual to supply the evidence in a disputed case.

In legal terms, a plaintiff is under a burden of proof to prove his or her case against a defendant. If the plaintiff accomplishes this, the burden of proof shifts to the defendant to disprove what has been offered. This principle is most familiar to the public in criminal proceedings where the prosecutor must prove the state's case beyond a reasonable doubt.

In most civil cases, however, the plaintiff is only required to prove his or her case by a preponderance of evidence. This burden must be met before any liability will be assigned. This merely means that the majority of the evidence must point toward proving the plaintiff's case.

In regard to administrative decisions, the burden of proof need only rest on a rational basis in fact. If there is a rational basis for an administrative decision, then any exercise of administrative discretion would be considered proper.

As applied to education, when dealing with a student and a disciplinary action contemplated against that student, the burden of proof rests with the administrator or school board. Obviously, this will not cause much difficulty when the discipline involves an afternoon's detention, but when a serious action such as expulsion from school is contemplated, then it behooves the school to have compiled a sufficient burden of proof to justify the action. In these cases, the burden of proof rests with the school. If, however, the school were to be sued by a parent, teacher or any outside agency, the burden of proof would rest with the litigating party. It should be remembered, however, that once they have presented their proof, the burden of proof then falls to the school to answer their charges.

In all cases, if properly established procedures are implemented, and the advice of board attorneys solicited and followed, the burden of proof should present no problem.

See Also: ACCESSORY; AGENT; ASSAULT; AUTHORITY, BOARD; AUTHORITY, PARENTAL; AUTHORITY, TEACHER; BREACH OF CONTRACT; CIVIL RIGHTS; CONFLICT OF INTEREST; CONSTITUTIONAL RIGHTS; DUE PROCESS; EXPULSION OF STUDENTS; LIBEL; NEGLIGENCE; NONFEASANCE.

BURGLARY

Burglary involves breaking and entering the place of another party with the intent to commit a felony.

Numerous schools have been burglarized. In some cases, trophies and school supplies of little financial value have been taken, while, in other cases, safes have been broken into and large sums of money, valuable school records or equipment taken.

A burglary in a school should always be reported to the local police. It is a wise practice to keep careful record of the serial numbers of projectors, TV's, record players, and other audio-visual equipment, as these often provide information that the police can use in tracking down the perpetrators. The quick reporting of a burglary and a listing of exactly what was taken are essential duties to be performed when this crime has been committed.

The schools can take some steps in order to prevent burglaries, or at least lessen their frequency. Adequate night-time lighting around the exterior of a building and at all exits is one such method that has proven to be a deterrent. Another method is to establish a policy that no more than a small amount of money, ten to fifteen dollars for example, is ever to be left in a school building overnight. Any amount beyond this would be removed from the building and deposited in the school's bank. This procedure and policy should be widely publicized, in order that all students are aware of it. Taking away a potential "target" is an effective deterrent.

In many of the larger school systems, security personnel have been hired to guard buildings during the hours when they are not in use. Whether or not a school system should go to this expense depends upon the past record of school burglaries and the degree of yearly loss from these crimes.

See Also: AUXILIARY PERSONNEL; AUXILIARY SERVICES; BUILDING; CASH; GROUNDS; KEYS; LIABILITY; PARENTAL LIABILITY; POLICE; RECORD KEEPING; SUPPLIES AND EQUIPMENT; THEFT; TRESPASSER; VIOLENCE.

BUS AND BUS DRIVERS

A school **bus** must meet state and federal minimum standards for school bus construction. All school buses, whether owned by the district or contracted, must be inspected monthly and must have a complete and thorough checkup yearly. These are established regulations that are necessary since the school bus carries children, and all care to make the bus as safe as possible must be implemented.

Since the **bus drivers** are responsible for the safety of the children in the bus during its operation, there are many guidelines for their selection and employment. A school system should thoroughly investigate each potential bus driver prior to employment for experience, previous driving and safety record, character, and such other personal qualities as may be deemed necessary. Also, all new drivers should be required to undergo a physical examination, and this should be a yearly requirement for all drivers. Newly hired drivers should undergo a training program consisting of both classroom and practical driving instruction.

Since a school bus driver often establishes close contacts with students and parents, it is highly recommended that all drivers periodically take part in some type of in-service training for their role as a bus driver and a member of the school community.

Board policy and regulations should clearly define the responsibilities and obligations of all people who are concerned with the child's safety while riding, boarding or exiting the school bus. These individuals include the bus driver, the classroom teacher, the parent, the administrative staff, and the student. In many systems, these rules and regulations are distributed to all individuals who must return a signed paper to the effect that they fully understand their part in the students' safety.

See Also: ACCIDENTS; AGENT; CLOSE OF SCHOOL; CONTRACTS; DISCIPLINE; DISMISSAL PROCEDURES (SCHOOL); EQUAL EMPLOYMENT OPPORTUNITIES; EXTRACURRICULAR ACTIVITIES; FIELD TRIPS; HANDICAPPED; INSURANCE; LIABILITY; NEGLIGENCE; PARKING; PRIVATE AND PAROCHIAL SCHOOLS; PUBLIC LAW 94-142; SAFETY; SCHEDULE; SPORTS; SUMMER SCHOOL; SUPERVISION (STUDENTS); TRANSPORTATION; TRIPS.

BUSING

Apart from the literal meaning of moving persons from one place to another, **busing** has a social and polit-

ical connotation in education. To many people, busing refers to the process of transporting students to a school other than the neighborhood school they would normally attend, in order to achieve racial balance. As such, it has been a source of controversy among parents.

It must be understood that school systems throughout the nation are under federal injunction to desegregate their systems with all possible haste. For many years, busing was used to keep the schools segregated and it has been upheld that school systems may use many methods, including busing, in order to implement the order to desegregate and achieve a racial balance in the public schools.

In the case of *Green v. County School Board of New Kent County* (391 U.S. 430 [1968]), it was held that school authorities had the affirmative duty to do whatever was necessary to eliminate discrimination "root and branch." It was ruled that the school board had a burden to establish a plan for desegregation that would work "now." In 1971, the case of *Swann v. Charlotte-Mecklenburg Board of Education* (402 U.S. 1) affirmed that cross-busing of students was a legitimate relief for *de facto* segregation.

Reaction to forced busing has often been violent as witnessed in such cities as Pontiac, Michigan and Boston, Massachusetts. Groups of parents and angered citizens have stopped buses, destroyed school property and created riot-like situations. In many cases, school enrollment dropped as parents withdrew children from school by either moving to the suburbs or placing their children in the many private schools that sprang up in answer to this demand. Busing remains an extremely "hot" issue, and any school system thinking about implementing such a policy must understand that there is bound to be controversy surrounding it.

See Also: AUTHORITY, BOARD; CIVIL RIGHTS; CONSTITUTIONAL RIGHTS; DEMONSTRATIONS; DISCRIMINATION; ETHNIC MINORITIES; FOURTEENTH AMENDMENT GUARANTEES; JURISDICTION; PETITIONS; POLICE; PRIVATE AND PAROCHIAL SCHOOLS; RACE RELATIONS; SAFE PLACE STATUTES; TRANSFERS; TRANSPORTATION; VIOLENCE; ZONING.

C

CAFETERIA

It has been held that the establishment of a **cafeteria** within a school is proper providing the cafeteria exists for the benefit of students and the convenience of faculty and staff members and not primarily for commercial gain. In preparing and serving nutritious meals to the student body, the cafeteria may be viewed as an auxiliary service. How well a cafeteria performs this function is a matter of some concern, since this service is the target of most student complaints, next to the classroom.

Most student complaints about the cafeteria center around the type and quality of the food served. One method used to combat this possible difficulty is to arrange a meeting between representatives of the student body and the person or persons in charge of the cafeteria. At such a meeting, both sides have an opportunity to express their views, and it is possible that the students may come away with a greater understanding of the problems faced by cafeteria workers. At the very least, students will not feel that their complaints are being ignored. It should be remembered, however, that, if left to individual preference, many students would eat a lunch composed of potato chips and cola, while the cafeteria's duty is to provide a balanced meal of nutritional value.

Cafterias also act as representatives of the school system, and as such, they should present a clean and neat appearance at all times. Often, the school cafeteria will be asked to serve food to adults during special activities at the school. The impression given to the public at these times can help build positive public relations.

School cafeterias are inspected regularly by local public health officials. The price of student food in a school cafeteria is often subsidized by state and federal funding. Consequently, certain items like milk, for example, may carry one price for students and a higher price for faculty or staff members.

See Also: AIDES; AUXILIARY PERSON-
NEL; AUXILIARY SERVICES; BUD-
GET; CAPACITY; CONTRACTS;
CUSTODIAL SERVICES; FEDERAL
AGENCIES; FEDERAL AID; FEDERAL
PROGRAMS; OPEN HOUSE; PUR-
CHASING; SCHEDULE; SUPPLIES
AND EQUIPMENT; VENDORS AND
VENDING MACHINES.

CALENDAR

A **calendar** is a register or schedule of events to be held during a school year.

Establishing the calendar of days when school shall and shall not be in session during the school year is usually the province of the board of education. In many systems, advisory councils have been established, composed of teachers from the district and even community members, in order to suggest a viable school calendar. The final calendar adopted by the board is often subject to some restrictions. Many states, for instance, impose a minimum number of days in which school must be in session in order to receive state aid. This number of days is usually exceeded on a school calendar in order to accommodate days when the school may have to close for emergency reasons such as inclement weather or failure of the boiler system. It is within the board's authority to add a provision to the calendar that, should the system fall below the required number of days, these days may be made up by extending the school year beyond the specified closing date, limiting vacation periods, etc.

Each school within a district may also publish its own calendar relating those activities to take place at the school during the school year. This task should be undertaken early in the school year or, whenever possible, before school opens. This calendar should list, as far as foreseeable, every activity, sports event, dance, etc., to be held along with the date, time and place of the performance. Obviously, this is no small task, and it will be necessary to glean information from many sources within the school in order to compile an effective calendar. One way to accomplish this is to call for a meeting of the coordinators of every activity in the school, advising them ahead of time of the purpose of the meeting in order that they may prepare a schedule of events for their activity.

Subsequently, the information should be arranged in a readable and usable manner suitable for duplication. Copies should be made and distributed to all students and faculty members, as well as to all staff members and parent groups. Several copies should be kept in the main office for distribution throughout the year to interested individuals who may have lost or never have received a copy.

Calendars serve to remind people of upcoming events, to allow faculty and parents to plan activities, and as public relations vehicles showing the amount and nature of activities within a school.

See Also: ACTIVITIES; ADVISORY COUNCILS; AMERICAN EDUCATION WEEK; ASSEMBLY PROGRAMS; BACK-TO-SCHOOL NIGHT; BOARD OF EDUCATION; CLOSE OF SCHOOL; CONVENTION; DANCE; DEPARTMENTAL MEETINGS; EXAMINATIONS; EXTRACURRICULAR ACTIVITIES; FACULTY MEETING; FIELD TRIPS; GRADUATION; NEWSLETTER; OPEN HOUSE; PARENT CONFERENCES; PROM; P.T.A.; REPORT CARDS; SCHEDULE; SPORTS; SUMMER SCHOOL; TRIPS; YEAR-ROUND SCHOOLS.

CAPACITY

Capacity refers to the maximum number of people that can be safely contained and efficiently managed within a given area.

To understand how capacity relates to education, one must remember that the capacity of a building does not refer to how many individuals can be placed in the building, but rather to how many can be safely and efficiently managed within the building. For example, the legal capacity of a theater is limited to the number of seats. Obviously, one could pack the theater by standing people in the aisles and exits. This would exceed capacity, however, since in this latter case, the people could not be safely and efficiently handled in an emergency.

It is inevitable that this principle be applied to class size in schools. Just because a room can physically hold 50 students and one teacher does

not mean that 50 students can be effectively managed by the single teacher. Consequently, merely having the room for students has not been held as a justification for larger class size.

The administrator is also faced with problems of capacity in relation to such activities as the cafeteria, assembly programs, playgrounds, etc. For example, if a cafeteria can safely and efficiently serve and contain 250 students during a lunch period, in a school of 750 students, the school day's schedule must obviously contain three lunch periods. While this scheduling of three lunch periods will undoubtedly present problems for the scheduling of the academic program, the capacity of the cafeteria demands that it be done or the administrator is left open to charges of inefficient management.

The principle of capacity will also dictate the manner in which classes are scheduled. For example, once a school has exceeded its capacity, it may be necessary to have the school put on split sessions in order to safely and efficiently manage the number of students attending. Needless to say, a concern for the proper learning environment and the safety of the students will be the motivating factor in any such decision.

See Also: ACTIVITIES; BUILDINGS; CAFETERIA; DANCE; FORESEEABILITY; GRADUATION; INSURANCE; NEGLIGENCE; PARKING; PLAYGROUND; SAFE PLACE STATUTES; SAFETY; SCHEDULE.

CAREER EDUCATION

Career education refers to those formal experiences through which students learn about work and various opportunities for employment in their future lives.

Career education developed as a reaction to the overemphasis on higher education during the late 1960s and the public feeling, as reflected in numerous polls, that the public schools should provide greater emphasis on the study of trades, professions and businesses. Also, during the 1970s, a projection was made that in 1980, two out of ten jobs would require higher education, while seven out of ten individuals were being given college training. Moreover, studies sponsored by the doctrine of affirmative action showed that females were not being shown career opportunities, other than those traditionally reserved for women.

The approach to career education is threefold. First, elementary school children should be introduced to the idea of work and shown how it relates directly to what they learn in the classroom. Second, secondary students should be given vocational training if they are *not* going on to higher education and should be allowed to examine career opportunities even if they *are* going on. Finally, during the later years of high school, students should be encouraged to make early career choices and be given guidance as to how to prepare for that career.

Career education should reflect the educational planner's concern for the practical application of knowledge.

See Also: ACADEMIC PROGRAM: ACCOUNTABILITY; AFFIRMATIVE ACTION; APTITUDE; COMPUTERS; CONSULTANTS; COUNSELING; CURRICULUM DEVELOPMENT; ELECTIVES; ENRICHMENT; SEXISM; VOCATIONAL PROGRAMS; WORKING PAPERS; WORK-STUDY PROGRAM.

CASH

Cash is often a problem in schools. The problem arises around the sad fact that as long as there has been cash, there have been people willing to steal that cash from others. Quite often, students report that lunch money or other cash they brought with them to school was stolen, either directly from their persons or from lockers or desks. In a like manner, teachers have had money stolen from their desks or pocketbooks and wallets, or taken from wherever they temporarily left them. Schools themselves have been burglarized and cash allocated to activity funds and other school functions have been taken.

These regrettable actions have led many schools to establish policies on cash. One of the most common policies is that no cash is to be left in the school building when school is not in session. Other policies require that any cash collected during the school day, such as money for trips, book clubs, or even milk money, be placed in the school safe within minutes of its collection. Moreover, many faculty handbooks advise teachers not to carry large sums of money in school, and, in some instances, although they are rare, teachers are asked to leave all wallets, purses, and/or loose cash in the school safe at the beginning of each day.

These policies are usually well-publicized so that all students are aware that cash is not easily attainable. Removing the target of a potential assault quite often acts as a deterrent.

See Also: BURGLARY; THEFT.

CENSORSHIP

Censorship is the act of reviewing material for its content, with the aim of removing all matter that the censor deems inappropriate for those people whom the material will reach.

As applied to the schools, the problem with censorship arises in such areas as which books shall or shall not be allowed in school libraries, in class, or on teacher-made reading lists; what shall or shall not be the content of assemblies or other school-sponsored programs; and what shall or shall not be allowed in student editorials or writings in school publications. There has been a great deal of controversy regarding censorship in each of these areas.

It should be remembered that under the principle of academic freedom, teachers have the right to discuss controversial issues in class. There exists, however, a very delicate balance. A teacher has the academic freedom to discuss communism, for example, but he or she may not advocate the violent overthrow of the government. In general, the same restrictions that apply to freedom of speech also apply to the censorship of a teacher in the classroom.

Regarding the use of books in the schools, the problem arises as to what shall be censored and who shall have the right of censorship. The Supreme Court has ruled that a book may be classified as obscene, and therefore able to be censored, if it violates prevailing "community standards." This ruling has been the subject of much controversy. For the administrator, this represents a problem when a group in the community calls for the censorship of a book. The question must be asked if this group does, indeed, represent community standards. In one famous case, a community group wanted the *Tarzan* books of Edgar Rice Burroughs banned from the school library because never was it mentioned in those books that Tarzan and Jane were legally married, and they were, therefore, "living in sin." Obviously, a call for the censorship of books should be an occasion for open hearings involving a totality of the academic and public communities.

In regard to the censorship of assemblies and school programs, it is to be remembered that students have the same constitutional rights to freedom of expression as any other citizens. With these rights, however, come attendant responsibilities, and the limitations that would apply to normal citizens apply to students as well. Hence, if an assembly program was libelous, disruptive or a potential cause of injury, the school officials would have the authority to censor and/or punish those responsible for the program.

With regard to the censorship of written materials in school-sponsored publications, the courts have ruled that school officials have the right to place "conditions" on the freedom of the press but not "prohibitions." Put in basic terms, this means that a student publication may be restrained from being obscene and libelous, but may not be restrained from airing controversial issues.

The right of prior review of school publications has been upheld, providing the school has established a clear policy on this matter that contains certain key elements. First, it must state that the policy is only applicable to distribution of the materials on school grounds or at school functions. Second, it must provide students the opportunity of knowing what they can or cannot write by clearly identifying what is forbidden. However, in prohibiting certain materials, the school must not have violated the student's right to free speech. Finally, there must be a procedure established for the submission of materials for approval. This procedure must define the word "distribution"; define *to whom* the

material will be submitted, *how* it is to be accomplished, and *who is responsible* for approving the material; specify a brief period of time after which a reply is forthcoming or the student is free to publish the material; provide a prompt and fully adequate appeal procedure; and state that the policy is not operable until all students in all affected schools have been informed of it.

See Also: ACADEMIC FREEDOM; AUTHORITY, BOARD; AUTHORITY, PARENTAL; AUTHORITY, TEACHER; BOOKS; CHURCH-STATE SEPARATION; CIVIL RIGHTS; COMMUNICATION; CONSTITUTIONAL RIGHTS; FIRST AMENDMENT GUARANTEES; FREE SPEECH; INSTRUCTION; LIBEL; MEDIA; POLITICS AND THE SCHOOL; PRIVACY; PUBLICATION; SEX EDUCATION; SPECIAL INTEREST GROUPS; STUDENT INFORMATION; TEXTBOOKS; YEARBOOK.

CENTRALIZED FILING

Centralized filing is a system of record keeping whereby all materials, correspondence, etc. are located in one main or central filing center.

In any large school system, centralized filing is usually found in the offices of the central administration. This is a convenient place to store such items as the personnel files of teachers and administrators throughout the district, contracts and bids, for example. Within a given school, it is quite often a necessity due to lack of space. In schools where there is space and pupil personnel services such as a guidance department, an administrator may wish to forego a method of centralized filing, in order to place items where they may be used most efficiently; for example, having a pupil's permanent record filed in the guidance offices, while such items as teacher assignment records would be kept in the main office.

The organization of filing within a school will be dictated by the space limitations and the philosophy of the administrator.

See Also: ATTENDANCE; BILL OF LADING; BULLETINS; CALENDAR; CLERICAL SERVICES; COMPUTERS; CONTRACTS; GUIDANCE; HEALTH; MONTHLY REPORTS; PERMANENT RECORDS; PERSONNEL FILES; RECORD KEEPING; REPORT CARDS; SCHEDULE; SECRETARY; SIGN-IN SHEETS; STUDENT INFORMATION; YEAR-END REPORT.

CENTRAL STAFF

The **central staff** is that group of professional educators who bear the responsibility for the administration and function of all the schools within a school system or district.

The central staff is headed by the chief school administrative officer who generally bears the title of superintendent of schools. He or she is usually aided by an assistant or deputy superintendent, under whom are various assistant superintendents who take charge of such areas as Business, Personnel, and Curriculum and Instruction. There may also be positions for directors of Finance and Accounting, Supplies and Research. Also included may be coordinators of Elementary, Secondary, Adult or Special Education; consultants and specialists in areas such as Guidance, Health, Attendance and Special Services; and special coordinators in subject-matter areas such as Art, Physical Education, and any of the academic subject areas.

The central staff assumes educational leadership for a school system or district. Its members are directly accountable to the board of education, who employ them. By projection, they are also accountable to the general community. Besides aiding in the physical functioning of the schools, they also function as leaders of the entire educational staff in striving for common educational goals and developing a unified, coordinated curriculum.

See Also: ACADEMIC PROGRAM; ACCOUNTABILITY; CHILD STUDY TEAM; CONSULTANTS; CURRICULUM DEVELOPMENT; DEPARTMENTS; GUIDANCE; HEALTH; INSTRUCTION; INTERVIEW; MONTHLY REPORTS; RECORD KEEPING; SPECIAL EDUCATION; SPECIAL SERVICES; SUPERINTENDENT OF SCHOOLS; YEAR-END REPORT.

CERTIFICATION

Certification refers to those documents that specify that the individuals named therein have met all the legal requirements that enable them to teach in the public schools of a particular state.

While laws vary slightly from state to state, generally a person may not perform teaching duties in a public school without proper certification. Indeed, a properly issued teaching certificate is essential for employment as a teacher.

Again, while laws governing the requirements for a teaching certificate do vary, generally, the state will require that the individual seeking certification shall have completed a prescribed course of study at an approved institution. Moreover, many states require that the individual meet various standards of character.

It is usually the province of the state board of education to approve the course of study and the institution. In some instances, however, they have delegated this authority to a commission composed of educators. This commission may grant certification as well as set minimum standards for institutions that prepare teachers.

In some instances, local boards of education have established standards for the employment of teachers that have gone beyond the minimum standards set by the state for certification. In general, this policy has been upheld by the courts, providing that the board's requirements were neither "arbitrary and capricious," nor violated the civil rights of potential employees.

Certification is also necessary for educational positions beyond that of teaching in the classroom. Hence, a supervisor's certificate may be called for, in addition to a teaching certificate for a position such as principal of a school.

See Also: ACCREDITATION; CONTRACTS; COUNTY SUPERINTENDENT; DECERTIFICATION; EQUAL EMPLOYMENT OPPORTUNITIES; FACULTY; PERSONNEL FILES; QUALIFICATIONS.

CHAIRPERSONS

Chairpersons are those individuals who head or direct a committee, council, or formal or informal group that gathers and/or distributes information and materials from one organizational level to another.

All chairpersons are bound by a level of authority. Hence, they may make decisions on matters pertaining to their own or lower levels of organization with approval from above, but they act only as advisors to the higher levels of organization. Therefore, chairpersons may not set policy.

In public education, chairpersons are usually at the midpoint between administrating and teaching. Indeed, they have been defined as instructional managers. Usually "in-house" appointees based on seniority, their numbers in a particular school will depend upon the size and division of the faculty. Chairpersons are more commonly found in secondary schools where they serve as coordinators for a department. If they exist in elementary schools, it is usually as a grade level coordinator.

See Also: AUTHORITY, TEACHER; CURRICULUM DEVELOPMENT; DE-PARTMENTAL MEETINGS; DEPART-MENTS; DIFFERENTIATED STAFFING; EMPLOYEE RELATIONS; FACULTY; GRADES; INSTRUCTION; MONTHLY REPORTS; NEEDS ASSESSMENT; RECORD KEEPING; SUPERVISION (STAFF); SUPPLIES AND EQUIPMENT; YEAR-END REPORTS.

CHANGE STRATEGIES

Change strategies are those techniques that may be effectively used to bring about alterations in any aspect of the educational system.

Within any educational system, there will be times when a past practice no longer works efficiently. At such times, change is called for. It then falls to an individual, acting as a *change agent,* to implement the alteration. At such times, there are various strategies a change agent may use in order to facilitate a smooth transition.

There are several strategies that have worked well in implementing change. First, the people who are to be affected by the change should have input and be involved in the planning and decision-making process. Second, change should be a cooperative effort, and all aspects of competition among groups should be abolished. Third, all change methods should be carefully thought out, have definite goals, and have definite established procedures for attaining those goals. Fourth, the change to be implemented should not be experimental in nature, but should appear to be a real answer to a real need. Fifth, everyone involved in the change should clearly understand all aspects of the change. Finally, the change agent must be careful not to "oversell" the idea, but rather, should allow the established implementation procedures to take effect as planned.

Change agents should be careful to follow the procedures they have outlined, since constant interference with a plan gives the impression that it was not well thought out to begin with. When planning for the change, the agent should be aware that there will be resistance, and he or she should plan in terms of those objections. Finally, change agents should remember that a plan is a guide and not a master. If, during the implementation of a change, something should occur to make the plan disastrous, the wisest course of action would be to drop it.

The optimum amount of time in which to implement a change is one year.

See Also: ADVISORY COUNCILS; CURRICULUM DEVELOPMENT; EMPLOYEE RELATIONS; FACULTY; INSTRUCTION; INTERDISCIPLINARY APPROACHES; NEEDS ASSESSMENT; NEW POLICY OR PROGRAM; RECORD KEEPING; SUPERVISION (STAFF); WORKSHOPS AND IN-SERVICE.

CHIEF STATE SCHOOL OFFICIAL

Chief State School Official is an all-encompassing term used to designate the executive head of the state or commonwealth department of education.

The chief state school official's relationship to the state or commonwealth board of education depends upon the policies or rules established by that body. They are usually appointed by the state or commonwealth board of education, but, in some instances, the official may be selected by popular vote. While qualifications for the office vary extensively, the most common qualification is the possession of a teaching certificate. Obviously, state boards of education will be looking for more extensive qualifications than mere certification, and a candidate will have to meet the board's requirements.

The term of office for the chief state school official will vary from state to state. The most common designation of the term of office is that the officer serves "at the pleasure of the board."

The chief state school official is known by various titles throughout the United States, such as state commissioner of education, director of public education, state superintendent of public instruction, etc.

See Also: ADMINISTRATOR; ADVISORY COUNCILS; CERTIFICATION; FEDERAL AGENCIES; FEDERAL AID; FEDERAL PROGRAMS; JURISDIC-TION; MONTHLY REPORTS; QUALIFICATIONS; STATE AGENCIES; STATE AID; STATE PROGRAMS; YEAR-END REPORT.

CHILD ABUSE

Child abuse refers to the mental or physical harm inflicted on a minor that is disproportionate to acceptable discipline.

There is no educator who can help but be affected by a case of child abuse. The problem of battered children is a grim one. Since the school may be the child's primary contact with adults outside the home, however, it is essential that educators be aware of the problem and take steps to deal with it.

The problem of child abuse may be the subject of an in-service or workshop course for all educators in a district. Local police and/or social service agencies will usually cooperate in providing information as to the extent of the problem, how to recognize victims and how to approach a suspected victim.

Educators realize that children are notorious for getting scrapes and bruises. The mere presence of a cut, bruise or black eye, therefore, does not automatically mean that the child is being abused at home. Educators must be very careful, therefore, before making an accusation that cannot be substantiated by fact.

There should be a policy established within a system for reporting cases of suspected child abuse. No single educator should take it upon himself or herself to deal personally with the problem. A teacher, for example, who contacts the home demanding to know if the child is being treated well could cause a great deal of harm; for if the child is being abused, the child will suffer all the more, and if not, the parents will be righteously angered at the accusation.

Rather, an agency of the school set up to handle this and other investigations, such as the child study team, should be notified and given all the information that has been gathered about the child. The more substantive evidence an educator can provide this agency, the better. This might include the dates and nature of the injuries observed, the replies and remarks of the child when questioned about the injuries, and any other indications of an unfavorable home situation.

Thereafter, the educator should stand ready to assist the agency in any way, including testifying in court, toward the alleviation of the problem.

See Also: BURDEN OF PROOF; CHILD STUDY TEAM; COUNSELING; FAMILY SERVICES; FIRST AID; HEARINGS; HEARSAY; LIBEL; MALICE; MALICIOUS MISCHIEF; NURSE; PARENTAL LIABILITY; PARENT CONFERENCES; VIOLENCE.

CHILD-CENTERED

Child-centered is a term used to describe those programs, curricula and services that are primarily based upon the needs, desires and behavioral growth of the child.

All children have special needs and desires that the school must meet if the goal of educating the total individual is to be accomplished. These areas include not only the academic side of school, but also the social and personal growth of the child. Developing children, for instance, not only need to be taught math, but also generally desire to be accepted, to have a freedom of choice, to have some say in their own education, and to be treated as individuals.

Toward the goal of meeting these needs and desires, schools have re-examined curriculum, counseling services, extracurricular activities, and instructional methods. This child-centered approach is reflected in such areas as career education, greater emphasis on elective courses, individualization, interdisciplinary approaches and team teaching, alternate school programs, the increasingly student-oriented role of extracurricular activities, and much more.

See Also: ACTIVITIES; AGE LEVELS; CHILD STUDY TEAM; CLUBS; COUNSELING; CURRICULUM DEVELOPMENT; FAMILY SERVICES; INDIVIDUALIZATION; LEARNING DISABILITIES; OPEN CLASSROOMS; PRIVACY; READINESS; SPECIAL SERVICES; VOCATIONAL PROGRAMS; WORK-STUDY PROGRAM.

CHILD STUDY TEAM

The **Child Study Team** is a group of educational specialists formed in order to study, classify and recommend courses of action for children with perceived educational difficulties.

Within any educational system, there will be those students with special needs that must be met if the schools are to provide a thorough education. Various programs have been established by individual systems in order to reach these students, and various criteria for entrance have been established. A problem arises, however, as to who shall determine if a child has met these criteria.

This is one of the major areas in which a child study team functions. Upon recommendation from the principal or a teacher, a student is studied and evaluated. Following the evaluation, the child study team usually issues a report on the child, recommending a program and possibly classifying the child in such a manner as to insure that the child has met the criteria for entrance into a special program. These classifications may include Neurologically Impaired, Perceptually Impaired, Emotionally Disturbed, Socially Maladjusted, and so forth. In many cases, a child may not be placed in any special program without prior classification by the team.

This process may take some time and may include reports from outside sources such as qualified physicians, special services, or child welfare agencies. A child study team may decide not to classify a child, but rather to recommend a particular course of action to be implemented by the teacher in the classroom.

A school system should be careful to fully delineate the power and scope of authority of the child study team, and also establish clear and precise procedures for the referral of a child to the team.

See Also: APTITUDE; CHILD-CENTERED; CONSULTANTS; DIAGNOSIS; EVALUATION; FAMILY SERVICES; HEARINGS; LEARNING DISABILITIES; MAINSTREAMING; MONTHLY REPORTS; NURSE; PARENT CONFERENCES; PERMANENT RECORDS; PRIVILEGED COMMUNICATIONS; PSYCHOLOGICAL STUDIES; PUBLIC LAW 94-142; RETARDED CHILD; SPEECH THERAPY; SPECIAL EDUCATION; SPECIAL SERVICES; YEAR-END REPORT.

CHRISTIAN SCIENTISTS

Christian Scientists are members of the religion, founded in 1866 by Mary Baker Eddy, known as The Church of Christ, Scientist.

It is a fundamental tenet of Christian Science that disease is caused by mental error and may be eliminated solely by spiritual treatment without medical aid. This has led to a number of cases where medical aid for a child has been refused by parents.

In terms of public education, it should be remembered that the right to freedom of religion is a basic constitutional right and may not be violated. Consequently, a student who has become ill on school property may not be sent for medical aid if he or she refuses it on the grounds of religious belief. To do so against the wishes of the child or his or her parents would be a clear violation of their rights. In some instances, the children may wish to have another child of the same belief read the Bible or pray with them, or may request such a service from an outside source. In all cases, this has been judged a legitimate request and should be honored.

The single exception is in the case of traumatic injury. The school may administer first aid and crisis care in these cases. Hence, an open gash may be bound and the blood flow stopped without violating the rights of the child or parent.

See Also: AUTHORITY, PARENTAL; AUTHORITY, TEACHER; BIBLE; CHURCH-STATE SEPARATION; CONSTITUTIONAL RIGHTS; FIRST AID; FIRST AMENDMENT GUARANTEES; HEALTH; IMMUNIZATION, INNOCULATION AND VACCINATION; NURSE; PARENTAL LIABILITY; PSYCHOLOGICAL STUDIES; STUDENT INFORMATION.

CHURCH-STATE SEPARATION

Church-State Separation refers to the constitutional concept that the government cannot establish or impose a religious belief upon its citizens.

The First Amendment guarantees citizens the right to freedom of religion. By implication, it also guarantees freedom *from* religion. That is, it guarantees that no government may impose a religious belief upon any-

one. In short, no one's religious beliefs may be violated, nor can they be required to espouse a religious belief or participate in a religious ceremony against their will.

The doctrine of church-state separation has had a profound effect upon public education. For instance, prayer and Bible reading have been prohibited in the public schools because it has been ruled that these activities violate this principle. (*Engel v. Vitale*, 320 U.S. 421, 425 [1962]). Moreover, the nature and content of certain assembly programs and projects has been altered, in order that their content be viewed from a strictly cultural context and not from any religious connotation. For example, schools are now presenting Spring Concerts rather than Easter Pagents.

In implementing these activities, there has often been confusion. For instance, what constitutes an imposition of a religious belief upon another? Would it be legal for an elementary school to decorate the hallways with pictures of Santa Claus and reindeer? What about a Nativity scene? A Cross? A Menorah? A Star of David?

The answers would appear to involve the matter of approach to the subject and equal time. First, anything of a religious nature should be presented in a cultural context. Hence, Christmas may be discussed in terms of the beliefs and practices of Christians around the world, and Hanukkah may be presented in terms of the beliefs and customs of Jews around the world. Therefore, there should be an allocation of time to all represented religions in a school, in order to insure that every child can participate.

It has also been upheld that separation of church and state applies to individuals who object to patriotic ceremonies on the grounds of religious freedom. Students may not be required to participate in patriotic activities such as the Flag Salute and Pledge of Allegience. *(West Virginia State Board of Education v. Barnette,* 319 U.S. 624, 644 [1943]) and *(State v. Linguist,* 278 A.2d 263 [MD. 1971]).

Moreover, some students and their parents have objected to participating in certain courses given in school on the grounds that participation would violate their religious principles. It has been upheld that this is a valid objection. Of course, it is within the authority of the school to verify that the religious objections are valid and not merely one student's way of getting out of a course.

There is, however, state aid to parochial schools. This has been upheld not to violate the principle of church-state separation under the child benefit theory, which states that where the state legislation is primarily for the benefit of the students themselves and the parochial school benefits only indirectly, the aid will be upheld. *(Everson v. Board of Education,* 330 U.S. 1 [1947]) Hence, secular textbooks and transportation may be provided to parochial schools where the main benefit falls to the student. In these cases the secondary

benefits to the school may be disregarded. On this matter, each school board must be subject to the laws of its state, and unless specifically directed by the state, may not be required to supply these services.

See Also: ACTIVITIES; ART; ASSEMBLY PROGRAMS; AUTHORITY, BOARD; AUTHORITY, PARENTAL; BIBLE; BOOKS; BUS AND BUS DRIVERS; CHRISTIAN SCIENTISTS; CONSTITUTIONAL RIGHTS; FEDERAL AGENCIES; FEDERAL AID; FEDERAL PROGRAMS; FIRST AMENDMENT GUARANTEES; FUNDAMENTAL INTEREST THEORY; JEHOVAH'S WITNESSES; NON-PUBLIC SCHOOLS; PLEDGE OF ALLEGIANCE; PRIVATE AND PAROCHIAL SCHOOLS; RELEASED TIME; SHARED TIME; SPECIAL INTEREST GROUPS; STATE AGENCIES; STATE AID; STATE PROGRAMS; TEXTBOOKS; TRANSPORTATION; STUDENT INFORMATION.

CIVIL RIGHTS

Civil Rights refers to those rights enjoyed by an individual by virtue of his or her citizenship.

The *Civil Rights Act of 1964* provided federal aid for various educational programs in such a manner as to insure individuals' freedom and equal opportunity. There have subsequently been several sets of guidelines issued by the Equal Employment Opportunity Commission. Basically, it was held that "no person in the United States shall, on the ground of race, color, or national origin, be excluded from participation in, be denied the benefits of, or be subjected to discrimination under any program or activity receiving federal financial assistance."

When the *Elementary and Secondary Education Act of 1965 PL89-10, 79 Stat. 27-65* was passed, it provided much in federal aid to the schools. The schools receiving this federal aid, however, were subject to compliance with all civil rights legislation as a requisite for receiving the aid. Consequently, several changes in policy were necessitated.

No longer could separate institutions for black and white students be maintained, no matter how equal they were in facilities or equipment. Segregation in any form had to be abolished, and subsequent cases held busing of students to be a legitimate tool for achieving racial balance in the schools. Discrimination on the basis of sex was unacceptable, and a number of cases based on sex discrimination, particularly in the area of school athletics, were filed and won, causing the schools to reevaluate physical education and sports programs. The principle of Affirmative Action came to the fore and its advocates challenged traditionally established school procedures. In short, there were a great many changes in schools in order to insure the civil rights of all citizens.

See Also: AFFIRMATIVE ACTION; ATHLETICS, SEX DISCRIMINATION IN; BUSING; DISCRIMINATION; ELEMENTARY AND SECONDARY EDUCATION ACT OF 1965; EQUAL EMPLOYMENT OPPORTUNITIES; FEDERAL AGENCIES; FEDERAL AID; FEDERAL PROGRAMS; OATHS; PETITIONS; POLITICS AND THE SCHOOL; RACE RELATIONS; SEXISM; SPECIAL INTEREST GROUPS; STUDENT INFORMATION; UNIONS; VOTING.

CLASS AND CLASS SIZE

A **class** is a group of students who are taught together according to subject, ability level, etc. **Class size** refers to the number of students within a class.

The class has traditionally been organized with the teacher as instructor and the students as observers. This concept has undergone radical changes. Now the teacher is viewed as the facilitator of and the students as the active participants in the learning process. One role of the administrator in the classroom process is to make certain that students are participating under the guidance of their teacher. By performing tasks in class, students should learn independence and responsibility. This involves both academic and non-academic tasks such as students selecting their own methods of study. Also, students should learn discipline through interaction in their classroom environment. Students should furthermore be exposed to new experiences through various units presented in class. Finally, members should learn to be interested in concerns outside the class.

Within a classroom, teachers are free to use the methods they judge best in implementing the philosophy of the school and its curriculum. This stems from the principle of academic freedom, but the philosophy of the school is basically derived from the administrator.

There will be various factors within a school that will determine the class size taught by a teacher. Some of these factors are the number of courses a teacher handles, the district's standards of instruction, the nature and level of difficulty of the course, the ability levels of the children in the class, and the availability of space. It had been theorized that the optimum class size was 30 students per 900 square feet of space. This standard, however, cannot hope to be maintained, since so many other factors must be considered in determining optimum size, not the least of which are the abilities of students and teachers. Ideally, a teacher should be able to spend time with individual students during a class period. Therefore, the time allotted to a period of instruction, along with the teacher's ability to reach the number of students within a class during that time, will also be a determining factor.

Again, it must be remembered that mere availability of space is not a justification for increased class size. Determining the class size within a school is never an easy process, and administrators must consider many factors before a decision can be made.

See Also: ABILITY GROUPING; ABILITY LEVELS; ACADEMIC FREEDOM; AGE LEVELS; AUTHORITY, TEACHER; CAPACITY; COURSE; DISCIPLINE; FACULTY; HABITABLE; INSTRUCTION; KINDERGARTEN; LEARNING CENTERS; OPEN CLASSROOMS; SCHEDULE; SELF-CONTAINED CLASSROOM; SPECIAL EDUCATION; SUPERVISION (STUDENTS); UNGRADED.

CLERICAL SERVICES

Clerical services are essential to the running of any school. The school secretary is usually the chief supplier of these services, but many other individuals may be involved as well.

The methods by which clerical services are supplied to schools within a system will vary. Some systems allow the building administrator to interview applicants and make recommendations for hiring. Other systems hire clerical workers by means of a central hiring source, usually a member of the central staff, and establish a "clerical pool," the members of which are then assigned to various schools or duties as the need arises.

In many schools, parents and/or interested community members perform clerical services within the classroom on a voluntary basis.

See Also: AIDES; ATTENDANCE; AUXILIARY SERVICES; BULLETIN; CALENDAR; CASH; CENTRALIZED FILING; COPYING SERVICES; EQUAL EMPLOYMENT OPPORTUNITIES; KEYS; MAIL; MONTHLY REPORTS; RECORD KEEPING; SECRETARY; TELEPHONE; VOLUNTEERS; YEAR-END REPORT.

CLOSE OF SCHOOL

Schools may be **closed** for a variety of reasons such as inclement weather, health or safety reasons, holidays, or the summer hiatus. These are usually times when neither students nor teachers are required to be present, although an administrator may have a contractual obligation to attend. A day when schools are closed does not count toward the minimum number of school days required by some states as a requisite for state aid.

Every school should establish procedures in order to make the closing of school as smooth a function as possible. As far as possible, everyone involved in the closing should be aware of his or her part in the process.

For emergency closing of schools where parents are not aware that school will not be in session (inclement weather, boiler breakdown, etc.), it is necessary to establish a method of informing the public. These methods might include announcements on local radio stations, the sounding of the town's fire signals at a specified time, or a telephone chain organized through a school's P.T.A. utilizing class mothers who will call the parents of the children in a particular class.

When closing school for a long period of time such as for the summer recess, care must be taken that all matters of business requiring student or teacher feedback are taken care of prior to the final dismissal. Therefore, administrative bulletins should outline procedures as to how, when and where teachers will turn in keys, final reports, all grades, and other such materials and forms as required by the school system. Teachers should also be made aware of any special supervisory duties or special circumstances required on the final day of school. In a like manner, students must be advised of the ways and means of settling debts, cleaning lockers, handing in keys and other school property, the procedures for the last day of school, and dismissal.

When everyone is fully aware of the role he or she will play in the procedure, the closing of school can be a smooth and painless process for all involved.

See Also: BULLETIN; CALENDAR; COMMUNICATION; DISMISSAL PROCEDURE (SCHOOL); P.T.A.; STUDENT INFORMATION; SUPERINTENDENT OF SCHOOLS; TELEPHONE; TRANSPORTATION; VOLUNTEERS.

CLUBS

Within the extracurricular activities program of a school, there will be many activities that classify themselves as **clubs.** These may include an Art Club, a Drama Club, a Stamp and Coin Club, a particular club that sponsors interest in the language and culture of a nationality such as a French or Spanish Club, Service Clubs, and many others. These clubs provide many benefits for members, including but by no means limited to, providing individuals the opportunity to share the society of people with like interests, to perform a service for the school, and to learn skills in socialization and group dynamics.

In formulating the criteria for student membership, faculty advisors and school authorities should be aware that the criteria must be based on interest and ability *only*. Hence, an ability to sing on key may well be a proper criterion for acceptance into a Glee Club. However, it would *not* be proper or legal, for that matter, to establish a rule that only males, or only Christians, or only Caucasians, or only individuals of middle European heritage be admitted.

There may also exist within a school clubs composed of faculty members. A faculty bowling league seems to be the most common of this type. If an administrator takes an interest in these activities, it goes a long way toward promoting good employee relationships.

See Also: ACADEMIC PROGRAM; ACTIVITIES; CULTURE; EMPLOYEE RELATIONS; EXTRACURRICULAR ACTIVITIES; FUNDS, SCHOOL; MUSIC; PERMISSION SLIPS; PHYSICAL EDUCATION; P.T.A.; SPORTS; STUDENT COUNCIL (STUDENT GOVERNMENT); STUDENT INFORMATION; VOLUNTEERS; YEARBOOK.

CODE OF ETHICS

The current **code of ethics** for the educational profession states ideals, principles and standards of indi-vidual conduct as related to professional duties and responsibilities. It also sets forth a specific set of standards of professional conduct that is approved and enforced by the membership of the professional group or association.

All major professional associations both for teachers and for school administrators have formulated codes of ethics and performance standards for their members.

See Also: ACCOUNTABILITY; PROFESSIONAL ASSOCIATIONS FOR SCHOOL ADMINISTRATORS; PROFESSIONAL ASSOCIATIONS FOR TEACHERS; RIGHTS AND RESPONSIBILITIES.

COLLECTIVE BARGAINING

Collective bargaining is a term covering the negotiation, administration and enforcement of written agreements between the employers and the employee organization, usually for a definite term, defining the conditions of employment and the procedures to be followed in settling disputes or handling issues that arise during the term of the agreement.

Collective bargaining is the main method of determining wages and other conditions of employment for those who earn their living by working for others. One of the chief points of contention in collective bargaining is the scope of the collective bargaining process. In education, while basic issues have long since been defined, greater emphasis is being placed on negotiation of such items as curriculum, class size and grievance procedures, among others. While there remain items that are the managerial prerogative of the board of education by law, there is a growing scope of permissible negotiations that a board must discuss, unless specifically prohibited by state statute or law. This will undoubtedly lead to negotiations in the future that will concern themselves with a wide variety of items previously classified as non-negotiable.

See Also: AGENT; ARBITRATION; AUTHORITY, BOARD; CONTRACTS; DEMANDS; GRIEVANCES; MEDIATION AND MEDIATOR; NEGOTIATIONS; REPRESENTATION; UNIONS; UNISERV.

COMMENCEMENT

See GRADUATION.

COMMITTEE

Committees provide a wide variety of services within the school. They can help to develop curriculum, screen possible textbooks, allow for the voicing of opinions by faculty and community members, and recommend solutions to problems. Quite often, committees provide increased morale among the faculty by acting as a forum for expressing opinions and dissatisfactions, and for opening up communications between ranks. This can also be said for the community where committees are composed of representative members of the public.

It should be noted, however, that a committee may also have a negative effect. For instance, if it should appear that the committee is merely a "rubber stamp" for the administration, that its composition is loaded toward one side, or that the entire process is a placebo intended to placate a faction by pretended representation where the findings of the committee are ignored, then the formation of the committee will have worse ramifications than if it were never formed in the first place.

Care should be taken, therefore, to establish a committee well in advance of difficulties (although *ad hoc* committees do serve a purpose in unforeseen situations) to see to it that representation is equally distributed by asking for volunteers, to advise the committee fully of the scope of its authority, to publish regular reports as to the progress of the committee, and to publish a full report at the conclusion of the committee's work as to its findings, recommendations and administrative reaction to the proposals.

When convened in good faith with a representative composition and with real work to do that will aid the school and the community, the committee is an invaluable tool in the educational process.

See Also: ADVISORY COUNCILS; BOARD OF EDUCATION; CHAIRPER-

SONS; CONSULTANTS; EMPLOYEE RELATIONS; FACT FINDING; FACULTY; HEARINGS; P.T.A.; RECOMMENDATION; SPECIAL INTEREST GROUPS; VOLUNTEERS.

COMMON SCHOOLS

The term **common school** is a legal term for what is most generally referred to as a public school. It is a school that provides a free education for all children within a given district. A common school is supported by public funds, usually derived through local taxes and/or federal and state aid.

The nature and extent of the education provided by a common school will be dependent upon the individual state laws, although basic minimums for literacy are fairly consistent. Grades 1 through 12 are covered under the term, with many states including kindergarten in the definition. With necessary statutory amendments, the term can also apply to adult schools and/or community colleges.

See Also: ACCREDITATION; ADULT EDUCATION; COMPULSORY EDUCATION; ELEMENTARY SCHOOLS; FEDERAL AGENCIES; FEDERAL AID; FEDERAL PROGRAMS; HIGH SCHOOLS; KINDERGARTEN; MIDDLE SCHOOLS; PRIVATE AND PAROCHIAL SCHOOLS; RESIDENCE; SUMMER SCHOOL; TAXES; TRANSFERS; VOCATIONAL PROGRAMS; YEAR-ROUND SCHOOLS.

COMMUNICATION

Communication is essential in any school system. It is not only desirable but a necessity that students, teachers and administrators be kept informed of what is going on so that they may function efficiently. Moreover, maintaining good channels of communications often prevents problems from occurring that might spring from misunderstanding or feelings of isolation were there no communication. Parents, for example, respond very positively to communications from schools that explain school policies and practices. Care and resentment often follows, however, when no attempt at communication has been made, and parents feel alienated and uninformed about this vital area in their children's lives.

Administrators and teachers should be aware that there are various barriers to effective communication. The biggest barrier exists when communications must pass through many levels. What is told at one level of authority may be subtly changed by the time it is passed on to the next. Moreover, in a communications chain that is too long, the last person receiving a message may get an entirely different one than was originally intended. Again, if a chain is too long, a communication may reach an individual long after it has a chance to do any good. In written communications, a reader may interpret the connotations of words in a manner never intended by the sender, or a reader may pick up some non-verbal cues that may or may not have been in the intent of the communicator. Great care should be taken, therefore, to be as precise and as positive as possible in all written communications, and to keep the chains of communications short and close between levels.

The process of communication is an active one. A sender decides upon a message to be sent, encodes that message and sends it via a medium to a receiver, who decodes the message, interprets it and sends some form of feedback to the sender. Communication is, therefore, a two-way process. Proper communication, properly constructed, can go a long way toward establishing rapport, disseminating information and establishing an efficient and smooth-functioning organization.

See Also: ACKNOWLEDGEMENT; ADDRESSES (SPEECHES); APPRECIATION, LETTER OF; BULLETINS; COMMITTEE; EMPLOYEE RELATIONS; FACULTY MEETING; GRIEVANCES; HEARINGS; INSTRUCTION; LIAISON; MEDIA; NEWS COVERAGE; NEWSLETTER; NEWS RELEASES; PARENT CONFERENCES; PRIVILEGED COMMUNICATIONS; PUBLIC ADDRESS SYSTEM; PUBLICATION; STUDENT INFORMATION; TELEPHONE.

COMPARATIVE NEGLIGENCE

Comparative negligence is the legal doctrine whereby opposing parties are compared as to the degree of negligence that contributed to an injury or incident.

Comparative negligence is a relatively new idea that was formulated in reaction to the principle of contributory negligence. Under the principle of comparative negligence, the actions of both parties are examined and a determination made as to the *degree* of negligence that each party contributed to the situation. Hence, *both* parties may be found to be at fault, or a greater or lesser degree of fault may be assigned to one of the sides.

For example, if a child were to be injured in school and the parents sued the school as being negligent because it did not provide adequate supervision, the school's defense would probably be that the child was running in the hallways, for example, which was a violation of the school rules. This, the school would contend, contributed to the accident, and the child was guilty of contributory negligence. It would then be up to the jury to determine if the child were or were not guilty of contributory negligence, and it would be on this determination that liability would be assigned. There would, of course, be many other factors considered.

Under the principle of comparative negligence, however, the actions of both parties would be examined for the degree of negligence involved. If it were determined that the child was equally as negligent in running as the school was in not providing supervision, then no damages would be assigned. If, however, it was determined that the school was 90 percent negligent in its lack of supervision and the child only 10 percent negligent in running, or if the opposite were determined, then damages might be proportionate.

Not all states have adopted the principle of comparative negligence, although many legal associations are in favor of it.

See Also: ACCIDENTS; AGENT; BURDEN OF PROOF; CONTRIBUTORY NEGLIGENCE; DAMAGES; FORESEEABILITY; IMPUTED NEGLIGENCE; INSURANCE; LIABILITY; NEGLIGENCE; NONFEASANCE; PARENTAL LIABILITY; REASONABLE AND PRUDENT; RIGHTS AND RESPONSIBILITIES; SAFE PLACE STATUTES; SAFETY; SPORTS; SUPERVISION (STUDENTS); TRANSPORTATION.

COMPETENCY-BASED PROGRAMS

Competency-Based Programs are those programs that are centered about the competency to be achieved by students, and which provide those experiences, methods, etc., which will help the learner achieve such a competency.

Competency refers to the ability to adequately perform the functions required for a task. With public concern manifested today in the outcry for a return to basics, along with the emphasis that has lately been placed upon the theory of accountability, the schools are increasingly focusing on competency-based programs that provide the learners with the compe-tency that has been determined necessary for adequate performance.

The competencies a school wishes to develop in its students may be ranked. First, there are *general competencies,* which are universal in fulfilling the needs of students. These competencies are multi-disciplinary in nature, and are necessary for the total functioning of the individual. Next, there are *program competencies,* which are those competencies necessary to functioning within a total program on a level-by-level basis. Third, there are *course competencies,* which are very specific and measurable and allow an individual to function adequately within a single course. Finally, there are *specific competencies,* which are necessary for accomplishing the objectives of a course. For instance, the competency to solve addition problems in a specific math class is necessary for the accomplishment of learning in that area.

With the appraisal of the competencies needed by students, there will then arise the necessity of developing programs and/or altering the curriculum in order to provide maximum opportunities for the attaining of these competencies by the students. This is often a long process involving input from various levels of the educational spectrum.

See Also: ACADEMIC PROGRAM; ACHIEVEMENT; BASICS; COMPENSATORY EDUCATION; COURSE OF STUDY; CURRICULUM DEVELOPMENT; EVALUATION; EXAMINA-

TIONS; GRADUATION REQUIRE-MENTS; INDIVIDUALIZATION; IN-STRUCTION; REMEDIAL INSTRUC-TION; STUDENT INFORMATION; SU-PERVISION, (STAFF); SUPERVISION, (STUDENT).

COMPENSATORY EDUCATION

Compensatory Education pro-grams are state funded programs in which the funds are strictly allocated for specific purposes. Compensatory education programs began as an at-tempt to compensate for disadvan-tages suffered by some percentage of the school population. For example, in 1965, Operation Headstart was founded as an attempt to provide ex-tremely young children with experi-ences that would otherwise have been reserved for children from a more privileged background.

Compensatory education came under Title VI of the education amendments of 1972, which restated the goals of the Elementary and Sec-ondary Education Act of 1965. The goal was to provide disadvantaged children with those cultural and social aspects that might inspire an equality of education. Project Headstart, Up-ward Bound, Job Corps and Man-power Training were all outgrowths of compensatory education.

The federal government also al-located money to individual states along strict federal guidelines to be administered by the state to the local levels in order to establish compensa-tory education programs.

See Also: ACADEMIC PROGRAM; BASICS; COMPETENCY-BASED PRO-GRAMS; CURRICULUM DEVELOP-MENT; ELEMENTARY AND SECOND-ARY EDUCATION ACT OF 1965; FEDERAL AGENCIES; FEDERAL AID; FEDERAL PROGRAMS; INSTRUC-TION; READINESS; REMEDIAL IN-STRUCTION; SPECIAL SERVICES; STATE AGENCIES; STATE PROGRAMS; STATE AID; UNDERACHIEVERS; YEAR-END REPORT.

COMPULSORY EDUCATION

Compulsory Education refers to those state laws (statutes and codes) mandating that all children within the state's jurisdiction shall attend school.

Generally, states compel the edu-cation of children from ages 7 through 16. This does not mean that a child must attend a common school; the child may be placed by his or her parents in a parochial or private school, or even be provided with tu-tors who are certified. However it is accomplished, every child must re-ceive an education.

There have been numerous chal-lenges to the doctrines of compulsory education. Cases have been brought before the courts on the grounds that compulsory education violates due process as guaranteed by state and federal constitutions and that it vio-lates religious freedom. While it has been upheld that the state has the right to compel education, it has also been upheld that this right is by no means absolute *(Wisconsin v. Yoder,* 406

U.S. 205 [1972]). The courts have indicated a willingness to review on a case-by-case basis.

See Also: ATTENDANCE; AUTHORITY, BOARD; AUTHORITY, PARENTAL; CALENDAR; CHURCH-STATE SEPA-RATION; COMMON SCHOOLS; ELE-MENTARY AND SECONDARY EDUCA-TION ACT OF 1965; JURISDICTION; PARENTAL LIABILITY; PRIVATE AND PAROCHIAL SCHOOLS; STATE AGEN-CIES; STATE AID; STATE PROGRAMS.

COMPUTERS

Computers are being in-creasingly used in education. They provide invaluable services and save a great deal of time and effort. Cur-rently, computers are being used to store data pertaining to personnel rec-ords, student records and the various purchases and financial transactions of the board of education. In many school systems, computers are also being used to handle attendance rec-ords and even to print and distribute student report cards. As the amount of information to be processed through individual school systems prolife-rates, it seems inevitable that more districts will be turning to computers for aid in correlating data and in data storage and retrieval. Computers may also be used to do projections that may be of value to a school board, such as projected population growth within a district.

Since the computer is becoming an entrenched part of American life,

many systems are beginning to offer introductory courses in computer pro-gramming and technology on the sec-ondary level, and computers are being used in elementary school as learning and teaching devices.

While initial investments may seem high, the very fact that com-puters free the time of teachers and staff members from routine clerical tasks and leave them free to devote more attention to educational matters seems more than enough justification for their installation.

See Also: ABSENCE; ATTENDANCE; BANK ACCOUNTS; CENTRALIZED FILING; CLERICAL SERVICES; EN-ROLLMENT; GRADES; INSURANCE; INTELLIGENCE TESTING; PERMA-NENT RECORDS; PERSONNEL FILES; RECORD KEEPING; SCHEDULE; STU-DENT INFORMATION; SUPPLIES AND EQUIPMENT; TRANSPORTATION; VO-CATIONAL PROGRAMS.

CONFLICT OF INTEREST

Conflict of interest refers to a situation in which an individual holds two positions, the interest of one being in direct conflict with that of the other.

As applied to education, it is generally held that no educator or member of a board of education may hold any position that conflicts in interest to the position held in educa-tion. Hence, teachers may, indeed, serve as members of a board of educa-tion, but they may not do this in the district in which they teach. It has been held that this presents a conflict of interest since the teachers would then be setting the policy under which they would work and thus would be in a position where they could determine their salaries, working conditions, etc. Consequently, a clear conflict of interest would occur.

This same principle applies to members of the board of education. They may not serve on a school board if they hold any other position that would conflict with their board duties. Hence, if the individual were, let us say, the representative for a Realtor anxious to sell certain properties to the local board, then it might be construed that the person's position indicated a conflict of interest since it would present an undue influence upon the board.

Exactly what represents conflict of interest is often debatable and may even be the subject of legislation. For instance, one state amended its position in order to allow teachers to serve as members of the state legislature. Previously, it had been felt that this would create a conflict of interest, but further investigation and argument allowed for the necessary amendments.

See Also: ACCEPTANCE OF DONATIONS; BOARD OF EDUCATION; CIVIL RIGHTS; CODE OF ETHICS; FACULTY; MEDIATION AND MEDIATOR; POLITICS AND THE SCHOOL; SPECIAL INTEREST GROUPS.

CONSOLIDATION

Consolidation involves a reorganization in which the boundaries of a school district are changed or the organizational structure of the system is altered in some manner.

There are many reasons why a school or school system would have to consolidate. Dwindling school enrollments may cause the consolidation of two schools into one, or it may necessitate the elimination of one or more classes on a grade level. Cutbacks in funding, rejection of budgets, or a general reduction of revenue base may also call for consolidation or retrenchment.

Consolidation may include such items as the closing of some schools, the reorganization of some schools, the termination of employment of some faculty members, the reduction in maintenance or other support services, the elimination of capital improvements, or the drastic reduction of athletic and other special interest programs. It should be remembered, however, that even after consolidation, the school must still provide those services and learning experiences which are required of it by state law or for proper accreditation.

See Also: ACCREDITATION; AUTHORITY, BOARD; BUILDINGS; ENROLLMENT; FINANCE; MORATORIUM; REDUCTION IN FORCE; SUPPLIES AND EQUIPMENT; TAXES; YEAR-ROUND SCHOOLS.

CONSTITUTIONAL RIGHTS

All citizens enjoy **constitutional rights,** and these rights may not be abrogated by any authority. Nor may the constitutional rights of an individual be waived by virtue of his or her employment or status. Consequently, administrators, teachers and students all have constitutional rights which must be maintained and protected in the daily functioning of the educational system.

There have been numerous test cases in education where individuals have felt that a board of education or a school has violated individual constitutional rights in its practices or policies. On a case by case basis, many of these have been upheld and the school or school system required to amend its policies or programs in order to implement full constitutional equity.

A board of education must be particuarly careful and diligent in policies of hiring, dismissal and educational regulations to see to it that the constitutional rights of all members of the educational community, including those of students, are fully recognized and protected.

See Also: BIBLE; CENSORSHIP; CHRISTIAN SCIENTISTS; CHURCH-STATE SEPARATION; DEMONSTRATIONS; DISCRIMINATION; DUE PROCESS; *EX POST FACTO;* FIFTH AMENDMENT GUARANTEES; FIRST AMENDMENT GUARANTEES; FOURTEENTH AMENDMENT GUARANTEES; FOURTH AMENDMENT GUARANTEES; FREE SPEECH; HEARINGS; JEHOVAH'S WITNESSES; LIBEL; MAIL; OATHS; PERMANENT RECORDS; PERSONNEL FILES; PETITIONS; PLEDGE OF ALLEGIANCE; POLITICS AND THE SCHOOL; PRAYER; PRIVACY; PRIVATE AND PAROCHIAL SCHOOLS; PUBLICATION; RESERVED POWERS; SEARCH AND SEIZURE; SELF-DEFENSE; SELF-INCRIMINATION; TAXES; VOTING.

CONSULTANTS

From time to time in the educational process, professional educators may wish to call in **consultants** for advice on certain topics of particular interest or concern. Hence, consultants may supply a number of services. A consultant may, for example, advise teachers on how to run videotape machines, how to set up a program of computer generated learning, the newest textbooks available within a particular discipline, or methods of facilitating a new policy or program.

Consultants need not be authorities from outside the school system, although they frequently are. Any faculty or staff member, coordinator or even a central staff member may serve in the capacity of a consultant should the need arise, provided that the person has the degree of expertise to serve.

See Also: ACTIVITIES; ADULT EDUCA-

TION; ADVISORY COUNCILS; AUXILI-
ARY PERSONNEL; CAREER EDUCA-
TION; CURRICULUM DEVELOP-
MENT; DIFFERENTIATED STAFFING;
EVALUATION; FAMILY SERVICES;
LEARNING DISABILITIES; MEDIA-
TION AND MEDIATOR; PSYCHOLOGI-
CAL STUDIES; RECOMMENDATION;
SPECIAL SERVICES; SUPERVISION
(STAFF); UNISERV; WORKSHOPS AND
IN-SERVICE.

CONTRACTED LEARNING

Contracted learning refers to a learning strategy in which a teacher and one or more students enter into an agreement as to what will be learned, what each party will do and how it shall be evaluated.

If a student has a need or difficulty in any particular area, a teacher may wish to enter into a contract with the student. In such a contract, what the student will do over a particular period of time is specifically spelled out. This may include what the child will do in terms of the subject matter, his behavior or a variety of other spects of the child's learning situation. While this in no way negates the resonsibilities of the teacher in the learning process, it provides the student with specific direction and delineation of his or her role in the procedure. It may also help to make the connection in the child's mind between his or her actions and their results.

Obviously, these contracts are informal and not legally binding.

They do serve, however, to pinpoint specific areas where change and/or application are needed. They have been referred to as vehicles for student accountability.

See Also: ACADEMIC FREEDOM; CHILD-CENTERED; EVALUATION; INDIVIDUALIZATION; INSTRUC-
TION; LEARNING CENTERS; PARENT CONFERENCES; RIGHTS AND RE-
SPONSIBILITIES.

CONTRACTS

A **contract** is an agreement, either oral or written, between two or more parties, which binds the parties to perform or refrain from performing some act or acts.

Both parties who sign a contract must have the legal capacity to sign a binding agreement, and the contract must be legal (for example, a contract cannot require a person to perform an unlawful act) in order to be binding.

For all educators, teachers and administrators alike, the contract is probably the single most important element of their employment. Contracts for educators should specifically delineate the services and duties to be performed by the educator and all other terms of employment. The specifics of an educator's contract will, of course, vary, but a contract for educators may include specifics on sick leave, time of employment, the granting of tenure, various rights such as the right to a hearing, grievance procedures, and even the school and level to which the educator will be assigned.

Today, quite often, a teacher's association, representing the teachers of a district in collective bargaining with the board of education, will enter into agreement for a "master contract" with the board. This "master contract" spells out all the specifics of procedures and terms of employment for all the teachers in a system. Thereafter, an individual educator signing an individual contract for employment becomes subject to all the terms in the "master contract" negotiated between the board of education and the local teacher's association.

See Also: ACCEPTANCE OF CONTRACTS; AGENT; AUTHORITY, BOARD; AUTHORITY, TEACHER; BREACH OF CONTRACT; COLLECTIVE BARGAINING; EQUAL EMPLOYMENT OPPORTUNITIES; MEDIATION AND MEDIATOR; NEGOTIATIONS; NON-RENEWAL OF CONTRACT; OFFER OF CONTRACT AND RECRUITING; RATIFICATION; RENEWAL OF CONTRACT; UNIONS; VOTING.

CONTRIBUTORY NEGLIGENCE

Contributory negligence is a term which basically means that if an injured party was himself or herself guilty of negligence, which in fact contributed to the injury, he or she may not hold the other party liable to legal action even if the other party was actually negligent.

Put in other terms, if a child in school were acting in a negligent manner and was subsequently injured, the child's parents may not collect damages from the child's teacher or the administrator, even if the teacher and administrator had been acting in a negligent manner.

Let us say that an administrator had not provided supervision of the halls during the passing of classes and a student was running down the hallway, pushing other students out of the way. Let us further imagine that this student crashed into an open locker door and injured himself. The parents may not hold the administrator guilty of negligence in not providing supervision, since the student was acting in a negligent manner by ignoring the rules of the school about not running in the hallways. Actually both are negligent, and therefore, neither one may be held for damages.

It should be noted, however, that in a court of law, it is sometimes very difficult to prove a child guilty of contributory negligence. While not a steady and fast rule, it has been generally assumed that a child under the age of seven cannot be guilty of contributory negligence, that a child over the age of fourteen could contribute to his own injury, and that between the ages of seven and fourteen, the child *might* be guilty. In any case, a jury will inevitably take into consideration the age, maturity and intelligence level of the child involved. The jury will be asked to determine if the child acted in a reasonable and prudent manner for someone of similar age and ability under similar circumstances.

The principle of contributory negligence is the single most common defense against a charge of negligence. This principle is being questioned with the establishment of the principle of comparative negligence in some cases.

See Also: BURDEN OF PROOF; COMPARATIVE NEGLIGENCE; DAMAGES; FORESEEABILITY; IMPUTED NEGLIGENCE; LIABILITY; NEGLIGENCE; NONFEASANCE; PARENTAL LIABILITY; PERMISSION SLIPS; REASONABLE AND PRUDENT; SAFE PLACE STATUTES; SAFETY; SPORTS; SUPERVISION (STUDENTS); TRANSPORTATION.

CONVENTION

Many school systems encourage professional staff members to participate in the **conventions** of their professional associations. Current views would seem to indicate that attendance at professional conventions is valuable because it is a means of appraising members of recent developments and trends within the profession, affords members an opportunity to contribute in leadership roles within the profession, and is a means for sharing and appraising certain practices that are currently in practice in the members' schools. Conventions are also valuable because educators may disseminate the ideas gained at these conferences by putting them into practice at the local level.

Many school systems provide for time off from school during the con-

vention of the professional organization.

See Also: ADDRESSES (SPEECHES); AMERICAN ASSOCIATION OF SCHOOL ADMINISTRATORS; AMERICAN COUNCIL ON EDUCATION; AMERICAN FEDERATION OF TEACHERS; CALENDAR; COMMUNICATION; NATIONAL EDUCATION ASSOCIATION; POLITICS AND THE SCHOOL; PROFESSIONAL ASSOCIATIONS FOR SCHOOL ADMINISTRATORS; PROFESSIONAL ASSOCIATIONS FOR TEACHERS; SPECIAL INTEREST GROUPS; UNIONS; WORKSHOPS AND IN-SERVICE; WORLD CONFEDERATION OF THE TEACHING PROFESSION.

COPYING SERVICES

Most schools provide some sort of **copying service** for the faculty and staff. These are usually in the form of mimeograph and/or spirit duplicators and photocopy machines. So common are these machines in school, that many publishers of educational materials are selling books of spirit duplicator master sheets already printed to run off and distribute to students.

One problem faced by many schools in regard to copying machines and services involves the use of these machines by unauthorized personnel. Strict guidelines should be established as to who is permitted to use the machines, as use by someone unfamiliar or partially familiar with them may cause a breakdown. In some schools, only the clerical staff or those trained by them may duplicate materials, while other systems allow the faculty access to the machines. In either case, the people who are allowed to run the machines should be thoroughly trained in their use.

Moreover, a policy should be set as to what may be duplicated. In order to save money and keep open access to the machines for educational use, many schools prohibit the use of machines for personal reasons such as duplicating directions to a party or making copies of birth certificates. Some systems provide coin operated dry copy machines for student use and the personal use of the faculty.

See Also: AIDES; AUDIO-VISUAL MATERIALS; BULLETIN; CLERICAL SERVICES; COPYRIGHT; SECRETARY; SUPPLIES AND EQUIPMENT.

COPYRIGHT

Copyright is a protection granted by national governments through statutory enactment covering the production, publication and sale of the content and form of literary and artistic works, and advertisements.

In 1976, the copyright laws of the United States were changed drastically (PL 94-553). Under this law, copyright extends for a period of fifty years following the death of the author. This allows the family or estate of an author to collect royalties for the use of the work for those fifty years. Most literary works contain warnings that the material is copyrighted and

may not be used without specific written authorization to do so.

As applied to education, there are guidelines for the use of copyrighted materials in the classroom. Educators may make single copies of chapters, articles, poems, and the like, provided that this material is used for the educator's preparation for the teaching of a class. The teacher can make multiple copies of short poems (less than 250 words), excerpts of longer poems (up to the 250-word limit), articles (less than 2500 words), parts of prose works (1000 words or 10 percent of the work), and *one* chart or graph, if and only if these are to be distributed to students on a one-copy-per-student basis.

There are restrictions that apply. Multiple copies may not be made of work for classroom use that has already been copied for work with another class. Work cannot be excerpted from the same author more than once per term. The same work cannot be excerpted more than three times per term, or more than nine times per term from a collected work. Multiple pages from workbooks cannot be duplicated.

It would be naive to suppose that these copyright laws are rigorously adhered to in all schools. Every school has a copying machine and every teacher has access to it. The most an administrator can hope for is to be aware of the guidelines, make certain that the faculty and staff are aware of them, and be on the lookout for flagrant abuses.

CORPORAL PUNISHMENT

Corporal punishment is any action that inflicts pain or harm upon a child's body as punishment for wrong-doing.

The inflicting of corporal punishment on children in school is a highly charged issue. Several states have laws banning the use of corporal punishment entirely. New Jersey, for example, has had anti-corporal punishment legislation since 1867. Other states allow corporal punishment, but only under controlled conditions. In these states, there are definite procedures as to what kind of corporal punishment may be administered and who may do the administering of it. The most common type of corporal punishment is spanking.

Even in states with anti-corporal punishment laws, it has been defined that physical force of a reasonable nature may be used to restrain a child who threatens physical harm to another person or school property, to gain the possession of a dangerous object or weapon in the possession of a child, for self-defense, or to protect another student or students. Personal physical restraint of a "reasonable and prudent" manner is not classified as corporal punishment.

Though there is a great push for anti-corporal punishment laws, the U.S. Supreme Court has held that those laws which permit corporal punishment under controlled conditions are valid.

It has generally been upheld that corporal punishment is valid when: the student knows why he or she is being punished; the state law allows corporal punishment; it is administered within the student-teacher relationship; it is administered without malice and for purposes of correction only; and it is not excessive, and takes into consideration the age and sex of the student.

There is also contention as to what constitutes corporal punishment. Such actions as standing a child outside the class in the hallway, a lengthy "punishment" assignment composed of writing, and standing in the corner have been interpreted as corporal punishment in some cases. As more and more legal actions are brought, there are bound to be increasing qualifications as to the nature of corporal punishment.

COUNSELING

Most schools provide some sort of **counseling** services for students.

These services are often provided by a full or part-time guidance counselor or, in larger schools, a staff of counselors. The counseling provided may be in the areas of what courses are needed for certain programs; possible career choices and preparations; selecting schools and applying for higher education; behavioral problems; social and/or home difficulties, or even those problems faced by students in the normal adjustment to school. Many systems provide counseling that involves parents in decision-making.

Counseling need not be formal in nature. Some of the best counseling takes place in the classroom, on an informal basis, where an empathetic, concerned teacher, to whom students can turn without fear of repudiation, provides a sounding board for student problems and offers sound advice when called upon to do so. Indeed, this can often be the most effective form of counseling for students, since the student perceives a need by the time he or she has asked the teacher for advice.

In this sense, all educators are counselors who provide counseling services to students.

See Also: ACADEMIC FREEDOM; AUTHORITY, TEACHER; CAREER EDUCATION; CHILD-CENTERED; CHILD STUDY TEAM; CONSULTANTS; FAMILY SERVICES; GUIDANCE; PARENT CONFERENCES; RECOMMENDATIONS; SPECIAL SERVICES; VOCATIONAL PROGRAMS; VOLUNTEERS.

COUNTY SUPERINTENDENT

A **County Superintendent** is an individual who may be either appointed or elected to perform various duties relative to the supervision and management of the public schools within a county, parish or district.

The usual term for a county superintendent is from two to five years. The position is known by various names throughout the United States such as county commissioner, division superintendent, or parish superintendent.

The duties and functions of a county superintendent vary widely from state to state. Generally, the county superintendent is the chief executive of the county board of education and must meet their requirements. The county superintendent must also meet such requirements as demanded by the state or commonwealth department of education. These are often of a statistical nature.

See Also: ADMINISTRATOR; CHIEF STATE SCHOOL OFFICIAL; JURISDICTION; QUALIFICATIONS; STATE AID; SUPERINTENDENT OF SCHOOLS.

COURSE

A **course** covers a specific time period, such as a semester or an entire school year. It is also necessary to delineate when the participants in a course shall meet and where the meeting shall take place. For most courses, this is not a problem. A typical course might be 9th Grade English, which meets Monday through Friday during Period Three of the school day, in Room 105. Some courses, however, may require more detailed planning. For example, Physical Education may meet during Period Two of the school day in the gym on Mondays, Wednesdays and Fridays, and in Room 98 on Tuesdays and Thursdays. Schedule planners must take the meeting days and places into consideration when planning.

It is understood, of course, that a course will be offered during more than one period of the day. The times when *one* of these courses will meet is important in an individual student's schedule.

It is also necessary to indicate what shall take place during the class meetings. This is referred to as the content of the course. Toward this end, each subject must follow the course of study outlined for it.

It might also be beneficial to explain what actions shall be taken during any particular cycle of the course. For example, a science class that meets for forty minutes a day, on a five-day-per-week cycle, may have a course requirement for a one-week cycle consisting of 40 minutes of lecture, 80 minutes of lab, 40 minutes of seminar or discussion, and 40 minutes of independent study, additional lab time or teacher conferences.

See Also: ACADEMIC PROGRAM; ASSIGNMENTS; AUTHORITY, TEACHER; CALENDAR; CLASS AND CLASS SIZE; COURSE OF STUDY; CURRICULUM DEVELOPMENT; ELECTIVES; INDIVIDUALIZATION; INTERDISCIPLINARY APPROACHES; INSTRUCTION; LESSON PLANS; MINICOURSES; SCHEDULE; SPECIAL EDUCATION; TEXTBOOKS; WORKSTUDY PROGRAM.

COURSE OF STUDY

A **course of study** is a plan. Within any particular subject, a course of study indicates how the learner shall achieve the objectives of the subject over a specified period of time. A course of study may take a learner from the beginning to the end of a school year, or from first grade through senior year in high school.

There are a number of steps in formulating an effective course of study. First, *goals and objectives* for learning within a specific subject area should be established. Second, it must be determined what *learning experiences* are necessary in order that a student achieve the objectives. Third, the planners must set about to *organize* the learning experiences in such a way that they are sequential and have a cumulative effect upon the learner. Fourth, individual courses (grade level, mini-courses, electives, etc.) within the course of study must be *scheduled* to facilitate the most effective use of teacher talent and student time. And, finally, there must be some vehicle of *evaluation* established in order to assess short- and long-term effectiveness.

The totality of the courses of study within a school forms the school's curriculum, which is part of the academic program of every school system.

See Also: ABILITY LEVELS; ACADEMIC PROGRAM; ACCOUNTABILITY; ASSIGNMENTS; AUTHORITY, TEACHER; BASICS; CAREER EDUCATION; CHILD-CENTERED; COMPETENCY-BASED PROGRAMS; COMPENSATORY EDUCATION; CURRICULUM DEVELOPMENT; EARLY CHILDHOOD PROGRAMS; ENRICHMENT; EVALUATION; GOALS AND OBJECTIVES; GRADES; GRADUATION REQUIREMENTS; GUIDANCE; INSTRUCTION; INTERDISCIPLINARY APPROACHES; KINDERGARTEN; REMEDIAL INSTRUCTION; SCHEDULE; SPECIAL EDUCATION; TEXTBOOKS; UNGRADED; VOCATIONAL PROGRAMS; WORK-STUDY PROGRAM; YEAR-ROUND SCHOOLS.

CREDIT UNION

A **credit union** is a cooperative association for pooling the savings of members and making loans to them at a low rate of interest.

A credit union is formed in order to meet the financial needs of individuals who share "a common bond of employment." Hence, a credit union may be composed of members who are teachers, public employees, or members of any group or profession. These credit unions offer a variety of financial services. However, individuals must show proof of the "common bond of employment" and become members of the credit union by "purchasing" at least one share ($5.00) in the union, before they can avail themselves of its services. These services include loans to members at a lower rate of interest than is usually found in a commercial bank.

Once a person becomes a member of a credit union, he or she remains a member as long as a single "share" is on deposit, even if the person should terminate his or her employment. The amount that may be loaned to members depends upon the amount of member "shares" on deposit with the union. A credit union cannot loan out more money than it has on deposit.

See Also: AGENT; EMPLOYEE RELATIONS; SPECIAL INTEREST GROUPS; UNIONS; WITHHOLDING.

CULTURE

Culture refers to the various concepts, habits skills, arts, folkways, mores, etc. of a given people.

The waves of immigrants that filled America brought with them various cultures. At one time, it was assumed that these cultures would fuse into one that would be representative of "American" culture. Indeed, the catchword was that America was the great "melting pot." That concept grew out of favor with the advent of the theory of "cultural pluralism," which saw America as a land rich with diverse cultural heritages existing side by side, each with a great deal to offer.

As far as the schools are concerned, current educational thinking would seem to suggest that all the cultural heritages represented within a school must be recognized. Consequently, no program, course of study, or type of instruction should, in any way, tend to lessen, disparage or dissolve the culture of any child or group. Children from a cultural heritage different from the prevalent culture in a school or system may need additional assistance, such as bilingual education, in order to function. They should not, however, be made to feel that they must deny their heritage and families in order to succeed in the dominant culture.

Toward this end, schools may conduct needs assessments within the community and the school staff to facilitate cultural representation. Schools might also wish to employ the services of a human relations consultant, in order to overcome inaccurate perceptions between cultures. In addition, the school's testing program should be reviewed to make certain that it does not discriminate against any culture. Finally, the staff, and particularly the guidance personnel, should include members of various cultures that are concentrated within the school.

Ethnocentrism must be avoided in public education, whether it stems from the majority or minority cultures within a school. It should be understood that a culture is neither better nor worse—merely different.

See Also: ACTIVITIES; BILINGUAL EDUCATION; CLUBS; CURRICULUM DEVELOPMENT; ETHNIC MINORITIES; EXTRACURRICULAR ACTIVITIES; FAMILY SERVICES; INSTRUCTION; LANGUAGE; LIBRARY AND MEDIA CENTER; MINI-COURSES; MINORITIES; MUSIC; NEEDS ASSESSMENT; PARENT CONFERENCES; SPECIAL INTEREST GROUPS; SPECIAL SERVICES; STUDENT INFORMATION; TEXTBOOKS; VOLUNTEERS.

CURRICULUM DEVELOPMENT

Curriculum Development refers to the ways in which the totality of the courses of study are developed within a school or school system.

There are many steps in developing curriculum. To begin with, members of the central staff meet and explore curriculum needs and problems. Then problem areas in the curriculum are discussed at various building levels. Third, a curriculum council is formed, composed of teachers, administrators, department coordinators, subject area coordinators, etc. These people then meet in order to determine the areas of critical need, to allocate time to work on the problem, to select resource people for various subject areas, and to formulate a budget for their services (consultant fees, summer salaries, etc.). This council reports back to the central staff on what areas they have decided to examine. Next the council initiates needs assessments within the community, staff and even among the students. They also call for volunteers to help in this work. Responses to the assessment are tabulated by the council, and they establish a center where curriculum materials may be gathered and stored. The council then establishes committees deemed necessary as by the responses to the needs assessment. The council meets and assimilates all the reports from the committees. They then issue bulletins on their progress, engage outside resources and keep the committees informed.

The council now goes to work by first examining the current state of the district's curriculum in the areas selected for study. They compile and duplicate the summaries of the existing curriculum in the area under study, copies of which are sent to the staff. Then they solicit reactions to the existing curriculum, and discuss these reactions in committee, with the committee reports being returned to the council. Upon investigation of these reports, the council reports its findings to the central staff. The various committees put together a written curriculum design, using desired competencies as criteria. Investigations are now conducted as to what textbooks, audio-visual aides, field trips, etc., will be used to implement the curriculum. The body of work is then edited by the council in terms of courses of study, and these are formally submitted to the central staff. If any further review is needed, additional time for work is allocated. The general staff is then provided with a full review of the work of the council. Finally, the coun-

cil sets up procedures for checking the curriculum throughout the school year.

See Also: ACADEMIC PROGRAM; ADVISORY COUNCILS; CENTRAL STAFF; CHANGE STRATEGIES; COMMITTEE; CONSULTANTS; COURSE; COURSE OF STUDY; DEPARTMENTAL MEETINGS; EVALUATION; FACULTY MEETING; GOALS AND OBJECTIVES; IN-SERVICE; INTERDISCIPLINARY APPROACHES; NEEDS ASSESSMENT; NEW POLICY OR PROGRAM; OBJECTIVES; OPEN COMMUNICATIONS; OPEN HEARINGS; RECOMMENDATION; SCHEDULE; SPECIAL INTEREST GROUPS; SUPERVISION (STAFF); TEXTBOOKS; VOCATIONAL PROGRAMS; WORKSHOPS AND IN-SERVICE.

CUSTODIAL SERVICES

Custodial services are necessary to the proper functioning of the school building. These services include the cleaning of classrooms, the maintaining of proper heating and/or cooling of buildings, the general upkeep and appearance of the school and grounds, and a host of other activities. Custodians are employees of the Board of Education under the supervision of the superintendent or business administrator of the district. They are generally assigned to the schools within a district. The number of custodial personnel within a building will depend upon the size, complexity, and needs of the individual structure.

Applicants for custodial positions should be screened and specific qualifications may be required. For example, a "Black Seal" license may be required if part of the custodian's work includes boiler operation and maintenance.

It should be remembered that a custodian is a member of the school staff, and as such, represents the school in terms of community relations. Care should be taken, therefore, to see to it that every custodial worker understands his or her role as a representative of the school system.

See Also: AUXILIARY PERSONNEL; AUXILIARY SERVICES; BUILDINGS; EMPLOYEE RELATIONS; EQUAL EMPLOYMENT OPPORTUNITIES; GROUNDS; KEYS; LAVATORIES; MONTHLY REPORTS; PLAYGROUND; RECORD KEEPING; SAFE PLACE STATUTES; SAFETY; SUPPLIES AND EQUIPMENT; UNIONS; YEAR-END REPORTS.

CUTTING

The **cutting** of classes occurs mainly on the secondary level, although it is far from unknown in the elementary schools. Students cut class for a variety of reasons, ranging from avoiding a test to the fact that it is spring and they wish to be out in the open air. Some class cutters stay within the school, "hiding out" in lavatories or stairwells, while others may leave the school grounds entirely.

The cutting of class can, of course, be a serious business, particularly for students, who absent themselves from valuable learning time. Consequently, schools have employed many methods aimed at discouraging student cuts. These methods have included establishing a policy on cutting that assigns specific penalities, including detention and even suspension; the closing down or patrolling of areas in which "cutters" congregate; and establishing quick communications channels whereby the presence of students who may be cutting class is ascertained.

See Also: ABSENTEEISM; ATTENDANCE; COMMUNICATION; COUNSELING; DETENTION; HALL DUTY; PARENT CONFERENCES; PASSES; RIGHTS AND RESPONSIBILITIES; STUDENT INFORMATION; SUPERVISION (STUDENTS); SUSPENSION; TARDINESS; TRUANCY; UNDERACHIEVERS.

D

DAMAGES

Damages are monetary compensations that may be recovered in the courts by any person who has suffered loss or injury because of the unlawful act or negligence of another.

In public education, there may be times when someone, usually the parents acting on behalf of a child, will enter suit against a school or an individual in the employ of the Board of Education in order to recover damages for an act that occurred on school property. There will, of course, be many factors that will enter into the final decision of the court, and both sides will be represented by legal counsel. If the parents should win, and liability is assigned to the Board employee or to the school system, then damages will be awarded to the plaintiff.

There are a number of types of damages that may be awarded. *Compensatory damages* are awarded in order to make an injured party whole and restore him or her to the position he or she held prior to the damaging act. Hence, if a student suffered a broken arm and compensatory damages were awarded the student, the guilty party would have to pay for all losses incurred by the student or his or her parents (medical bills, doctor's fees, etc.), as well as the costs of restoring the student to his or her former state of good health. *Punitive damages* may be awarded that are far beyond the amount of compensatory damages, in order to punish the guilty party for the wrongful act. This decision is rare in the case of negligence, and is usually reserved for punishment of an outrageous act where clear malice was intended by the wrongdoer. Finally, *nominal damages* may be awarded. These are small amounts usually awarded to merely prove the point of the plaintiff's case, usually in instances where no real harm occurred.

See Also: ACCIDENTS; AGENT; AUTHORITY, PARENTAL; BATTERY; BURDEN OF PROOF; FORESEEABILITY; HABITABLE; IMPUTED

NEGLIGENCE; INSURANCE; JUST COMPENSATION; LIABILITY; MALICE; NEGLIGENCE; NONFEASANCE; PARENTAL LIABILITY; SAFE PLACE STATUTES; SAFETY; SEXISM; SUPERVISION (STUDENTS).

DANCE

The **dance** is an entrenched part of the social life of a school. Although more common on the secondary level, one can find dances being held in elementary schools. A dance may be sponsored by the school or by an organization directly connected to the school such as the Student Council or the P.T.A. A dance may have no admission charge or else a nominal charge may be made for admittance, with the revenue going toward defraying the cost of the band, decorations and refreshments.

Since the dance takes place under the school's auspices and on school property, the event should be properly supervised. Interested faculty members, administrators and parents make excellent chaperones on a voluntary basis. Some schools enlist faculty members as chaperones and offer monetary compensation for their time. It is also wise to employ the services of a police officer for the occasion. This person is usually hired for the evening from a list of local police officers who offer their services. The officer is compensated by the school or group that sponsors the dance.

It should be understood by all chaperones and students that the normal rules of the school apply to all student functions held on school property.

See Also: ACTIVITIES; BAND; BUILDINGS; CALENDAR; CAPACITY; COMMITTEE; DRESS CODES; DRINKING OF ALCOHOLIC BEVERAGES; DRUGS; FUNDS, SCHOOL; HEALTH; INSURANCE; LAVATORIES; LIABILITY; MUSIC; NEGLIGENCE; PARENTAL LIABILITY; PARKING; POLICE; PROM; SAFETY; STUDENT INFORMATION; SMOKING; SUPERVISION (STUDENTS); VOLUNTEERS.

DEBTS

The ability of a school board to incur a **debt** is a matter of state legislation and varies greatly from state to state. Therefore, it behooves each school board to thoroughly check its state's statutes regarding this matter. Where the state does permit the board to incur a debt, there will be limitations placed upon the board. These limitations will include the purpose for which the debt is to be incurred, the procedures which must be followed for incurring the debt, and the maximum amount of allowable indebtedness which a board may incur.

The maximum amount of indebtedness is usually derived through a formula based upon a percentage of taxable property within a district. The most common method of incurring such a debt is through the issuance of bonds.

See Also: AUTHORITY, BOARD; BONDS; BUDGET; EXPENSES; FINANCE; PURCHASING; TAXES.

DECENTRALIZATION

Decentralization is the dispersal of authority, either downward or parallel, through the organizational hierarchy.

Traditionally, all schools were centralized. That is, there existed a central staff of a school system from whom all ideas filtered downward to the schools they controlled. Hence, all schools shared the same textbooks, for example, and a decision made at the administrative level applied to all schools within the district.

While the majority of American schools still operate under this system, there has been a growing push, particulary in large districts, for decentralization. Under decentralization, it is believed that there are variations in the staff and pupils which, in turn, require variations in programs from school to school; that a faculty has the right to voice an opinion about programs for its school, and will, consequently, show a greater commitment to the implementation of these programs; and, that communication is more effective in a decentralized setup, so matters can be handled more quickly and efficiently.

Where decentralization exists, the schools within a district become *almost* autonomous. The central staff of a district still exists, but their roles change to the point where they become coordinators, planners and facilitators. They are still the final decision-makers, but the individual schools now have the authority to implement and adapt their programs to their particular needs. An individual school may have programs, textbooks and methods of instruction that differ widely from a similar school in the same district. They must, however, still conform to the basic curriculum established for the district.

It must be understood that, while decentralization is an attempt to make the schools more responsive to the communities they serve, the central staff is still responsible for seeing to it that basic literacies are taught, and that no federal or state laws are violated. There exists a real need, therefore, in a decentralized setup, to establish clear policies that detail those decisions which can clearly be delegated.

See Also: ACADEMIC FREEDOM; ACADEMIC PROGRAM; ADVISORY COUNCILS; ASSIGNMENTS; AUTHORITY, BOARD; AUTHORITY, TEACHER; CENTRAL STAFF; CHANGE STRATEGIES; COMMITTEE; CONSULTANTS; CURRICULUM DEVELOPMENT; DIFFERENTIATED STAFFING; JURISDICTION; NEEDS ASSESSMENT; POLITICS AND THE SCHOOL; P.T.A.; REPRESENTATION; SPECIAL INTEREST GROUPS; SUPERINTENDENT OF SCHOOLS: SUPERVISION (STAFF).

DECERTIFICATION

Decertification of a teaching professional is the ultimate penalty.

Unlike dismissal, in which an individual merely loses a position, decertification classifies a person as unfit to teach. In effect, it ends a person's career in education.

There are four basic grounds that have been recognized in most state statutes as legitimate bases for decertification. Decertification may occur if an individual has been convicted of a crime involving moral turpitude, has been convicted of a crime that involved various sexual offenses, has been found guilty of gross neglect of duty or gross unfitness, or has been found guilty of knowingly making false statements when originally applying for certification. While these four are more or less basic to every state, it should be noted that individual states may add to this list as they choose.

It must be understood that an individual who is the subject of decertification proceedings is entitled to due process, and his or her constitutional rights must not be abrogated. Moreover, the burden of proof is on the complaining body.

In the case of *Morrison v. State Board of Education* (461 P.2d 375, 378 [CA, 1969]), the court held that there must be a clear connection between the conduct of the individual under review and the ability of that individual to perform as a teacher. Providing that the conduct was noncriminal in nature, it must be proven that the conduct directly interfered with the person's ability to teach in order for decertification to take place. Consequently, the mere fact that a person is a homosexual, cohabits with a member of the opposite sex or belongs to the Communist Party, for example, is not sufficient grounds for decertification by itself. While these may, in some cases, be grounds for dismissal, in order for decertification to occur, they must be *criminal* in nature or so interfere with the person's ability to teach that he or she can no longer function as a teacher.

See Also: BREACH OF CONTRACT; BURDEN OF PROOF; CERTIFICATION; CODE OF ETHICS; DISMISSAL OF PERSONNEL; HEARINGS; MORAL TURPITUDE; PERSONNEL FILES; QUALIFICATIONS.

DEFAMATION

Defamation is the abrogation of an individual's right to enjoy his or her reputation free from false or injurious remarks.

Defamation may also mean inciting adverse, derogatory or unpleasant feelings or opinions toward an individual.

As Shakespeare said, "he that filches from me my good name/robs me of that which not enriches him/and makes me poor indeed." (*Othello*, Act III, Scene III) In modern terms, defamation is the term used to indicate the destruction of a person's good name or reputation. This may be done by spreading false, derogatory information about a person, or by disclosing something that is true and derogatory, if it is done with malice.

For instance, to spread a false rumor that a teacher had been convicted of robbery would be defamation. It would also be defamation to spread such a rumor even if the teacher had, indeed, been convicted of robbery in the past (let us say as a youth) if the rumor was spread with malice: for instance, if this were done to turn the faculty against the teacher, or to make the situation so uncomfortable as to force his or her resignation.

Defamation is subject to action in the courts. As applied to education, the question often arises as to the possible defamatory nature of comments made by educators about students. This is particularly true in the area of comments made on student records and report cards. It may, however, also appear as verbal statements made in public about a student. In general, statements made about students can be considered defamatory only if they are not made in good faith (that is, made with malice) and fall outside the educator's scope of duties and authority. For instance, should a principal write to or tell another principal that the student the other principal is about to have transferred to his school has been sent to the office for disciplinary reasons 24 out of the last 30 school days, this is not defamation, if it is a statement of fact that one educator, acting in good faith, feels that the other educator should know. If, however, the first principal were to add that the student is obviously a sociopathic criminal with manic-depressive overtones, that would be defamation, for the principal has stepped outside his scope of duty and authority.

It should be noted that defamation does not occur when remarks are made in privileged situations such as when testifying before a court, when aiding a Child Study Team in the psychological evaluation of a student, or in a conference where it is clearly understood that strict confidentiality shall be observed.

See Also: ADDRESSES (SPEECHES); BURDEN OF PROOF; CENSORSHIP; DAMAGES; HEARINGS; HEARSAY; LIABILITY; LIBEL; MALICE; MALICIOUS MISCHIEF; PERMANENT RECORDS; PERSONNEL FILES; PRIVACY; PRIVILEGED COMMUNICATIONS; PSYCHOLOGICAL STUDIES; REFERENCES; REPORT CARDS.

DEMANDS

A **demand** is a peremptory exercise of authority that calls for something which is almost considered as the right of the demanding party.

In public education, educators are constantly being bombarded with demands from all sectors of the school and community. It may be the students of a school that "demand" a smoking area; it may be parents who "demand" that a teacher be fired; it may be a civic group that "demands" that the curriculum be changed; it may be a religious group that "demands" that a book be removed from the library shelves as immoral; or, it may be the faculty who "demands" smaller class size or more teacher aides. Whatever the group and whatever the demand, the administrator is usually the first person who must deal with the demanding group or individual. How an administrator handles the situation quite often determines all future dealings with the group or agent.

It should be remembered that, when faced with a recalcitrant, heels-in-the-dirt attitude, to adopt a similar attitude merely leads to a standoff in which no one wins and everyone is unhappy. Rather, an administrator should acknowledge that the feelings behind the demands are genuine, then set about seeking an equitable solution where lines of communication are established and the problem is thoroughly investigated.

This is often easier said than done, but the establishment of an advisory council, in order to investigate the demands at hand, is one method that allows for recognition while opening up communication between factions. If this method is used, it should be remembered that great turmoil is bound to result if the council established even hints at being weighted to one side or the other, or if it appears that it is nothing but a placebo. Therefore, the council should be equally composed of representatives of all sides pertinent to the demands in question. Hence, the council might be composed of educators, members of the community, members of the group that brought the demands, and even students from the affected school. Moreover, their pur-

pose and procedures should be made clear, and all reports and findings of the council published and widely distributed, as should any final decisions and the bases on which these decisions were formulated.

Good lines of communication and a genuinely concerned attitude on the part of the administrator go a long way toward facilitating the smooth handling of demands.

See Also: ADVISORY COUNCILS; CHANGE STRATEGIES; COMMITTEE; COMMUNICATIONS; FACT FINDING; GRIEVANCES; HEARINGS; MEDIATION AND MEDIATOR; NEGOTIATIONS; PETITIONS; REPRESENTATION; SPECIAL INTEREST GROUPS; STUDENT COUNCIL (STUDENT GOVERNMENT); UNIONS.

DEMONSTRATIONS

Although they were more common in the 1960s and early 1970s, **demonstrations** by groups continue to be a point of contention for school administrators. Demonstrations may occur at any time and may involve students, teachers and members of the community. They may take the form of picketing outside a school building, sit-ins within the school building itself or "rallies" held at some other location.

While a school surrounded by citizens, each voicing his or her opinion, is far from a comforting sight, it must be remembered that the Constitution of the United States guarantees citizens the rights of association and assembly. This means that a group basically has the right to peaceful demonstration.

There have been numerous rulings by the courts as to what is permissible in a "peaceful" demonstration. First, the demonstrating group must have *the right to be at the location where the demonstration is taking place*. For instance, they may not demonstrate on private property where they would not normally be allowed, but they may demonstrate on school property, since it is public property. Next, the demonstration must be *peaceable* in nature. The term "peaceable" has three main points: (1) no destruction of property may occur; (2) demonstrators may not deny access to "legitimate others," for example, stopping students or teachers from entering a school building; (3) they cannot stop "the conducting of proper business." For instance, as long as a group allows students and teachers to enter a school and conduct classes, they are not stopping the "conducting of proper business," no matter what signs they may be carrying or what names they may call the principal when he or she enters the school.

Other forms of demonstrations may include sick-outs, work slowdowns, work stoppages, job actions, mass resignations, and strikes.

See Also: ACCESS RIGHTS; CIVIL RIGHTS; CONSTITUTIONAL RIGHTS; DEMANDS; FREE SPEECH; JOB ACTIONS; PETITIONS; POLICE; POLITICS AND THE SCHOOL; SPECIAL INTEREST GROUPS; STRIKES; TRESPASSER; UNIONS.

DEMOTION

Demotion means the reduction in rank, grade or salary of an individual.

In public education, a demotion would be said to occur if, for example, a principal were to be assigned as a classroom teacher rather than as an administrator, or if a teacher were to be assigned as a teacher's aide. These moves would entail a reduction in status from former positions, as well as a decrease in salary.

By the terms of most contracts which result from collective bargaining, demotion of an individual is illegal. This does not mean to say that a 6th grade teacher cannot be assigned to teach 3rd grade, or that a teacher may not be transferred to another school in the township. Demotion only occurs when there is a lowering of salary as a result of the assignment. It has been held, however, that assigning a teacher to a new position requiring additional certification and where the teacher must pay for his or her own training in order to keep the new position, does impose a hardship and may be construed as a demotion.

In general, a demotion occurs where there is a reduction in salary, where additional certification is required for which the individual must pay, or where a grave hardship is imposed. In all cases involving demotion, due process must be observed.

See Also: ASSIGNMENTS; AUTHORITY, BOARD; DUE PROCESS; EMPLOYEE RELATIONS; HEARINGS; PERSONNEL FILES; SALARY; UNIONS; UNISERV.

DEPARTMENTAL MEETINGS

Within any departmentalized system, it will be necessary to have the members of a particular department gather from time to time in order to conduct business that is pertinent to the smooth functioning of the department and, by projection, to the school as a whole. These meetings may be used to discuss various topics such as textbook requisitions, reports on new teaching methods within a discipline, or the preparation of necessary reports and reviews. The departmental meeting may also be used to disseminate information from the administrative level to the faculty.

Some systems schedule departmental meetings on a regular basis, while others call them only when necessary. Although usually held after regular school hours, many systems prefer to hold them in the mornings before the start of school. Whenever held, an agenda of topics to be covered should be issued to each member of the department well in advance of the meeting, and sufficient notice of the meeting itself should be given in order to allow department members to adjust their schedules.

It would also seem necessary to allocate a part of each meeting for department members to voice their concerns or to bring up topics which may be of interest to them.

See Also: AUTHORITY, TEACHER; BULLETIN; CALENDAR; CHAIRPERSONS; COMMITTEE; COMMUNICATION; DEPARTMENTS; FACULTY MEETING; SUPERVISION (STAFF).

DEPARTMENTS

A **department** is the third echelon within a school district, coming after the central staff and the school administration; it is the second level of authority within a school building, often acting as liaison between faculty and administration. A department is directed by a department head, leader, chairperson, or coordinator, who may be either appointed or elected, and who must have proper credentials and/ or longevity. Departments exist almost entirely on the secondary level.

Members of a department perform numerous tasks besides teaching. Within their particular discipline, department members often generate extracurricular activities, Open House programs, assembly programs, and Career Education programs; they help carry out testing programs; they assist in decisions regarding the placement of students within the program; they provide input to Guidance; they generate ideas for curriculum development; they help carry out research within their area of expertise; they lend their expertise to the district's Adult Education programs; they help establish goals and objectives for planning and course development, and they may also have input into setting the philosophy of the department in relationship to the entire academic program of a school.

Members of a department may also perform such tasks as helping to orient new department members, cooperating with student teacher programs from local colleges, coordinating resources and learning materials, and even assisting substitute teachers. As an organizational body, departments also help facilitate budget preparation, and supply requests and other information that may be required by the school administration.

Departments also hold regular meetings under the direction of the department head, in which matters of concern to the members of the department are explained or discussed. Department members may also gather to witness demonstration lessons or review books pertinent to their area.

See Also: ACADEMIC PROGRAM; ACTIVITIES; ASSIGNMENTS; BULLETIN; CHAIRPERSONS; CHANGE STRATEGIES; CLUBS; COUNSELING; COURSE; COURSE OF STUDY; CURRICULUM DEVELOPMENT; DEPARTMENTAL MEETINGS; DIFFERENTIATED STAFFING; FACULTY; GOALS AND OBJECTIVES; GUIDANCE; INSTRUCTION; INTERDISCIPLINARY APPROACHES; MINI-COURSES; MONTHLY REPORTS; RECOMMENDATION; RECORD KEEPING; SCHEDULE; SUPERVISION (STAFF); SUPPLIES AND EQUIPMENT.

DETENTION

Teachers have been assigning **detention** and students have been "staying after school" for a long, long time. It has been held that detention is a perfectly justifiable action when taken along certain guidelines, and the term may also be used to cover such activities as withholding a child's recess or a play period privilege as well as the more traditional detention after school.

There are, however, certain restrictions that have been placed on the practice of detention which must be observed if the detention is to be legal. First of all, the detention must be *reasonable*. This has been interpreted to mean that a teacher must have probable cause and reasonable grounds for issuing the detention. Further, the detention must come as a result of some act on the part of the student and not as a result of caprice or the ill will of the teacher. In addition, the detention must not be unreasonable in length. In regard to the last part, a "reasonable" length of time for a detention is time equal to a regular teaching period.

Next, the child must be *properly supervised* while in detention. Lack of proper supervision could result in a charge of negligence should the child be injured. Also, the child must have a way of *getting home safely* after the detention. Should such a way not be available, and the teacher volunteers to take the child home, it should be remembered that if anything happens to the child while in the teacher's car, the teacher might be held liable.

Detention may be held by an individual teacher in the teacher's classroom or some other room of the school. Some schools have established a room and procedures for "central detention," to which every student who has been assigned detention for that particular day reports and serves the detention under the supervision of a teacher.

Rules for detention vary greatly from school to school, and often revolve around the school day's schedule and the buses serving an individual building. Hence, individual schools may set up a policy regarding the maximum length of detention and the procedures for notifying parents of the action which is also required for legality.

Without the presence of all of the above factors, the detention might be interpreted as false imprisonment and punitive damages might be assessed the teacher who made the assignment.

See Also: AUTHORITY, TEACHER; COMMUNICATION; CORPORAL PUNISHMENT; DISCIPLINE; PARENT CONFERENCES; STUDENT INFORMATION; SUPERVISION (STUDENT); TRANSPORTATION.

DIAGNOSIS

Diagnosis refers to the careful investigation of facts in order to determine the nature of something, with the subsequent report of the findings based on that investigation.

There is a wide range of diagnostic techniques available to educators for a variety of purposes. Administrators can use a number of techniques for the overall improvement of the school. The results of *Standardized Tests,* for example, may be used to diagnose the effectiveness of new programs, new teaching methods or changes in the curriculum by comparing the results of the tests before and after the implementation of the new policy or program. *Time-Analysis Methods* may be used to diagnose the time needed for programs or units in the future by comparing the time estimated for a unit with the time actually consumed on an average basis. *Aptitude-Achievement Parallels* can help diagnose the effectiveness of student placement within various programs.

For teachers and school units like the child study team, there are other various diagnostic techniques available. Instruments such as the *Metropolitan Reading Readiness Test* and the *Wide Range Achievement Test* are used for diagnostic purposes in the placement of students. In diagnosing learning difficulties, a number of instruments can be used to help diagnose the intelligence level along with the physical, emotional, social, and experiential development of the child. To diagnose reading difficulties there are such tools as the *Peabody Picture Vocabulary Test* and the *Gates-MacGinitie Primary Reading Test.*

The instruments named above are but a few of the many tools available to educators. Diagnosis of the component parts of any problem is the first step toward its solution.

See Also: ABILITY GROUPING; ABIL-
ITY LEVELS; ACHIEVEMENT; APTI-
TUDE; CHANGE STRATEGIES; CHILD-
CENTERED; CHILD STUDY TEAM;
CURRICULUM DEVELOPMENT;
EVALUATION; EXAMINATIONS; IN-
STRUCTION; INTELLIGENCE TEST-
ING; LEARNING DISABILITIES;
NEEDS ASSESSMENT; OBSERVATION;
PRIVILEGED COMMUNICATIONS;
PSYCHOLOGICAL STUDIES; READI-
NESS; RECOMMENDATION; SPEECH
THERAPY; SPECIAL SERVICES; STU-
DENT INFORMATION.

DIFFERENTIATED STAFFING

Within a decentralized setup, authority is often diffused through various levels, with each one responsible
for developing those programs that
meet the needs of its students. **Differentiated staffing** is often used at
the instructional level to promote professional growth and expertise.

Differentiated staffing always involves some form of teaming. First,
educators are recognized as having
various levels of competency. Upon
review, they are placed in a hierarchy
of staff structure. For example, one
model has the following structure:
first is the instructional specialist who
works in curriculum; second is the
master teacher or department head;
third is the line, staff or general classroom teacher; fourth is the certified
associate teacher, who has taught for
at least one year but does not have
tenure; and fifth is the "intern"
teacher who is certified but has no
previous experience.

Once these classifications have

been determined, a further determination is made as to who shall be teamed
with whom in order to form the most
effective combinations to promote
growth among students and teachers.

When determining the combinations for teaming, strict guidelines are
usually observed. For example, in the
model used above, "intern" and associate teachers may be teamed with
line teachers but seldom with each
other; the line teacher may work with
the master teacher but probably not
with the instructional specialist; and
the master teacher would work with
the instructional specialist.

In this way, it is hoped that both
the students and the teachers involved
would profit from the associations.

See Also: ASSIGNMENTS; AU-
THORITY, TEACHER; CHAIRPER-
SONS; CURRICULUM DEVELOP-
MENT; DECENTRALIZATION; DE-
PARTMENTS; PROBATIONARY
TEACHER; QUALIFICATIONS; STU-
DENT TEACHER; SUPERVISION
(STAFF); TENURE.

DIPLOMA

Each school district has the right
to determine whether or not a student
has completed the course work required to obtain his or her **diploma.** It
has been held that no other reason can
be used for withholding a diploma,
other than the fact that a student has
not met these requirements.

Although diplomas are usually
issued during a formal ceremony with
faculty and parents in attendance, the

diploma can be given under any circumstance that the school district deems appropriate.

Diplomas should be ordered well in advance of graduation, and if names are to be printed on them, a thorough check should be made in order to insure and correct spelling.

See Also: GRADUATION; GRADUATION REQUIREMENTS; STUDENT INFORMATION.

DISCIPLINE

Discipline refers to internal self-control, orderliness, character, and the methods used to bring about such results in an individual.

Educators have long recognized the need for discipline and good class management within the schools. In almost all systems, the chain of discipline flows downward, from superintendent over principal over teacher over student. Consequently, since most discipline problems are student-caused, the teacher is the first line of discipline within a school. Good class management, however, is not parceled out with a teaching certificate. Therefore, administrators and supervisors must frequently review the class management techniques of teachers through observation, workshops and in-service training.

School-wide rules, as well as the rules of individual teachers, should also be reviewed periodically. For instance, if a large number of disturbances or disciplinary problems are occurring in one particular area or violate one particular rule, it might be useful to examine the rule. Individual teacher's rules should also be examined and adapted to conform with school policy, and be altered if necessary.

When reviewing or adapting school policy on discipline, it would be helpful to involve as many parties as possible. Students may be involved indirectly through the participation of Student Council or Student Government representatives. Parents can become involved by the use of questionnaires or by being solicited as volunteers from the Parent-Teacher Association. Also, there are always respected members of the faculty who may be enlisted to serve on advisory councils.

The policy on discipline and the rules of a school should be written in extremely clear language. Moreover, these rules should be kept visible, and, if possible, every student, teacher and parent should have a copy of them.

With regard to the enforcement of discipline, the administrator only intercedes when remedial action is needed (if a civil law is broken, if a major fight occurs, or if vandalism is detected) and, upon occasion, if problems of class management surface (such as excessive class disruption, obscene language, constant lack of preparation, etc.). In the latter case, the administrator can often find him- or herself spending a disproportionate amount of time handling minor classroom management problems. Therefore, the administrator quite often provides for the separation of the student and the teacher, in order to provide time for each to gain a perspective on the situation. Thereafter, he or she may wish to work with the teacher in order to provide guidance in the handling of future disciplinary problems with that student.

It should be understood that all disciplinary actions taken within a school must conform to the law and must not violate the civil or constitutional rights of students.

See Also: ASP (ALTERNATE SCHOOL PROGRAM); AUTHORITY, TEACHER; COMMUNICATIONS; CORPORAL PUNISHMENT; DETENTION; EXPULSION OF STUDENTS; IN-SCHOOL SUSPENSION; PARENT CONFERENCES; STUDENT COUNCIL (STUDENT GOVERNMENT); STUDENT INFORMATION: SUPERVISION (STAFF); SUPERVISION (STUDENT); SUSPENSION.

DISCRIMINATION

Discrimination is an obvious difference in treatment of an individual on the grounds of race, color, sex, religion, or national origin.

Discrimination in schools is a serious business. Not only is it reprehensible because it violates the freedoms guaranteed by the Constitution, but also, the *Civil Rights Act of 1964,* (74 Stat. 86 1971, 1975, 1977) states that "no person in the United States shall on the grounds of race, color or national origin, be excluded from participation in, be denied the benefit of, or be subjected to discrimination under any program or activity receiving federal financial assistance." Consequently, a school system found guilty of discriminatory actions can find federal funds withheld.

It should be understood that the definition also includes discrimination on the basis of sex. Indeed, recent cases have involved sex discrimination in athletic programs, as well as unequal pay or opportunity of promotion on the basis of sex. It has also been upheld, for example, that if a school system grants maternity leave for women, it must also grant paternity leave for men.

Also forbidden by this Act is discrimination based on religion. While it is obvious that no school system would deny a child or teacher the right to practice his or her religion, it has been upheld that the refusal to employ, grant leave or dismiss an employee on the grounds of absenteeism based on the number of days missed for religious observance is *de facto* discrimination.

Consequently, school systems must be particularly careful that the policy or rules established by them afford equality of treatment on all levels. They should examine the purpose behind each rule and determine if any individual is hampered or prohibited from any aspect of education based upon any classification such as race, sex, etc. All the policies of a school district should be in line with federal guidelines on discrimination.

DISMISSAL OF PERSONNEL

An employee of the board of education may be **dismissed** by the board, but only for very specific reasons. The most common reason for dismissal is *incompetence*. This charge is rather vague, however, and proof of the charge will have to be clearly documented. It has been held that this proof cannot be based on a single instance, nor can it be derived from hearsay.

The next most common ground for dismissal is *immorality*. This is a rather touchy area, however, since concepts of what constitutes immorality will vary, sometimes from person to person. In the case of *Burton v. Cascade School District, Union High School No. 5 (Oregon, 1973)* (353 F. Supp. 254 [U.S. Dist. Ct. OR 1973]), it was brought out that the board must have *objective proof* that the action they consider to be immoral directly interferes with the ability of the person so charged to teach.

It has been completely upheld that the *conviction of an individual for a felony* is proper grounds for dismissal, as is conviction of a crime involving moral turpitude (indecent exposure, for example) even if that crime was not a felony.

Insubordination, which is the refusal to obey the just rules of the administrator or the board of education, is also grounds for dismissal. This can be challenged, however, if it can be proven that the rule was not a "just" rule. Quite often, these problems become the center of established grievance procedures rather than formal dismissal actions.

A person may be dismissed for *mental or physical disability,* but the board must show that the individual is no longer capable of performing his or her duties because of the disability.

Finally, *inadequate performance* is often used as a grounds for dismissal. In this case, the board must prove that although an individual is capable of performing his or her duties, he or she has not been doing so. As in the case of incompetence, proof is by a "preponderance of evidence."

Whatever the grounds for dismissal, certain principles must be followed in order for the dismissal to be legal. An individual must be afforded due process, and there must be a fundamental fairness in all proceedings. Objective proof against a specific charge leveled at the person must be taken. Statutory dismissal procedures must be followed to the letter, or else there is a real possibility that the final decision will be overturned.

Statutory dismissal procedures may be formulated by local school boards in some states, but the majority have established state-wide procedures. Whatever the case, these procedures must be formally phrased in writing.

There are a number of steps involved in statutory dismissal procedures. First, an individual may be suspended temporarily without a hearing, so that the charges may be investigated. Then, written notice of a recommendation to dismiss must be filed by the superintendent with the school board. After an investigation has been conducted, the individual so charged must receive written notice of the intention to dismiss him or her, and this written notice must contain the reasons and evidence of why this is being done. The individual then has the right to a hearing in which he or she has the right to cross-examine witnesses and dispute evidence, as well as to present evidence or witnesses on his or her own behalf.

There are further safeguards that protect an individual's rights during such a hearing. For instance, the hearing is to be open unless requested by the person. Evidence is given under oath, and court procedures apply. The burden of proof lies with the board of education. The accused individual has the right to counsel and the right of review (the decision may be appealed).

It has been held that non-tenure teachers have the same rights regarding dismissal as do tenure teachers. It should also be noted that should a school board instigate dismissal procedures and then retract them, the individual under consideration might have grounds for a suit against the board for defamation of character.

See Also: ABSENTEEISM; BREACH OF CONTRACT; BURDEN OF PROOF; CIVIL RIGHTS; CONSTITUTIONAL RIGHTS; DUE PROCESS; FIFTH AMENDMENT GUARANTEES; FIRST AMENDMENT GUARANTEES; FOURTEENTH AMENDMENT GUARANTEES; GRIEVANCES; HEARINGS; INCOMPETENCE; INSUBORDINATION; MORAL TURPITUDE; NONFEASANCE; PROBATIONARY TEACHER; SELF-INCRIMINATION; SEVERANCE PAY; SUPERINTENDENT OF SCHOOLS; SUPERVISION (STAFF); TARDINESS; TENURE; UNIONS; UNISERV.

DISMISSAL PROCEDURES (SCHOOL)

School dismissal procedures are those procedures established for the safe and prompt dismissal of students from the school building at the end of the school day or during an emergency requiring evacuation.

Particularly in schools with a large student population, it is often necessary to establish procedures for a mass exodus from the school building such as would occur at the close of the school day. Such factors as the place of arrival of buses, the physical placement of exits in relationship to streets, and the number of students in any given area of the building at the time of dismissal will all play a part in the exact procedures established by a particular school.

The main factor of concern in establishing dismissal procedures is that safety be maintained and that no one area become so congested as to hinder progress, cause students to miss boarding their assigned buses, or threaten the physical safety of any child. Consequently, a school administrator may design procedures in which all students on the second floor exit from one door while all those on the first floor exit from another; where all "walkers" exit one way while all bus riders exit another way; or where all students return to "homeroom" at the end of the day and then are dismissed by room on a staggered schedule.

It is also wise to provide for supervision in the hallways at the time of dismissal. Parents should be advised of the school's dismissal procedures, and, if possible, a special place should be established for parents who wish to personally pick up children after school.

Dismissal procedures will vary from school to school, depending on physical limitations and the ages of the children involved. Whatever procedures are established, they should be strictly enforced, and everyone involved should thoroughly understand the process.

See Also: AGE LEVELS; AUTO-MOBILES; BUS AND BUS DRIVERS; CLOSE OF SCHOOL; COMMUNICATION; FORESEEABILITY; HANDI-CAPPED; LIABILITY; PARKING; PUB-LIC ADDRESS SYSTEM; SAFETY; SCHEDULE; STUDENT INFORMA-TION; SUPERVISION (STUDENTS); TELEPHONE; TRANSPORTATION; VOLUNTEERS.

DRESS CODES

Dress codes for students and teachers were a long-established part of the school scene in America, and some of them seem fairly humorous by modern standards. For instance, in 1915, one school system required teachers to wear no bright colors, at least two petticoats, and no dress more than two inches above the ankle; while in 1928, a group of teachers in West Virginia were forced to sign contracts in which they vowed to fasten their galoshes all the way up. Dress codes were heavily challenged, however, during the 1960s and 1970s, with almost universal success on the part of the challengers.

The courts have held that every person is an individual and is entitled to express him- or herself as he or she deems proper. Consequently, it was deemed improper and unlawful for a school or school system to establish rules that regulated a person's appearance such as the length of hair, the wearing of beards, the use of jewelry, the color and style of clothing, etc. It was also upheld that whatever applied to students applied to the teachers as well, and restrictive dress codes for teachers were also struck down.

The courts did hold, however, that dress codes were legitimate in three areas, but only in those three areas. Schools may regulate dress and/or appearance for reasons of *health*. Schools, for instance, may not prohibit long hair, but they may require that the hair be clean in order to prevent lice. Schools may impose codes for *safety*. For example, a school may not prevent a child from wearing a long necklace or scarf, but the child may be required to remove the necklace or scarf when operating machinery in an Industrial Arts class. Finally, codes may be imposed on dress that causes *substantial disruption*. This last classification is somewhat vague, however, and needs interpretation.

What is substantial disruption? In 1971, a female teacher was dismissed for wearing a bikini while teaching swimming to a group of male and female students. The courts ordered the teacher reinstated when it was proven that none of the students had complained, nor did any of them consider the teacher's attire a distraction or disruption. Consequently, the burden of proof of a substantial disruption falls on the complaining body, and it would have to be proven that the dress or appearance was a disruption *to the students* and caused a disruption of learning *on the part of the students* before such a charge would be valid. (Heather Martin, #8156 [NY Comm. of ED. Aug. 3, 1971]). Although a teacher or administrator may be personally offended by a mode of dress, this is not sufficient reason to claim that it is a disruption that should be banned.

Finally, for other than those three reasons, no dress codes may be imposed. It has been upheld, however, that requiring uniforms to be worn for participation in an activity does not impose a dress code. Consequently, members of the band may be required to wear band uniforms, and the members of a choral group may be required to have neat, combed hair and wear white tops and black bottoms, for example.

See Also: BURDEN OF PROOF; CIVIL RIGHTS; CONSTITUTIONAL RIGHTS; DUE PROCESS; FREE SPEECH; PRIVACY; SAFETY; STUDENT INFORMATION.

DRINKING OF ALCHOLIC BEVERAGES

The **drinking of alcoholic beverages** refers to the consumption, storing and possible sale of alcoholic beverages by minors while on school property or during school activities.

When a student or students drinks alcoholic beverages during the school day or stores these beverages in his or her locker, and then either distributes or sells them to other students, the school, as well as the student, faces a very real problem. The abuse of alcohol by children at younger and younger ages, sometimes down to the middle grades of elementary school, is an increasingly serious problem throughout the United States.

It should be understood that the student who brings in a bottle of liquor once to impress his peers or to gain attention *once* is not a serious problem and can be handled through normal disciplinary procedures. Rather, the concern is for the student who is involved in serious alcohol abuse, who comes to school intoxicated, or who secretly drinks during the school day and becomes increasingly incapable of functioning in a normal manner. It is generally understood that it is within the school's authority to deal with this student for the student's good, as well as for the good of the other students in the school.

Teachers should be taught to recognize the symptoms of alcohol abuse. Teachers should never directly accuse the student of drinking, but the child should be referred to the school nurse. The nurse, in turn, should be thoroughly trained in spotting the problem and dealing with its immediate and long-term effects. This might include informing the student's parents, holding conferences with the student and his or her parents, or even referring the student to an outside agency.

Teachers should be encouraged to incorporate units on alcohol abuse into their curriculum. Toward this end, there are many excellent filmstrips, movies and programmed units available on the topic. These units should be "real" and should carry a powerful, personal message to the students in the class. Alcoholics Anonymous, as well as its teenage division, ALATEEN, are extremely cooperative in providing materials, advice and aid for schools in preventing alcohol abuse.

It should be noted that any alcoholic beverages found on school grounds may be legally confiscated since alcohol is considered to be part of the universal contraband for schools.

See Also: CHILD STUDY TEAM; CONSULTANTS; COUNSELING; FAMILY SERVICES; GUIDANCE; HEALTH; NURSE; PARENT CONFERENCES; PSYCHOLOGICAL STUDIES; SAFETY; STUDENT INFORMATION; SUPERVISION (STUDENTS).

DROPOUTS

A **dropout** is an individual who leaves school prior to or after the age of sixteen without having completed the course of study and receiving a diploma.

The dropout can present a real problem for school systems throughout the United States. While statistics vary, the dropout rate, particularly in larger city school systems, can run as high as between 50 and 60 percent in an individual district. This often sets up an economic cycle that is difficult to break. The more dropouts within a school system, the smaller the economic base for federal aid becomes. The less aid that is received, the less money there is available for programs. The less programs there are, the less interest in the schools. The less interest in the schools, the more dropouts. And so it goes.

There have been many reasons proposed as to why students drop out of school. Noting that the *vast* majority of dropouts comes from the lower socio-economic strata, it has been proposed that one reason for dropouts would seem to be a matter of perspective. Historically, education in the United States went from a privilege to a right to an obligation. Today, the upper class still views education as a privilege, while the middle class looks on it as a right, while the lower socio-economic class sees it as an obligation for which they are merely forced, by law, to attend school even though they can see no value or benefit to them.

Consequently, various solutions have been propounded to make school more relevant to the potential dropout. These ideas include changing the curriculum in order to offer courses that are more relevant to the immediate needs of the student (Consumer Education, Knowing the Law, etc.) while still providing instruction in the basics with an eye toward achieving at least basic competencies. Even for the student who has already dropped out, there are programs such as Job Corp and Manpower Training, which approach education from the point of view of providing job skills rather than traditional literacy.

It is a general contention that the dropout may be spotted long before the actual incidence of dropping out occurs. Such characteristics as a poor self-concept, a high degree of frustration with school work, the possession of values that are in direct conflict with those of the school, and difficulties in both verbal and nonverbal communication have been identified as early warning signs of the dropout, and educators have been urged to recognize these symptoms and try to deal with them during the early years of education.

Programs for the prevention of dropouts inevitably require money, however, and in many districts, this money is either unavailable or else the system does not perceive the problem to be of sufficient gravity to justify the cost in light of its other priorities.

It is interesting to note that Germany, faced with a high dropout rate, began putting its money into improving the housing, clothing and other living conditions of potential dropouts rather than putting it into such items as free tuition or textbooks. Over a two-year period, their national dropout rate fell from 57 percent to 17 percent.

See Also: ABSENTEEISM; ASP (ALTERNATE SCHOOL PROGRAM); CAREER EDUCATION; COMPETENCY-BASED PROGRAMS; COUNSELING; CULTURE; ENROLLMENT; ETHNIC MINORITIES; FAMILY SERVICES; GUIDANCE; JUVENILE DELINQUENCY; LANGUAGE; LEARNING DISABILITIES; MAJORITY, AGE OF; PARENT CONFERENCES; PREGNANT STUDENTS; PUPIL; REMEDIAL INSTRUCTION; SOCIAL PROMOTION; TRUANCY; STUDENT INFORMATION; UNDERACHIEVERS; VOCATIONAL PROGRAMS; WORKING PAPERS; WORK-STUDY PROGRAM.

DRUGS

Drugs are those narcotic substances that are used by an individual without a valid prescription from a medical authority. Here, we are using the term "drugs" to indicate those substances that are part of the universal contraband for schools, and not those substances that are medications legitimately prescribed.

The use and abuse of drugs in our nation's schools constitutes the number one threat to student safety and well-being. It is an extensive problem that reaches every level of society. Once thought to be a problem limited to the lower socio-economic areas and classes, many educators closed their eyes to it until it began to infiltrate the middle and upper socio-economic levels. By the end of the 1960s, drug use and abuse had become a recognized problem in all schools, and the problem continues to grow.

There are no predictors or common factors that will identify the potential drug user. Spinoza once remarked that "we always strive toward that which is forbidden and desire the things we are not allowed to have." That, however, is only part of the problem. Such factors as the threat of nuclear holocaust, increasing social and economic pressures, and the general challenging of traditional values have all been proposed as possible explanations of the increasing use of drugs.

Whatever the causes, schools have realized that, while they cannot relieve the pressures of everyday life, they can make an attempt to reach students with alternatives to drugs and show the detrimental effect that drugs have had on individuals.

In formulating drug prevention programs, schools should start with the assumption that students may already be using drugs or may have tried them. They should try to show students where drug use and abuse has led others, but they should be truthful about it. To tell students, for example, that smoking a marijuana cigarette will lead them to ruin would destroy the validity of the program, since the students well know that there are a number of individuals who smoke marijuana and function quite well, and some of them are well-known. To know this, all they have to do is to read the newspaper or look at some interviews on television. Rather, this should be admitted, but alternatives to this use should be stressed and a connection established that there are individuals who have been destroyed by drugs. An examination should be conducted as to why drugs have destroyed these people. Toward this end, a program may include trips to drug clinics or visits from rehabilitated drug addicts. Wherever possible, students should help other students, with the older ones working with the younger ones.

Educators should be trained to recognize both the general and specific symptoms of drug use and abuse, and the school should set specific policies for dealing with the use, possession and sale of drugs on school property. The occasional user should receive counseling, which can take place within the school. The chronic user and possessor should also receive counseling, but is quite often referred to agencies outside the school that are better equipped to handle the problem. The seller of drugs is another matter.

It is generally held that the drug seller (also called the dealer, pusher or connection) is the most dangerous student in school, and there should be no thought of leniency for someone who engages in this activity. Again, it is a general consensus that a first offender in selling drugs should have his parents notified, possibly have the police involved, and both the seller and the buyer should receive stern punishment. If the offender is caught a second time, he or she should be suspended and the police should definitely be involved. A third offense of this nature should warrant expulsion and criminal charges should be filed with the police. Expulsion of a student under these circumstances has been upheld in the courts under the principle that the school is acting for the safety and welfare of the other students in the school.

If a student claims that drugs found in his or her possession are legitimate prescription drugs, it is within the school's authority to require verification in the form of a note from the parents and/or a prescription from a doctor.

See Also: AUDIO-VISUAL MATERIALS; CHILD STUDY TEAM; CONSULTANTS; COUNSELING; EXPULSION OF STUDENTS; FAMILY SERVICES; GUIDANCE; JUVENILE DELINQUENCY; MEDICATION; NURSE; PARENT CONFERENCES; POLICE; SAFETY; STUDENT INFORMATION; SUSPENSION; SUPERVISION (STUDENTS).

DUE PROCESS

Due process refers to the following of legal and prescribed procedures in the taking of legal or quasi-legal actions against an individual or group of individuals.

When the Fourteenth Amendment was ratified on July 9, 1868, Section One guaranteed that no individual would be deprived of "life, liberty or property without due process of the law." This Amendment guaranteed that all citizens were entitled to all the protections of the Constitution and civil law to the date of a legal action.

Consequently, due process is not a law of itself, but merely a guarantee that anyone who is accused of a crime, or against whom a legal action has been brought, shall be afforded all the protections and processes of the law to which he or she is entitled and which have become part of the legal proceedings to date. For example, our Founding Fathers never indicated in the Constitution that a person arrested for a crime had to be advised of his or her rights. When the Supreme Court issued its decision, however, the "Miranda Warning" became a legal part of arrest procedures, and anyone who was not informed of his or her rights when arrested was, from that date forward, being denied the "due process of law."

As applied to public education,

there will be many cases in which legal or quasi-legal actions are instigated against individuals. These may include all aspects of the dismissal of personnel, punishment of students, suspension and expulsion of students, etc. Consequently, all educators should be aware of their legal rights and responsibilities, in order to assure that due process is afforded in every case.

All individuals who are accused or a crime, or against whom an action is taken, are entitled to the due process of law. The denial of due process during a proceeding is, in and of itself, more than sufficient grounds for reversing and/or overturning the final decision.

See Also: AFFIRMATIVE ACTION; BURDEN OF PROOF; CIVIL RIGHTS; CONSTITUTIONAL RIGHTS; DISMISSAL OF PERSONNEL; EQUAL EMPLOYMENT OPPORTUNITIES; FIFTH AMENDMENT GUARANTEES; FIRST AMENDMENT GUARANTEES; FOURTEENTH AMENDMENT GUARANTEES; FOURTH AMENDMENT GUARANTEES; FREE SPEECH; GRIEVANCES; HEARINGS; IN-SCHOOL SUSPENSION; PUPIL; RIGHTS AND RESPONSIBILITIES; SEARCH AND SEIZURE; SELF-DEFENSE; SELF-INCRIMINATION; STRIKES; STUDENT INFORMATION; SUSPENSION.

E

EARLY CHILDHOOD PROGRAMS

Early Childhood Programs are those programs that aim at providing developmental instruction and care to children prior to the start of the formal educational process.

Early Childhood programs include nursery school programs, Project Head Start, and kindergarten.

Kindergaretn programs are generally administered through the public school system and require certified personnel. The same is true of preschool programs that are part of a district's educational programs, although aides may be, and quite often are, used. Many private nursery schools do not have these criteria, although they, too, must meet certain state requirements in order to be licensed. Educators are seeking legislation that would insure that Early Childhood educational programs would be administered through the public school system.

Such programs that exist within school systems should be publicized to the community, and limitations, requirements and criteria should be established for entrance. In many cases, formal registration is required, and formal procedures for parental involvement are established.

See Also: ACADEMIC PROGRAM; AGE LEVELS; AIDES; CERTIFICATION; COMMON SCHOOLS; FEDERAL AGENCIES; FEDERAL AID; FEDERAL PROGRAMS; IMMUNIZATION; INSTRUCTION; KINDERGARTEN; PLAYGROUND; PRIVATE AND PAROCHIAL SCHOOLS; READINESS; SUPERVISION (STUDENT); VOLUNTEERS.

EASEMENT

An **easement** is the right given to travel on, over or through land adjoining one's own; or to use it for specific purposes such as utility rights-of-way, pole easements, party walls, etc. An easement may be either temporary or permanent, and they generally come with the land when it is sold, unless prohibited by deed restrictions.

An easement may be granted to property holders whose land adjoins the school. This may include such items as the right of access while public roads are being repaired, etc. Also, easements of school property may be granted for the placing of telephone lines, transformers and other necessary equipment.

If the school grounds contain easements, the students should be advised of their responsibility to avoid blocking an access way, trespassing on private property, or tampering with public property such as a telephone pole.

See Also: ACCESS RIGHTS; GROUNDS; JURISDICTION; LEASE OF SCHOOL PROPERTY; ZONING; ZONING BOARD.

EDUCATION COMMISSION OF THE STATES

The **Education Commission of the States** is a nonprofit organization formed by interstate compact in 1966, in order to provide mutual assistance in solving the educational problems of member states.

The original idea for an Education Commission of the States (ECS) came, in 1964, from James Bryant Conant, Harvard President emeritus. The idea was to further working relationships among state educational and political leaders. The Compact for Education envisioned the need for, and created, the Education Commission of the States to fulfill five essen-tial functions; first, to *undertake policy research* and surveys to improve state policy decisions; second, to *provide a clearinghouse* of *information* and ideas for state leaders; third, to *sponsor forums* on significant educational policy issues; fourth, to *provide technical assistance* and training for state officials; and fifth, to *represent states' interests* in the national arena.

Through ECS, legislators exchange ideas with educators, and governors discuss current issues with school officials. ECS is the only national organization that brings both political and educational leaders together on a continuing basis and affords them the opportunity to share ideas, information and solutions to many of education's critical problems with their counterparts from other states.

ECS offers a number of services to its membership, which currently includes 48 states, American Samoa, Puerto Rico, and the Virgin Islands. It offers a source of trained talent to help explore policy issues, program evaluation, and the creation of new educational approaches; a clearinghouse for educational information, data, ideas, and successful programs across state lines (inquiries are answered within 24 hours); a national forum for the dissemination of ideas and experiences among legislative, executive, and education leaders; a liaison between political, educational, and federal organizations; a source of policy alternatives on educational issues of the times; and, a voice to the federal government that is respected and heeded so that federal policy and programs reflect state needs.

ECS also provides periodic surveys of educational issues, advanced leadership seminars for legislators, state education officials and others; and the National Assessment of Educational Progress (NAEP), the only nationwide program to determine what children know in major subject areas.

Through ECS, each dollar appropriated by member states is matched by up to seven dollars from other sources such as federal grants and grants from various foundations, in order to provide service that states need but probably could not otherwise obtain for the cost of the individual membership fee.

For further information contact:

*Education Commission
of the States*

Suite 300

1860 Lincoln Street

Denver, Colorado 80295

(303) 830-3600

See Also: ACCREDITATION; CHIEF STATE SCHOOL OFFICIAL; FEDERAL AGENCIES; FEDERAL AID; FEDERAL PROGRAMS; NATIONAL ASSESSMENT; POLITICS AND THE SCHOOL; STATE AGENCIES; STATE PROGRAMS; STATE AID; U.S. DEPARTMENT OF EDUCATION.

ELECTIVES

Electives are courses within a plan of study that teach similar skills from different points of view.

All schools establish academic requirements for graduation. Traditionally, this meant a course of study into which each student was locked. Today, however, elective courses are becoming more and more popular and have even been found to better fit academic requirements in some cases.

There are four classifications of elective courses. There are *revolving electives,* parts of a system in which one elective leads to a second, which may not be taken without the first. An example of this would be Spanish I, which is a prerequisite to Spanish II, which is a prerequisite to Spanish III, etc. There are *mini-courses,* a group of which make up a body of knowledge. These are short, highly-concentrated courses that collectively constitute a body of knowledge. Hence, Literature may be composed of mini-courses in Poetry, Black Writers, American playwrights, etc. There are *independent projects or studies,* which are often open-ended in duration. An individual studies and develops at his or her own pace under the system. And, finally, there are *straight electives,* which are offered as part of the academic program, such as Band or First Aid.

These classifications may be further broken down into five types of electives. First, are the *common learning electives,* which apply to courses of study in "the basics." Hence, History is required, but students may elect to take courses such as U.S. History, Problems in American Democracy, etc. Second, are the *vocational electives,* in which particular talents or job skills are developed such as woodworking, ceramics, stenography, etc. Third, are the *personal interest electives* such as Music Appreciation, Fine Arts, etc. Fourth are the *social/emotional developmental electives,* which teach values or decision-making skills in such areas as Debate, Psychology, etc. Finally, are the *recreational electives* such as Tennis, Gymnastics, etc.

Electives will probably continue to play a major role in American education, because they have been proven to have relevance, guarantee student interest, provide a "fresh start" to students more often, and allow for greater use of teacher expertise.

The problems surrounding electives, particularly in a school that offers a great many of them, come not from their educational soundness, but from the attendant difficulties in scheduling classes. Educational planners must consider the number of students, the number of teachers, the basic requirements for any given school year, and the time limitations imposed within the traditional setup. All of these factors must be assessed and accommodated, in order to insure a proper academic program for all.

See Also: ACADEMIC PROGRAM; BASICS; CONTRACTED LEARNING; COUNSELING; COURSE; COURSE OF STUDY; CURRICULUM DEVELOPMENT; ENRICHMENT; GRADUATION REQUIREMENTS; GUIDANCE; INDIVIDUALIZATION; INTERDISCIPLINARY APPROACHES; MINI-COURSES; SCHEDULE; UNGRADED; VOCATIONAL PROGRAMS.

ELEMENTARY AND SECONDARY EDUCATION ACT OF 1965

The **Elementary and Secondary Education Act of 1965** (PL89-10, 79 Stat. 27) (ESEA '65) is the act passed by Congress that aims toward helping the educationally deprived and providing for equality and cooperation in education.

With the passage of the Elementary and Secondary Education Act of 1965, certain actions were taken. A nationwide system of university-based research and development centers were established to engage in problem-oriented research. A system of regional laboratories was also established to undertake programs that would help create and disseminate improvements in education. It was further established that these research and development centers would do basic research, draw on interdisciplinary research done in universities, supplement and codify research and theory, fit all usable data into systems for use in further development, and apply the research to the classroom.

Also, with the passage of the ESEA '65, educational decision-making passed once and for all from the local to the national level. Now federal funds were available for all schools. However, schools receiving federal aid had to comply with federal guidelines on education or risk the loss of these funds.

ESEA '65 was aimed primarily at urban districts, and there was an immediate outcry from suburban and rural districts that they were being slighted. There was, consequently, an immediate clarification that the act applied to all districts in all states, and any of the formulas inherent in the act could be applied to everyone.

ESEA '65 was updated in 1972 and became ESEA '72 (Pl 92-318). This action created the National Institute of Education (NIE) and established the goal of bringing the same degree of intellect, intensity and direction in education that had been brought to health, space and agriculture. It retained all the original provisions of ESEA '65, but strengthened them significantly. Further updates, also called Eduational Amendments, occurred in 1976 (PL 94-482) and 1980 (PL 96-374).

ESEA operates under seven Titles:

TITLE I—A program to aid school districts with impoverished children. The Title defines "impoverished" as children from families with an income under $2,000 or who are already on welfare. The federal grants were given on the basis of the following formula: the number of low income children, times 50 percent of the *state's* average expenditure, per child, in the state. The states could use the money in any way they wished, but had to aid non-public school students as well. Compensatory Education is one of the programs under Title I.

TITLE II—Provided for the purchase of tangible materials for education. This included such items as books, textbooks, audio-visual equip-

ment, library and media center equipment, and much more.

TITLE III—Provided for education centers and research for model programs. From this came such items as pre-school programs (Project Head Start), supplemental education and needs assessment mandates.

TITLE IV—Provides funds for services that local school districts cannot, both in actual programs and training. This might include anything from teacher aides to field trips to new school buses.

TITLE V—Provided for the strengthening of the states' Departments of Education. Under this title, state Departments of Education were provided with funds in order to educate migrant children, aid in school district consolidation, generate, evaluate and conduct educational assessments, and provide cooperation between the state and local, and state and national levels.

TITLE VI—Provided that civil rights shall pervade education. It adopted, *in toto*, the Civil Rights Act of 1964 (PL 88-352). Under ESEA '72, programs for the handicapped were added under this title.

TITLE VII—Generally provided that all civil and constitutional rights shall apply in education. ESEA '72, for example, issued the ruling that a student could not be excluded from the classroom because of pregnancy. Also, affirmative action statutes are based upon this title.

These titles were originally in the ESEA '65. Because education is a viable entity, there continue to be numerous updates, clarifications and additions.

ELEMENTARY SCHOOLS

An **elementary school** is a school, public or otherwise, containing grades kindergarten or first through sixth.

An elementary school usually has two or more sections per grade, depending on class size. The optimum sizes are 15 students per kindergarten class, and 25 through 30 students for the other grades. Classes generally are self-contained with one teacher, but there may also be teacher aides and team-teaching. The "neighborhood" elementary school usually contains 300-500 students. If schools in a district contain less than this number, they usually consolidate. On a national average, however, elementary schools were found to have 700 students. Any school containing a population that approaches 1,000 is considered too large and should be divided.

Elementary staffing is usually divided into several sections. There are the *regular classroom teacher,* the *"special" teacher* (Art, Music, Physical Education, etc.), and *the specialists* (supervisors, consultants, etc.) with one per curriculum area as the norm, such as guidance counselors, remedial instructors and learning disabilities specialists.

It is generally considered that one of the most important educational tasks of the elementary school is teaching reading, which is fundamental to all future academic success. Indeed, with current emphasis on the "basics" and their importance, many elementary schools have gone to an ungraded program below third grade. Sometimes known as a "continuous progress" program, this usually consists of teachers who instruct in the curriculum related to K-3. Students merely stay in the program, progressing at their own pace, until they have mastered the requirements of this area. In this way, it is hoped that each child will gain a firm foundation in the basics required for all further education.

There is also a growing concern for guidance facilities on the elementary school level. Unlike secondary guidance, with its emphasis on life choices, elementary guidance aims at personality development, handling peer relationships and developing study habits. The aim of elementary guidance counselors is to minimize the establishment of habits that would be difficult to break later on.

A child's experiences in elementary school are often causative factors in that child's later success or failure in secondary school. Consequently, the importance of good elementary schools cannot be overstressed.

See Also: ACADEMIC PROGRAM; AGE LEVELS; CLASS AND CLASS SIZE; CONSULTANTS; CURRICULUM DEVELOPMENT; EARLY CHILDHOOD PROGRAMS; GUIDANCE; KINDERGARTEN; OPEN CLASSROOMS; SELF-CONTAINED CLASSROOM; SUPERVISION (STAFF); UNGRADED; VOLUNTEERS.

EMPLOYEE RELATIONS

Employee relations is a collectivized term for the communication, morale and diplomatic functions of the administrator in dealing with all levels of the staff.

At one time, the school administrator carried the image of an authoritarian, unapproachable enforcer of the rules whose word was law and who brooked no interference. Today, this image has drastically changed, as have the images of all educators and education in general. It is generally recognized that the most efficient schools are those having a positive working relationship between the administrator and the faculty. Indeed, several national studies have concluded that schools run better where

teachers have input and feel needed. Moreover, the role of positive employee relations is being stressed more and more in graduate courses in administration and supervision.

For example, while faculty members do not need to feel that they are liked by an administrator, they should feel that they are respected and that their contributions are recognized. Therefore, those administrators who know each member of the faculty, who solicit opinions and offer congratulations, who appear generally concerned about the welfare of the faculty and the quality of education in the school, usually run schools where morale is high and education flourishes.

With increasing teacher militancy, such procedures were set up as the grievance, which aimed at handling complaints against administrators who many teachers felt were unresponsive to their needs. Without positive employee relations, these feelings can lead to an "us and them" attitude between faculty and administration within a school, thus threatening the effectiveness of education.

Working toward positive employee relations, where the faculty feels that it is genuinely contributing to the school and is, in turn, recognized, appreciated, and treated with respect, is a course of action that benefits everyone.

See Also: ACKNOWLEDGEMENT; ADMINISTRATOR; ADVISORY COUNCILS; APPRECIATION, LETTER OF; COMMUNICATION; FACULTY; GRIEV-

ANCES; LIAISON; SUPERVISION (STAFF).

ENRICHMENT

Enrichment is an educational concept that students should be exposed to as many "new" ideas and learning strategies as possible. Further, all students, especially the bright, gifted or talented ones, should have the opportunities to explore these new ideas, reasonably unencumbered by traditional time sequences and schedule limits, to their full potential of learning.

Never has a single word caused as much disturbance to education as has the word "enrichment." Administrators ask, "How is it possible?" Teachers state that they are doing the best they can for *all* their students. Further, the community becomes embroiled in the argument of who shall be enriched, how shall the enrichment be accomplished, and who is going to pay for it.

The lines are clearly drawn. There are those, both inside and outside of education, who advocate that schools should teach the "basics," with few extraneous frills as possible. No student, for example, needs a swimming pool; if the parents wanted him to learn to swim they would have taken him to the Y.M.C.A. There is no need for TV or radio stations, Broadway-type stages, or auto-repair shops. On the other side are those who assert that students must learn to live in the "real" world. The schools must have, therefore, film and media libraries, good and abundant science equipment, fully-stocked art and music programs, etc., because students must have exposure in learning to deal with all the aspects of the "real" world.

On the secondary level, enrichment is handled fairly easily through the use of electives and mini-courses. On the elementary level, however, enrichment is harder to plan for, since the students have less general knowledge.

Administrators should encourage teachers to fit as many enrichment activities as possible into their daily lesson plans. If there are students within the school who might profit from special enrichment programs, the establishment of such in-depth studies should be investigated, with the criteria for student placement being aptitude and achievement, parental requests and teacher recommendations.

See Also: ACADEMIC PROGRAM; ACCELERATION; ACCOUNTABILITY; ACHIEVEMENT; ACTIVITIES; ASSEMBLY PROGRAM; AUDIO-VISUAL MATERIALS; CHILD-CENTERED; CLUBS; COURSE OF STUDY; CULTURE; CURRICULUM DEVELOPMENT; ELECTIVES; EXTRACURRICULAR ACTIVITIES; FIELD TRIPS; INDIVIDUALIZATION; INTERDISCIPLINARY APPROACHES; LEARNING CENTERS; LIBRARY AND MEDIA CENTER; MINI-COURSES; MOVIES; PARENT CONFERENCES; TRIPS.

ENROLLMENT

Enrollment is the number of students who have been formally enrolled in a school and who have been present in it for at least one day.

There are many factors affecting a school's enrollment. One such factor would be the *number of births* in an area. Based on this data, projections can be made for enrollment in the next seven years. Another factor is *migration* into and out of an area. If a community is particularly attractive, offering a low tax base, many community services and open land, for example, then it is safe to project that larger numbers of families will be moving into the area, with a proportionate increase in school enrollment. If, however, there are community factors such as high taxes, an increasing crime rate, the clsoing of plants and businesses, excellent private schools for the lower grades but a high dropout rate at the upper grades, and parents within the 28- to 38-year-old age bracket (proven to be the families with the most mobility), then it is likely that enrollment will decrease. Finally, one must *consider housing starts* and the *type of housing* within a district. Housing developments, trailer courts and apartments are likely to increase enrollment that will be very fluid in nature, whereas high-priced homes, high-rise apartments and condominiums may not have as great an effect upon enrollment.

The state of a school system's enrollment or projected enrollment may necessitate several important decisions. These decisions may center about the need for consolidation or expansion. For example, if the sending districts create a bulga at the high school level, the district might consider building an intermediate, middle or junior high school.

These decisions are often based on formulas. One such formula would be the *Enrollment vs. Capacity Formula*. In this case, one takes the projected enrollment and the present capacity of the system. A decision is made as to the optimum class size. This is divided into the present number of students, and the result tells you whether the enrollment is under, at or above capacity. This, in turn, affects the decision to build or consolidate.

Precise enrollment figures are extremely important, since they act as the basis for federal aid, state aid, and possible fluctuations in local taxes.

See Also: ADDRESSES (RESIDENCE); ATTENDANCE; CAPACITY; CLASS AND CLASS SIZE; COMMON SCHOOLS; CONSOLIDATION; FEDERAL AGENCIES; FEDERAL AID; FEDERAL PROGRAMS; STATE AGENCIES; STATE AID; STATE PROGRAMS; TAXES; TRANSPORTATION.

EQUAL EMPLOYMENT OPPORTUNITIES

The **Equal Employment Opportunities** Commission (EEOC) was set up specifically to handle cases of the denial of fair and equal employment on the basis of sex, race, belief, and national origin. If a person believes that he or she has been denied a job because of discrimination as a result of one or more of these factors, a complaint may be lodged with the EEOC, and a full investigation will be launched. If a complaint should be made against a school system and the school system is found guilty, federal funds may be withheld from the district.

It has been held that the only basis for employment within the school system should be the ability to do the job. Should the case arise where there are two applicants for a position and both are equally qualified, obviously a decision will have to be made. The decision, however, must be based on acceptable reasons. For instance, the chosen applicant may be the one with more experience, but he must not be chosen because he is a man and the superintendent feels that a man can better handle difficult classes.

Equality of employment also refers to promotions within the system itself. An applicant for a better position cannot be rejected on any grounds other than his or her capacity to adequately perform in the position.

Applicants can be required to fill out an application and supply references. Also, the system can set up reasonable requirements and standards for employment, as long as these do not violate anyone's civil or constitutional rights. Equal employment opportunities apply not only to the professional staff, but are also in

effect for custodians, clerical workers and the entire group of support personnel within the schools.

See Also: AFFIRMATIVE ACTION; APPLICATION; CERTIFICATION; CIVIL RIGHTS; CONSTITUTIONAL RIGHTS; CONTRACTS; DISCRIMINATION; DISMISSAL OF PERSONNEL; FEDERAL AGENCIES; FEDERAL AID; FEDERAL PROGRAMS; GRIEVANCES; HEARINGS; INCREMENTS; POLITICS AND THE SCHOOL; PROMOTION; QUALIFICATIONS; REINSTATEMENT; SEXISM.

ESTIMATES

See BIDS.

EVALUATION

Evaluation is the chief method of finding out whether or not specific goals have been achieved. The goals will, of course, vary, depending on what is being evaluated, but they may include such items as program effectiveness, curriculum effectiveness, the quality of teaching, and the effectiveness of administrative and supervisory procedures.

Particular methods of evaluation might include observation, review of test results, filling out of questionnaires, etc. The data compiled from these methods is then reviewed and interpreted.

There are five steps in any evaluation. First, the *specific objectives* that are to be evaluated must be formulated. In other words, the evaluation must be purposeful. Second, *a spectrum along which evaluation will proceed* must be established. By "spectrum" is meant a rating system for each particular aspect such as "Seldom-Frequently-Always," the numbers 1 through 10, or "good" to "poor," with gradations in between. Third, the *procedures as to who will do what and when* must be established. Fourth, the actual evaluation procedure established in step three must be *implemented*. Finally, the findings must be *interpreted and published*. Publishing the findings can mean anything from submitting a teacher observation to the central staff office, to publishing the results of a program evaluation in the local newspaper. It is in the fifth step that the most difficulties often arise, the interpretation of data often being a subjective matter.

Evaluation can be used to look for the success or failure of a person or program, or it can be used to promote change by looking for strengths and weaknesses with an eye toward correcting the weaknesses. Problems often arise, however, when individuals under evaluation feel that they are being threatened or attacked. Every effort should be made, therefore, to assure personnel that individual evaluations are merely one part of a continuing school and district-wide evaluation procedure, which is ongoing and which aims at continual improvement. It is also necessary that those being evaluated have the right or

review on the final outcome and are provided the opportunity to express contrasting opinions or explanations.

See Also: ACADEMIC PROGRAM; AUTHORITY, BOARD; AUTHORITY, TEACHER; CHANGE STRATEGIES; CHILD STUDY TEAM; CURRICULUM DEVELOPMENT; DIAGNOSIS; DIFFERENTIATED STAFFING; GOALS AND OBJECTIVES; IN-SERVICE; INSTRUCTION; NEEDS ASSESSMENT; NEWS RELEASES; OBSERVATION; PSYCHOLOGICAL STUDIES; RECOMMENDATION; SUPERVISION (STAFF); WORKSHOPS AND IN-SERVICE.

EXAMINATIONS

Examinations may be given at various times. Within a subject area, examinations may be given at the end of a unit of study or at various times during the unit. Examinations within a course of study may fall at mid-term and the conclusion of the school year. Whenever they are given, examinations provide the instructor with feedback as to the effectiveness of the methods of instruction used and/or the individual progress of a specific student.

Examinations should always be given to find out how much a student knows. Consequently, overly complex or "trick" questions should be avoided. Also to be avoided are questions that test obscure or esoteric areas within the course of study. An examination should test for the ability to recall a substantial amount of the general knowledge to be gleaned from the course material.

Examination questions may be *objective* such as true or false, matching or multiple choice, or they may be *subjective* such as short answer or essay. Objective questions allow no leeway in marking the paper, whereas essay-type answers are often open for interpretation by the corrector.

See Also: ACADEMIC PROGRAM; ACCOUNTABILITY; ACHIEVEMENT; BULLETIN; CALENDAR; COURSE; COURSE OF STUDY; DIAGNOSIS; GRADES; PERMANENT RECORDS; RECORD KEEPING; REPORT CARDS; RETENTION OF STUDENTS; STUDENT INFORMATION.

EXCEPTIONAL STUDENTS

See ACADEMICALLY TALENTED; GIFTED STUDNETS; HANDICAPPED; MARRIED STUDENTS; PREGNANT STUDENTS; PUBLIC LAW 94-142; RETARDED CHILD; TRAINABLE CHILD.

EXPENSES

Expenses are the actual or potential outlay of funds involved in the operation of a school or school system.

Education does not come cheaply. Each year, school systems throughout the United States face increasing expenditures in order to maintain the school system and provide quality education for all students. Such factors as the high rate of inflation, increases in salaries across the board, the outcry for new and more relevant programs, and federal and state requirements have all combined to raise the expenses faced by the modern school system to an all-time high.

Each state sets its own laws relative to the financing of education within the particular state. This is usually expressed in the amount of money provided per student. This amount reflects the widest of variations from state to state, from just over $500 per student to well over $1,500 per student. Federal aid is also available within certain guidelines and can add to the funds available for meeting expenses within school districts.

Projections of expenses for a school system can be made. One tabulates the *fixed expenses* and combines this total with the *estimated expenses* for any given period of time. The resultant figure is then compared to the projected revenues for the same time period. The comparison should give an indication of whether or not expenses will be met by revenue. In cases where expenses apparently overlap revenue, decisions will have to be made by the school board as to ways of increasing revenue or cutting expenses.

See Also: AUTHORITY, BOARD; BANK ACCOUNTS; BIDS; BILL OF LADING; BUDGET; CASH; DEBTS; FEDERAL AGENCIES; FEDERAL AID; FEDERAL PROGRAMS; FEES; FINANCE; FUNDS, SCHOOL; HOSPITALIZATION; INSUR-

ANCE; *PER DIEM;* PURCHASING; SALARY; SEVERANCE PAY; STATE AGENCIES; STATE AID; STATE PROGRAMS; SUPPLIES AND EQUIPMENT; TAXES; TEXTBOOKS; TRANSPORTATION; VANDALISM.

Ex Post Facto

Ex Post Facto refers to any retroactive legislation or rule that has the effect of substantially prejudicing the rights of the accused or convicted party in a criminal proceeding. The law further states that no legislation may be passed that would increase the penalty for a crime an individual already commited and was convicted of.

While the principle of *Ex Post Facto* applies primarily to criminal law, it does find application in education. For example, let us suppose that a student who was in charge of the school newspaper published an editorial which was offensive to the Board of Education. Let us further assume that the student went through all the established procedures required by school policy for review prior to its publication. Now let's say that the offended Board members demand that the student be suspended. If the student is suspended, both the principal and the Board members are guilty of *Ex Post Facto* violations.

This is so because it was not illegal for the student to print the material since he or she followed the *established rules and procedures,* and because within those rules, there was

no penalty attached to the printing of material that had been cleared. The board may establish new review procedures and, in certain cases, attach penalties to their violation *from this point forward.* However, the student in the example may not be penalized since he or she was operating under the previous standards.

See Also: CIVIL RIGHTS: CONSTITUTIONAL RIGHTS; DUE PROCESS.

Expulsion of Students

There are several valid reasons that have been upheld by law as grounds for the **expulsion** of a student. These are *stealing,* but only after the second or third offense; *vandalism* involving damage of over $1000; *truancy; calling in false fire alarms or making bomb threats; extortion* or "shakedowns" with or without a weapon; the *sale, possession or use of any of the universal contrabands for schools* such as weapons, drugs, alcohol, and pornography and, the *breaking of community laws* such as arson, burglary or murder. All of these have been upheld under the principle that to have such a student in the school would recklessly endanger the safety and well-being of the other students.

In the process of expelling a student, the most important factor to note is that the student is entitled to due process of the law. Before a student can be expelled from school, he or she is entitled to a formal hearing.

The hearing must operate under certain very stringent rules. Rules of procedures must be in written form and everyone involved must have a copy. The student is entitled to written notice of the charges against him or her. This must include a statement of the evidence and the possible punitive results. A student must be informed of his or her rights under the law. These rights include the right to legal counsel, the right to inspect the evidence against him or her, the right to present evidence in his or her favor, the right to present witnesses in his or her own behalf, the right to confront and cross-examine witnesses against him or her, and the right to protection against self-incrimination (Fifth Amendment). Precise records and transcripts should be kept of all proceedings. Finally, the student must have the right to appeal the decision.

When a student under the age of sixteen is expelled, it has been upheld that the school board must provide an alternate method of instruction for the student until that student reaches the age of sixteen.

The expulsion of a student is a serious business, but the keynotes of the entire process are "fairness and legality." If the expulsion procedures have been based on hard facts, if the student has been provided with every legal protection of his or her rights, and if the entire procedure provided for the due process of law, then the final decision will stand.

See Also: DUE PROCESS; FIFTH AMENDMENT GUARANTEES; FOUR-TEEN AMENDMENT GUARAN-TEES; HEARINGS; JUVENILE DELIN-QUENCY; SAFE PLACE STATUTES; SAFETY; SELF-INCRIMINATION) STUDENT INFORMATION; SUPERVI-SION (STUDENT).

EXTRACURRICULAR ACTIVITIES

Extracurricular activities are those activities students engage in on a voluntary basis, that are organized and sponsored by the school, which fall outside the regular curriculum.

Extracurricular activities provide a variety of benefits for the students of a school. They help students to develop friendships; they help sponsor positive student interest in school; they teach students how to win, lose and cooperate; they inspire school or class loyalty and spirit; they provide a worthwhile use of the student's free time; they often develop closer relationships with teachers on a different level; they frequently provide for a greater willingness on the part of the students to accept constructive criticism; and, they allow students to gain information not usually taught in curricular courses.

Participation in extracurricular activities should always be voluntary, although guidance personnel can often suggest various activities to students. A student's participation in an activity should become part of that student's permanent record.

Sponsorship of an extracurricular activity by a teacher should also be voluntary wherever possible. This sponsorship should be considered part of the total work load of teachers.

Extracurricular activities should be free of community pressure. All such activities should receive equal but proportionate funding from the Board of Education, and both athletic and nonathletic activities should be accorded the same status and honor. Moreover, such factors as the scheduling of extracurricular activities should receive the same attention as other phases of program development.

The number and type of extracurricular activities offered by a school may expand or contract, depending on many factors such as student interest, availability of funding, availability of sponsors, the size of the school, the number and type of activities offered within the community, and the general attitude about extracurricular activities among students, teachers, administrators, and the community.

Extracurricular activities fall into many classifications. Historically, sports were the first extracurricular activities offered by schools, and they continue to hold a prominent position. School subjects inspire activities such as a Math Club, Science Club, French Club, etc. Service organizations such as the Student Council or Student Government have always been popular. Also, activities centered around particular interests such as Stamp and Coin Clubs, Garden Clubs, Cooking Clubs, are always in demand. Finally, there has been growth in extracurricular activities that center around the language and customs of a particular ethnic heritage, for example, Spanish Clubs, Italian Clubs, etc.

Extracurricular activities continue to play a valuable role in American education, and their potential for student involvement and personal development will undoubtedly increase in the coming years.

See Also: ACADEMIC PROGRAM; ACTIVITIES; ASSEMBLY PROGRAM; BAND; CLUBS; CULTURE; ENRICHMENT; FUNDS, SCHOOL; GUIDANCE; HOME ECONOMICS; INSURANCE; MUSIC; PERMANENT RECORDS; PERSONNEL FILES; PROFILE SHEET; SCHEDULE; SCHOLARSHIP; SPECIAL INTEREST GROUPS; SPORTS; STUDENT COUNCIL (STUDENT GOVERNMENT); STUDENT INFORMATION; SUPERVISION (STUDENTS); SUPPLIES; TRANSPORTATION; VOLUNTEERS; YEARBOOK.

EXTRACURRICULAR DUTIES

Extracurricular activities must be supervised. There is no contention on that point. A difficulty often arises, however, when the question of who shall supervise them is brought up. Ideally, the sponsorship of an extracurricular activity should be voluntary. A teacher with an avid interest in drama, let us say, who volunteers to produce the school play will undoubtedly do an excellent job, the students will learn and prosper under his or her guidance, and everyone will be happy. What happens, however, if there are more activities than there are teachers willing to sponsor them?

The assignment of an **extracurricular duty** to a teacher who does not want it has been a bone of contention for a long time. There have been cases in which teachers have refused extracurricular duties and have subsequently been dismissed. Whether or not the assignment of the duty was, in fact, legal, and whether or not the dismissed teacher should be reinstated have often been the subject of court cases. The decisions in these cases tend to point out a number of variables.

The key point seems to be the "reasonableness" of the assignment. The assignment, for example, should not present an excessive number of hours; the students must benefit from the activity and the assignment of the particular teacher; the assignments should be distributed equally among all teachers, must be professional in nature, and should relate to the teacher's field of certification and interest. These qualifications have been held to be "reasonable" qualifiers of an extracurricular duty assignment.

For example, one court held that a teacher could not be forced to collect tickets at a ball game because it was not "professional," in that it was a task anyone could have performed *(Todd Coronway v. Lansdowne School District No. 785,* Court of Common Pleas of Delaware County, PA, 1951). In another case a teacher was dismissed for refusing to take a bowling club. He was ordered reinstated, and the court declared that the activity was not so related to the school program as to justify the assignment *(Pease v. Millcreek Township School District,* [195 A.2d 104 108] Pa, 1963).

However, it has been held that "reasonable extracurricular assignments" that fall under the guidelines detailed above are considered implied duties under teacher's contracts. Consequently, they can be assigned given that all the provisions for a "reasonable assignment" are met. Moreover, because they have been defined as "implied duties," they need not be compensated. Let us hasten to add, however, that compensation for extracurricular duties as well as the nature and scope of extracurricular duty assignments can be, and very often are, matters of negotiation between the representative teacher's group and the Board of Education in contract talks.

See Also: ACCEPTANCE OF CONTRACTS; ASSIGNMENTS; EXTRACURRICULAR ACTIVITIES; FACULTY; JUST COMPENSATION; NEGOTIATIONS; QUALIFICATIONS; SALARY; SUPERVISION (STUDENTS); TRIPS; VOLUNTEERS.

FACT FINDING

Fact finding refers to the process of investigating a disputed area, usually involving labor or contract negotiations, by an individual or group of individuals specifically appointed to do so.

Within the scope of contract or labor negotiations, impasses frequently occur involving areas that are disputed by both sides. Often, but not always, these areas revolve around projected salary demands as opposed to management's ability to meet these demands. When such disputes arise, it is a fairly common practice for both sides to call for a fact finder's report.

Fact finding is a fairly formal process. An individual, or a panel of individuals, goes through a process of gathering information from all parties involved in the dispute, holding hearings, and, ultimately, issuing a report that makes a formal recommendation based on the information gathered for the settlement of the dispute. It should be noted, however, that unless both parties to the dispute formally agree to abide by the fact finder's decision, the findings and recommendations are not binding for either side.

Most often, the fact finder's report is made public. Because of this, the report often shapes public opinion about the dispute and this provides powerful incentive toward the resolution of the difficulty. Fact finding is a frequent part of negotiations between boards of education and local teacher's associations.

See Also: ADVISORY COUNCILS; ARBITRATION; AUTHORITY, BOARD; COLLECTIVE BARGAINING; CONTRACTS; DEMANDS; DUE PROCESS; EMPLOYEE RELATIONS; MEDIATION AND MEDIATOR; NEGOTIATIONS; RECOMMENDATION.

FACULTY

A **faculty** is a group consisting of all the properly certified professional teachers in a given school or educational institution.

Technically, administrators and supervisory personnel are not classified as members of the faculty, but rather as members of the professional staff. This is often a small distinction, however, since many administrators, for whatever reason, may carry out teaching as well as administrative assignments, especially in smaller school systems. Moreover, Guidance personnel are considered part of the faculty, even though they may teach no classes.

In public education, all faculty members must be properly certified to teach by the state. Faculty members are hired by, and serve as employees of, the school district's board of education or school board. The assignment of individual teachers to the faculty of any particular school is usually a prerogative of the board, as is the transfer of teachers within the district from one faculty to another, although certain stipulations may be imposed on these actions as a result of contractual obligations.

The overall quality of a faculty, its cooperation with and involvement in the affairs of the school, and the quality of the working relationship between the faculty and the administration are all contributing factors to the educational excellence of a school. Acting as a body, the faculty of a school can exert a powerful influence upon policy and performance.

Faculty members also act as representatives of the school system. Consequently, many school districts provide in-service courses in effective public relations techniques for faculty members that emphasize the part faculty members play in the overall image of the school system in the community.

A board of education may impose standards and requirements for faculty members as long as these are legal and do not violate the constitutional and civil rights of an individual. Within the chain of command, the faculty is the primary controlling agent of the student body, subject, in turn, to the administrative and central staff as well as the Board of Education.

See Also: ACCOUNTABILITY; AMERICAN FEDERATION OF TEACHERS; ASSIGNMENTS; AUTHORITY, TEACHER; CERTIFICATION; COLLECTIVE BARGAINING; CONTRACTS; DIFFERENTIATED STAFFING; DISMISSAL OF PERSONNEL; EMPLOYEE RELATIONS; FACULTY MEETING; *IN LOCO PARENTIS;* LEAVE OF ABSENCE; NATIONAL EDUCATION ASSOCIATION; NONFEASANCE; PROFESSIONAL ASSOCIATIONS FOR TEACHERS; QUALIFICATIONS; REDUCTION IN FORCE; SUPERVISION (STAFF); SUPERVISION (STUDENTS); WORLD CONFEDERATION OF THE TEACHING PROFESSION.

FACULTY MEETING

The number of **faculty meetings** held during a school year, as well as the duration of these meetings, may be at the discretion of the administrator or they may be a matter of contractual regulation as a result of collective bargaining. Faculty meetings may be held after or before regular school hours, or students may be dismissed early so that the meetings can be held during the time when school might normally be in session. These variables are all matters of policy within individual school systems.

The topics covered during a faculty meeting will also vary. These may include instruction in the preparation of the budget or other forms, the clarification of procedures for upcoming events, in-service type exposition of educational methodology, the conducting of surveys and the gathering of statistical data, *ad hoc* meetings to solve particular problems, and a variety of other reasons.

Notice of faculty meetings should be given well in advance and an agenda for the meeting should be published. Faculty members should feel that they have input into these meetings and that the meetings are purposeful. While faculty meetings should not become "gripe sessions," faculty members should be given the opportunity to voice their concerns and offer advice and constructive criticism.

Faculty meetings that are well-planned, that cover topics of importance and concern, and that allow for consideration of the faculty's opinion and provide opportunities for faculty comments are generally well-attended and productive.

See Also: ADVISORY COUNCILS; BULLETINS; COMMITTEE; COMMUNICATION; DEPARTMENTAL MEETINGS; EMPLOYEE RELATIONS; FACULTY; LIAISON; PARLIAMENTARY PROCEDURE.

FALSE IMPRISONMENT

See DETENTION.

FAMILY SERVICES

No educator would underestimate the importance of the family in the education of the child. The family has been and remains the primary socializing instrument in the child's life. It is recognized that children who come from homes where education is prized, where parents supply supportive reinforcement of education, and where there is a high degree of motivation for success in education, generally do better in school than children who come from family situations where these elements are lacking. Indeed, the famous Coleman Report (1966) indicated just how powerful an influence the family can be.

Consequently, many educational agencies and institutions have taken a compensatory approach in which the school or agency endeavors to make up for those qualities which might be lacking at home. Such programs as Project Head Start and Higher Horizons were attempts at introducing children to curriculum subject areas and cultural experiences that would not have been a part of their normal experiences within the family. Moreover, many school districts supply a variety of services which they list under titles such as "Special Services" or **"Family Services,"** which aim at dealing with the home situation in order to beneficially affect the child's relationship to the school and education in general. Members of these "special" teams may include psychologists and social workers, as well as educational specialists.

Family services offered by schools and by cooperating social agencies within the community may include such items as day care centers. Public health facilities, home tutoring teams, social welfare agencies and many others. Collectively, these agencies are listed with the state departments of youth and family services (names vary) across the nation.

See Also: ADVISORY COUNCILS; AUTHORITY, EXPRESS AND IMPLIED; AUXILIARY SERVICES; BUDGET; CHILD ABUSE; COMMUNICATION; CONSULTANTS; COUNSELING; CULTURE; DIAGNOSIS; DRINKING OF ALCOHOLIC BEVERAGES; DRUGS; EARLY CHILDHOOD PROGRAMS; FEDERAL AGENCIES; FEDERAL AID; FEDERAL PROGRAMS; HEALTH; HOME INSTRUCTION; IMMUNIZATION; INNOCULATION AND VACCINATION; LEARNING DISABILITIES; MARRIED STUDENTS; MIGRANTS; PARENT CONFERENCES; PRIVILEGED COMMUNICATIONS; PSYCHOLOGICAL STUDIES; SPECIAL SERVICES; TRUANCY; UNWED MOTHERS; WELFARE.

FEDERAL AGENCIES

FEDERAL AID

FEDERAL PROGRAMS

The Federal Government of the United States administers a variety of programs relative to education in America through the U.S. Department of Education. Moreover, the Government supplies financial assistance to school districts along federal guidelines for school aid.

Traditionally, the administrator was faced with some confusion in trying to implement a federal program within a school district. In order to obtain funding for a school lunch program, for example, one had to contact the U.S. Department of Agriculture and was then referred to the Federal Surplus Commodities Corporation. What's more, once contact had been made, the administrator might find that the agency has shifted, virtually overnight, to another department. School lunches, for example, left the Department of Agriculture when the Federal Surplus Commodities Corporation became part of the U.S. Department of Labor.

With the goal of alleviating this type of confusion and consolidating all federal agencies and programs *relative to education* under one agency, the Department of Education Organization Act (PL 96-88) was signed on October 17, 1979. This Act authorized the creation of the U.S. Department of Education, which had its official opening on May 4, 1980.

With the formation of the Department of Education, access to **Federal Agencies, Aid, and Programs** became standardized.

The Department of Education maintains programs through which federal funds are disbursed to local school districts in various forms. Following are the types of federal assistance, both financial and nonfinancial, which relate to education:

TYPES OF FEDERAL AID/ASSISTANCE

Formula Grants—Also known as entitlement awards, these are allocations of money to states or their subdivisions, in accordance with a formula based on the numbers of children to be served, or the amounts of Federal or state money available, for activities of a continuing nature not confined to a specific project.

Project Grants—The funding, for fixed or known periods, of specific projects or the delivery of specific services or products without liability for damages from failure to perform. Project grants include fellowships, scholarships, research grants, training grants, traineeships, experimental and demonstration grants, evaluation grants, planning grants, technical assistance grants, survey grants, construction grants, and unsolicited contractual agreements.

Direct Payments for Specified Use—Financial assistance from the Federal Government provided directly to individuals, private firms and other private institutions to encourage or subsidize a particular activity by conditioning the receipt of the assistance on a particular performance by the recipient. Contracts are awarded to bidders submitting proposals that best meet the requirements of the announced work, within a competitive budget range. This does not include solicited contracts for the procurement of goods and services for the Federal Government.

Direct Payments with Unrestricted Use—Financial assistance from the Federal Government provided directly to the beneficiaries who satisfy Federal eligibility requirements with no restrictions being imposed on the recipient as to how the money is spent. Included are payments under retirement, pension and compensation programs.

Direct Loans—Financial assistance provided through the lending of federal monies for a specified period of time, with a reasonable expectation of repayment. Such loans may or may not require the payment of interest.

Guaranteed/Insured Loans—Programs in which the Federal Government makes arrangement to indemnify a loaned-against part, or all, of any defaults by those responsible for repayment of loans.

Sale, Exchange, or Donation of Property and Goods—Programs that provide for the sale, exchange, or donation of Federal real property, personal property, commodities, and other goods including land, buildings, equipment, food, and drugs. When setting the sales price, the secretary may take into account any public benefit that has or will accrue as a result of implementing the proposed educational program.

Provision of Specialized Services— Programs that provide federal personnel who perform certain tasks for the benefit of communities or individuals. These services may be performed in conjunction with personnel who are not federal, but they involve more than consultation, advice or counseling.

Advisory Services and Counseling—Programs that provide federal specialists to consult, advise or counsel communities or individuals including conferences, workshops or personal contacts. This may involve the use of public information, but only in a secondary capacity.

Dissemination of Technical Information—Programs that provide for the publication and distribution of informational data of a specialized technical nature, frequently through clearinghouses or libraries. This does not include conventional public information services designed for general public consumption.

Some of the aforementioned are outright grants with or without restriction; others involve combined money or "matching funds"; still others involve just personnel and services.

The U.S. Department of Educa-

tion administers programs through its various offices:

The Office of Elementary and Secondary Education administers programs that provide services for children in public and private elementary and secondary schools. Its largest program is the Compensatory Education program for disadvantaged children under Title I of the 1965 ESEA. It also administers the Indian Education Act, which funds programs to meet the special needs of Indian students. In addition, it administers programs to help teachers improve classroom skills, career education, and school administration. The OESE also has programs that encourage and assist desegregation efforts, as well as programs that provide financial assistance to school districts whose tax base is seriously affected by federal activity, and to schools damaged by financial disasters. For more information contact:

Office of Elementary and
  Secondary Education
U.S. Department of Education
Washington, DC 20202
(202) 245-8720

The Office of Bilingual Education and Minority Languages Affairs supports education programs for some 300,000 children and adults who use English as a second language. Its programs were detailed in the entry, BILINGUAL EDUCATION earlier in this book. For further information contact:

The Office of Bilingual Education and Minority Language Affairs
U.S. Department of Education
Washington, DC
(202) 245-2600

The Office of Special Education and Rehabilitative Services helps states give handicapped children the education that best meets their needs. It also helps to support state-operated centers and other services for the rehabilitation of disabled adults. It provides federal aid to locate, evaluate and provide learning programs for disabled children and provides teaching materials for children who are blind, deaf or have one or more disabilities. In addition, over a million disabled Americans, mostly adults, receive vocational training, counseling and physical therapy through state rehabilitation centers. For further information contact:

The Office of Special Education and Rehabilitative Services
U.S. Department of Education
Washington, DC 20202
(202) 472-2455

The Office of Post-Secondary Education furthers the nation's commitment to give every financially needy young person who wants to go to college, or get post-high school vocational training, the support to do so. The OPE programs also offer academic support to disadvantaged students in order that they might earn degrees. The Cooperative Education Program helps students find jobs closely related to their field of study while they are working toward a degree. There are also programs that provide funds to graduate and professional schools to recruit more women and minorities, as well as helping selected colleges strengthen their academic programs, upgrade faculty, improve administration, and expand student services. The OPE's international education programs funds training to develop specialists in many languages and regions of the world. For further information contact:

The Office of Post-Secondary Education
U.S. Department of Education
Washington, DC 20202
(202) 245-9274

The Office of Vocational and Adult Education helps states and communities offer young people and adults the specialized training that leads to good jobs, both in traditional fields and in the newer technologies. Programs provide instructors, equipment, textbooks, and other teaching materials in high schools, colleges and area vocational-technical centers. Services also include career counseling, remedial reading and mathematics for students, as well as in-service training for teachers and other members of the school staff. It also supports community education projects. For further information contact:

The Office of Vocational and Adult
Education
U.S. Department of Education
Washington, DC 20202
(202) 245-8166

The Office of Educational Research and Improvement operates almost 50 research and demonstration programs, pre-school through graduate school. The OERI also supports projects of national concern on the elementary, secondary and college levels. The OERI aids libraries, provides assistance in the production of high-quality media educational programming, and disseminates information about research developments and innovative programs to all interested parties. For further information contact:

The Office of Educational Research
and Improvement
U.S. Department of Education
Washington, DC 20202
(202) 472-5753

The Office of Civil Rights is responsible for seeing that schools, colleges and other education institutions receiving federal aid comply with laws barring discrimination against students or employees because of their race, national origin, sex, handicap, and age. The OCR also administers the Civil Rights provisions of the Emergency School Aid Act, an annual grant program in the Office of Elementary and Secondary Educa-

tion. ESAA gives federal aid to elementary and secondary schools to encourage the voluntary elimination, reduction or prevention of minority group isolation. For further information contact:

The Office of Civil Rights
U.S. Department of Education
Washington, DC 20202
(202) 245-7680

Department of Education programs are described in detail in an annually printed booklet entitled "19xx Guide to Department of Education Programs." Single copies of reprints are available free by writing to:

EDGuide—XX (Insert digits of
current year.)
U.S. Department of Education
Washington, DC 20202

Dealing with federal agencies, becoming involved in federal programs, and applying for federal assistance can be an extremely complicated process, especially since the programs and regulations may change rapidly. Indeed, many school districts specify one member of the central staff to deal with all aspects of federal funding and aid within the district. Moreover, many districts seek the services of people who are experts in applying for and obtaining grants from the federal government.

See Also: ELEMENTARY AND SEC-ONDARY EDUCATION ACT OF 1965; MONTHLY REPORTS; PUBLIC LAW 94-142; RECORD KEEPING; STATE AGENCIES; STATE AID; STATE PRO-GRAMS; TAXES; U.S. DEPARTMENT OF EDUCATION; YEAR-END REPORT.

FEES

Fees that are charged by persons or agencies outside of public education such as consulting psychologists, speakers for in-service sessions and the like are usually handled through the board of education. Individual schools within a district often receive funds under the classification of "Activities," "Professional" or a number of other designations with which to meet the fees of persons or agencies who provide special assembly programs, in-service sessions for individual schools, social, and other special activities.

In regard to the school itself, the question often arises as to whether or not a school district may charge fees for participation in certain academic activities. These fees often include such items as textbook fees, lab equipment charges for science classes, "towel" fees for participation in physical education and a host of others. While public education in America is mandated to be free to all, certain fees have been upheld as legal, but these vary greatly from state to state and are largely dependent upon the Constitutional requirements and restrictions of the individual states.

Whatever the case, it behooves an administrator to check thoroughly for particular restrictions before imposing any fee.

One thing that has been almost universally upheld is the fact that a school district may not charge tuition for residents, but may impose a tuition fee for nonresidents of the school district.

See Also: ACTIVITIES; CAFETERIA; CASH; CONSULTANTS; COPYING SERVICES; EXPENSES; FIELD TRIPS; FUNDS, SCHOOL; GRADUATION; LI-BRARY AND MEDIA CENTER; NON-RESIDENT, ADMISSION OF; PARK-ING; SPORTS; STUDENT INFORMA-TION; TRIPS.

FIELD TRIPS

Field trips are a very valuable part of the educational process. They help to promote and foster learning, supplement the academic program, expose students to a variety of social and cultural experiences, and much, much more. Field trips to places within the community can also act as positive public relations vehicles as well as acquaint students with the resources of their communities.

Field trips should be planned well in advance. All arrangements for transportation, tickets, variables such as where students shall eat lunch, times of departure and return, and arrangements for supervision should all be taken care of well before the actual event. Teachers are usually the main source of supervision, but it should be remembered that parents are often anxious to volunteer and their involvement can enhance school and community relations.

The parents of all children going on the field trip should be informed of all the particulars of the trip, especially the time of return in the event that this is later than normal school dismissal time. Parents should also be required to sign a paper granting permission for the child to participate in the field trip. These papers should contain the details of the trip and a statement such as, "I hereby relieve (name of school district) of all responsibility beyond that of normal supervision." These papers should be collected from each child prior to leaving on the field trip.

See Also: ACADEMIC PROGRAM; AIDES; APPRECIATION, LETTER OF; AUTHORITY, BOARD; AUTHORITY, EXPRESS AND IMPLIED; AUTHORITY, PARENTAL; AUTHORITY, TEACHER; BUDGET; CALENDAR; COURSE; CULTURE; ENRICHMENT; EXPENSES; FEES; FUNDS, SCHOOL; INSTRUCTION; INSURANCE; INTERDISCIPLINARY APPROACHES; LIABILITY; MORATORIUM; PERMISSION SLIPS; SAFETY; SUPERVISION (STUDENTS); TRANSPORTATION; TRIPS; VOLUNTEERS.

FIFTH AMENDMENT GUARANTEES

The **Fifth Amendment** to the U.S. Constitution provides to citizens several guarantees and provides safeguards that may be applied to education:

1. "No person shall be held to answer for a capital, or otherwise infamous crime, unless on a presentment or indictment of a grand jury...." Consequently, a teacher or student accused of a breach of conduct by the board must be fully apprised of the complete actions and charges to be brought against him and be accorded a review hearing on those charges.

2. "...nor shall any person be subject for the same offense to be twice put in jeopardy of life or limb...." Double jeopardy is a well-understood concept that applies to students and educators in actions such as suspension or revocation of certification, as well as in criminal proceedings.

3. "...nor shall be compelled in any criminal case to be a witness against himself...." Consequently, the burden of proof falls upon the body bringing the action, and a student or teacher's silence in the matter cannot be construed as evidence of guilt.

4. "...nor be deprived of life, liberty or property, without due process of law...." Any student or educator accused of a breach of conduct has an absolute right to all the protections of existing law.

5. "...nor shall private property be taken for public use, without just compensation." This section is particularly applicable to school systems that want to expand the current system.

In short, it has been held that students and educators do not abrogate their civil and constitutional rights because of their positions. They are fully entitled to all the protections and guarantees of the Constitution.

See Also: ACCESS RIGHTS; BURDEN OF PROOF; CIVIL RIGHTS; CONSTITUTIONAL RIGHTS; DUE PROCESS; EASEMENT; *EX POST FACTO;* HEARINGS; JUST COMPENSATION; LEASE OF SCHOOL PROPERTY; OATHS; SELF-INCRIMINATION; SEVERANCE PAY; ZONING; ZONING BOARD.

FIRE DRILLS

The holding of **fire drills** is an important part of school procedures. In the event of an actual emergency, the time spent practicing the swift and safe evacuation of the school could well pay off in the number of lives saved.

The main objective of a fire drill is to move the entire school population out of the building as quickly and safely as possible to a place that is hazard-free. Toward this end, the location of classrooms in relationship to building exits should be thoroughly studied and a flow pattern ascertained that will allow all classrooms to exit in a swift but orderly fashion, without the possibility of a "traffic jam" at any one exit.

Once the evacuation procedure has been established, the faculty should be familiarized with it, as well as their role of supervision. Moreover, they should also be informed as to requirements such as ensuring that windows are closed and lights and electrical appliances turned off. They should also impress upon students the seriousness of the exercise.

Ideally, every classroom and area of the school, including cafeterias and gymnasiums, should contain a poster or plaque with the evacuation directions from that particular area. For example, a typical poster might read, "Fire Drill, Room 211, turn right; use center stairs to Exit 3." Teachers using the room or area should familiarize students with the evacuation route.

Once outside the building, it is generally held that students should be moved to a position at least 200 feet from the building and to such a place where they will not hamper fire fighting and emergency vehicles. Students should, of course, be properly supervised during the entire procedure.

The frequency of fire drills, as well as other specific requirements, is often a matter of local and/or state law.

See Also: BUILDINGS; CAPACITY; CLASS AND CLASS SIZE; DISCIPLINE; FIRST AID; FORESEEABILITY; INSURANCE; LIABILITY; MONTHLY REPORTS; NURSE; POLICE; PUBLIC ADDRESS SYSTEM; SAFE PLACE STATUTES; SAFETY; STUDENT INFORMATION; SUPERVISION (STUDENTS); TRANSPORTATION.

FIRST AID

First aid is the reasonable and prudent emergency treatment given in the face of injury or illness by un-licensed laymen or a licensed profes-sional if the need is immediate.

All administrators feel responsi-ble for the safety and well-being of their students. Consequently, school boards assign professional nurses on a full- or part-time basis to each school in their jurisdiction. The administrator and nurse are then responsible for the health care provided. Further, the ad-ministrator can also disseminate first aid information to all members of the faculty and staff.

In many instances, the school nurse will provide first aid kits for each room with instructions on how these kits are to be used. In many schools, a schedule of workshops is arranged for teachers in fundamental first aid measures. Some schools also provide for a course in first aid to be taught to students as part of either their Physical Education or Health curricula.

The most difficult aspect of first aid, aside from knowing what to do, is knowing when and when not to ad-minister aid. Some religious sects and secular groups can refuse first aid on religious and/or constitutional grounds. However, the courts have held that the school *can* act if the situation is "life-threatening" to the individual. This has further been in-terpreted to encompass situations where the injury or illness is severe, such as a broken limb, even though it may not be a life-or-death situation. Indeed, a good first aid program, administered under the proper super-vision of a health professional, has become an integral part of the en-vironment of almost all schools.

See Also: ACCIDENT, AUTHORITY, EX-PRESS AND IMPLIED; CHRISTIAN SCIENTISTS; CONSTITUTIONAL RIGHTS; FACULTY MEETING; FIELD TRIPS; FUNDS, SCHOOL; HEALTH; *IN LOCO PARENTIS;* INSURANCE; JEHOVAH'S WITNESSES; NURSE; SAFE PLACE STATUTES; SAFETY; SPORTS; STUDENT INFORMATION; SUPERVISION (STAFF); SUPERVISION (STUDENTS); WORKSHOPS AND IN-SERVICE; X-RAY REPORT.

FIRST AMENDMENT GUARANTEES

The **First Amendment** to the Constitution provides citizens several guarantees and safeguards that may be applied to education:

1. "Congress shall make no law respecting an establishment of re-ligion, or prohibiting the free exercise thereof. . . ." Parents can send children to parochial schools and fulfill com-pulsory education laws. Further, federal aid to parochial schools is based on the Child Benefit Theory of direct versus indirect aid. Direct aid is contrary to the Amendment, while indirect aid is permitted. Released time is permitted because it is consid-ered an accommodation, not an aid *(Zorach v. Clauson,* 343 U.S. 306 [1959]). The Supreme Court has fur-ther held that one may not spend an inordinate amount of time on religion or "the pall of orthodoxy" *(Keyishian v. Board of Regents,* 385 U.S. 589, 603, 604 [1967]).

2. "...or abridging the freedom of speech...." The courts have ruled *(Tinker v. Des Moines Independent Community School District,* 393 U.S. 502, 503, 506, 508-511 [1969]), that freedom of speech may be restricted "only where it materially and substantially interferes with the requirements of appropriate discipline in the operation of the school." (See FREE SPEECH.)

3. "...or of the press...." Teachers cannot be fired for what they write. Moreover, by implication, it would seem that a teacher cannot be dismissed for what he does not write. It would not be surprising if the so-called "publish or perish" regulations usually applied to higher education were to be challenged in the foreseeable future.

4. "...or the right of the people peaceably to assemble...." Educators have the right to join unions. Moreover, they have the right to assemble with their peers. It is to be understood that the key word here is "peaceably," and as long as the assembly is peaceful, it may not be stopped by any authority.

5. "...and to petition the Government for a redress of grievances." This has been interpreted to mean the right of protest, strike, demonstration, job actions, etc. It is to be understood, however, that these rights may be restrained by court injunction. Thereafter, the grievance will be tried in court. This section of the First Amendment also guarantees the right of teachers to establish grievance procedures within school systems.

See Also: ACADEMIC FREEDOM; AUTHORITY, TEACHER; CENSORSHIP; CHRISTIAN SCIENTISTS; CHURCH-STATE SEPARATION; CONSTITUTIONAL RIGHTS; CREDIT UNION; DEMANDS; DEMONSTRATION; DRESS CODES; FIFTH AMENDMENT GUARANTEES; FOURTEENTH AMENDMENT GUARANTEES; FREE SPEECH; FUNDAMENTAL INTEREST THEORY; GRIEVANCES; INSTRUCTION; JEHOVAH'S WITNESSES; JOB ACTIONS; OATHS; PETITIONS; PLEDGE OF ALLEGIANCE; POLITICS AND THE SCHOOL; PRIVATE AND PAROCHIAL SCHOOLS; PROFESSIONAL ASSOCIATIONS FOR SCHOOL ADMINISTRATORS; PROFESSIONAL ASSOCIATIONS FOR TEACHERS; PROTEST; PUBLICATION; RELEASED TIME; SHARED-TIME; SPECIAL INTEREST GROUPS; STATE AID; STRIKES; STUDENT COUNCIL (STUDENT GOVERNMENT); STUDENT INFORMATION; TEXTBOOKS; TRANSPORTATION; UNIONS.

FORESEEABILITY

Foreseeability is the responsibility to reasonably foresee that an injury might occur if a particular condition is not corrected or perventative action not taken.

There are a number of implications to foreseeability. The person must take appropriate actions to correct the condition prior to the injury occurring: (1) If the person *sees the danger but does nothing,* he is liable; (2) If *he doesn't see but should have,* he is equally liable.

There are easy applications of foreseeability. These would include seeing to it that a substitute teacher is employed when the regular teacher is absent, providing supervision during recess, etc. There are, however, cases in which the doctrine of foreseeability is a bit more involved. They stem from the court's ruling that a teacher or administrator has a "higher standard of care and should be able to foresee an accident more than could 'the average man on the street.'" Here, the latter part of the definition is the most crucial.

Obviously, there are hundreds of places within a school building where an accident *could* occur. The very obvious dangers (jagged glass, loose bannister, etc.) are usually reported and fixed immediately. There are however, those conditions which, being human, teachers and administrators learn to "live with." A light that "blinks" occasionally, a door that "sticks" when it rains, or a public address speaker that garbles the words in one room, are annoyances which do not appear dangerous on the surface. However, let the blinking light explode, let the door stick during an emergency, let an emergency message be misunderstood, and there is serious trouble.

Responsibility as regards foreseeability depends upon who last reported the possible danger. To avoid finding oneself in court as a defendant in a negligence action, taking *reasonable precautions* and placing all complaints *in writing* to the next highest superior whether or not *they* act, is enough to end liability. A copy of all such correspondence should be kept. If all steps are properly followed and an accident occurs, the board must then bear the liability.

See Also: ACCIDENTS; ASSIGNMENTS; AUTHORITY, EXPRESS AND IMPLIED; BUILDINGS; CAPACITY; DAMAGES; DISMISSAL PROCEDURES (SCHOOL); GROUNDS; HABITABLE; INDUSTRIAL ARTS; IMPUTED NEGLIGENCE; LIABILITY; NEGLIGENCE; NONFEASANCE; REASONABLE AND PRUDENT; RIGHTS AND RESPONSIBILITIES; SAFE PLACE STATUTES; SAFETY; SUPERVISION (STUDENTS); TRANSPORTATION.

FOURTEENTH AMENDMENT GUARANTEES

In reaction to the "Black Codes," the Thirteenth Amendment was ratified in 1865. When this failed to accomplish its purpose, Congress adopted the Civil Rights Act of 1866 (PL 39-31 [14 Stat. 27]) and sustained the Act with the ratification of the **Fourteenth Amendment** in 1868. This Amendment, and the Thirteenth and Fifteenth Amendments (1870), are sometimes called the *Anti-Discrimination Amendments*. These state that citizenship rights cannot be limited based on race, color, or previous conditions of servitude. Coupled with the Nineteenth Amendment (1920) and various Civil Rights Acts such as those of 1870 (PL 41-114, Sec. 18 [16 Stat. 140]), 1871 (PL 42-22 17 [Stat.

13]), and 1964 (PL 88-352), this body of legislation once and for all states that *all citizens of the United States are equal before the law.*

The Fourteenth Amendment to the U.S. Constitution provides citizens several guarantees and safeguards that apply to education. These are specifically stated in various sections:

1. SECTION I: "All persons born or naturalized in the United States and subject to the jurisdiction thereof are citizens of the United States and of the State wherein they reside. No State shall make or enforce any law which shall abridge the privileges or immunities of citizens of the United States; nor shall any State deprive any person of life, liberty, or property, without due process of law...." Due process, mentioned in the First Amendment, was reinforced in the Fourteenth for the states. Furthermore, the states police power could be exercised, according to the courts, in the areas promoting "health, morals and safety," and could *in no way* infringe, disrupt or abridge an individual's right to liberty, justice and property. *Liberty* has been defined by the courts to mean a person's right to have "a good name, reputation, honor or integrity." Consequently, an educator can argue on charges of disloyalty, incompetence, insubordination, etc. The courts have defined *property* as a person's job and his or her right to it.

The Fourteenth Amendment is the basis for the constitutional rights of teachers and administrators. Even though local school boards do the actual hiring, the state is the employer of public school teachers and administrators. The school board acts as an agent of the state, as do the employees as they perform their duties. Therefore, school boards and officials are prohibited from enacting any rules or regulations that substantially infringe on an individual's constitutional right's, be they administrator, faculty, staff, or student.

Eight of these rights have been tested in the courts and upheld. These are freedom of speech outside the school environment; freedom of speech within the classroom; freedom from undue restrictions on personal appearance; freedom to live life in privacy; freedom of association; freedom of religion; protection from arbitrary, capricious or discriminatory actions or dismissals on the part of the local board; and due process.

2. SECTION I: "...nor deny to any person within its jurisdiction the *equal protection of the law.*" (emphasis added) This clause has been taken to protect married or pregnant students, pregnant teachers; prevent sex discrimination; ensure maternity leaves, paternity leaves, protect the handicapped, and aid in a large number of other cases. These equal protection cases are fought in the courts on two grounds. Both must be valid for the ruling or regulation to stand. The first ground is *purpose:* if the purpose of a regulation is health, morals or safety, there is a possible chance that the regulation may be upheld. The second ground is *classification:* if a

regulation applies to anyone based on race, religion, sex, age, national origin, etc., the regulation is on shaky grounds to begin with. While each case is tried individually, the purpose of the courts is to guarantee everyone the equal protection of the law.

3. SECTION II: While this section, which guarantees the right to vote, does not particularly apply to education, it was further amended by Amendments 16, 19, and 26. The Twenty-Sixth Amendment lowered the age of majority to 18. This has application to high school students, many of whom have reached this age. Consequently, they are adults, with every implication of the word.

4. SECTION V: "Congress shall have the power to enforce, by appropriate legislation, the provisions of this article." Consequently, if a state or its agent does not comply with the provisions of this amendment or any legislation leading out of it, federal funds for that state or district may be withheld.

See Also: ACADEMIC FREEDOM; AFFIRMATIVE ACTION; AGENT; ATHLETICS, SEX DISCRIMINATION IN; BOARD OF EDUCATION; BUSING; CENSORSHIP; CIVIL RIGHTS; CONSTITUTIONAL RIGHTS; CONTRACTS; DEMOTION; DISCRIMINATION; DISMISSAL OF PERSONNEL; DRESS CODES; DUE PROCESS; ELEMENTARY AND SECONDARY EDUCATION ACT OF 1965; EQUAL EMPLOYMENT OPPORTUNITIES; FEDERAL AGENCIES; FEDERAL AID, FEDERAL PROGRAMS; FIFTH AMENDMENT GUARANTEES: FIRST AMENDMENT GURANTEES; FOURTH AMENDMENT GUARANTEES; FREE SPEECH; GRIEVANCES; HEARINGS; JURISDICTION; LEAVE OF ABSENCE; MAJORITY, AGE OF; MARRIED STUDENTS; OATHS; PERMANENT RECORDS; PERSONNEL FILES; POLITICS AND THE SCHOOL; PRIVACY; SEARCH AND SEIZURE; SELF-INCRIMINATION; SEXISM: STATE AGENCIES, STATE AID, STATE PROGRAMS; STRIKES; TENURE; UNIONS; UNWED MOTHERS.

FOURTH AMENDMENT GUARANTEES

The **Fourth Amendment** to the U.S. Constitution provides citizens with several guarantees and safeguards that apply to education:

1. "The right of the people to be secure in their persons, houses, papers, and effects, against unreasonable searches and seizures, shall not be violated...." This guarantees the right to *privacy.* Consequently, a teacher cannot be fired because of his private life style, as long as it does not interfere with his teaching. As applied to students, a teacher or administrator cannot go through a student's pockets or purse, or, strictly speaking, read or act upon a note from one student to another.

2. "...and no Warrants shall issue, but upon *probable cause*, supported by Oath or affirmation...." (emphasis added) This "probable cause" clause is the one on which the most Fourth Amendment cases are brought before the courts. Who shall

determine probable cause? What action can be taken? The courts have ruled in conflict with each other to such an extent that administrators are faced with no better knowledge of their authority than before the rulings. On one hand, the courts have ruled that a student, teacher or staff member is "inviolate in their person" and unless "a clear and present danger" has been established, no action can constitutionally be taken. On the other hand, if the administrator is acting on written guidelines and acting as an agent of the state, action may be taken. This would apply to such items as locker searches and personal searches.

3. "...and (without) particularly describing the place to be searched and the person or things to be seized." In the strictest sense of the word, this guarantee prevents "fishing expeditions" by administrators, police or any other authority. However, police entering the school with a statement such as "We have reason to believe that a bomb in a shoebox has been placed in one of your lockers," has been deemed enough to warrant a complete locker search. However, if, during the search, anything other than a shoebox with a bomb in it is found, that item cannot be touched.

See Also: AGENT; AUTHORITY, EXPRESS AND IMPLIED; CIVIL RIGHTS; CONSTITUTIONAL RIGHTS; *IN LOCO PARENTIS;* LAVATORIES; POLICE; POLITICS AND THE SCHOOL; PRIVACY; REASONABLE AND PRUDENT; SAFETY; SEARCH AND SEIZURE; STUDENT INFORMATION; SUPERVISION (STAFF); SUPERVISION (STUDENTS).

FREE SPEECH

Free speech is the right to speak freely, to express oneself without undue restraint, to question the decisions of the government, to campaign openly against it, to enter into free and open debates whether as an individual or as a member of a group. Free speech implies not only the right to speak, but also the right of others to hear.

In education, free speech is considered to be part of academic freedom and is protected by the First, Fourth, Fifth, and Fourteenth Amendments. This means that educators, like all citizens, are privileged against self-incrimination, loyalty oaths, etc. Further, silence can never be construed as an admission of guilt to any charge.

There are two major aspects of freedom of speech, relative to education, which have been tested and upheld in the courts. First, as regards freedom of speech outside the school environment, a teacher cannot be liable for views held outside the classroom. The courts decided, however, that two and only two grounds for dismissal were possible: first, that the statements were made *harmful to a substantial public interest,* and second, that the statements rendered the person *unfit to teach.* Disruption of the public interest occurs when the statements "materially and substantially interfere" with the order and efficiency of the operation of the school. This came from the Pickering decision *(Pickering v. Board of Education,* 391 U.S. 563 [1968]) in which the Court further stated that an individual could not be fired for what he says or writes, provided he doesn't disrupt working relationships, breech loyalty or confidentiality, disrupt public service, indicate the unfitness of another, and/or fail to comply with established grievance procedures.

Second, freedom of speech within the classroom was upheld. Classrooms are used as a marketplace of ideas. Therefore, arguments, even noisy ones, must be tolerated and can only be restricted when they "materially and substantially interfere" with appropriate discipline *(Tinker v. Des Moines Independent Community School District,* 393 U.S. 501-524 [1969]). The criterion for whether or not to restrict speech in the classroom depends on how closely the argument or discussion comes to serving an educational purpose. For example, discussing a controversial social issue may be perfectly valid for a History, Civics or Psychology teacher, whereas a Math teacher may have a difficult time justifying the discussion. If the topic is relevant, however, no view can be restricted. If it is irrelevant, however, the teacher or student may be disciplined. In one famous set of cases, a student was suspended for saying the word "fuck" in class, and a teacher was dismissed for using the same word in his class.

The student's suspension was upheld, because the student's remark served no educational purpose, while the teacher was ordered reinstated because the teacher had used the word as an example during a lecture on the improper use of the English language. *(Mailloux v. Kiley,* 448 F.2d 1242).

Under this principle, no student or teacher can be forced to lead or participate in the Pledge of Allegiance, loyalty oaths or anything that does not serve a strict educational purpose.

The courts have further held that freedom of expression as manifested in such variables as hair length, wearing of arm bands, style of dress, etc., is protected under the principle of free speech and restricted in the same manner.

See Also: ACADEMIC FREEDOM; CIVIL RIGHTS; CENSORSHIP; CONSTITUTIONAL RIGHTS; DEMONSTRATIONS; DRESS CODES; DUE PROCESS; FIFTH AMENDMENT GUARANTEES; FIRST AMENDMENT GUARANTEES; FOURTH AMENDMENT GUARANTEES; FOURTEENTH AMENDMENT GUARANTEES; GRIEVANCES; INSTRUCTION; OATHS; PETITIONS; PLEDGE OF ALLEGIANCE; POLITICS AND THE SCHOOL; PRIVACY; PUBLICATION; RIGHTS AND RESPONSIBILITIES; SELF-INCRIMINATION; UNIONS.

FUNDAMENTAL INTEREST THEORY

Fundamental Interest Theory is the belief that equal educational opportunities are guaranteed by the "equal protection" clause of the Fourteenth Amendment and cannot be denied on the basis of religion, socioeconomic background, or race.

The Child Benefit Theory, as stated in the decision on of *Borden v. Louisiana State Board of Education* (123 So. 655) fostered the idea that education could neither be denied nor abridged because of religious background or affiliation. A series of cases further tested the Fourteenth Amendment guarantees concerning the social status and financial dispersements of taxes to schools. The case of *Serrano v. Priest* (487 P.2d 1241, [CA, 1971]) established the concept that the "fundamental interest" should be the schooling of the child, regardless of where that child resides or the wealth of his parents and/or community. Denial of state revenue because of a poor local tax base was also declared to be unconstitutional under this theory *(San Antonio Independent School District v. Rodrigues,* 93 S.Ct. 1278, [1973]). While closely allied with the Child Benefit Theory, the Fundamental Interest Theory can be applied to any anti-discrimination case, regardless of how the discrimination may be accomplished or against whom it may be aimed. The right to a free and appropriate education has been stated as a constitutional privilege of every child in the United States.

See Also: BOARD OF EDUCATION; BONDS; BUDGET; BUSING; CHURCH-STATE SEPARATION; CIVIL RIGHTS; CONSTITUTIONAL RIGHTS; DIS-CRIMINATION; ELEMENTARY AND SECONDARY EDUCATION ACT OF 1965; FOURTEENTH AMENDMENT GUARANTEES; MIGRANTS; PRIVATE AND PAROCHIAL SCHOOLS; RACE RELATIONS; RELEASED TIME; SHARED-TIME; TAXES.

FUNDS, SCHOOL

School funds are usually generated by local taxes and fees. In some cases, however, under some state statutes, these funds are mingled with state and federal aid funds, but generally there is a separation between the two. Income received from student activities, such as athletic events and school plays, are legally considered school funds subject to control by and under the responsibility of the school board.

One of the first questions to be asked about school funds is, "Who shall govern them?" They are governed by state statutes only. Authority over them is granted through the statutes to local school boards.

These statutes expressly state the purposes for which school funds may be spent. Authorized expenditures must be listed in writing and on file in the state's attorney general's office. Common authorized expenditures include: athletic equipment and facilities; doctors, dentists and nurses to diagnose but not treat; insurance for employees; legal counseling; insurance of school property; cafeterias; nonprofit school stores; speaker's fees; school buses and drivers; architects, and band uniforms.

The question of who shall be allowed to spend these funds rests with the school board, which may not delegate its discretionary authority to employees of the district, a single member of the board, or a committee of the board. While some states permit some specific purchasing authority to the district superintendent or business administrator, unless clearly stated in writing, the board of education is not bound by the purchases unless those purchases are ratified by the entire board. While practicality has led to some loosening of this purchasing authority, the courts will not recognize any purchasing debt unless it is stated in the statutes. Consequently, a board employee may find himself liable for the debt.

See Also: AUTHORITY, BOARD; AUTHORITY, EXPRESS AND IMPLIED; BAND; BANK ACCOUNTS; BUDGET; CASH; DEBTS; EXPENSES; FEES; FINANCE; MORATORIUM; PURCHASING; SUPERINTENDENT OF SCHOOLS; TAXES.

G

GAMBLING

Within the school environment there would seem to be no place for **gambling,** either by students or staff. However, any experienced educator would agree that gambling not only exists, but at certain times of the year, it is rampant. Major sporting events such as the World Series, the Super Bowl, NCAA basketball tournament, engender faculty "pools" of many forms. The administrator is then faced with the dilemma of choosing between a "there-shall-be-no-gambling-in-school" policy and the camaraderie that exists within the faculty at such times. Most administrators questioned have adopted an unwritten policy of "I know it's happening, but as long as it does not disrupt classes or involve students, and I cannot actually see it taking place, I will not stop it."

It is interesting to note that there have been no court cases involving gambling among *just* the faculty or staff. However, when faculty and students engage in gambling "pools" or anything where money and/or "specie" are risked, the educators become liable to charges of contributing to the delinquency of minors. Therefore, there are usually well-written and explicit policies prohibiting gambling among students.

Student gambling is most prevalent on the junior high and high school levels because of an accessability of meeting places or quiet places, the availability of free time, and the possession of money or specie. Middle and elementary school children usually do not have the same interest that would lead them to gambling. Again, "pools" on the upper levels seem generally to be "officially" ignored, while actual "games" (Craps, poker, numbers, etc.) are dealt with more severely. Student handbooks should have a policy statement on gambling, but it should be noted that since gambling is not as serious a problem in most schools as smoking, alcohol or drugs, the penalties should be proportionate to the offense.

Perhaps it should be noted that there is a great deal of perceived difference between a "pool," in which an individual places a set sum on a one-time basis and wins or loses, according to the vagueries of chance, with no one outside of the wagerers making a profit, and a "numbers operation," in which one is encouraged to wager more and more, with the return to winners only a percentage of the amount taken in. These factors, along with the amount and severity of the gambling within a school, must all be taken into account by the administrator and a fitting judgment made based on these factors.

See Also: DISCIPLINE; EMPLOYEE RELATIONS; STUDENT INFORMATION.

GIFTED STUDENTS

A **gifted student** is one who has the innate ability to grasp one or more subjects in the school curriculum.

Gifted students are seldom disruptive, and consequently, until very recently, have been largely ignored. Educational funds previously have been granted mostly to the lower achieving students and Special Education rather than to the gifted. Lately, educators have realized that this is a seeming waste of natural resources and talent. Consequently, many programs have been instigated for such students. Guidance staffs, curriculum supervisors and Special Services are now working with staff and faculty personnel to encourage freedom of expression and imaginative problem-solving for the gifted.

There would seem to be four basic types of gifted students:

The Uni-Subject Gifted—This child seems to learn intuitively in one subject area. There seems to be no extraordinary motivation, intellectual background or increased skills, yet the child learns at a phenomenal rate. He just seems to "know" it, because "it has to be that way."

The Trans-Subject Gifted—This child seems to do well intuitively in all his subjects. There is no pressure here, nor an inordinate amount of effort on the part of the student. He or she just does well. There is very little you can ask of him or her that cannot be done.

The Manually Gifted—This child can do anything with his hands. This is the child who may not be able to use the microscope, but he can take it apart and put it back together and tell you how it works. There is nothing, given the materials, he can't fix or build. His sense of spatial relationships, design and the way things fit together to work make him unique.

The "Outcast" Gifted—This child is out of step with his surroundings. This is the child who, while he may be gifted in one or all ways, does not get along with his peers, teachers, parents, or himself. He is basically the unhappy misfit. He is intolerant and intolerable. He is also brilliant.

Gifted students may be given independent study programs, learning centers may be established for their use, they may be given "open-ended" assignments in which they are encouraged to investigate questions generated by their own curiosity, and they may be used in the classroom as supplemental teachers or as tutors for slower students.

See Also: ABILITY LEVELS; ACADEMICALLY TALENTED; ACCELERATION; ACHIEVEMENT; APTITUDE; COUNSELING; CURRICULUM DEVELOPMENT; ELECTIVES; ENRICHMENT; INDIVIDUALIZATION; INTELLIGENCE TESTING; LEARNING CENTERS; MINI-COURSES; STUDENT INFORMATION; UNGRADED.

GIFTS

It is not uncommon for students to form a genuine attachment and affection for their teacher. Consequently, students, particularly in the lower grades, quite often want to present **gifts** to their teachers, especially at times associated with gift-giving such as Hanukkah or Christmas.

While patently innocent, and even endearing in the majority of cases, concern is sometimes expressed as to the nature and purpose of gifts given to teachers by students. The major concerns about gift-giving are that the gifts may be construed as bribes (Money, for example, whether ten cents or ten dollars, should never be accepted as a gift.), that the cost of the gifts may impose a financial hardship on the students or on their families, or that other students who may not be able to give gifts may be made to feel inferior or unworthy.

Consequently, many school systems have established specific policies on gifts given to educators. These policies may indicate the type of gifts that may be accepted, may set a financial limit as to the assumed cost of the gifts, and may even specify at what times during the school year it would be proper to accept gifts. Thereafter, should any questionable gifts be offered, they may be gently refused by referring the gift-givers to the school policy.

When refusing a gift, however, extreme care should be taken that there is no misunderstanding on the part of a student that his or her gift is being rejected because it isn't "good enough" or because the student is "unworthy." Such misunderstandings could have a decidedly negative effect.

Obviously, the matter of gifts given to teachers is a tightrope that must be walked with care and concern. An established policy on the matter, coupled with tact and the common sense of the experienced educator, will go a long way toward ameliorating the problem.

See Also: ACCEPTANCE OF DONATIONS; APPRECIATION, LETTER OF; CASH; EMPLOYEE RELATIONS; STUDENT INFORMATION.

GOALS AND OBJECTIVES

Goals are the broadest statements in the expected learning outcomes of a competency-based curriculum. **Objectives** are the most specific formal statements that are made about those expected learning outcomes. Objectives are the behavioral descriptions of learning skills.

Put in other terms, goals are where you want to go, and objectives are the observable criteria to determine if you've gotten there.

Between goals and objectives, lie the areas of instruction or competencies. Once a goal has been established, that goal will generate the competencies that will lead to the attaining of the objectives.

A goal is an assumption and hope for all students who will be educated in a particular school system, grade or class. Therefore, all members of a faculty or staff must be aware of these goals and be made to understand how each thing they accomplish will lead the students to the final objectives. This calls for constant goals clarifications within the school. When everyone is aware of how he or she must function, and understands the value of what another is doing, day-to-day conflicts of schedules, space and priorities are greatly reduced. When a group defines goals, it gives substance to what people feel is important. Their feelings, attitudes and expectations are crucial to achieving the goals and objectives of the curriculum. If the faculty and staff believe in the goals, they will expend the time and effort necessary to teach the competencies and thus generate the motivation for success visible in the completed objectives. Goals clarification can re-

lease the creative energies of a school staff, and...effective planning can translate vision into reality.

Objectives are seen as indicators of how well the program is progressing toward a goal. They make concrete what might otherwise be vague. A well-stated objective will provide specific guidelines for activities and plans, and it will clarify what it is that the faculty and staff must do to reach their goals.

See Also: ACADEMIC PROGRAM; ACCOUNTABILITY; CHANGE STRATEGIES; COMPETENCY-BASED PROGRAMS; CURRICULUM DEVELOPMENT; EVALUATION; INSTRUCTION; LESSON PLANS; NEEDS ASSESSMENT; SUPERVISION (STAFF).

GRADES

A **grade** is a mark or rating on an examination, work or body of work in a course, based on some scale, either alphabetical or numerical.

Perhaps the most visible expressions of success or failure, relative to the student's academic progress, are the grades he receives. The very concept of grades, however, has come under careful scrutiny in the past few years because of several factors. First, if there is the presence of a bell-shaped curve for marking (e.g., A through F), then there is the built-in assumption that some students will fail. Second, there is the question of to what or whom the student is being compared when he is graded. Is the grade an indication of what he has learned, or is it an indication of what he has learned in comparison to others? If it is the latter, are the grades then valid? Third, there is rarely a consensus as to what is meant by any grade. Since standardization of grades is seemingly impossible from year to year, or even from teacher to teacher in the same year, how can either the child, his parents or even the school know if he is progressing properly. Finally, can or should any teacher be held responsible for what a child does or does not do? This is the argument that arises when accountability is based on grades only.

All members of the academic community agree that there must be some tangible sign to show what a student has accomplished. Many studies have shown that grades are an incentive to performance for some students. Also, poor performance, indicated by slipping grades or even failure, is an indicator to some students and their teachers that more concentrated effort is needed in some particular area of the curriculum. The reaction against grades, then, comes from using a grading system as the *entire* means of evaluation. This is the crucial flaw perceived by both professional educators and laymen. Therefore, open communications on the use of grades for evaluation is essential. Also, workshops to bring all faculty grading systems into line with each other are equally essential.

See Also: ACCOUNTABILITY; AUTHORITY, TEACHER; EVALUATION; INSTRUCTION; NEEDS ASSESSMENT; PARENT CONFERENCES; PERMANENT RECORDS; PROMOTION; REPORT CARDS; SOCIAL PROMOTION; STUDENT INFORMATION; SUPERVISION (STAFF); UNDERACHIEVERS; UNGRADED; WORKSHOPS AND IN-SERVICE.

GRADUATION

Graduation is the exercise, ceremony or service that honors those students who have completed a prescribed course of study and are now eligible to be granted whatever degrees to which this completion entitles them.

Any experienced educator whose purview encompasses the completion of an academic step, whether it be elementary school, high school or college, will agree that *planning* is the key to successfully handling this very important duty. Some very basic steps can help insure success:

1. Order all diplomas, caps, gowns, and other trappings well in advance. Some educators order such supplies during the first few months of the school year in order to avoid "panic" in June.

2. Start with the basic assumption that all students in the graduating class will graduate. Multiply that number by two, add twenty more for good measure, and add this number to your list of graduates. This gives a figure of how many people to reasonably expect to attend the ceremony. If the number exceeds the largest indoor

area available, then it must either be held outdoors or attendance must be limited to "invitation only."

3. Decide on two dates for graduation. If the graduation is to be held indoors, a single date may suffice, but outside graduations usually have a rain date. This rain date can be one to four days beyond the set date.

4. Provide ample time for all speakers to prepare. Notify all participants at least three weeks in advance.

5. Practice, practice, practice. If a school has twenty students in the graduating class, a simple "walk through" may be enough. If, however, the graduation entails 600 or so students, an entrance by faculty members, the marching band, the Mayor, the Superintendent, and other dignitaries, the logistics demand sufficient rehearsal.

6. It should be remembered that a major purpose of the graduation ceremony is to allow the students to take pride in their accomplishments, to foster positive memories and to allow students to enjoy themselves.

See Also: ACKNOWLEDGEMENT; ADDRESSES (SPEECHES); CAPACITY; DIPLOMA; FEES; GRADUATION REQUIREMENTS; MEDIA; NEWS COVERAGE; NEWSLETTER; NEWS RELEASES; PARKING; PUBLIC ADDRESS SYSTEM; SCHEDULE; SPECIAL INTEREST GROUPS; STUDENT INFORMATION.

GRADUATION REQUIREMENTS

There is no national policy on required competencies for **graduation.** Instead, the requirements are provided by each state's Department of Education for all school districts, common, private and parochial within its jurisdiction. While these may vary from state to state, the usual requirements are four years of English; two years of U.S. History; four years of Physical Education; one half year of Career Education; one year of Performing, Creative or Fine Arts; the passage of a Minimum Basic Skills test on the ninth grade level; completion of a course of study of 75 credits, including the above for a three-year school, or completion of a course of study of 100 credits, including the above for a four-year school. Also, the local districts may make further requirements. For example, an individual district may require two years of Math, one year of Science, and a total required course of study of over 120 credits.

The discretionary power of a board may not set requirements below those of the state, but they may set them above. Some individual courses of study such as "College Prep," may have other requirements for graduation, for example, two years of a foreign language, and a half-year of Typing, Stenography or Business. These special course requirements are all set by the school district's board of education.

See Also: ACADEMIC PROGRAM; CHIEF STATE SCHOOL OFFICIAL; COMPETENCY-BASED PROGRAMS; COURSE OF STUDY; GRADUATION; GUIDANCE; PERMANENT RECORDS; STUDENT INFORMATION.

GRAFFITI

Graffiti is as old as history itself. It seems from the dawn of time, if there has been a wall, there has been someone with an urge to write upon it. There are four basic reasons for graffiti. They are, in ascending order, *boredom,* which usually finds an outlet in "doodling"; the *expression* of a *private, passing thought* such as writing a telephone number on a wall beside the booth, or jotting a homework assignment on the page of the textbook; *shock value* such as writing the obscenity on the desk or wall, and since this graffiti is conscious, this is usually large and vivid; and, *disrespect* or *protest,* which may involve personal invective and is done in such a manner as to be permanent such as carving into a desk or spray-painting on a wall.

Students involved in the first two types of graffiti should be assigned task-oriented discipline that should be relatively mild such as being made to clean the particular desk or erase the pages in the textbook. Students involved in shock-value graffiti should receive a proportionately more severe punishment such as cleaning all the desks in a room, painting the lavatory walls with the supervision of the custodians, etc. Disrespect or protest graffiti, however, should be treated as any other form of vandalism, and the punishments should be specifically delineated in the Student Handbook.

Some schools and classrooms have established "Scribble Walls" or "Graffiti Sheets." These are places where students may legitimately place graffiti, according to whatever guidelines are dictated by the school or teacher.

See Also: BUILDINGS; DAMAGES; DISCIPLINE; LANGUAGE; PARENTAL LIABILITY; STUDENT INFORMATION; VANDALISM.

GRIEVANCES

A **grievance** is a statement of dissatisfaction, usually made by an individual, but sometimes made by an employee organization or by management, concerning the interpretation of an agreement or work-related matter involving the internal operation of the school.

In several states, the judicial authority for handling grievances is an administrative agency. This takes grievances out of the courts and keeps them internal, within the school or district. New York and New Jersey, for example, are exemplary in this regard in that they grant their Commissioners of Education extensive authority to render decisions in school disputes.

Where conflicts exist within the internal operation or handling of the school, the teacher may be required to follow internal grievance procedures before "going public." This restriction is only valid if there is a *reasonable* chance that the conflict can be solved by these procedures. If the procedures are vague, non-existent, unknown to the staff or faculty member, or, as in past practices, have been inconclusive, it has been held that teachers are not required to comply.

Administrators can set an environment where criticisms and grievances can be looked upon as opportunities for problem-solving, rather than a place where conflicts are avoided, which lowers morale.

There are a number of ways to handle grievances, each with its advantages and disadvantages:

STAFF MEETINGS—Grievances may be handled in meetings involving the entire staff of a school. The advantages of this are that all staff members have the right to give their opinions, that problems aired can then be sent to subcommittees, that there is usually great interest since only those staff members involved with a problem will seek solutions, and that there is a great openness to complaints and their solutions. There are, however, disadvantages such as the fact that time is usually too short, and snap judgments are thus made; too much time can be taken on a problem that only affects one or two staff members, thus boring others; some people with genuine complaints may exhibit shyness in large groups; and some administrators may not know how to use groups effectively.

ADMINISTRATOR/TEACHER CONFERENCES—The advantages are that this method provides for one-on-one contact with teachers and their problems, and it is probably the best and easiest way to solve simple conflicts. The disadvantages are that there are no real solutions without a great deal of trust, and there will be none

unless this trust has been previously established; also, without tapes or written notes, there is no real commitment to the solution.

GRADE LEVEL MEETINGS—Advantages include that the group has similar interests and shares similar problems, the members of the group share responsibilities and resources, problems are put into perspective by peers, and usually a single report is forthcoming to the administrator, rather than many. Disadvantages include the fact that if an administrator is unsupportive, the expectations for success will be lowered and the group may produce only half-hearted attempts. Also, if the group is weak, someone with a major grievance will become very frustrated. On the secondary level, these grade level meetings are replaced by departmental meetings.

INTEREST GROUPS—These are groups made up of interested individuals who work toward a specific goal or try to settle a specific grievance on a short-term basis. The advantages are that such groups are highly committed, vocal and seek workable solutions. The major disadvantages are that the group dissolves once a solution is found, and there may be problems of jurisdiction as to which group shall handle what problems.

TEAMS—This involves the establishment of a long-standing team, such as a Liaison Committee, to which the faculty brings problems that are discussed in turn by the committee with the administrator. Advantages include: cohesive staff responsibility, with everyone knowing his or her part in the procedure; expertise gained because of the length of time served on the committee; greater faculty involvement, if members of the team are selected by the faculty for a term of from one to three years; and the fact that teams tend to have much broader goals as well as the ability to see the entire picture. Disadvantages include personality difficulties, particularly if a member of the committee or the administrator has "an axe to grind"; and the fact that this type of committee seems to sponsor an "us-and-them" mentality on the matter of grievances.

See Also: ACADEMIC FREEDOM; ADVISORY COUNCILS; CHANGE STRATEGIES; COMMITTEE; COMMUNICATIONS; DEMANDS; DIFFERENTIATED STAFFING; EMPLOYEE RELATIONS; MEDIATION AND MEDIATOR; HEARINGS; NEGOTIATIONS; PETITIONS.

GROUNDS

The **grounds** of a school consist of all the land owned by the board of education that surrounds a particular school.

Some schools have very little attendant property, while others may have wooded areas, large lawns or even sports fields as part of the grounds on which the school is located. Quite often, the condition of the school grounds is a decisive factor in the image of the school that is held by community members. For example, school grounds, that are unkempt, that are littered with paper and debris, and that have a sloppy or uncared-for appearance cannot help but produce a negative impression within the community, which may have implications in terms of eroding community support.

Besides the appearance of the grounds, care must also be taken to make sure that they are as safe as possible for student use. Consequently, sharp objects such as rocks, broken glass, broken concrete, etc., should be removed or cleaned up, and potential dangers such as holes on the grounds or in the pavement should be recognized and repaired.

In some schools, maintenance of the school grounds falls within the duties of the custodial staff. In many systems, however, the school district maintains a "groundskeeping" staff or crew that is responsible for the repair, maintenance and upkeep of all school grounds within the district. This crew moves from school to school on an established schedule.

See Also: AUXILIARY SERVICES; BUILDINGS; CUSTODIAL SERVICES; EASEMENT; INSURANCE; LEASE OF SCHOOL PROPERTY; PARKING; PLAYGROUND; SAFE-PLACE STATUTES; SAFETY.

GROUPINGS

See ABILITY GROUPING; HETEROGENEOUS GROUPING; HOMOGENEOUS GROUPING.

GUARDIAN AND GUARDIANSHIP

A **guardian** is one who accepts responsibility for a minor's well-being, safety and support. This guardianship may be by an agency or a person. Legally, the title of guardian is assigned to someone other than the minor's natural parent or parents.

Schools continuously seek the written permission of parents before allowing children to participate in certain activities such as sports, field trips, and the like. If the school child, for whatever reason, has no parents, the school is within its rights to require the child's legal guardian to sign these papers and permission slips. This has been a traditional practice in education.

The school accepts responsibility for the child's safety and well-being from the time the child enters the school until he leaves. The school also has the responsibility of notifying the child's parents or guardian of special situations where possible injury, moral or religious issues, and legal rights and protections are involved. Permission for the child to participate traditionally was given through various forms bearing the signature of an adult. The assumption in the past has been that the adult was the child's natural parent, adopted parent or legal guardian (usually a family member such as an uncle, grandparent, etc.).

This assumption, however, does not hold up in all cases today. Indeed, if the school does work on this assumption, administrators may find themselves in court facing liability and negligence charges brought by whoever really does have the guardianship or parental rights over the child. This is so because children in foster homes, in county or municipal crisis-care agencies, or in homes of people who have no legal or family ties to the child, are living with people who take care of them, but have no legal guardian status. Therefore, if one of these people signs a permission slip and the child is injured, the school may bear the liability for that injury.

In order to protect themselves because a student does not have to inform the school that he is a foster child or living with someone other than his parents, many school systems require that there be a *"Certificate of Domicile"* filed for each student. This is a legal document, authorized and notarized, which states that the signator will be legally responsible for the child. See below for typical example.

This type of certificate shows that the school is acting in good faith, and the signed documents that arrive

(Name of Child) is now domiciled in (Name of District), and said child has been and will be under my care and supervision as though the child were my own. I am supporting the child, and I have assumed all personal obligations for (Name of Child) relative to school requirements, and intend to keep and support (Name of Child) for a longer term than merely through the school term.

thereafter from the guardians legally release the school from liability.

If the child in question is a foster child, the school may wish to obtain the same type of certificate from the Division of Youth and Family Services that placed the child.

See Also: ADDRESS (RESIDENCE); COMPULSORY EDUCATION; FAMILY SERVICES; INSURANCE; LIABILITY; PARENTAL LIABILITY; PARENT CONFERENCES; PERMANENT RECORDS; PERMISSION SLIPS; REPORT CARDS; SPECIAL SERVICES; STUDENT INFORMATION; WELFARE.

GUIDANCE

Guidance is a program designed to assist each pupil to become all he or she is capable of being; it is a structured, professional system of nurturing, caring, and counseling a person toward this potential.

In the elementary school, a Guidance program aspires to form good work, study and personal habits and concepts; to find and help the exceptional child at all ends of the spectrum; to destroy stereotypical job choices; and to place greater emphasis on child development and individual and age differences. An elementary Guidance program should have one full-time and one part-time person for every 400 students.

In the secondary schools, a Guidance program's purpose is to help the students choose their curriculum, overcome deficiencies, develop special interests, cultivate intellectual interests, impart occupational information, give advice on occupational choices, help secure employment, and help choose the proper college. A typical secondary Guidance program should have one full-time person per 300 students.

It should also be remembered that the majority of the programs such as drugs or alcohol-abuse prevention, summer job programs, and local employment programs also come out of the Guidance offices.

According to a recent nationwide study, a good Guidance program has counselors who seek out those students who need help, rather than waiting for the students to come to them; has clearly established policies that are discussed with the faculty; has sufficient available funds for personnel; has adequate office space and clerical help; shares institutional research and findings with the faculty and administration; has continuing evaluations; shows everyone the success of the program; has an appropriate counselor-per-pupil ratio for the school; keeps complete and up-to-date records on each student; understands the need for understanding, rather than competition with all educators, both within and outside of the building; has adequate materials available for counselors; has available current occupational data; has community involvement and support; and has visible and active administrative support.

See Also: CAREER EDUCATION; CENTRALIZED FILING; COUNSELING;

FAMILY SERVICES; MARRIED STU-
DENTS; MENTAL HEALTH; MONTHLY
REPORTS; NEWS RELEASES; PARENT
CONFERENCES; PERMANENT REC-
ORDS; RECORD KEEPING; SCHED-
ULE; SCHOLARSHIP; SPECIAL EDU-
CATION; STUDENT INFORMATION;
VOCATIONAL PROGRAMS; WORKING
PAPERS; WORK-STUDY PROGRAM;
YEAR-END REPORT.

H

HABITABLE

Habitable means capable or fit to be lived in; the word denotes not only a dwelling that would sustain life, but also one that may be occupied in reasonable comfort, safety and enjoyment.

It is generally understood that a school must be habitable in order for it to be used. Indeed, should a building fall below certain standards for safety or care, to the point where it may legally be classified as not habitable, it can be legally closed. It behooves all school systems, therefore, to maintain habitable conditions in all schools.

See Also: BUILDINGS; GROUNDS; LIABILITY; SAFE PLACE STATUTES; SAFETY.

HALL DUTY

Hall duty is an assignment, usually handled by a teacher, in which the individual is responsible for the supervision of a designated area of the school during a specific period of the school day.

The purpose behind assigning a teacher to hall duty is to provide active supervision in the hallways of a school at the time when the halls are not in general use and the majority of teachers are with their classes.

The specific duties of an individual assigned to hall duty will vary from school to school. Specific requirements may include challenging students to produce a pass and escorting them to the office if they do not have one; checking the lavatories; helping out in situations where a substitute teacher may have difficulties; assisting visitors to the school; assisting teachers who may have special activities in progress; and relieving regular teachers who may find it necessary to leave the classroom.

Having someone on hall duty is seen as a deterrent to vandalism, class cutting, and possible violence that might occur were the area not super-

vised. The importance of the assignment should be impressed upon the
person receiving it.

See Also: ACCOUNTABILITY; ASSIGN-
MENTS; IMPUTED NEGLIGENCE; LI-
ABILITY; MINISTERIAL ACTS; NEG-
LIGENCE; NONFEASANCE; PASSES;
SAFETY; STUDENT INFORMATION;
SUPERVISION (STUDENTS); VAN-
DALISM.

HANDICAPPED

In this entry, we are dealing with
the **physical handicap** only, not the
mental or cultural handicap.

A physical handicap can cause
great difficulties for the student, his
teachers and school administrators.
Different students are different, and
common sense is the best guide to
schedules, privileges and interactions. However, no rights may be
denied the handicapped student, no
matter how well-intentioned. A child
in a wheelchair, for example, cannot
be kept inside during recess because it
is inconvenient to move the child's
wheelchair outside, or because the
teacher or administrator feels that it
would only sadden the child to see the
others at play. The child in the wheelchair has the same right to recess as
any other child in the school.

Handicapped children are permitted all freedoms because of the
"equal protection clause" of the Fourteenth Amendment. Each case must
be treated as if it is the child's difference that is considered for special
attention, rather than the child. There-

fore, there are many agencies, counseling services etc., which can aid the
administrator in making sure that the
student participates in all aspects of
his or her education.

A handicap is never just physical, for being different can scar the
emotional makeup of the child as
well. There are, however, several suggestions for handling the handicapped
child. First, *be understanding,* but do
not pity. Second, *be encouraging* and
helpful when needed, but do not
overdo it so as to single out the
individual. Third, try in all respects,
except those directly related to the
handicap itself, to *treat the student as
you do the others.* Fourth, if the
student needs to talk, *be a good listener;* if asked for suggestions, give
them. Finally, *never condescend to do
the work* for them, or any other task
that they are capable of doing themselves, for this is interpreted as pity
and can, in fact, become a trait that
these students will expect in others.

See Also: CIVIL RIGHTS; CONSTITU-
TIONAL RIGHTS; CONSULTANTS;
COUNSELING; ELEMENTARY AND
SECONDARY EDUCATION ACT OF
1965; FAMILY SERVICES; FOUR-
TEENTH AMENDMENT GUARAN-
TEES; INSURANCE; MAINSTREAM-
ING; PUBLIC LAW 94-142; STUDENT
INFORMATION; SUPERVISION (STU-
DENTS); TRANSPORTATION.

HEALTH

Health is a state of physical and/
or mental well-being or soundness; it

is also freedom from defect, disease or harm.

Each state sets health requirements, and the schools, as agents of the state, can then require and/or provide such health regulations and services as they deem necessary in cooperation with the local boards of health.

There are three main aspects of health in the schools: first, under the directive that schools be *"habitable,"* they must maintain and provide such services as heating, an adequate number of seats, good plumbing, and adequate enclosure, in order to provide a habitable atmosphere. Second, there are those aspects of health that come out of school funds, including *periodic checkups* by visiting doctors or dentists, vision and hearing tests, etc. These are usually items that are diagnosed but not treated. Finally, there are collective *"Medical Services"* and their programs. These include medical facilities such as Health Rooms, diagnostic materials such as eye charts and stethoscopes, first aid treatments and kits, and professional health personnel. They also provide auxiliary services such as athletic trainers and team doctors. The programs provided under Medical Services include Sex Education, Nutrition, First Aid and Safety, and Drug and Alcohol Prevention Programs.

If a student wishes to be excluded from any periodic checkup, he or she must present to the health personnel a note from another physician that such tests have been conducted. In the case of religious and/or constitutional conflicts, the courts have stated that if non-treatment endangers others, then the treatment can be a prerequisite to the child's returning to school.

See Also: AUTHORITY, EXPRESS AND IMPLIED; AUXILIARY PERSONNEL: AUXILIARY SERVICES; CHRISTIAN SCIENTISTS; CONSTITUTIONAL RIGHTS; DIAGNOSIS; FAMILY SERVICES; FIRST AID; HABITABLE; IMMUNIZATION, INOCULATION AND VACCINATION; INSURANCE; MEDICATION; NURSE; PERMISSION SLIPS; PERMANENT RECORDS; PHYSICAL EDUCATION; PSYCHOLOGICAL STUDIES; PREGNANT STUDENTS; RECORD KEEPING; SAFE PLACE STATUTES; SAFETY; SEX EDUCATION; SPORTS; STUDENT INFORMATION; SUPERVISION (STUDENTS); SUPPLIES AND EQUIPMENT.

HEARINGS

A **hearing** is a formal process having the main purpose of allowing a person to offer evidence in his own behalf and fully reply to any charges leveled against him. In education, hearings are primarily used in procedures for dismissal of nontenured teachers, and/or nonrenewal of contract cases for non-tenured teachers. A hearing is a formal procedure before the school board or its surrogates. There have been several states where this has been seen as a conflict of interest, in that the administrator who brought the action is officiating over the hearing. Several states have placed hearings in the courts, before panels of educators only, or before panels of educators and the public. More and more states are heading in this direction as a protection of due process and as a way of eliminating the conflict of interest.

The question of whether a hearing should be open or closed is subject to interpretation. A teacher has the right to an open hearing, and only he or she may decide if it should be closed. This is so because it is always assumed that if the board brought the action, the teacher has nothing to hide. However, in some states, the boards feel that discipline or the smooth operation of the school may be upset by an open hearing. At this point, state statutes allow for the hearings to be brought before the courts. There is then a judgment as to whether the hearings will be open or closed, but there is no judgment of the case itself. The defendant, in this case the teacher, is always given the right of appeal, while the plaintiff, in this case the board, usually is not.

See Also: BURDEN OF PROOF; CIVIL RIGHTS; CONSTITUTIONAL RIGHTS; DISMISSAL OF PERSONNEL; DUE PROCESS; FIFTH AMENDMENT GUARANTEES; FIRST AMENDMENT GUARANTEES; FOURTEENTH AMENDMENT GUARANTEES; PRIVILEGED COMMUNICATIONS; QUORUM; UNIONS; UNISERV.

Hearsay

Hearsay is a statement made by a witness, the validity of which is not based on the witness' personal observations or knowledge, but on the observations or knowledge of someone else not present in the courtroom or hearing.

Usually the courts take a dim view of "rumor and gossip" as testimony. The main examples of hearsay are those statements which begin "I heard she did..." or "I was told that...." If no *objective* evidence of the behavior can be found, the testimony is inadmissible. If there are several pieces of *prima facie* evidence and one or two hearsay corroborations, the testimony *may* be allowed.

See Also: BURDEN OF PROOF; DEFAMATION; DUE PROCESS; HEARINGS; LIBEL.

Heterogeneous Grouping

Heterogeneously grouped classes actually have some similarities, such as age, place of residence, and general likes and dislikes. What is really meant by the term is the unevenness of ability-levels in the class makeup. One child might do fine in Spelling but may do poorly in Reading, while another might excel in Reading and not be very good at Math. No particular criterion is used to place the students of each level together in a class.

Heterogeneous grouping has several advantages. First, in such groups, students often teach other students. Second, there is an interdependence of instructional techniques, since teachers tend to approach heterogeneous groups with a wider variety of methods. Third, poorer students tend to do better in such groups since they are exposed to more knowledge. Fourth, these classes are easier to schedule. Finally, this type of grouping tends to remove the stigma of ranking classes. Students feel that there are no "dummy" classes.

Heterogeneous grouping has several disadvantages as well. First, there is the possibility that the brighter students may become bored. Second, multiple groupings tend to develop within the class, and this means more planning for the teacher. Third, many teachers complain that it is harder to help slower students in these groups. Finally, grades may be crushing to slower students as they begin to feel that they cannot hope to compete.

Heterogeneously grouped classes lend themselves to greater individualization techniques such as Individually Prescribed Instruction (IPI) for Math or SRA for Reading. If a school is committed to individualization, then heterogeneous grouping would seem to be the logical choice.

See Also: ABILITY LEVELS; CONTRACTED LEARNING; GRADES; INDIVIDUALIZATION; INSTRUCTION; SCHEDULE.

HIGH SCHOOLS

High schools were developed in answer to those demands for further schooling not found except in academies who were interested in preparing their students for colleges and universities. The common or "public" high schools were then formed to teach those students who did not need this classical background. More and more states began endorsing the "common" schools and the academies declined.

The final step in establishing the American system of high schools came with the case of *Charles E. Stuart, et al. v. School District #1 of the Village of Kalamazoo, et al.* (Michigan, 1874) which granted that a district has a right to maintain a high school to "...furnish a liberal education to the youth of the state in schools brought within the reach of all classes (since) ... education, not merely in the rudiments, but in an enlarged sense, was regarded as an important practical advantage to be supplied ... to rich and poor alike, and not something pertaining to culture and accomplishment ... (for) those who accumulated wealth, enabling them to pay for it." Now, along with the grammar school, the courts had established a school "system," including an elementary and a high school for all.

In modern education, we also find places such as middle schools, intermediate schools, and junior high schools, but the high school was the first major division and proved that the United States felt that all its citizens had the right to be fully educated.

See Also: ACADEMIC PROGRAM; ACCREDITATION; COMMON SCHOOLS; CURRICULUM DEVELOPMENT; ELECTIVES; GRADUATION; GRADUATION REQUIREMENTS; SCHEDULE;

VOCATIONAL PROGRAMS; WORK-STUDY PROGRAM.

HIRING PRACTICES

See EQUAL EMPLOYMENT OPPORTUNITIES.

HOME ECONOMICS

Home Economics is the science and art of homemaking, including nutrition, clothing, budgeting, and child care.

Traditionally, as part of the high school and then junior high school curriculums, Home Economics was looked upon as another way that education prepared its students for life. Girls were expected to run households, and the schools felt responsible for giving them a full background in the skills they would need. Further, support was given to such programs, because it was felt that, with this new background, standards of care, health and nutrition would reach the homes of the students and their families as well as into their own homes later on as adults, thereby improving the quality of life itself in the United States.

Major Home Economics programs began to be introduced into American education in the 1930s. Originally, all these programs centered around "how to" cook and sew, and whatever else was considered the "fundamentals." Changes began in the mid 1960s and 1970s, as more emphasis was placed on child care, meal planning rather than preparation, money managing, and running a house while engaged in work outside the home. Still, the Home Economics program was designed for the female student.

With the advent of the late 70s and 80s, the Home Economics curriculum fell victim to cries of sexism. Girls could no longer be assigned to Home Economics while their male counterparts took Industrial Arts. Now, both males and females take both. With this change came a further modification in the basic Home Economics course. Minor home repairs such as fixing a toaster, changing a washer; and more Consumer Education courses, home management techniques, and mutual child care strategies are now basic parts of Home Economics.

Education is still committed to raising living standards, but administrators must be very careful to integrate into their programs *all* aspects for *all* of their students.

See Also: ACADEMIC PROGRAM; CURRICULUM DEVELOPMENT; ELECTIVES; SEXISM; SUPPLIES AND EQUIPMENT; VOCATIONAL PROGRAMS.

HOME INSTRUCTION

Home Instruction is instruction by a properly certified teacher, given to a student in the student's home, during the period when the student is unable to attend regular school due to physical incapacitation.

The instruction given to such a student will parallel the instruction the student would have received were he or she able to attend school. The textbooks and the curriculum are usually the same as those of the grade level he or she would normally attend in school. Indeed, the objective of Home Instruction is to allow the student to return to class at the same level as his or her fellow classmates when deemed physically able to do so.

The criteria for a child to receive Home Instruction will vary from district to district, but generally, a child is eligible if he or she will be absent from school for such an extended period of time that his or her academic progress would be jeopardized by a lack of formal instruction. Obviously, an absence of one day to one week would not fit this definition, while an absence of a month or more would fall within the boundaries. Many districts require a formal, written request from the child's parent or guardian, as well as certification from a doctor of the child's physical status.

Financial compensation for teachers involved in Home Instruction is made through the board of education, which may also establish criteria for Home Instruction, including, but not limited to, such items as written reports of progress, validation of actual time spent in instruction, and written reports to the child's classroom teacher.

See Also: CERTIFICATION; COMPULSORY EDUCATION; PUBLIC LAW 94-142; RECORD KEEPING; SPECIAL SERVICES; STUDENT INFORMATION; VOLUNTEERS.

HOMEWORK

It is perfectly legal for teachers to assign **homework** and discipline to those who do not satisfactorily complete their assignments in school. However, the homework must be reasonable and may not substantially interfere with the student's private life. For example, it might be all right to assign a one-hour lesson, but it is not permissible to tell the student that he must do it between seven and eight p.m.

When questioned on homework, parents showed great approval of that which the children could understand and see a reason for, of that which truly supplemented the work being done in school, of that which individualized home study to benefit those students who have special interests or need special work, or of those assignments which gave children a choice.

The things parents and teachers generally disapproved of about homework were those assignments that had little educational value for the time spent (ultra-neat notebooks), had vague instruction, made demands on parents' time that seem unreasonable (Billy is required to collect 20 shells from the beach), that left homework unchecked, that was "piled on," that were to be done over vacations and holidays, and of which the purpose is not clear.

TIME ALLOTTED FOR HOMEWORK ASSIGNMENTS		
GRADE	**TIME PER DAY/PERIOD**	**TIME PER WEEK**
1-3	**15-30 minutes**	**1-2½ hours**
4-6	**30-45 minutes**	**2-4½ hours**
7-9	***45 minutes-1 hour**	***3-8 hours**
9-12	***1 hour +**	***4-6**
*more time is added when projects or unit work is assigned		

The amount of homework assigned to a child is often debated by educators. Generally, the seeming consensus is reflected on the table above.

Homework should never be used as a punishment. School is the student's occupation, and if the student is constantly shown that work is punishment, he or she may have the seeds of negativism toward work planted in them. If homework is useful, helpful, interesting, and practical, then work becomes rewarding.

See Also: ACCOUNTABILITY; AGE LEVELS; AUTHORITY, EXPRESS AND IMPLIED; AUTHORITY, TEACHER; CONTRACTED LEARNING; DETENTION; GOALS AND OBJECTIVES; INDIVIDUALIZATION; INSTRUCTION; PARENT CONFERENCES; REASONABLE AND PRUDENT; REPORT CARDS; STUDENT INFORMATION.

HOMOGENEOUS GROUPING

Children are grouped homogeneously according to some criteria. These criteria may include reading scores, standardized achievement test scores, individual subject interests, and departmentalized learning. Students are then placed in classes with others of like ability.

Homogeneous grouping has several advantages. First, it makes possible more consistent planning of activities and use of material for these groupings. Second, the methodological choices are easier. Finally, there is more relaxation from stress among teachers and students.

There are several disadvantages to homogeneous grouping as well. A child may progress to the point where he is out of step with the rest of the group, but homogeneous grouping does not allow for him to go anywhere within the group. Also, teachers are locked into their strategies, whether high or low. Even if a student falls below or rises above the class level, the teacher's goal is to teach the level of the homogeneous group; thus, the child may suffer. Finally, in homogeneous grouping, there is an almost automatic ranking of groups that children are particularly adept at noticing.

Homogeneously grouped classes lend themselves to lectures, labs and group activities. They do not work well with an individualized setup. Consequently, schools that are not very concerned about individualization often tend toward homogeneous groupings.

See Also: ABILITY GROUPING; ABILITY LEVELS; ACHIEVEMENT; APTITUDE; DEPARTMENTS; INSTRUCTION; INTELLIGENCE TESTING; LESSON PLANS; SCHEDULE; UNDERACHIEVERS.

HOMOSEXUALS

The courts have ruled that teachers' rights include the right to live their lives in privacy. This privacy includes sexual activity and preference for both the **homosexual** and the heterosexual employee. To determine whether or not an action is sufficient for a teacher to be dismissed, proof must be shown that such action makes the individual "unfit to teach." There must exist some connection between the conduct complained of and the teacher's ability to perform his or her necessary duties. "The private conduct of a man (or woman), who is also a teacher, is a proper concern to those who employ him (her) only to the extent that it mars him (her) as a teacher.... Where his (her) professional achievement is unaffected, where the school community is placed in no jeopardy, his (her) private acts are his (her) own business and may not be the basis of discipline." *(Jarnella v. Willoughby-Eastlake City School District,* 233 N.E. 2d 143, 146 [OH, 1967]).

This is now the "fitness as a teacher" test, against which all such cases of discipline are based. The connection must be objectively proven.

Heterosexual activity has been tested in the courts *(Morrison v. State Board of Education,* 461 P.2d 375, 386-387 [CA, 1969]), but homosexual activity specifically has not. However, "immorality" as a grounds for dismissal was judged to be constitutionally vague in the Morrison case. This, plus the case of *Burton v. Cascade School District, Union High School #5,* 353 F. Supp. 254 (U.S. Dist. Ct. [OR. 1973]), showed that homosexuals have the same rights to appeal dismissal.

The following have been stated by the various court decisions. First, the board can consider a teacher's conduct *outside* the classroom, but only as far as that conduct effects the teacher's conduct *inside* the classroom. Second, if the board can show no such connection, the courts will not uphold dismissal. Finally, the courts have ruled that the right of privacy comes from the constitutional rights of freedom of speech outside the classroom, and freedom of expression and freedom of association as protected by common law, state constitutions and the U.S. Constitution, particularly, the Fourth and Fourteenth Amendments.

See Also: BURDEN OF PROOF; CIVIL RIGHTS; CONSTITUTIONAL RIGHTS; DISCRIMINATION; EQUAL EMPLOYMENT OPPORTUNITIES; FOURTEENTH AMENDMENT GUARAN-

TEES; FOURTH AMENDMENT GUAR-
ANTEES; FREE SPEECH; NON-RE-
NEWAL OF CONTRACT; PRIVACY;
SPECIAL INTEREST GROUPS.

HONOR ROLL

The concept of having an **honor roll** in school has risen and declined in favor in a rather predictable swing. When curriculum areas are in favor, so are honor rolls; when individualization is in favor, then the honor roll is seen as an effete, chauvinistic display having no educational value.

The efficacy of an honor roll is generally seen by administrators as somewhere in between. The key point made by administrators is that honor rolls are good when they are handled as rewards in *many* areas, and serve very little value as incentives.

In each school, the honor roll should be reviewed to determine exactly how it is perceived by the students, faculty, central staff, and community. If these perceptions are not keeping with its expected educational value or the academic program of the school, a total review of the practice would seem in order.

See Also: ACTIVITIES; GOALS AND OBJECTIVES; GRADES; NATIONAL HONOR SOCIETY; REPORT CARDS; SCHOLARSHIP; STUDENT INFORMATION.

HOSPITALIZATION

Hospitalization refers to the insurance that provides payment for the facilities of a hospital, and the attendant expenses therof, for the subscriber and usually the members of his or her immediate family.

Many school systems provide employees with health care or hospitalization insurance. While it is not mandated by law that this be done, some form of hospitalization for employees is the rule rather than the exception. Usually a district provides hospitalization as a result of collective bargaining between the board and the local teacher's association. The board of education generally arranges coverage on a group basis through a recognized insurance company. The board may pay for all, or a percentage of, the premium for its employees. The insurance may cover just the employee, the employee and the spouse, or the employee and the entire family, including any children. Coverage may include full expenses, expenses on a fixed scale, or a percentage of expenses. Furthermore, some policies include coverage of all or part of the physician's fee, prescription drugs, home health care, and the like. These variables are also often a matter of collective bargaining within negotiations.

With the already astronomical costs of medical care still rising, it seems likely that hospitalization insurance will become a regular part of employee benefit packages.

See Also: BUDGET; CONTRACTS; EMPLOYEE RELATIONS; INSURANCE; MEDIATION AND MEDIATOR; NEGOTIATIONS; WITHHOLDING.

HOUSE SYSTEM

A **house system** is an organizational method for handling management difficulties in an extremely large school.

With increases and shifts in population come the consolidation of school districts and the establishment of "regional" high schools. It is not uncommon to find in these schools a student population of several thousand pupils. Moreover, the building itself may have several "wings" and may cover a space of several acres. In schools this large, even simple administrative procedures such as recording attendance can be a monumental task.

In some districts, a house system has been established. Under this system, the school is divided into sections or houses. This division may be by grade level, by wing of the building, by floor, or by any other division the administrator deems appropriate.

Each house is then placed under the charge of an administrator, usually a vice-principal or an administrative assistant. This person is in charge of collecting and correlating data relative to attendance and other requirements for that particular house. This data is then transmitted to the central office for school-wide record keeping.

Moreover, the particular administrator is often in charge of the discipline within the house, handling all but the most serious cases or those the principal wishes to handle personally. Reports of these discipline procedures are also recorded in the central office.

The main advantage of a house system is that it allows for the efficient handling of an exceedingly large student population and frees the main or central office from unnecessary confusion.

See Also: DIFFERENTIATED STAFFING; ENROLLMENT; MINISTERIAL ACTS; RECORD KEEPING; STUDENT INFORMATION; SUPERVISION (STAFF); SUPERVISION (STUDENTS).

I

ILLNESS

See ABSENCE; ABSENTEEISM; HEALTH IMMUNIZATION, INOCULATION, AND VACCINATION; MEDICATION; NURSE.

IMMUNIZATION, INOCULATION, AND VACCINATION

The state has the power to protect the "health, morals and safety" of its inhabitants. By extention, so do the schools as agents of the state. This includes *all* schools—nursery, play, common and parochial—at any level or in any place within the state.

Immunization laws exist in several states. These laws place on record, that attendance in the schools is dependent on immunization. Others use existing statutes as an "umbrella" for the schools.

The most common **vaccinations** and **inoculations** required are smallpox, diphtheria, and polio. However, some states include *all* existing pre-

ventative vaccines available: influenza, whooping cough, measles, etc.

Expenses for the vaccinations and inoculations are borne by the parents or guardians of the pupil. In almost all states, however, free inoculation clinics are available.

While parents who refuse to immunize their children may do so on religious and/or constitutional grounds, the courts have held that this refusal, because it is tied to school attendance, places the parents in violation of compulsory education statutes, and the parents' cases have not been upheld.

Faculty and staff members, whether permanent or temporary, are also bound by the same dictum. Further, all employees of a board of education may be required to have a tuberculin sensitivity test during each school year. They, too, do not have the right to refuse.

See Also: AUTHORITY, BOARD; AUTHORITY, EXPRESS AND IMPLIED; CHRISTIAN SCIENTISTS; CIVIL RIGHTS; COMPULSORY EDUCATION;

CONSTITUTIONAL RIGHTS; HEALTH; JEHOVAH'S WITNESSES; PARENTAL LIABILITY; PERMANENT RECORDS; PERSONNEL FILES; STUDENT INFORMATION.

IMPASSE

In collective bargaining procedures between a board of education and a local teacher's association, there may be a point in negotiations at which neither side sees the possibility of coming to a satisfactory conclusion or compromise. This may be for any number of reasons, and may revolve around one specific item or the entire negotiation package. Usually, both sides have put in a great deal of time and effort, and neither side feels that it can compromise any further.

At such a point, both sides may decide to declare an **impasse.** This is a formal declaration that both sides are deadlocked, and negotiations can proceed no further. At this time, an impartial third party acceptable to both sides is brought in. This person, called an arbitrator, mediator or fact finder, studies the situation, taking testimony from all sides, and appraises the objective evidence. Based solely on this evidence, the fact finder or arbitrator issues a report making specific recommendations, usually in the form of a compromise, for the settlement of the area of impasse.

It is interesting to note that unless both sides involved in the impasse formally agree to abide by the recommendations, they are not bound by

the findings, and should either side reject the proposals, other avenues of approach to the impasse will have to be investigated.

See Also: ARBITRATION; COLLECTIVE BARGAINING; CONTRACTS; FACT FINDING; MEDIATION AND MEDIATOR; MEET AND CONFER; NEGOTIATIONS; UNIONS; UNISERV.

IMPUTED NEGLIGENCE

Imputed negligence is negligence that is not directly attributable to the person himself, but which is the negligence of a person who has shared knowledge with him, and with whose fault he is charged.

This concept is of vital importance in education. On one level, it is the protective shelter that covers the administrator from being sued for the negligent actions of a faculty or staff member. On another level, it protects the child to have the school acting in his best interests at all times. This apparent contradiction can be explained by an example.

Mary is on the playground. She trips while playing and breaks her arm. Her parents bring suit for unsafe or unsupervised conditions. Mary's teacher admits that she could not see Mary from the other side of the playground. The teacher is solely liable. But, the teacher, in her own defense, states that she had told the principal that there should be another teacher to help her on playground duty. Now, because the administrator was aware of the danger, she, too, is liable. If her defense is that there was no money to hire another adult to supervise the playground, the board may be added to the suit.

Not all states agree in just how far the negligence can be spread. The reason is a secondary concept called "governmental immunity." This is the belief that agencies cannot be held liable for any injuries caused in carrying out their functions.

Depending on the statutes of the state, the level of imputed negligence to the board can be set according to any of the following four categories:

1. *Complete Right to Immunity*—This means the board cannot be sued. If a student is injured while a teacher or administrator was acting within the scope of his or her duties, the suit can only be brought against the teacher or administrator. In these states, the teacher or administrator should secure personal liability insurance.

2. *Governmental v. Proprietary Acts Immunity*—In these states, the board is only liable if the act was done for the purpose of raising or saving money, time or some other convenience not directly covered by statute. They are not liable if the act was required by state law.

3. *Liability Insurance Purchase*—In the first two categories, no insurance for the board is allowed. Under this category, the immunity is anything not specifically named in the board's insurance policy. Teachers and administrators in these states, for their own protection, should know what is covered and take out personal liability insurance to cover everything else they think is possible.

4. *Waived Immunity with "X" Number of Dollars*—In this, the state will cover any liability up to "X" number of dollars. The teachers and administrators are responsible for anything over this amount. In some states following this approach, the agency (board) must pick up all costs of defending the teacher or administrator. In others, the agency does not. Insurance in states using this approach is imperative.

A copy of the state statutes pertaining to liability and the policy of the local school board on imputed negligence should be kept in the board office, the superintendent's office and the building administrator's office. This protection can prevent headaches and ulcers in the crisis time of the suit.

See Also: ACCESSORY; AGENT; AUTHORITY, BOARD; AUTHORITY, EXPRESS AND IMPLIED; AUTHORITY, TEACHER; CHIEF STATE SCHOOL OFFICIAL; COMPARATIVE NEGLIGENCE; CONTRIBUTORY NEGLIGENCE; DAMAGES; FORESEEABILITY; HABITABLE; INSURANCE; JURISDICTION; LIABILITY; MINISTERIAL ACTS; NEGLIGENCE; NONFEASANCE; SAFETY; SUPERVISION (STAFF); SUPERVISION (STUDENTS); UNISERV.

INCOMPETENCE

Incompetence means to be without adequate ability, knowledge, or fitness; failing to meet requirements; being incapable, unskilled, or not legally qualified.

If a teacher rightfully possesses a teaching certificate, it is considered sound *evidence of competency.* It shows for the record that the teacher is *capable of instruction, supervision* and *providing a safe environment* for the students placed in his or her care. To find that the certificate itself is invalid is a clear violation of trust, and can be, of itself, grounds for dismissal on the charge of incompetence. However, this instance is very rare.

Much more common is the charge of incompetence brought because of a teacher's inability to perform one of the three functions of a competent teacher mentioned above. Here, too, the courts require strict adherence to "true" evidence. A single incident cannot be used as the grounds for dismissal. There must be a "preponderence of evidence" usually in the form of a written log of offenses. Also, testimony can be taken from administrators or fellow workers, but hearsay is usually not permitted, because it may be prejudicial.

Because incompetence is a subjective judgment, the proof against the teacher must be *trustworthy* and, wherever possible, written. All incidents must also be explained *at the time* as to why the administrator is recording them as incompetent acts.

The administrator has another requirement in building the case. The teacher whose actions are under question must be *notified* that such evidence is being gathered. On their own behalf, teachers should also begin recording instances in which they feel their actions might be reviewed. While this record should include the reasons for their actions, the teachers should remember to place any pertinent information such as who else was present, what was said and by whom, where were various items and people positioned in relation to the incident, and *any* outside or extraneous circumstances that might be needed in the future to understand the "environment" of the incident. This "journal" is admissible as defense evidence if it was written *at the time* of the incident.

The burden of proving incompentency is on the board of education. A complete and open hearing is required if dismissal procedures are to be initiated. Also, the teacher can request a review of the procedure or charge by the grievance structure in the district.

See Also: ACCOUNTABILITY; BURDEN OF PROOF; DECERTIFICATION; DISMISSAL OF PERSONNEL; DUE PROCESS; GRIEVANCES; HEARINGS; NONFEASANCE; OBSERVATION; PERSONNEL FILES; QUALIFICATIONS; SUPERVISION (STAFF).

INCREMENTS

It is quite usual that the single largest and most hotly-contested item in negotiations between boards of education and local teachers' associations is salary. When that item is finally settled, it is usually represented in a "salary guide" for the district. This guide lists the starting and top salary within various classifications, as well as the number of years of service required to go from the bottom to the top of the guide and the particular salary at each step. The difference in salary between one step and another is generally referred to as the **increment** for that particular step.

Increments may be "weighted." That is, larger increments may be placed toward the beginning of the scale with smaller increments toward the top, or the reverse may be the case, or the larger increments may be in the middle with smaller increments on either end. *Weighted increments* are often negotiated by Teachers' Associations when the majority of the teachers in a district fall within a particular area of the scale. Hence, a district in which most teachers have ten to fifteen years of experience would negotiate to have the increments weighted toward the top of the scale, which the most people would benefit from.

Many systems also provide for *Longevity increments,* which are special increases given after a certain amount of service within the district. A system may decide to add longevity increments for example, at the 14th and the 23rd step. This would mean that a teacher would receive a longevity increment starting with his or her fourteenth year within the school system, and then again upon reaching the twenty third year of district service.

Another form is the *Educational Advancement* increment. The district recognizes, with a certain added "bonus," the teacher's continued graduate school course work. After steps such as BA + 10, + 20, or + 30, or Master's and Master's + 10, + 20, + 30, etc., are added as incentives for staff members to strive for and receive higher degrees.

See Also: COLLECTIVE BARGAINING; NEGOTIATIONS; SALARY.

INDIVIDUALIZATION

Precisely what is meant by **individualization** is often difficult for administrators to pin down. Various educational leaders often profess varying concepts of applying this term to methods of instruction of the schools. Currently grouped under the title of individualized instruction one may find such programs as Individually Prescribed Instruction (IPI), Teaching by Prescription (TIP), Learning Activity Packages (LAP), Continuous Progress, Flow Scheduling, Individual Scheduling, and Independent Study.

Ideally, an individualized program doesn't just happen because a principal, supervisor or teacher thinks it's a good idea. It only works if objectives are clearly defined for each unit, each skill and each concept, and are extremely specific (performance-based objectives); the evaluation techniques are constantly employed at small, regular intervals (student achievement); and a complete and thorough inservicing is accomplished, at least one year in advance of the start of an individualized program, and is maintained on a schedule of four per year for the first year and several per year for every year thereafter (staff education).

Individualization may include such items as identifying student needs; developing lesson plans that put primary stress on what the learner will accomplish, rather than on what the teacher will attempt; selecting proper appraisal criteria; establishing one-to-one contact between teacher and student; a single subject or topic area handled by a whole class from their own points of view, or collective work done by students to make a whole project; picking a subject or area of interest to complete a course or course of study; and offering a wide variety of behaviors and study habits from which students are free to choose.

Evaluation processes should be as individualized as the instructional program. Appraisal should be in terms of exactly what was done successfully or not *by the student*, and not by the rest of the class or group. Clearly, this individual progress must show just what effort the student put forth. Performance can be a part of evaluation, but the processes and objectives completed are what should be evaluated. It is not individualization in the true sense to place a chart on the wall and give higher grades to students who went up three levels than those who only went up two levels. The student who went up two levels

may have *learned* more than the child who *performed* three levels.

In individualization, the teacher doesn't teach the student, but acts as a guide to his or her learning what he or she needs to learn. In other words, they direct the student to learn, and they do not teach subject matter. This direction is given by means of a four-step method of evaluation. First, there is a *pretest* given by the teacher on the subject matter that the child needs to know. Then, there is an *interim test,* either created by the teacher or the student, made up of objectives toward learning that material. Next, there is a *self-evaluation test,* made up by the student, explaining what he or she knows about what was on the pretest. Finally, there is a *post-test* given by the teacher to see if the student has learned the material. Then, the cycle begins again.

The major advantages of individualization are that it provides specialized help for special interests and remediation of special needs; it shows a good and solid progression at the pace of interest and ability; it provides unsupervised drill for rote subjects; and it opens avenues of exploration for individual students without having to wait for the group. In many cases where individualization is a school-wide concept, it has eliminated barriers of age, grade level and ability.

Its major disadvantages are that it may provide too much or too little free time for a student during the school day; the planning involved in individualization is often monumental; the "difficult" student or the student who is not a self-starter may find it a problem; and, since students can plan when they want to do something, teachers cannot easily plan group activities.

Administrators should be fully aware of all sides of the question of individualization before they make a decision to incorporate it as part of their academic program.

See Also: ACADEMIC PROGRAM; AIDES; CHANGE STRATEGIES; CHILD-CENTERED;COMPETENCY-BASED PROGRAMS; CONTRACTED LEARNING; CURRICULUM DEVELOPMENT; EVALUATION; GOALS AND OBJECTIVES; GRADES; INSTRUCTION; LESSON PLANS; LEARNING CENTERS; OPEN CLASSROOMS; RECORD KEEPING; REPORT CARDS; SCHEDULE; SUPERVISION (STAFF); UNDERACHIEVERS; UNGRADED; WORKSHOPS AND INSERVICE.

INDUSTRIAL ARTS

Industrial arts is the study of the correct handling of the tools, materials and processes used in construction and allied mechanical technologies.

Industrial Arts should not be confused with Vocational Education. The latter involves in-depth studies within a particular area of expertise, while Industrial Arts is basically avocational in nature. Hence, within Industrial Arts a student may be taught the various grades of wood, the use of woodworking tools, and be encouraged to undertake some woodworking projects, but it would be under Vocational Education that carpentry and everything that that title entails would be fully taught.

Industrial Arts classrooms are often referred to as "shops," and often involve the operation of mechanical equipment. Strict safety rules are established for these shops and should be strictly enforced. Besides this "hands-on" experience, there are classroom sessions as well. An Industrial Arts curriculum may include classes in woodworking, metal working, small engine repair, mechanical drawing, plastics, architectural design, and electrical systems.

Traditionally, Industrial Arts was taught to male students under the assumption they would need these skills for their work in life, while female students would marry and run a home, and thus were assigned to Home Economics. With society's reappraisal of stereotyped sex roles and the advent of affirmative action, however, Industrial Arts courses have been opened to both male and female students. It is very common nowadays to see girls in Industrial Arts classes and boys taking Home Economics. This is a trend that will undoubtedly continue.

See Also: ACADEMIC PROGRAM; CURRICULUM DEVELOPMENT; ELECTIVES; EXPENSES; HOME ECONOMICS; PURCHASING; SEXISM; SUPPLIES AND EQUIPMENT; VOCATIONAL PROGRAMS.

INJUNCTION

An **injunction** is a mandatory or prohibitive writ issued by a court; a court order which restrains individuals or groups from committing acts which, in the court's opinion, will do irreparable harm; a court order which compels an individual or group to do an act which, in the court's opinion, is necessary to prevent irreparable harm.

Injunctions may be used for a number of reasons. A board of education may apply for an injunction against a strike by teachers on the grounds that such an act would do irreparable harm to the educational progress of the students under their assigned care. Also, an individual citizen or group of citizens can petition the court to issue an injunction prohibiting the school from violating a right that they feel is protected by common, civil or constitutional law.

If the court agrees with the petitioner, an injunction to cease and desist the action will be issued. Failure to comply with the injunction order is a court offense, namely contempt of court. The punishment spelled out for this offense varies according to local statutes.

See Also: AUTHORITY, BOARD; AUTHORITY, PARENTAL; AUTHORITY, TEACHER; COMPULSORY EDUCATION; HEARINGS; JOB ACTION; JURISDICTION; PETITIONS; STRIKES; UNISERV.

IN LOCO PARENTIS

"In loco parentis" is a Latin phrase that literally means "in the place of parents"; it is a legal doctrine established by the courts in order to give school officials the necessary authority to regulate student conduct.

In essence, the doctrine of *in loco parentis* means that when a student is within the jurisdiction of the school, a school official may *discipline, instruct, supervise,* and *provide for the safety of the student* as if the student were his or her own child.

The courts have defined the jurisdiction of the schools as that time when the student is on school premises, or present at school-sponsored activities or school-related functions such as school club activities, school athletic events, field trips, school buses and bus stops, the playground, classrooms and buildings, and other school property. It has also been held that the school's jurisdiction does not extend to the time when the child is coming to or going home from school, unless the child is on a school vehicle or school property.

The greatest arguments involving *in loco parentis* have come in the area of discipline and punishment. Traditionally, the doctrine was the justification of the right to use reasonable force to correct student conduct because the teacher stood in the place of the parent, and the school had the express and implied authority to set such rules of conduct as were necessary to maintain a safe, controlled and educationally productive environment. The point of contention comes from an interpretation of what is meant by "reasonable."

Obviously, what is "reasonable" will need definition. A teacher who disciplines his or her own children by spanking them may feel it is reasonable to do the same thing in the classroom, while the parent of the child so disciplined may hold a vehemently opposite opinion. This is why *in loco parentis* is not defined by state statutes but is defined by court decisions. Indeed, specific state statutes may prohibit any form of corporal punishment in a school, and a teacher using corporal punishment in such a place cannot argue that he is justified under *in loco parentis*.

See Also: ACCOUNTABILITY; AUTHORITY, EXPRESS AND IMPLIED; AUTHORITY, TEACHER; DISCIPLINE; HEALTH; IMPUTED NEGLIGENCE; JURISDICTION; REASONABLE AND PRUDENT; SAFETY; SUPERVISION (STUDENTS).

IN-SCHOOL SUSPENSION

In-school suspension is a type of disciplinary action in which a student who has been suspended from school serves the suspension time in the school building, but apart from regular classes.

Suspension from school has been used as punishment for serious disciplinary infractions for some time. During the time of the suspension, usually measured in a number of days, the student is barred from attending school. It is hoped that this separation from peers and the normal school activities will cause the student to reappraise his or her attitude upon return.

There are, however, several problems with this philosophy. For the more "hardened" cases, suspension is often looked upon as merely a vacation from school. If there is a lack of supervision or reinforcement in the home, the disruptive student will be free to "roam the streets," getting into even more serious trouble. Moreover, the student's academic progress stops during the period of suspension.

Many schools, therefore, are turning towards some form of in-school suspension. A room is established under the supervision of a qualified teacher, and the suspended student reports directly to this room upon entering the building. The student's teachers send the student's assignments for the day to the room, and the student stays there, under supervision, and continues with his or her academic work. Usually, lavatory facilities are adjacent to the room, and the student's lunch may be brought to the room and eaten there. The student does class work all day and does not leave until regular dismissal time. This procedure is repeated through the entire period of the suspension.

Consequently, proponents believe that the suspension now becomes meaningful. It is no longer a "vacation"; the student is under the school's authority and supervision, and his or her academic status is maintained, if not improved. Moreover, the teacher in charge often has the opportunity to enter into meaningful dialog with the student, possibly affecting positive changes in the student's attitude and/or behavior.

See Also: ASP (ALTERNATE SCHOOL PROGRAM); DETENTION; DISCIPLINE; SUPERVISION (STUDENTS).

INSTRUCTION

Instruction has been defined variously as "an arranging of conditions of learning that are external to the learner"; "aiding the student to learn until the student does"; "an authoritarian art based from beginning to end on teacher judgment of student needs"; and "teacher-transmitted information."

It is a general consensus that good instruction should promote personal learning that the school can support as private life choices and not attempt to either influence or monitor; should present controversies that present cultural alternatives without concordance, and that the school can monitor for process integrity but not conclusions; and should provide personal survival skills that can be systematically taught and vigorously evaluated for performance.

A good instructional program is one in which the students begin building one "block" at a time to a larger "building" of knowledge that the teacher did not specifically design. Sequential "blocks" are added in a free-flowing progression that is relevant and usable to the student's "building." New material is introduced and "hinged, cemented and attached" to old "blocks" at as many points as possible so that the "building" is ever growing.

Some instructional processes that help facilitate this goal are broad curriculums, the collection and use of a wide range of materials, competency and relevancy-based education, homework assignments, marking systems, examinations, and guidance systems.

The biggest changes in instruction in the past few years have been in techniques and practices. The role of the teacher in the instructional process has changed because there has been a shift in emphasis from teacher behavior to the characteristics of the learning environment and the ways in which students learn. For example, in all but a very few cases, the "lecture method" has all but disappeared. The teacher is now looked upon as the facilitator, the guide, the mitigator, if you will, in the educational process, and instruction is dictated by the individual student's needs. Indeed, it has been said that today, "teachers teach students, not classes."

Traditionally, the principal of a school was viewed as the "master instructor," who provided guidance in the art of instruction to students and teachers. However, the administrator's instructional role has all but disappeared, because other demands are leaving very little time for it. Moreover, as instruction in individual classes becomes more and more specifically geared to those students in the particular class, the concept that the administrator could step into any class and teach it has gone by the boards.

See Also: ACADEMIC FREEDOM; ACCOUNTABILITY; AUTHORITY, TEACHER; CLASS AND CLASS SIZE; COMPETENCY-BASED PROGRAMS; COURSE; COURSE OF STUDY; CURRICULUM DEVELOPMENT; EXAMINATIONS; GOALS AND OBJECTIVES;

GRADES; HOMEWORK; INDIVIDUAL-IZATION; INTERDISCIPLINARY AP-PROACHES; LEARNING CENTERS; LESSON PLANS; OBSERVATION; OPEN CLASSROOMS; REMEDIAL IN-STRUCTION; REPORT CARDS; SUPER-VISION (STAFF); SUPERVISION (STU-DENTS).

INSUBORDINATION

Insubordination has been and is used as a grounds for the dismissal of a teacher. A teacher who fails to comply with the reasonable rules set by an administrator is, in fact, guilty of insubordination. Should the teacher feel that the rules are not "reason-able," this must be handled through existing grievance procedures. A teacher cannot use the fact that he or she feels that the rules are unreasona-ble as a justification for disobedience.

The charge of insubordination against a teacher, however, must be fully documented and can apply only to what the teacher does or does not do within the school or classroom. An administrator, for example, cannot tell a teacher not to join a political group and then charge insubordination if the teacher does. This, indeed, would be a clear violation of the teacher's con-stitutional rights, and the administra-tor would be the one in trouble. Indeed, a charge of insubordination cannot be sustained for the refusal to follow a rule that violates an individ-ual's civil or constitutional rights.

See Also: ASSIGNMENTS; AU-THORITY, BOARD; AUTHORITY,

TEACHER; CIVIL RIGHTS; CONSTITU-TIONAL RIGHTS; DISMISSAL OF PER-SONNEL; GRIEVANCES; JOB ACTION; NONFEASANCE; NONRENEWAL OF CONTRACT; PETITION; PRIVACY; PUBLICATION; REASONABLE AND PRUDENT; STRIKES.

INSURANCE

Insurance is a legal and social device designed to eliminate pure risk; a device by which a person or group is financially protected from ruin should a tragedy occur.

All school districts have the im-plied power to insure school property and to take out *liability insurance*. Indeed, in the increasingly legalistic society in which we live, for a school system not to take out insurance would be to invite disaster.

Insurance for a school district is issued through a recognized insurance company, usually after an appraisal and investigation of the needs within the district. This will determine the nature and type of the insurance is-sued, as well as the premium to be paid by the district. Insurance com-panies are controlled by state insur-ance departments and the statutes of the state in which they operate.

A school district may purchase property insurance on school build-ings and equipment and such insur-ance as will cover liability within buildings, on school-owned vehicles, on all school property, and during school-sponsored events and ac-tivities. Schools may legally require employees to have their vehicles covered by automobile insurance within certain limits of liability before operating them on school grounds. Schools may also offer parents the opportunity to purchase student insurance for their children during the time they are in school, as long as this insurance purchase is strictly voluntary.

Insurance for a school district is issued on the basis of a fiscal year rather than a school year. This provides for year-round coverage, whether or not the school is in session.

See Also: HOSPITALIZATION; WITHHOLDING.

INTELLIGENCE TESTING

It is generally understood that whatever the test given, the interpretation of its results is of foremost importance. One must consider such factors as the validity and reliability of the test being used, as well as the population on which the test was standardized. One must remember that a test is neither good nor bad, but rather, that it is in the area of its application and interpretation that difficulties often arise.

If **intelligence test** results are used as the sole criteria for a child's placement within a track or ability group, the courts have held that this is a violation of constitutional rights. The courts have held that some tests may measure intelligence gained through cultural experience and not innate intelligence (*Hobson v.*

Hansen, 408 F2d.175 [1969]). Nor can a test be used if the test is not in the basic language of the child being tested. These tests may be used, however, if they are in the child's basic language, if an interpreter is provided, and if the safeguards outlined under the *Hobsen v. Hansen* case are observed (*Diana v. State Board of Education,* Civil #C-70 37 RFR CA 1970). Moreover, besides intelligence testing, the courts have held that there must be other factors considered in the placement of students (*Moses v. Washington Parish School Board,* 456 F.2d 1285, [1972]). It is likely that the courts will continue to define the uses of intelligence testing.

Some of the more common intelligence tests used are Stanford-Binet, Wechsler Intelligence Scale for Children (WISC), Slosson Intelligence Test for Children and Adults, the Peabody Picture Vocabulary Test, and the Developmental Test of Visual-Motor Integration (VMI).

See Also: ACHIEVEMENT; APTITUDE; DIAGNOSIS; LEARNING DISABILITIES; PERMANENT RECORDS; STUDENT INFORMATION.

INTERDISCIPLINARY APPROACHES

A student who cannot read has difficulty in everything. Teach that child to read, however, and suddenly he or she finds that his or her grades improve in courses besides Reading, because now that skill is being used in other disciplines. Teach a student good handwriting as a separate course and it will soon be forgotten, but if every teacher in every subject demands good handwriting, the skill will be used forever. These are just two examples of the uses of **interdisciplinary approaches.**

It stands to reason that more skills can be introduced and maintained by students if these skills are reinforced from many angles. An interdisciplinary approach attempts to reinforce the skills taught by one discipline in all the other disciplines to which the child is exposed in school. In its simplest form, when a schoolwide objective such as the correct use of English is taught and reinforced in all classes, interdisciplinary learning is taking place.

Proponents of interdisciplinary approaches see them as the saviors of the curriculum basics, because through them, one can tie one subject to everything else. A skill taught in Math, that is immediately reinforced in Science, and, later in the day, in Physical Education, and still later in English, for example, is likely to be remembered. Obviously, this will take some coordination and a great deal of cooperation on the part of teachers, but the reinforcement provided seems to merit the effort.

Interdisciplinary approaches provide meaningful links between seemingly isolated ideas; they provide flexibility in the use of time and space through teaming, shared objectives and cross-curriculum planning; they promote student-to-student learning as students discover the link between

subjects; the curriculum is viewed as a continuum, and everyone tends to see his or her place as a part of the whole; and a subject can become a vehicle for complete study, with technical and social skills making it possible to integrate life with learning.

See Also: ACADEMIC PROGRAM; CHANGE STRATEGIES; COURSE; COURSE OF STUDY; CURRICULUM DEVELOPMENT; DIFFERENTIATED STAFFING; GOALS AND OBJECTIVES; GRADES; INSTRUCTION; LEARNING CENTERS; SUPERVISION (STAFF); UNGRADED; WORKSHOPS AND IN-SERVICE.

INTERMEDIATE SCHOOLS

See MIDDLE SCHOOLS.

INTERVIEW

Interviews are used for many purposes in education. From the screening of potential applicants for a position to a conference about educational problems to an investigation of disciplinary infractions, the interview provides an opportunity for all parties to appraise the situation and each other. Indeed, in most school systems, a personal interview is a prerequisite to hiring.

While there is no set formula for conducting an interview, there are several guidelines which, when followed, allow for a smoothly flowing and productive interview. First, every interview should have a definite and defined purpose, and all parties involved should be aware of that purpose. This avoids confusion and determines the thrust of the proceedings. Second, the interview should be held in a quiet place, relatively free from interruptions, where participants can concentrate on the matters at hand. Third, a relatively relaxed and informal atmosphere should be maintained, which allows all parties to be at ease. Fourth, sufficient time should be allotted for the interview so that neither party feels rushed and that all items for discussion may be investigated thoroughly. Fifth, the interview should be so structured that some definite conclusions or at least a determination of the next steps to be taken can be made. Finally, immediately upon the completions of the interview, the person conducting the interview should make a complete, written record of the proceedings and the impressions gleaned.

An interview that is well-conducted, where all parties are at ease, and where there is a definite purpose and plan, can be a valuable tool for every administrator.

See Also: APPLICATION; COMMUNICATION; EMPLOYEE RELATIONS; EQUAL EMPLOYMENT OPPORTUNITIES; PARENT CONFERENCES.

J

JEHOVAH'S WITNESSES

Jehovah's Witnesses are a Christian sect founded by Charles T. Russell. The major tenets of the faith are opposition to war and/or nationalism, refusal to accept the authority of any government in matters of religious conscience, and belief that the only true authority comes from God (Jehovah) to whom they owe their testimony (witness) of His Law, as set forth in the Old Testament and affirmed in the New Testament.

This group is quite vocal in its adherence to the First Amendment guarantees concerning church-state separation in the U.S. Constitution. Further, they believe in the literal interpretation of the Fifth Amendment guarantees of free speech. They hold that not only does this guarantee them the right of free speech, but also, that no one can force them to say anything they do not wish to say. Therefore, the courts have upheld the Jehovah Witnesses in their opposition to the flag salutes, the pledge of allegiance, and the practice of Bible reading and prayers in school. The courts are still reviewing Jehovah's Witnesses' objections to compulsory education, sex education and disciplinary actions in the schools on a case-by-case basis.

Usually, the best course for the administrator or board of education to follow is to hold conferences with the parents who belong to this sect. This allows the two parties to state their points of view *in the beginning,* perhaps avoiding later misunderstandings in the classroom. Great care should be taken to avoid any restrictions of their constitutional and/or civil rights.

See Also: AUTHORITY, PARENTAL; BIBLE; CHRISTIAN SCIENTISTS; CIVIL RIGHTS; COMPULSORY EDUCATION; CONSTITUTIONAL RIGHTS; FIFTH AMENDMENT GUARANTEES; FIRST AMENDMENT GUARANTEES; FOURTH AMENDMENT GUARANTEES; FREE SPEECH; OATHS; PARENT CONFERENCES; RELEASED TIME; RELIGION; SELF-INCRIMINATION; SPECIAL INTEREST GROUPS; STUDENT INFORMATION.

JOB ACTION

A **job action** is a measure designed to stop a violation of either the spirit of, or the actual adherence to, a contract, law, statute, or code.

As teacher unions and associations have become larger and stronger, negotiations have sometimes produced rising tensions that have led them to job actions. Also, an alleged mishandling of a grievance, misunderstood dismissals or transfers of personnel, or even a mispoken word can sometimes seemingly touch off such a reaction. It should be quickly noted, however, that in these latter instances, the culprit is usually poor communications and deeper or hidden feelings of ill will. Whatever the case, when a job action occurs, the school board, central staff, and building administrators still must handle the situation.

Job actions fall into two categories. The first involves *administrative disruption*. Suppose that a contracted workday is 6 hours and 45 minutes long. With the extracurricular duty period after school, the day comes to 7 hours and 30 minutes. A job action might be that, on one or two days, *all* teachers would sign out precisely at the 6-hour and 45-minute mark, and no one would participate in the extra period. This job action, while certainly an inconvenience, does not constitute a detriment to instructional time that should be given to students. Instead, it is aimed solely at "management" functions. The second category, however, involves *work stoppages*. These can be very disruptive. One example is the "Blue Flu," so named for the actions taken by some police unions, which has *all* employees calling in sick for a particular day. This action is particularly abhorrent when used against school boards, for it interrupts the instructional process and the progress of the students and the school.

The only way to alleviate the deleterious effects of job actions is to defuse the situations that lead to them. This may be easier said than done, but effective liaison committees and fair grievance procedures are a good start in that direction for the administration.

See Also: DEMONSTRATIONS; EMPLOYEE RELATIONS; GRIEVANCES; LIAISON; NEGOTIATIONS; PETITIONS; STRIKES; UNIONS.

JUNIOR HIGH SCHOOL

See MIDDLE SCHOOLS.

JURISDICTION

Jurisdiction is the scope of authority held by a court as to the type and reasons for the cases it may hear and on which it can render decisions.

Given that education is primarily for the purpose of the schooling of children, there are still many situations that can lead administrators to seek judicial solutions and clarifications. The most salient decision in the judicial process is before which court to present the case.

The most common, and, indeed, the most often used, are the district or circuit courts. These are *courts of general jurisdiction* and are usually organized on a county or parish basis. The judge hears cases on state, county, and district matters generally, as they apply to state law and/or county statutes. The state court system also has a *court of appeals* and a *court of last resort,* usually the state supreme court, or in some areas, the state superior court.

The state court system is separate from, but can be connected to, the federal court system. Here, the *courts of general jurisdiction,* called U.S. District Courts, review cases concerning federal laws and statutes and questions on constitutional law. There are 87 such courts for the fifty states and territories. The U.S. Courts of Appeal, of which there are 11, hear appeals from these courts. The *court of last resort* in the federal court system is the U.S. Supreme Court.

Needless to say, very few school districts need to pursue a case to either the state supreme court or the U.S. Supreme Court, but it is a good idea to decide just what kind of results the school wishes to have at the conclusion of the litigation. An injunction to end a school strike could be best handled in the state court system, while a case on whether or not the school has the right to require a particular style of dress, conduct or performance might belong instead in the federal court system.

It is for questions of this type that most school districts employ a board lawyer. The courts are there to serve the people, and knowing in which jurisdiction to bring suit will insure that the district is best served.

See Also: CIVIL RIGHTS; CONSTITUTIONAL RIGHTS; HEARINGS; INJUNCTION; UNISERV.

JUST COMPENSATION

There are several aspects of the concept of **just compensation** that apply to education. First, and most common, is the salary paid to faculty or staff for work accomplished *over and above* that for which they have contracted. For example, suppose a staff member has been asked to handle playground supervision at a time that would normally be part of his or her lunch hour. The board might pay a "supervision fee" to compensate for the loss of the teacher's free time. Also, some districts compensate faculty and staff members for attending conferences, lectures and workshops that they will "reteach" to the rest of the faculty and staff.

This type of compensation is not to be confused with salaries for contracted extracurricular activities. A teacher under contract to produce a play is salaried for that position. A teacher, however, who gives up his Saturdays for a month in order to work on curriculum, and who received an "honorarium" in appreciation, may feel that he is receiving just compensation.

The term "just compensation" also applies to the damages awarded by the court in a legal action.

See Also: ACTIVITIES; ASSIGNMENTS; DAMAGES; PLAYGROUND; SALARY; SUPERVISION (STUDENTS).

JUVENILE AUTHORITIES

See FAMILY SERVICES.

JUVENILE DELINQUENCY

A **juvenile delinquent** is a minor who either is legally classified as "in need of supervision" or who commits an adult crime.

The first classification of juvenile delinquency is made of a minor who has been legally classified as *"in need of supervision."* This is a legal term meaning that the minor has committed an offense which would not have been an offense, had the person not been a minor. Truancy is a common example. If a person is 18 years of age and does not wish to attend school, there is nothing anyone can do about it. If a person under 18 decides not to go to school, he is a truant. If the minor is a truant, or, for that matter, commits any noncriminal act such as upsetting a neighbor's garbage cans, swearing at his parents or becoming intoxicated, any one of a number of authorities such as the school, the police, the parents, a neighbor, or any adult can make out a complaint against him or her.

The second classification of juvenile delinquency describes the minor who *commits a crime* that would be a criminal action no matter who committed it. Just as with adults, these crimes may be misdemeanors or felonies. The complaint for this type of offense is sworn out either by the injured party or the police.

The normal procedure for handling a minor classified under either type of juvenile delinquency is as follows: a complaint must be signed by someone; the minor is then either remanded immediately to his or her parents, sent to a juvenile shelter for no longer than 24 hours, or held in juvenile detention for no longer than 72 hours, pending a hearing. After the complaint has been filed, an "intake officer" (IO) reviews the complaint. If it is noncriminal, he will set up a conference with the parent(s), the minor, and such family and community services as he feels might help mitigate the situation. They then meet until there is a resolution (no judge is involved). If the intake officer is handling the second classification of juvenile delinquency, he decides whether the minor should go before the juvenile court for a formal or an informal hearing. The informal hearing is used for the juvenile who is either a repeated, noncriminal offender, or it is used for one who has committed a lesser criminal offense such as malicious mischief with little damage or first-offense petty larceny. This informal hearing is held before a judge, with the court clerk, the child's parents and the child present (legal counsel is not necessary). The minor at the informal hearing must plead guilty or not guilty. If he pleads guilty, the judge may give disposition immediately and, at this point,the child may be remanded back to the parent, be put on probation, or be remanded to family services. If the minor pleads not guilty, he is sent to a formal hearing and a court date is set. If, however, the intake officer feels that a formal hearing is necessary, another procedure is set in motion. The child may be at home, with his or her parents, or may be at the juvenile shelter; but, in either case, the intake officer notifies the minor's parents of the time of the hearing, advises them to secure legal council, and petitions the court that a summons to appear be issued. This is obviously used for the more serious crimes. The case then comes before the court and is handled as any other matter of this type.

The first step, once a child has been referred to or has had a complaint signed against him as a juvenile delinquent, is that he is remanded to his parents' custody. Obviously, if it was the parents who signed the complaint, there are great frustrations inherent in the situation and the child may have to be housed in some juvenile facility. In this case, the child may be taken out of his or her regular school and may continue his or her education at the facility. Most juvenile facilities in the United States now have certified teachers on staff in order to continue the minor's education and comply with compulsory education laws.

See Also: BATTERY; BURGLARY; COMPULSORY EDUCATION; DRINKING OF ALCOHOLIC BEVERAGES; DRUGS; FAMILY SERVICES; GUARDIAN AND GUARDIANSHIP; MAJORITY, AGE OF; MALICIOUS MISCHIEF; PARENTAL LIABILITY; POLICE; TRESPASSER; TRUANCY; VANDALISM; VIOLENCE.

K

KEYS

Within any school, there will be uses for a myriad of **keys.** Students may require keys for lockers, teachers need keys to the room or rooms in which they teach, custodians need keys for the building's doors, storerooms, etc., and administrators require keys to various offices and rooms.

There are also master keys that open all the locks produced by the same manufacturer. Hence, there may be a master locker key, a master classroom key, a master office key, and a master building key. Care should be taken in distributing these master keys, since the more master keys that are circulated, the greater the chance of one being lost or stolen, thereby leaving the school vulnerable.

As a general rule, master keys should only be given to those individuals who require them in order to perform their jobs. For example, custodians may need a master key to rooms in order to clean them; a teacher on hall duty might need a master locker key to accommodate students who have forgotten their keys; a guidance counselor might need a master office key in order to have access to records; and, the head custodian and all administrators would require master keys to everything.

A master list should be kept of the serial numbers of all keys used in a school, as well as the names of the persons to whom they have been assigned, along with the specific doors or locks opened by them. Keys should be distributed at the start of the school year and collected at its conclusion. All keys to be turned in to the Main Office should be tagged with the serial number and identification of the lock opened by it such as "177843B—Door, Room 102." These keys should then be sorted and stored in the school safe until needed in the fall.

See Also: LOCKERS; MINISTERIAL ACTS; RECORD KEEPING.

213

KINDERGARTEN

In 1858, the Boston School Committee stated, "[All children should have] hours of instruction, of active exercise of the mind, and of the personal influence of the teacher on the mind and the heart of every pupil...taking children at random from a great city, undisciplined, uninstructed, often with inveterate forwardness and obstinacy...forming them from animals into intellectual beings; giving to many their first appreciation of what is wise, what is true, what is lovely, and what is pure...." Certainly, our rhetoric has changed a great deal since then, and today, one can find **kindergarten** defined as a place where "multicentered universes meet with other universes." The basic philosophy remains, however, and most educators perceive of kindergarten as the primary socializing step for the youth of our nation.

Indeed, study after study has shown that the kindergarten and first grade teachers are probably of extreme importance. Children pick up from these teachers the socialization that will shape their entire educational lives. Proper selection of these teachers, therefore, is of primary importance to every administrator.

Since the kindergarten experience will help shape the child's educational career, many schools place great emphasis on the process of entry itself. There is an increased emphasis on the involvement of parents in the process; one- or two-day orientations prior to the actual start of school; "buddy" systems in which older children escort younger ones through a school day; tours of the school, and the like. In all of these activities, the rapport and the personality of the teacher cannot be stressed too highly.

Generally, the public schools have resisted the expansion of classes below kindergarten level. Indeed, many studies have shown that the gains made from other, formal preschool programs have generally been lost once the child enters formal kindergarten classes. Consequently, the shift has been toward bringing children into kindergarten at an earlier age. The national average age for those attending kindergarten is now five.

School districts can set requirements such as immunization, toilet training and the like for entrance into kindergarten. A district will also establish certain days for registration. This should be well-publicized throughout the community.

See Also: ACADEMIC PROGRAM; AGE LEVELS; EARLY CHILDHOOD PROGRAMS; INSTRUCTION; READINESS; STUDENT INFORMATION; SUPERVISION (STUDENTS).

L

LANGUAGE

Language, its uses and abuses have long been a concern of the school. While schools, as well as teachers in almost all disciplines, have tried to instill correct grammatical usage in countless generations of children, schools have also been concerned with the abuse of language as manifested in vulgarities and obscenities. The courts have held that schools may set rules for the use of language not in the extent of what is said, which would be an infringement on free speech, but as to how it is said; that is, the words used to express the thought.

Consequently, a student or teacher who uses obscene language in the classroom may be disciplined. It must be understood, however, that if the disciplinary action is legally challenged, the courts will take into consideration the context in which the word or words were used. In one famous case, a teacher was dismissed for writing "fuck" on the blackboard.

He was ordered reinstated when the court determined that this was done as part of a lesson on language, was treated academically, and was therefore not obscene, *(Mailloux v. Kiley,* 448 F.2d 1242 [1st Cir. 1971]). A student who used that same word in class was suspended, however, and that suspension was upheld, because the court determined that the word was used only to shock.

Besides language abuses, schools are also concerned about children whose primary language is other than English. Many schools employ the services of an ESL (English as a Second Language) specialist to deal with children who have problems with English. Moreover, the courts have held that such items as intelligence and ability tests may be used with these children only when special provisions are made for children who are not fluent in the language of the test.

See Also: ADDRESSES (SPEECHES); BILINGUAL EDUCATION; COMMUNICATION; CULTURE; FREE SPEECH;

215

LANGUAGE ARTS; PRIVILEGED COMMUNICATIONS.

LANGUAGE ARTS

In many school systems and particularly in the lower grades, students take a course designated in the curriculum as **Language Arts.** This designation replaces what was formally called "English." This originally came about because it was felt that Language Arts was a broader term that incorporated more along the lines of training in communications than was understood under the term "English."

Language Arts students may study the traditional English curriculum including grammar, penmanship, spelling, letter writing and the like, as well as those aspects of communication that are a part of today's scene. These might include aspects of media, informed TV viewing, parts of consumer education, writing with specialized requirements such as job applications, and a host of other language-related activities.

In some schools, reading is considered part of the Language Arts curriculum, while in other schools it is treated as a separate subject. Beyond the point of instruction in the basic skills of reading, the processes involved in the interpretation and study of literature generally fall under the Language Arts classification.

Proper skills in communication are among the most important if not *the* most important skills a child learns in school. The Language Arts curriculum, therefore, is an extremely important part of any academic program.

See Also: ACADEMIC PROGRAM; BASICS; COMMUNICATION; LANGUAGE; LIBRARY AND MEDIA CENTER; MEDIA; READING; SUPERVISION (STAFF).

LAVATORIES

All schools must provide **lavatory** facilities. Indeed, without them a school would not be considered habitable. The failure of a sewage line, for example, which would make the lavatories inoperable, would be enough reason to close the school until repairs were effected.

The problem with lavatories in schools lies not with their use but with their abuse. This abuse can take many forms, from smoking in the lavatories during classes, to major vandalism of commodes and sinks, to students being pulled into the lavatories and robbed, extorted, beaten, and even killed. While these latter cases are extremes, they have happened, and the administrator must be aware of these unhappy possibilities.

Consequently, lavatory use is often limited by requiring students to obtain a pass from a teacher for use of the facilities. Moreover, teachers on hall duty are often required to check the appropriate lavatory on a periodic basis. (It should be understood that a male teacher should never enter the

Girl's Room and vice versa; that causes too many problems.) In schools where there is or has been a great deal of violence or crime, many systems are hiring security guards, some of whom have the specific assignment of supervising the lavatories.

It must be noted that an educator cannot deny a child the use of the lavatory. If it is believed that the child is abusing the right, then some form of supervision or investigation may be required, but under no circumstances can a teacher or administrator refuse to let a child go to the lavatory.

It is interesting to note that many schools have reduced lavatory vandalism by allowing students, under supervision, to paint or decorate the lavatories with designs or colors of their choosing. It is felt that, in this way, students take a personal interest in preserving what they feel is theirs.

See Also: HABITABLE; HEALTH; PASSES; PRIVACY; SAFETY; SUPERVISION (STUDENTS).

LEARNING CENTERS

A **learning center** is a concentrated placement of materials to aid student discovery of either academic concepts or developmental skills.

Basically, a learning center is a package of materials. These may be standardized materials or teacher-prepared materials, but everything in the package is geared toward the teaching or reinforcing of one particular concept or skill. The materials may include dittos, games, skill cards, tests, and the like. They are geared for individual use. A student goes to the learning center, explores the materials, does the activities, and, with appropriate teacher aid where needed, assimilates the concept or skill.

Learning centers have a variety of uses. They can, for instance, make excellent use of student-activated time to teach, reinforce or test concepts taught to the whole class. Moreover, they are prime targets for contracted learning, where a child may enter into a contract to do "X" amount of learning centers work successfully, over "X" amount of time. In addition, the centers function extremely well in the open classroom, in which the teacher is primarily viewed as the facilitator. Finally, learning centers need not concentrate only on academic subjects, but also may be used for such developmental concepts as decision-making, self-concept, values clarification and more.

Learning centers have advantages and disadvantages. On the plus side, they are virtually self-motivating, they provide for constructive use of student time, and they are student-centered. Conversely, they present some difficulties for children who are not self-starters, and too much freedom of choice allows some students to lose too much time on tasks.

Beyond the middle school, the concept of the learning center is usually seen expressed in individual projects utilizing the library or media center.

See Also: CHILD-CENTERED; CONTRACTED LEARNING; ENRICHMENT; INDIVIDUALIZATION; OPEN CLASSROOMS.

LEARNING DISABILITIES

Learning disabilities are any one of a number of conditions a child may have which inhibit his or her normal educational processes.

Historically, the concept of learning disabilities developed with the establishment of Child Study Teams. These teams addressed themselves to the problem of why some children cannot learn. From this arose the concept of learning disabilities, and from this, the concept of formulating a way to help children with these problems.

Once a child is suspected of having a learning disability, he or she is referred to an LDS (Learning Disabilities Specialist), sometimes called an LDTC (Learning Disabilities Teacher Consultant). The child is then tested with such instruments as the *Schlosson Battery, Torrence Creativity, WISC, WRAT,* and a host of others. If, as a result of this testing and evaluation by the LDS, the child is determined to be learning disabled, the child is then classified by the LDS. These classifications fit under three headings:

1. *Physical or Accuity Disability*—The child has impaired sight, loss of hearing, etc.

2. *Perceptual and/or Pattern Disability*—The child is physically normal but perceives reality incorrectly; dyslexia is an example.

3. *Social or Emotional Disability*—The child's social integration or emotional and/or environmental pressures prevent learning.

Some classifications that may be used are Neurologically Impaired, Perceptually Impaired, Socially Maladjusted, and Emotionally Disturbed.

Once a child has been classified, the law states that the child is no longer bound by the grade, schedule or time restrictions that bind other children in the school. The LDS writes an individual prescription for the child's learning, which is then implemented by the classroom teacher and the LDS. It is part of the LDS's duties to establish a Resource Center where classified children may be helped. Once a child has been classified, part of the prescription will be time spent outside the classroom environment in the Resource Center, where the LDS teaches via the individual prescription. There are restrictions on the Resource Center, however. Usually, no more than 25 children per school year may be placed there, and they may be no farther than four grade levels apart. The rest of the time, the children are mainstreamed whenever possible.

In differentiated staffing, the LDS has the same classification as the staff supervisor, unit coordinator or administrative teaching assistant, while in the hierarchical system, they are classified as administrative assistants. This sometimes causes problems when working with the implementation of individual prescriptions made by the classroom teacher. LDS's are legally bound under Title VI to provide the individualized education (IEP) prescriptions, which will allow a child to reach his or her full educational potential.

See Also: ACCOUNTABILITY; CHILD-CENTERED; CHILD STUDY TEAM; DIAGNOSIS; DIFFERENTIATED STAFFING: HANDICAPPED; MAIN-STREAMING, PSYCHOLOGICAL STUDIES; PUBLIC LAW 94-142; RE-MEDIAL INSTRUCTION; RETARDED CHILD; SPECIAL EDUCATION; SPECIAL SERVICES; SUPERVISION (STAFF); SUPPLEMENTAL EDUCATION.

LEASE OF SCHOOL PROPERTY

The school is public property. As such, it must abide by the same requirements imposed upon all public establishments. If school property is leased to groups for their use outside of education, then the right to **lease the school property** cannot be denied to any group legitimately qualified to do so.

Usually, this presents no problem. Girl Scouts, Boy Scouts, adult recreation groups and the like regularly use school property and no one is upset. There have been cases, however, when a group that is patently

racist has made application to use school property for rallies, political speeches, etc., and this *has* upset members of the school and public communities. Since the school is a public building, however, refusal to lease school property to such groups must be on grounds other than their philosophical or political beliefs. Often, situations of this sort have ended in the courts.

Certain restrictions may legitimately be placed on those who lease school property. The school may prohibit the group from using alcoholic beverages on school grounds, prohibit the group from using school property while school is in session, or even, in some cases, require the purchase of limited insurance.

See Also: CIVIL RIGHTS; CONSTITU-TIONAL RIGHTS.

LEAVE OF ABSENCE

A **leave of absence** is usually granted to a teacher or administrator by the board of education upon review of the application for such leave. If granted, for whatever time is specified, the educator is free from all educational duties, as if he or she were not employed by the district; however, upon his or her return, his or her position is made available and the educator may resume that position as if there had been no interruption.

Leaves of absence are granted for many reasons. *Sabbatical leave* is granted for the purpose of obtaining a graduate degree. *Maternity and paternity leave* involves leave for the purpose of having and caring for a child. *Medical leave* is granted for recovery from extensive illness or injury. Moreover, leaves may be granted for any other reason that a board of education feels may merit the action.

A leave of absence may be without pay, with pay, or at a percentage of pay. There may also be criteria set by the board for the granting of a leave. For example, sabbatical leave may be limited to a set number per year within the district, and applicants may be required to have taught a set number of years within the district and guarantee that they will serve an additional set number of years upon their return from leave. These variables are often a matter of individual board policy.

See Also: AUTHORITY, BOARD; MATERNITY LEAVE; MILITARY LEAVE; PATERNITY LEAVE; SABBATICAL LEAVE.

LESSON PLANS

The basic arguments over **lesson plans** center around the questions of for whom are they written, why are they written, and what should be their content. Most educators agree that effective lesson plans cannot be written in isolation from the learner. The student is the person for whom the planning is done. Therefore, a lesson plan should not show what the teacher will accomplish, but rather what the student will accomplish. The traditional method of lesson planning centered on what the teacher anticipated accomplishing in a given class day or period. More recently, the thrust has aimed at what the students will accomplish. For example, a traditional lesson plan for Math might read, "pages 23-44; do problems 16-27." Now, the lesson plan covering that same material might read, "students will be able to add three-digit numbers using pp. 23-44, the Math learning center, and small group instruction and drill." This latter type of plan now becomes a guide for student learning rather than teacher performance. This student-oriented planning allows for individual differences and individualized teaching. This also helps alleviate "gapping," which is the problem often found in traditional lesson plans where the class goes faster or slower than the teacher expected. With the new system where mastery is the key, time spent by the students on various tasks will change, but the objectives will be met.

Originally, lesson plans were a means of guaranteeing that the curriculum for any given grade was taught between September and June of a school year. Again, this was content-oriented. Lesson plans are now written to connect curricular demands with student needs and skills. Consequently, exposure of material is seen not in terms of one year, one day, one week, etc., but in terms of relevant usages for a lifetime. Consequently, two teachers teaching the same grade could not possibly have the same lesson plans, but they probably will have the same objectives.

As far as the content of lesson plans is concerned, if they are content-oriented, the bulk of them will be made up of page numbers, quiz dates, exercises to be done, etc. If they are concept and student-mastery oriented, there will be a great deal of overlapping, flexible scheduling, ability grouping, etc. Anyone certified as a teacher could take the first set of plans and teach from them given a certain expertise in the subject matter, and accomplish this without knowing the class or its needs. With the second set of plans, this could not be done. Teaching from those plans requires a highly specific knowledge of the individuals in the class, their needs and their masteries.

Administrative review of lesson plans can be a touchy subject. Part of a teacher's authority is to instruct his or her students in whatever manner deemed appropriate. Consequently, some groups look upon administrative review as restraining this freedom. However, if instead of looking at content, administrators review plans in order to assist the teachers use of concept development, these same groups are more willing to accept administrative review.

See Also: ACADEMIC FREEDOM; ACCOUNTABILITY; AUTHORITY, TEACHER; CHILD-CENTERED; COMPETENCY-BASED PROGRAMS; CONTRACTED LEARNING; EVALUATION; GOALS AND OBJECTIVES; GRADES; INDIVIDUALIZATION; INSTRUCTION; LEARNING CENTERS; RECORD KEEPING; SUPERVISION (STAFF) UNGRADED.

LIABILITY

Liability is the state of being legally bound, as to make good any loss or damage that occurs in an action, transactions, contract, or communication.

The theory of liability pervades education. Some examples of its application are that teachers do not have to insure student safety, but liability exists where injuries result from a teacher's failure to exercise reasonable care and precaution; school boards are liable for all contracts they sign; individual school board members do not incur personal liability because the board acts as a body, but they do have personal liability if a member supercedes his authority and causes some injury; a student is held to be liable for his or her actions, but they are "judgment proof"—any debts or damages incurred by the minor become the liability of the parents or guardians.

Test cases have been offered, but no judgments made on the liability of a principal who uses students in "supervisory positions" such as safety patrols, crossers, parking lot facilitators, etc. The test cases are often based on whether or not the principal acted in good faith.

For Guidance counselors, Child Study Teams, and any school group or individual that delves into the personal lives of students, the liability is often expressed in terms of invasion of privacy. Consequently, any record that could possibly be opened at some point in time should be written in such a manner that anyone could read it. Any notes, conference reports or first-hand data should be kept separated, only to be divulged at the demand of the court.

When checking liability, teachers and administrators must be sure they understand the immunity statutes regarding imputed negligence in their particular state.

See Also: ACCESSORY; ACCIDENT; AGENT; AUTHORITY, EXPRESS AND IMPLIED; COMPARATIVE NEGLIGENCE; CONTRIBUTORY NEGLIGENCE; DAMAGES; FORESEEABILITY; GUARDIAN AND GUARDIANSHIP; IMPUTED NEGLIGENCE; NEGLIGENCE; PARENTAL LIABILITY; PRIVACY; SAFE PLACE STATUTES; SUPERVISION (STUDENTS).

LIAISON

Liaison refers to a group or individual who acts as an intermediary between groups within a school or system.

A liaison committee may be an *ad hoc* affair formed to handle a particular problem, but more often it is a standing committee whose membership changes but whose purpose continues. A standing liaison committee is often part of a school's structure.

One of the major communications problems within any school is the fact that administrative actions and decisions are sometimes viewed by the faculty as arbitrary, capricious and without consideration of the needs or feelings of the faculty. Such feelings, if left to fester, can produce disastrous results. It is in situations such as this that a liaison committee can function best.

A committee is established, composed of teachers who will represent every grade or department within a school. Usually, these representatives are freely chosen by the faculty. This committee then meets on a regular basis with the administrator, discusses the problems and concerns of both sides, and reports back to the faculty.

In this way, the faculty feels they have some impact on administrative decision-making, are better able to understand and appreciate administrative actions and problems, and are able to contribute to those outcomes that will affect the school environment and their professional lives. Because of this, an active, functioning liaison committee can establish open lines of communication, foster positive employee/employer relations, and help promote the general feeling that each teacher is a functioning, important and necessary part of the whole.

See Also: ADVISORY COUNCILS; COMMITTEE; DEMANDS; EMPLOYEE RELATIONS; GRIEVANCES; PETITIONS.

LIBEL

Libel is the written, printed, published, and distributed defamation of one person by another, presented before or open to the review of a third person or persons.

Educators, like any other citizens, are restricted from committing libel in their private lives. However, their positions as teachers and administrators leave them open to exposure to libel charges that may not be seen by the general public.

First, in the role of *publisher* of newsletters, student newspapers, yearbooks, etc., educators are given the responsibility to "reasonably review" such publications for libel. This duty can bring them into conflict with censorship restrictions if the policies of "prior review" are not clearly understood by everyone involved.

Second, in the role of the *writer* of recommendations, educators are protected from libel if they are acting in good faith. Further, they must assume that the person requesting the information or recommendation is also acting in good faith and will continue to do so in the future. The recommendation, while not strictly a privileged communication, *is* expected to be used for a specific purpose and not for "open publication." Once it has served the specific purpose, the recommendation should not be used for any other.

Finally, in the capacity of *observer* or recorder, educators are expected to write opinions on permanent records and/or personnel files. Here, too, they are protected from libel, provided three conditions are met. First, that the opinion is *part of their duties;* second, that it was *given in good faith;* and third, that it *serves a real purpose* in the educational process. Once the conditions are met, no libel occurs.

See Also: CENSORSHIP; DEFAMATION; PERMANENT RECORDS; PERSONNEL FILES; PRIVILEGED COMMUNICATION; PSYCHOLOGICAL STUDIES; PUBLICATION; RECOMMENDATIONS; REFERENCES; STUDENT INFORMATION.

LIBRARY AND MEDIA CENTER

Libraries and media centers are an integral part of the school plant. They serve not only as depositories but also as dispensers of books, materials and motivational ideas. Indeed, they are both the motivators and the facilitators of many skills.

The American Library Association (ALA) and the National Education Association (NEA) have set standards for libraries and media centers. While the standards are difficult and often impractical for most school districts, the criteria are used as excellent guides by administrators. These standards suggest approximately 7,000 books per 250 students; periodicals of interest to the bulk of the students within the school, with several at either end of the grade or age spectrum; four or five newspapers containing local, national and international news; and filmstrips, tapes, records, etc., in sufficient quantities to allow and promote easy access for the students. Some districts have also added video tape recorders, closed circuit TV and computer terminals.

The library and media center performs several functions. A good library and media center serves both the students and the professional staff within a school. It provides consultant services to improve learning and instruction; it improves learning through printed and AVA materials; it makes information available on new educational developments; it creates and produces new materials for students and teachers; it assists classes and individuals in doing investigations and explorations; it provides work areas and equipment for use with their materials; and, finally, it promotes an atmosphere of open-ended skill growth on the part of the entire school.

Most library and media centers are funded under individual school expenditures, with additional support from federal aid through grants issued under Titles II through V of ESEA '65. Expenditures per school usually remain stable from year to year, with a cost of living or inflation extention built in.

Guidelines for the use of books, materials and resources should be a clearly-defined policy known to all educational levels.

See Also: AUDIO-VISUAL MATERIALS; BOOKS; COMPUTERS; CULTURE; EL-EMENTARY AND SECONDARY EDUCATION ACT OF 1965; FEES; MEDIA; MOVIES; READING; STUDENT INFORMATION; SUPPLIES AND EQUIPMENT; TEXTBOOKS; VOLUNTEERS.

LOCKERS

Never was an unknown person so roundly condemned as he who brought **lockers** into the schools. Educators have found that these small spaces can cause large headaches.

There are several specific problems with lockers. First, there is the very management of them. There are keys and combinations, space allocations, etc., to deal with. Usually lockers are assigned to students of a specific class or homeroom teacher on a yearly basis. Keys and/or combinations are then given out by the teacher to his or her students. However, since individual student schedules may vary within the particular homeroom, locker locations may not be convenient for all students. The most common excuse for class tardiness is, "I had to go to my locker." To avoid this, some administrators have established "locker times" interspersed throughout the day, when *all* students may go to their lockers.

Lockers also get dirty. Teachers may check them periodically for sanitation, but they may not search the lockers. They may, however, require a student to remove the lunch he or she left there three months ago.

People also steal from lockers. Administrators have handled this by making up certain guidelines, including the rule that a locker combination should not be shared; that unless there is a shortage, the lockers themselves should not be shared; and, that valuables such as clothing, jewelry or other such materials should be kept in the locker unless the student wishes to put them in the school safe.

Lockers also are vandalized. Because of this, teachers on hall duty should be made aware that lockers in proximity to lavatories, exits, libraries, drinking fountains, etc., are most susceptible to vandalism and theft. Consequently, they should be the ones most closely watched.

Students often keep contraband in lockers. There should be established policies on what may be kept in a locker. Teachers on hall duty should watch for the same students congregating at the same places at the same times over a number of days and notice what types of materials are passing through their hands. If there is a suspicion of wrongdoing, procedures for a locker search may be instigated (See SEARCH AND SEIZURE).

Finally, lockers often create problems with the flow of students. Students congregating around lockers can block a hallway. Usually, gentle but firm reminders of imminent bells, buses, etc., can move students on their way.

See Also: HALL DUTY; KEYS; PASSES; PRIVACY; SEARCH AND SEIZURE; STUDENT INFORMATION.

LOYALTY OATH

See OATHS.

MAIL

Educators are quite often besieged with **mail.** They receive magazines, book club brochures, announcements of graduate courses, advertisements for equipment, books and supplies, and a host of other materials, almost all unsolicited. This mail arrives daily at school, sometimes in such volume that larger schools may require two mail deliveries a day.

Once the mail has arrived at the school, it is the duty of the clerical staff to sort it and place the pieces in the appropriate teacher's mailbox. These mailboxes are often a series of cubby holes with teachers' names affixed and which serve as repositories for mail, bulletins, notices, memos, etc. The sorting and placing of mail may be done by the school secretary, and sometimes trustworthy student aides are used to perform the service.

Most schools have arrangements with local postal offices whereby outgoing mail from the school is picked up at the time when a delivery is made. This is quite a convenient arrangement, and both faculty and staff appreciate the convenience of being able to post personal mail directly inside the school.

Many school systems have also established procedures for inter-office mail, whereby mail that is going to another school, office or agency within the school district is picked up at individual schools on a daily basis, sorted at the central administrative offices, and delivered to the appropriate place the following day. This practice can mean a substantial savings in postage.

See Also: ADDRESS (RESIDENCE); APPRECIATION, LETTER OF; BULLETIN; CLERICAL SERVICES; NEWSLETTER; SECRETARY, SCHOOL.

MAINSTREAMING

Mainstreaming is the concept of setting academic programs for classifiably handicapped students in regular classroom placements, in order to present opportunities for maximum educational, social and emotional growth.

With the passage of Public Law 94-142, educators were faced with a complete review of the educational development of "different" students. For many years, districts had had Special Education classrooms for students who were classified. Usually, these classifications were made of mental and/or physical handicaps. Trainable, educable, paraplegic, blind, or deaf students were kept in self-contained classrooms. There may have been one or two of these classrooms for the entire district. The regular classroom teacher had little or nothing to do with the education of these children. The public's attitude towards this was almost, "Do the best you can for these poor children; we can't expect too much, though." The mainstreaming concept dramatically changed this outlook.

Under Title VI of the law, all students were to be given "the best educational opportunity possible." Students were to be examined by the child study team, classified along strictly written guidelines, and then moved into the mainstream of the school "whenever possible and as prescribed by the child study team."

Changes immediately appeared in schools. Students with physical handicaps could now attend regular classes, and the schools had to adapt their environment to permit access. The stereotypical view that a physical handicap equalled a mental develop-

mental difference was destroyed forever. Once a period of adjustment had passed, most classroom teachers took the presence of handicapped students in their classes for granted.

The severely mentally handicapped were still kept in self-contained rooms, but they were taken to assembly programs, to movies shown in regular classrooms, etc. They became exposed to the social environments and aspects of the school.

This still left the "new" classifications to be dealt with. Perceptually Impaired, Neurologically Impaired, Socially Maladjusted, Emotionally Disturbed, Minimal Brain Dysfunction—these became terms with which educators had to become familiar.

Depending upon a district's needs and desires, mainstreaming may be implemented from two points of view. Students may all be assigned to regular classes, and those classified by the child study team may be *"pulled out"* into resource rooms and supplemental education classes for special help. Or, classified students may be placed in self-contained settings and *"released"* into classes with nonclassified students for one or two periods a day.

Most difficulties with mainstreaming come from communications lapses. For instance, if a classified student is placed in a regular classroom and the teacher hasn't been told that this student will be in the class, or what the classification is and what it means, or how to implement the "prescribed academic program" (generally the Individualized

Educational Program written by the Learning Disabilities Specialist) for the child, or what to do when the child can't cope, then there are going to be serious problems. Proper communication among the LDTC, the child study team and the teacher is a must.

Mainstreaming can be one of the most complex ideas with which the administrator must deal. Several steps should be implemented to aid everyone's basic understanding. First, the administrator should fully understand the laws, classifications and options for mainstreaming that are open to the district. Second, the child study team must not only classify, but also act as support personnel, facilitating the understanding of all those who work with these special students on all levels. Third, workshops and in-service training should be provided for *all* teachers, before, during and after their mainstreaming experiences. These workshops should be conducted by child study team members, outside agencies who specialize in various types of handicaps, and other teachers who have had classified students. These sessions lend a feeling of cohesive support to teachers who may feel overwhelmed and, in addition, convey voluntary information for future mainstreaming experiences. Finally, administrators should share, through publication, addresses, conventions, and meetings, the expertise they developed while working with the day-to-day realities of main-streaming.

Finally, an administrator's familiarity with the individual classified students and their problems, as well as their knowledge of the classroom teachers with whom these students come in contact, can help avoid severe scheduling conflicts. While teachers are willing to help all students, some seem to work better with classified students than with others. Certainly this is one aspect of the educational environment that must be considered. Mainstreaming was designed to help students, and if properly managed, it is a bright and shining hope for the classified student.

See Also: ACADEMIC PROGRAM; CHANGE STRATEGIES; CHILD STUDY TEAM; COMMUNICATION; DIAGNOSIS; HANDICAPPED; INDIVIDUALIZATION; INSTRUCTION; INTELLIGENCE TESTING; LEARNING DISABILITIES; PARENT CONFERENCES; PUBLIC LAW 94-142; RECORD KEEPING; RETARDED CHILD; SELF-CONTAINED CLASSROOM; SPECIAL EDUCATION; SPECIAL SERVICES; WORKSHOPS AND IN-SERVICE.

MAJORITY, AGE OF

The **age of majority** is the chronological age at which a society allows a person to become a citizen.

Education deals with children, and often the question arises as to when that child becomes an adult. Under Federal laws prior to the 26th Amendment, the age of majority was 21. However, after January 21, 1971, that age was lowered to 18. Accordingly, 18-year-olds could enter into contracts, grant loans, accept debts, vote, and otherwise exercise the rights of citizenship.

Therefore, it would seem that there is a standard age of majority, but not so. Most state compulsory education laws list 16 as the age at which a student need no longer attend school. After that age, the child can "act as an adult and no longer is within the requirements of public education." Further, states vary ages as applied to such items as permission slips, insurance coverage, records examination, prosecution of various crimes, and the like, not to mention drinking, driver's licenses, marriage, and legal suits.

While very few cases arise in which the age of majority is of vital concern to the administrator, a written record of what ages constitute majority, for which actions, should be available in the central office for easy access when these questions do arise.

See Also: ABSENCE; ATTENDANCE; CENTRALIZED FILING; COMPULSORY EDUCATION; LIABILITY; PARENTAL LIABILITY; PERMANENT RECORDS; STUDENT INFORMATION; WORKING PAPERS.

MALPRACTICE

See NONFEASANCE.

MALICE

Malice is the intent to injure, or the actual injuring, for spiteful purposes.

The legal implication of malice is that a person charged with it did so for the express purpose of harming the other person. There are no extenuating circumstances or accidents under the charge of malice. Therefore, the charge will only be upheld if the *intent* can be proved "beyond any reasonable doubt."

In education, cases are rare in which charges of slander and libel, unfair dismissal procedures and negligence are enhanced by the additional charge of malice. For malice to occur, the accused person would have to have gone out of their way to abuse the defendant. Seldom is this possible, since malice implies deep-seated animosity, which causes delight in seeing others suffer or in making them suffer. Such behavior seems diametrically opposed to the behavioral concepts present in education.

See Also: BURDEN OF PROOF; DISCRIMINATION; DISMISSAL OF PERSONNEL; MALICIOUS MISCHIEF; VANDALISM.

MALICIOUS MISCHIEF

Malicious mischief is the intentional act or disturbance done by a person or persons seeking revenge or wanting to spite.

Administrators and teachers come in contact with many types of student misconduct and disturbances. Rarely, however, do these misconducts qualify, under law, as malicious mischief. As was stated in the entry

MALICE, intent must be proved "beyond a reasonable doubt." Therefore, vandalism, which is the most common type of malicious mischief, can be shown to be intentional, while shouting, fighting or otherwise disrupting a class usually is not.

If an educator wishes to proceed with a charge of malicious mischief, the police must be notified and a complaint must be made against the perpetrator. At that point, the procedures outlined under JUVENILE DELINQUENCY apply.

See Also: JUVENILE DELINQUENCY; LIBEL; MALICE; PARENTAL LIABILITY; VANDALISM; VIOLENCE.

MANDATORY EDUCATION

See COMPULSORY EDUCATION.

MARRIED STUDENTS

As early as 1929, schools were trying to decide how to treat those individual students who had **married** prior to finishing their education. Attitudinal changes were slow in coming, but the courts have spoken clearly and often on the rights and responsibilities of these students.

There are several points to consider about married students. First, schools cannot bar married students from attending classes merely because they are married (McLeod v. State of Mississippi, 122 So. 737 [MS, 1929]). Nor can a school suspend students merely because they are married *(Board of Education of Harrodsburg v. Ventley,* 343 S.W. 2d 677 [KY, 1964]). Nor can a married student who is pregnant or has had a child be barred *(Alvin Independent School District v. Cooper,* 404 S.W. 2d 76 [TX, 1966]). As well as not being able to bar married students from attending, neither can schools force them to attend school under state compulsory education laws. This is because it has been held that marriage emancipates the minor from having to attend school. In short, married students must legally be treated as adults.

Perhaps the most controversial aspect of married students in public schools is the right to participate in extracurricular activities. While cases and circumstances have to be tested in the courts, *(Davis v. Meek,* 344 F. Supp. 298, 301 [U.S. Dist. Ct., OH, 1972]), the present educational feeling is that while extracurricular activities are not part of "students' rights," exclusion from them had better be on grounds that do not violate their civil or constitutional rights.

With drop-out rates soaring and social problems entering the public school environment, another shift of thought came in during the mid '70s. Not only married students, but also their offspring were welcomed back into the schools. This, say the proponents of open schools, broadened the scope of education, providing access to more students on a fairer basis, in an atmosphere more conducive to the free and open exchange of ideas. This thinking led to the establishment of day-care centers and flexibile scheduling. Not all educators, however, agreed with this new freedom of attitude because they felt that schools are still primarily interested in education, not social problem-solving.

The goals and objectives of each school must be the overriding criteria as to how far a particular district will go to facilitate the education of its married students.

See Also: CIVIL RIGHTS; CONSTITUTIONAL RIGHTS; MAJORITY, AGE OF; PREGNANT STUDENTS; STUDENT INFORMATION.

MATERNITY LEAVE

Educational views on pregnancy have come a long way from the days when female teachers had to swear that they were not married or planning to be married in order to obtain and keep their teaching positions. Indeed, even after school boards accepted married female teachers, they continued to dismiss them if they became pregnant. By all standards of today's education, these past practices seem archaic and primitive.

The rules and guidelines governing most states' handling of maternity leaves are based on the Equal Protection Clause of the Fourteenth Amendment, the Civil Rights Act of 1964, Equal Employment Opportunities Legislations, and numerous test cases.

Present practices in most states regarding maternity leave are: the teacher, both tenured and non-tenured, must give notice of wanting such a leave 30 days prior to ending service; a doctor's certificate may also be required; payments during the leave may be either totally suspended or the person may receive payments for the length of accumulated sick leave only; a teacher cannot be forced to end her teaching at any particular date, but some states have required that a pregnant teacher take maternity leave if she is due within the first two months of a school year; a teacher may return to teaching whenever she is declared fit by her physician, but some states bar her return within a month of the school's closing; and, depending upon the state, jobs will be kept for at least one chronological year from the date of the leave only, or for one school year only, or for one chronological/school year with only one extension allowed.

Whatever the rules and requirements in a particular state, the single biggest change in the granting of maternity leaves has been that pregnancy is now legally handled as an *illness and not a disability.* As such, the teacher's rights are more securely held and understood.

See Also: CIVIL RIGHTS; CONSTITUTIONAL RIGHTS; FOURTEENTH AMENDMENT GUARANTEES; LEAVE OF ABSENCE; PATERNITY LEAVE; PERSONNEL FILES; TENURE.

MATHEMATICS

Often, **Mathematics** or Arithmetic is classified as one of the basics in an academic program. From kindergarten through senior high, a student is exposed to various aspects of this course of study.

There are many disciplines within the core Math curriculum. In the primary grades, the operations of addition and subtraction and the concepts of consecutive counting, currency, number placement, and telling time are given emphasis. In the middle grades, studies of the operations of multiplication and division and the concepts of fractions, decimals, blind equations, and shape and size theorems are begun. Also, logic and word problems are used to enhance problem-solving and deductive reasoning skills. In the high schools and even in some middle schools, Algebra, Geometry, Trigonometry and Calculus are incorporated. Also, alternative counting systems for computers are part of innovations along with others such as alternate bases (New Math) and Metrics, which always keep Math current within a changing technocracy.

Math is not only an integral part of the overall school curriculum, but constitutes one of the "life skills," the attainment of which gives evidence that a person is "educated" according to society.

See Also: ACADEMIC PROGRAM; BASICS; COMPUTERS.

MEDIA

When one thinks of the term **"Media,"** one inevitably thinks of television, radio and newspapers— the so-called "mass-media." Educators often have first-hand knowledge of the workings of these media as a result of interviews and articles in which they are the central points of discussion, either willingly or unwillingly. Indeed, unfavorable media exposure within a district can make an administrator's life distinctly hectic, while favorable attention from the media can help produce passed budgets and positive community support.

Media is a relatively new subject to be taught in the schools. There was no real definition of the word "media" as we know it today prior to 1960, and media as a school subject did not enter the national curriculum until 1972. Today, however, it is not uncommon to see courses in media in general, as well as specific mediums such as TV Production and Filmmaking in the schools, particularly the larger ones.

Media also attempts to study words, their meanings and their connotations. Consequently, media would incorporate the study of propaganda, advertising, consumer education, and various other means of verbal persuasion.

Most media courses are taught under the auspices of the English or Language Arts Department. Advocates of media study claim that in today's world, with the ever-increasing prominence of communications technology and with the mass media playing an increasingly greater role in the daily life of every citizen, a firm knowledge of media is fast becoming a survival skill.

MEDIATION AND MEDIATOR

Mediation and mediator refer to the process of bringing, or the person who brings, two disputing parties together, in order that a settlement may be reached.

In most cases, face-to-face nego-tiations will result in acceptable con-tracts, salary guides and other terms of employment. Occasionally, how-ever, the parties are so far apart that there is the chance of impasse. At that point, or sometimes just before, a mediator may be called in to get the parties back to the bargaining table.

Unlike the fact finder, who can often compel a solution to the dispute, the mediator usually has no power or force, but can only recommend possi-ble solutions. Also, the mediation process carries none of the compunc-tions present in binding arbitration. Even without this power, however, mediation serves a primary purpose in listening "with an open ear" to the grievances of both sides and then placing the parties' focus back on the problem at hand. This "listener," who has no vested interest in the outcome of the dispute, can often defuse an otherwise volatile situation.

Education is finding other uses for the mediation process. Sometimes an "outsider" type of advisory com-mittee is established to bring elements of the community, special interest groups and/or juvenile services to-gether with classroom teachers, su-pervisors, curriculum-coordinators, and administrators to promote better understanding *before* major disputes can develop.

MEDICAL SERVICES

See HEALTH.

MEDICATION

Although actual statutes may vary from state to state, there are very strict guidelines for the use or admin-istering of **medications** in the school. Each school board must get *in writing* all orders concerning recommended first aid procedures, supplies in the health room and acceptable medical practices from the board-appointed school doctor. Once these orders have been signed and distributed to the various health professionals in the dis-trict's schools, most liability has been lifted from the individual health pro-fessional unless the order is exceeded.

When dealing with medication, the guidelines are even stricter.

Dear Parents:

If under exceptional circumstances a child is required to take any medication during school hours, and his attendance at school would not be detrimental to the health or physical well-being of others, the following procedures shall be followed:

1. Wherever possible, the parent shall administer the medication.
2. If the parent is unable to be at the school, medication shall only be administered by the school nurse or other authorized personnel after the following have been received:
   a. A written statement from the parents giving permission to give the medication prescribed by the attending physician.
   b. A written order from the attending physician that shall include:
      i) The child's name and the name of the medication.
      ii) The purpose of the medication, its dosage, and its termination date.
      iii) The possible side effects.
      iv) The medication shall be in its original container.
3. The parents of the child shall assume responsibility for informing the school nurse of any change in the child's health or medication.

The school nurse shall:

1. Inform appropriate school personnel of the medication.
2. Keep a record of the administration of the medication.
3. Keep medication in a locked cabinet.
4. Return unused medication to the parent only.

The school district retains the right to reject requests for the administration of medicine.

Thank you for your cooperation.

Sincerely yours,

Nothing (not tea, aspirin or antacids) can be given to a student by the health professional without *written* orders. Verbal confirmation or permission is not enough either. The health professional must have such written consent *in hand*.

To be certain that they are handling the medication properly, most districts have issued policy statements such as the example shown above, setting procedures that must be followed.

See Also: AUTHORITY, BOARD; AU-THORITY, EXPRESS AND IMPLIED; DRUGS; HEALTH; IMPUTED NEGLIGENCE; LIABILITY; NURSE; PERMISSION SLIPS; STUDENT INFORMATION.

MEET AND CONFER

Meet and confer refers to those statutes that require school boards and representatives of the employee organization to meet, discuss, debate, and decide on conditions of mutual interest in order to reach an agreement.

Most "meet and confer" statutes are falling to compulsory arbitration laws because of a basic flaw in the "meet and confer" concept. Under the strict interpretation of "meet and confer," the boards were only required to listen to employees, *not act.* Once they had listened, the boards could then do whatever they wanted, regardless of the recommendations from employees.

Actually, under "meet and confer," there is a distinct division of roles. Employers will act and employees will recommend. Later interpretations have added "meet and confer in good faith." Still, this left employees trusting to the kindness of the benevolent board. With stronger employee and teacher unions, this was not enough legal commitment to insure that they would get what they felt they should have.

In almost all states, "meet and confer" statutes are now backed by collective bargaining procedures.

See Also: ARBITRATION; BOARD OF EDUCATION; COLLECTIVE BARGAINING; FACT FINDING; GRIEVANCES; HEARINGS; LIAISON; NEGOTIATIONS; PETITIONS; REPRESENTATION; UNIONS.

MENTAL DISTRESS

Mental distress is the result of an action or conduct that constitutes mental stress or pressure and exceeds any reasonable bounds of proper conduct in society; it includes a calculated endangerment of mental well-being, through either intent or negligence.

This relatively new actionable offense has increasingly found its way into education. It strikes at two aspects of administration. First, in *employee relations,* charges of harassment, sexism, prejudicial and/or preferential treatment may all carry a supplementary charge of mental distress. At one time, physical injury had to be shown as a manifestation of mental distress, but this is no longer true. Consequently, working in unsafe conditions, without proper supervision, or with some restriction on "proper teaching" may be used to prove mental distress. There have been several cases of teachers claiming disabilities due to mental distress. While there have been no blanket cases dealing with mental distress, the courts have shown a willingness to review on a case-by-case basis.

The second instance of mental distress concerns the *disciplining of students.* Here again, proof of mental distress used to come from some physical injury, but now the charge can stand alone. The following conditions test for a case of mental distress: was the action in question reasonable, prudent, and in keeping with societal limits, mores and acceptabilities? Therefore, reprimanding a child in front of his peers is acceptable and causes no mental distress, while placing him in a locked coat closet is not. While no physical injury may occur, unreasonable exposure to fear *is* considered injury or mental distress. So far, the courts have no rulings as to the actual limits of mental distress on students, but special interest groups as well as professional educational associations are becoming increasingly aware of actionable offenses.

See Also: ASSAULT; ATHLETICS, SEX DISCRIMINATION IN; CHILD ABUSE; CORPORAL PUNISHMENT; DAMAGES; DEFAMATION; DISCIPLINE; DISCRIMINATION; HABITABLE; HOMOSEXUALS; LIBEL; MALICE; MALICIOUS MISCHIEF; SEXISM; SPECIAL INTEREST GROUPS; SUPERVISION (STAFF); SUPERVISION (STUDENTS).

MENTAL EXAMINATION

A **mental examination** is a test or battery of tests which demonstrate the mental processes of the person being tested.

There are many mental tests used by personnel directors in the business world to show the mental outlook of potential employees. In education, these tests are rarely used, and if given at all, they are done under several rigid restrictions. While a school board may ask a perspective administrator, teacher or staff member to take a mental examination, that examination may *not* contain any part of an intelligence test. Further, because aptitude is one reason for pursuing a career, a completed and validated teaching certificate has been held to be *prima facie* evidence of this aptitude. Therefore, before a school board may give a mental examination,

it must present a valid reason other than checking the intelligence and aptitude of the person being tested. Also, in some cases, the local teacher's association may negotiate the taking or not taking of these tests. It should be noted that school boards do have the right to give such tests. It is only their content and usage that may be discussed.

See Also: APPLICATION; AUTHORITY, BOARD; CERTIFICATION; EQUAL EMPLOYMENT OPPORTUNITIES; PERSONNEL RECORDS; PRIVACY.

MERIT PAY

There are two classifications of **merit pay** that have entered education. One covers increments, steps, or longevity; the other covers incentive, bonuses, or performance. Most districts use the first kind of merit pay. In this instance, the word *pay* in "merit pay" is more important for understanding. For example, two English teachers performing the same duties may receive different salaries. One teacher has been with the district for four years, while the other has been employed for fifteen. The assurance under this type of merit pay is that when the newer teacher reaches the length of service of the older teacher, he or she will also receive a higher salary rate. The differentiated salary guides are very objective. Nothing but longevity, educational status (BA, BA + 10, MA, etc.) or position (department heads, extra contracts, administrators, etc.) are taken into consideration for the differences in pay. The "merits" are known to all, and are under no discussion or "judgments" of others.

In the second type of merit pay, the word *merit* takes more weight. Under this form, teachers could receive increases in pay reflecting differences in performance, changes in supply and demand, and the unequalness of academic fields in comparison with noneducational employment. Here, there are no clear guidelines. Unlike the two previously-mentioned teachers, there is no guarantee, either written or implied, that the newer teacher would ever attain the salary of the older one. Proponents of this kind of merit pay feel that monetary increases should be made available in order to increase the desire for professional improvement and competency. Also, they see these rewards as a means of getting and keeping the best practitioners in education, instead of losing them to the business world. The opponents see merit pay as a threefold problem. First, how and by whom will the teacher be "judged," in order to receive the increased pay? Second, the philosophies of "equal treatment" and "opposition to ranking" are considered cornerstones of American education. Opponents feel that these philosophies could be destroyed. Finally, opponentts see a built-in flaw in performance-based merit pay. Namely, if a teacher does a good job one year and his or her pay goes up, could his or her pay be decreased the next year if the "judge" were not satisfied?

Much is still to be decided on this pivotal question of payment for teaching services.

See Also: DIFFERENTIATED STAFFING; EMPLOYEE RELATIONS; EVALUATION; INCREMENTS; QUALIFICATIONS; SALARY; SUPERVISION (STAFF).

METRICS

See MATHEMATICS.

MIDDLE SCHOOL

A **middle school** is a structure, plant, or philosophy of educational instruction for students, usually in grades 4-8. This is alternately called intermediate school or junior high school.

In the mid 1950s, the need for a further division of the American educational structure was met by the building, staffing, and instigation of the middle school. Elementary schools were presenting the basics in rote and skill learning, and high schools were presenting opportunities for students to apply this material to life expectations, either for further education or careers. The educators of the period were asking for the development of a system of practicing these skills *before* career choices were ready to be made.

Therefore, a basic program was developed for the middle school, namely, a curriculum based upon *experiences*. The aim was not perfection of all skills, but rather multiple samplings of experiences. It was felt that these samplings would then allow the student to develop and pursue those skills, aptitudes and choices that were best suited to his or her needs. Then, upon entering high school, the student would have a better idea of what he or she could do and where he or she was headed, in order to get the most out of the specialized courses given at that level.

The greatest characteristic of the middle school is change. The widest range of extremes are found here, too. The changes that affect the student and society are reflected in extremes of behavior and expectations. The changes in curriculum and evaluation are reflected in the extremes of high and low performances and career/educational goals. The middle school is a progression of knowledge. The student is expected at some later date to be at point "X"; the middle school provides the tools, emotional support, materials, and choices to help the student get there.

Middle schools may be structured along several lines. The most common are the closed traditional type and the open-ended type. Under the closed traditional type, there is teacher-selected content, cognitive-based, teacher-oriented demands, standardized testing, and student conformance to teacher-functioning or behavioral demands. In an open-ended format, there is staff-student use of self-appraisal, staff-student

identification of satisfactory performance levels, the involvement of students in the selection of learning activities, and the implementation of a learner-oriented, personalized classroom.

Within the middle school structure, the "support" personnel of a school district are most active. Since some of the inherent goals of a middle school are the teaching of self-reliance, the building of self-esteem, the nurturing of respect, and the meeting of individual needs, special services, guidance counseling and various supplementary programs are usually present in the school. Also, extracurricular activities, clubs, student government, and student committees are seen as necessary training programs for the social development of the students. Finally, parents are usually very involved in the day-to-day progress, in addition to serving on various committees for influencing the middle school.

See Also: ACADEMIC PROGRAM; AGE LEVELS; CHANGE STRATEGIES; CHILD STUDY TEAMS; CONTRACTED LEARNING; ENRICHMENT; EXTRACURRICULAR ACTIVITIES; GUIDANCE; INDIVIDUALIZATION; LEARNING CENTERS; MINICOURSES; OPEN CLASSROOMS; PARENT CONFERENCES; P.T.A.; SELF-CONTAINED CLASSROOM; STUDENT COUNCIL (STUDENT GOVERNMENT).

MIGRANTS

A **migrant** is a person who is eligible to receive PL96-374 Title I migrant funds because he has moved across school district, county or state lines within the last year for agricultural or food-related processing work.

The plight of traveling workers and their families has historically presented major difficulties for both the migrants themselves and for the educational systems that must deal with them. In order to recognize and somehow ameliorate the educational situation of this group, the federal government passed, as early as 1965 (PL89-10), legislation to provide funding for this project. Many programs were generated by the Departments of Health, Education and Welfare (HEW) and the Department of Labor. The state departments of education, sensing the need for coordinated information, used part of these funds to present the *Migrant Student Record Transfer System* (MSRTS) to the National Diffusion Network for validation. This was accomplished, and all state education departments are now connected by MSRTS to a home computer in Little Rock, Arkansas.

The system was designed to facilitate social and educational continuity for every school-aged migrant child. *The Home-School Liaison-Recruiter* goes to the employer's business or farm and enrolls children in the program. The parents sign a *Migrant Student's Enrollment Form* (MSEF) in order to make their children validated migrant students. At the point of enrollment, the child is assigned a computer number. Complete health records are placed on one computer data sheet and complete social and educational information is placed on another. Each sheet may include contact personnel on the bottom. Recently, a third sheet was added under the *Skills Information System* (SIS). This sheet gives the exact skill mastery attained by the student, from grades pre-K to 12, in Reading, Math, Early Childhood, etc. This data is then entered into the main computer. Working with the Home-School Liaison-Recruiter, the present employer and the next employer, MSRTS can provide a school district with complete records on any migrant child about to enter their district. The information can be made available within 48 hours of the request. The system is constantly and completely monitored to insure accuracy and effectiveness.

Migrant students and their families affect every state and constitute a moving population of as many as six million. Therefore, any local district needing aid may contact and receive assistance from their state MSRTS coordinator.

See Also: CHIEF STATE SCHOOL OFFICIAL; ELEMENTARY AND SECONDARY EDUCATION ACT OF 1965; NONRESIDENTS, ADMISSION OF; PERMANENT RECORDS; STUDENT INFORMATION; TRANSFERS.

MILITARY LEAVE

Military leave is leave granted to a teacher or administrator who has been drafted or who is required to perform duties for the National Guard or military reserve.

Once a staff member has been employed for more than six months, the granting of military leave is mandatory. No salary is required during the time of absence, but the position must be held until the teacher returns. The only exception is that the board may impose a time limit on the absence. If that time limit is overextended, the board may reserve the right to hire a permanent replacement.

See Also: LEAVE OF ABSENCE.

MINI-COURSES

A **mini-course** is a short, concentrated, curricular block of information taught over three to six weeks.

The mini-course is a relatively new scheduling device being used from middle school through high school and college. This device provides several advantages for both students and faculty. The greatest advantage is the "fresh start" offered with the beginning of each new mini-course. A student's enthusiasm usually remains high because of new material and/or new teachers, and also has the allure of choice. He is there because he selected the course. The second advantage is the ability to explore, in-depth, a particular body of facts that might otherwise have been superficially treated in a year-long course. The advantage to the teacher is that of teaching one or two courses

of great personal interest. Some schools offer mini-courses specifically designed around the particular expertise of their faculty, even if this expertise crosses disciplinary lines. For example, a Math teacher may be an expert on Elizabethan Theater and could teach a mini-course in this field rather than one in Math.

Flexible scheduling, highly-motivated students, and involved faculties have made mini-courses an exciting addition to the school's curriculum.

See Also: ACADEMIC PROGRAM; COURSE; COURSE OF STUDY; CURRICULUM DEVELOPMENT; ELECTIVES; ENRICHMENT; INTERDISCIPLINARY APPROACHES; SCHEDULE.

MINISTERIAL ACTS

Ministerial acts are duties that are private in nature, that can be carried out by anyone, *without having to make a decision among various factors,* and thus may be delegated.

The key words of this definition, *"without having to make a decision among various factors,"* are what can either make an administrator liable or remove liability from him or her. If he or she delegated authority to a teacher for any action that required the teacher to make a decision, the administrator is liable for any subsequent result under the concept that there was no authority to delegate that decision in the first place. If, on the other hand, the administrator had assigned a task that could have been performed without making a decision and an accident or unlawful incident subsequently occurred, the administrator is not liable.

Basically, an administrator is within the boundaries of ministerial acts when he assigns a duty that could be carried out equally by any member of the school staff. Within the day-to-day running of a school system, many decisions are made by many people. To insure the full protection under ministerial acts and express and implied authorities, the administrator should become aware of the school board's policy on the delegation of authority and adhere to it carefully.

See Also: ASSIGNMENTS; AUTHORITY, EXPRESS AND IMPLIED; LIABILITY; NEGLIGENCE; SUPERVISION (STAFF).

MINOR

See MAJORITY, AGE OF.

MINORITIES

See ETHNIC MINORITIES or SPECIAL INTEREST GROUPS.

MONTHLY REPORTS

Monthly reports are compilations of materials generated on a monthly basis, within individual buildings and facilities of a school district, for use by the central staff, local school boards, state, or federal authorities.

Few things appear more vexing and time-consuming for the administrator than the preparation of monthly reports. Every day, hundreds of decisions are made by administrators. Also, papers are generated, signed and filed, and then the process is repeated in every office and department in the school. These papers ultimately come to the administrator's attention. Programs implemented within the building need to be monitored. The accounting of money received and spent needs to be made. The list goes on and on.

Each month, the building administrator must formalize these activities in order to report them to the central staff office. There, the central staff must disseminate this information through its own reports, to either the board, the state, or the federal government.

While there will obviously be variations from district to district and from state to state, the most common information included in monthly reports is: *building reports* (maintenance and repairs); *building requisition forms* (non-consumables such as desks, file cabinets, etc.); *attendance* figures (students entered, left, moved within the building, or transferred in or out of the district); *child study team reports* (tests given, students seen, conference reports, decisions reached); *supplemental education report; handicapped children's needs assessment sheet* (also, special classes needs assessment sheet); *total district attendance* (figures of students entered and left); a *suspension list* (of both in- and out-of-school suspensions), assignments to an ASP program, and indications of the beginnings of expulsion procedures; *student activities accounts reports* (deposits, debts and balances); the *attendance officer's report* (on absentees and truants); reports of *milk and lunch money reimbursements; Home Instruction informations; pending court cases* and *decisions* (involving students and teachers); *health reports* (number of students using health office and for what reasons, physicals, visual and auditory testing, and the number and types of communicable diseases); and, *monitoring reports* on any state or federal programs being implemented in the school.

It becomes obvious that there is a need for good record-keeping procedures in all schools.

See Also: CENTRALIZED FILING; CENTRAL STAFF; CLERICAL SERVICES; SECRETARY, SCHOOL; STUDENT INFORMATION; SUPERVISION (STAFF); YEAR-END REPORT.

MORAL TURPITUDE

Moral turpitude is conduct that is contrary to honesty or good morals.

In the military, grounds for detachment are sometimes stated as, "conduct unbecoming...." Charges of moral turpitude are as close as Education comes to this concept. Basically, moral turpitude is the charge against a teacher or administrator, of behavior that interferes with the performance of their duties and responsibilities.

To support this charge for dismissal, however, at least one of three major criteria must be proven: *conviction of a crime of a sexual nature;* knowingly having made *false statements concerning application for a certificate;* and, *gross negligence or gross unfitness.* Because an individual may consider proper a conduct that the community does not, the courts are quite anxious that the teacher/administrator's rights to privacy are not violated. The board must prove that the conduct in question has prevented the employee from fulfilling some *educational* duty. If this cannot be proven, the court will not permit the dismissal.

See Also: BREACH OF CONTRACT; BURDEN OF PROOF; CODE OF ETHICS; DISMISSAL OF PERSONNEL; FIFTH AMENDMENT GUARANTEES; FOURTH AMENDMENT GUARANTEES; PRIVACY; SELF-INCRIMINATION; SPECIAL INTEREST GROUPS; SUPERVISION (STAFF).

MORATORIUM

A **moratorium** is a legal authorization, usually by a law or an order passed in an emergency, to delay payment or services for a specified period.

When budgets are planned, school boards attempt to make expenditures last for an entire school year. Bills are paid as they occur. Occasionally, however, particularly in times of high inflation or emergencies, the budgetary estimates fall short of actual requirements. At these times, the budgetary agent, either local boards or even state and federal agencies, may call for either a suspension of services or a delay of payment if the services are considered essential.

For example, a local board may have allocated fifteen thousand dollars for field trips. If the allotment is greatly depleted by November, the board may wish to place a moratorium on field trips until May or June. In fact, if all monies are tight in a district, field trips may be suspended for the rest of the year, until September.

Likewise, if the allocation for fuel oil is insufficient because of unexpectedly cold weather, a board may delay payment to the oil company while still receiving fuel, until such a time as the weather changes or other funds are made available.

Moratoriums are rare occurrences, but procedures for them should appear as a regular part of the policy statements of the board. Then, if an emergency does arise, implementation can be clear and precise.

See Also: AUTHORITY, BOARD; BUDGET; DEBTS; FINANCE; PURCHASING.

MOVIES

Movies are a valuable part of the audio-visual aids used in teaching. Since a movie involves both auditory and visual senses and is usually professionally produced, it is likely to inspire a high level of retention in the viewer. Moreover, an enormous number of movies are available to educators on the widest variety of subjects for all levels, from kindergarten through graduate school. These movies are made available through various educational supply houses, either by direct purchase or rental. Also, many community and county libraries maintain movie libraries from which educators may borrow, either free or at a nominal charge. Both the supply houses and the libraries often publish catalogs that describe the content of the film, indicate whether it is produced in black and white or color, and give the time length of the presentation.

Movies are often used as part of assembly programs. It must be remembered that no admission may be charged as a prerequisite for viewing the film if it is presented as part of a school-wide assembly program or during normal school time. Admission may be charged, however, as a fund-raising event if the movie is shown after regular school hours.

It is always wise to preview all movies shown to students. No educator would wish a child to be embarrassed because of a racial or ethnic stereotype as sometimes occurs in older movies, nor would an educator wish children to be exposed to material that might be intended for a more mature audience.

In many schools, courses in Film

Making and Movie Appreciation are part of the Media or Language Arts curriculum.

See Also: AUDIO-VISUAL MATERIALS; LIBRARY AND MEDIA CENTER; MEDIA; SUPPLIES AND EQUIPMENT.

Music

Music is a part of the curriculum for grades K-12. It is felt that Music is an experience that should be shared by every student in the school. Many aspects of musical expression are, therefore, available in most schools. Assembly programs and concerts usually include either whole-school singalongs or classwide performances. Special clubs for vocal or instrumental music are also available for those interested. In some districts, actual course credit may be given for choral activities.

As with band activities, choral groups may appear as representatives of the school at outside events. Public performances of student groups are seen by educators as excellent opportunities for acquainting the public with the quality and results of its academic program. Also, merely taking part in such performances acts as incentives for excellence, growth in self-esteem and interest in school on the part of students.

The school may set qualifications for special music groups, but if it does, it must *only* use ability as its criteria. Also, it has been held that requiring certain attire for concerts or other performances does not violate a student's right to free expression in dress.

Music is another example of the "life experiences" offered in the schools.

See Also: ACADEMIC PROGRAM; BAND.

N

NATIONAL ASSESSMENT

The **National Assessment of Educational Progress** is a continuing national survey of the knowledge, skills, understanding, and attitudes of young Americans in major learning areas usually taught in the schools. It represents a unique, cooperative undertaking by the education community and the federal government.

The National Assessment of Educational Progress (NAEP) has been in existence since 1964. Although its initial planning and development phase (1964-69) was funded by foundations (the Carnegie Corporation, the Ford Foundation, and the Fund for the Advancement of Education), funding shifted to the federal government when NAEP began collecting data in 1969. Because of concern about federal control, NAEP was administratively placed with the Education Commission of the States (ECS), an interstate compact of 48 states, American Samoa, Puerto Rico, and the Virgin Islands, whose goal is the improvement of education at all levels. Composed of governors, chief state school officers, legislators, and educators, ECS established an Assessment Policy Committee for NAEP to make it accountable and responsible to both the public and the educational community.

NAEP was initially funded by the U.S. Office of Education through a grant. In 1973, The National Center for Education Statistics assumed federal administrative responsibility and funded it through a sole-source contract. As part of the Educational Amendments Act of 1978, a statutory basis for National Assessment was explicitly established; an independent NAEP governing body with subscribed membership was established to remove any doubts about federal control; and federal administrative responsibility for the program was transferred to the National Institute of Education (NIE). The Education Commission of the States was awarded a four-year grant by NIE to continue national assessment through 1983.

The objectives of NAEP are to collect census-like data on the educational attainments of major portions of our nation's youth, and to measure the growth or decline in educational attainment that takes place over time in key learning areas. The assessments were not intended to be another kind of standardized testing program. There are no norms, scores, standards, or comparisons of individuals, school districts or states. They were not intended to state what students *should* know, but rather to compile accurate information on what students actually *do know and are capable of doing*.

NAEP develops "exercise packages" to assess Art, Career and Occupational Development, Citizenship/Social Studies, Mathematics, Music, Reading/Literature, Science, and Writing. During each data collection effort, the "exercise packages" for one or more learning areas are administered to nation-wide sample samples of 9-, 13-, and 17-year-olds. Young adults, ages 26 through 35, are also surveyed periodically. Scoring and analysis of the exercises are done in terms of how well the nation and groups of people within the nation are meeting desired goals established by scholars, educators and concerned lay people in each of the learning areas. Results are reported for each assessment exercise, and are also summarized to show the relative performance of certain groups. At each age-group, results are available by sex, race, geographic region, community size and type, and parental education.

Controversy over the concept of a national assessment continues. Proponents state that with a national assessment, everyone, at all educational levels, would have a chance to influence educational goals and, consequently, would become more involved with them. Also, this faction states that more monies could be applied to those areas of greatest need (i.e., areas and/or groups with low national averages). The opponents contend that national assessments logically lead to an imposition of curricular changes to conform with national requirements. They are quick to point out that education is the constitutional responsibility of the states and not of the federal government, and that national assessment is just another way to weaken the control of local districts over their own schools. Finally, they claim that comparisons, rankings and other distinctions could be detrimental to the well-being of the students.

Whatever the controversy, NAEP does perform many valuable services. Results published by National Assessment are being used by many national organizations involved in teaching in the schools, by local and district administrators, by curriculum coordinators, etc. For further information, inquiries may be made to:

National Assessment of
  Educational Progress
1860 Lincoln Street
Suite 700
Denver, Colorado 80295
(303) 830-3732

See Also: CHIEF STATE SCHOOL OFFICIAL; EDUCATION COMMISSION OF THE STATES.

NATIONAL EDUCATION ASSOCIATION

The **National Education Association** (NEA) is a professional organization of educators founded in 1857.

The NEA's stated goals are to serve as the national voice of education, to advance the cause of education for all individuals, to promote professional excellence among educators, to gain recognition of the basic importance of the teacher in the learning process, to protect the rights of educators and advance their interests and welfare, to secure professional autonomy, to unite educators for effective citizenship, to promote and protect human and civil rights, and to obtain for its members the benefits of an independent, united teaching profession.

The NEA is composed of various committees who work in conjunction with state and local teacher organizations to promote their goals.

Chartered by Congress in 1906, the Association has a growing membership of over two million educators throughout the nation.

Inquiries may be addressed to:

National Education Association
1201 16th Street, N.W.
Washington, DC 20036

See Also: AMERICAN ASSOCIATION OF SCHOOL ADMINISTRATORS; AMERICAN COUNCIL ON EDUCATION; AMERICAN FEDERATION OF TEACHERS; NEA-PAC; PROFESSIONAL ASSOCIATIONS FOR SCHOOL ADMINISTRATORS; PROFESSIONAL ASSOCIATIONS FOR TEACHERS; UNISERV; WORLD CONFEDERATION OF THE TEACHING PROFESSION.

NATIONAL HONOR SOCIETY

Excellence in scholarship and achievement has always been given a high priority in most school systems. The first honor society aimed at promoting high scholarship in America's secondary schools was Phi Beta Sigma, founded in 1903 at South Side Academy in Chicago. In 1921, the Department of Secondary School Principals' National Education Association founded the **National Honor Society,** which today is sponsored by the National Association of Secondary School Principals. Thousands of high schools maintain local chapters, and hundreds of thousands of students have become members.

There are other national organizations, among which are the National Thespians, the National Forensic League, and the Quill and Scroll. Certain commercial firms and civic groups have gotten the idea of fostering additional organizations that purport to be national in scope. Some have not been too successful, but the effort is a commentary on the effectiveness of national achievement societies such as the National Honor Society.

One advantage of having a chapter is that students with particular talents are given official recognition. Also, members are often dedicated to rendering service to worthwhile school and community endeavors such as assisting in tutorial services, working in the library and assisting with youth groups.

It is important to establish standards and develop objective techniques for electing students to honor groups. Problems may develop when the student body, the parents and/or the community are given the impression that only conforming students or "teacher's pets" will be selected. This difficulty can be avoided by spelling out conditions for membership and providing sufficient public information concerning selection processes.

See Also: ACHIEVEMENT; ACTIVITIES; CLUBS; GIFTED STUDENTS; HONOR ROLL; QUALIFICATIONS; RECOMMENDATION; SCHOLARSHIP; STUDENT INFORMATION.

NEA-PAC

NEA-PAC is an abbreviation that stands for the National Education Association Political Action Committee.

This organization, which functions at the national level, has the stated objective of aiding in the election to federal office of those candidates who support federal legislation that is consistent with the policies established by the NEA.

Funds for the support of NEA-PAC come chiefly from the contributions of the membership. The NEA formally requests a one-dollar yearly contribution from every teacher, and the various state associations are free to develop their own systems of soliciting contributions.

NEA-PAC helps federal candidates whom they classify as "friends of education." They may, for example, make a financial contribution to the campaign of such a candidate. Whether or not the contribution is made, they will send a letter endorsing the candidate to members and media, urging his or her election.

Candidates are endorsed by NEA-PAC upon study by the parent body (NEA) and a recommendation of acceptance from the appropriate state affiliate.

See Also: NATIONAL EDUCATION ASSOCIATION; POLITICS AND THE SCHOOL; SPECIAL INTEREST GROUPS.

NEEDS ASSESSMENT

When an administrator senses that a change is needed either in structure, scheduling, curriculum, or a social aspect of a school or district, a series of decisions is called for. While these decisions can, indeed, be made solely on value judgments, the success of the change is more likely if a formalized system of evaluation is used. This is called **needs assessment.**

A needs assessment has four steps. The first step is to *identify areas of concern*. To do this, one would either draw up a questionnaire, take lists of concerns from small group discussions, or take formal reports from advisory committees at various educational levels. This list of concerns is then divided into specific areas such as curriculum, methods of instruction, conduct, etc. Then the areas are ranked along some span such as highly important to not important. The highest ranked items then become the concern of the needs assessment.

The second step is to *determine what the conditions are* (the reality of the present). Data is gathered in order to determine what exists. This data gathering is formally delineated as to the personnel involved and the methods and duration of the process. Accuracy is vital; statistical proof is not. Hence, the group may use informal observations, formal and informal conversations, and any records available.

The third step is called *values clarification* (hopes of the future). All goals set by the board, the state, the curriculum, and the teachers are formally set down. These goals are examined to see if they were valid in the first place, and if they accurately reflected what everyone wanted. These goals are then changed, added to or deleted, in order to bring those goals into line with the priorities of the present.

The final step is to *list the needs* as expressed in the differences between what is presently done and the goals expected. The goals that show the widest difference from what is presently done should be the point of attack for the first series of changes. Concrete decisions should then be made as to how the gaps should be closed. And, finally, a time limit should be placed to insure a further study to see if what was needed was done.

Once the process is familiar, implementation of a needs assessment or any other change strategy affords the administrator unparalleled opportunities for involvement, relevancy and educational growth at all levels of the school.

See Also: CHANGE STRATEGIES; EMPLOYEE RELATIONS; EVALUATION; GOALS AND OBJECTIVES; STUDENT INFORMATION; SUPERVISION (STAFF); WORKSHOPS AND IN-SERVICE.

NEGLIGENCE

Negligence is the unintended doing, or the lack of doing an act that subsequently causes wrongful injury to another; it is the failure to use reasonable care to avoid injury.

The concept of negligence is not generally defined by statute, but rather has developed through the precedents of court decisions.

There are four components to the charge of negligence. Again, by precedent, each has been defined. The first factor is *duty*. Since the student is considered a "ward" of the school, it is deemed the duty of a teacher or administrator to eliminate dangerous conditions, protect the students and come to their aid. The main definition of this court-defined duty is "maintenance of safety."

The second factor of negligence is *violation*. Here, the court asks the question, "Did the person charged with negligence act in a way which any reasonable and prudent teacher/administrator/peer would have acted in the same or similar circumstances?" If the answer is yes, then no negligence occurred; if not, this constitutes a *violation*.

The third factor is *cause*. Now the court asks, "Did the act, for which the charge is brought, occur because of something that was done or not done by the person charged?" In some cases, it is easy to prove *sole cause,* while in others, contributory, comparative or imputed negligence may be present.

The last factor is *injury.* Without injury, there is no liability. Damages are awarded relative to the injuries incurred. Punitive damages are rare, but may be awarded if grievous mental or physical injury exists and/or there was gross negligence.

All factors of negligence must be present, for if any are missing, the charge will not be upheld.

See Also: COMPARATIVE NEGLIGENCE; CONTRIBUTORY NEGLIGENCE; IMPUTED NEGLIGENCE; LIABILITY; NONFEASANCE; PARENTAL LIABILITY; SUPERVISION (STAFF); SUPERVISION (STUDENTS).

NEGOTIATIONS

Negotiation is the process that may be used in any face-to-face conflict. Practitioners and theoreticians alike agree that the process is vital to any decision-making machinery present in the school.

Many areas are presently being handled through negotiations, not just the more publicized areas of teacher salaries and welfare. In fact, no listing of items negotiated during any given year at all levels of education is possible, for whatever people can discuss from different points of view can be placed into negotiations. Generally, wages, hours, and terms and conditions of employment, as well as anything not specifically denied under state bargaining laws, are negotiable. The few items listed as "inherent managerial policy" are still not considered negotiable, because school boards have been upheld on a review of their needs for discretionary powers. Still, there are more elements of education on the table than ever before.

At the present time, there are over two million teachers involved in some type of professional association. This has had a profound effect on personnel administration. First, the board/central staff can no longer make unilateral decisions and expect them to be carried out without discussion. Second, negotiating teams can be and are selected from many levels of interest. Third, presently bilateral or even multilateral discussions take place before, during and after any major decision is made.

Because of the expectations of "good faith" dealings (ofttimes codified under Meet and Confer Statutes), negotiations may not always have the sting of collective bargaining, compulsory arbitration, fact finding, etc. It is only when one or both parties feel that the "good faith" binders are not enough that the process gets more legalistic and formal, sometimes reaching the stages of impasse, strikes and injunctions.

The traditional parties involved in negotiations are the local board of education and central staff on one side, with the teachers and staff organizational representatives on the other. This has left the building administrators in a very awkward position, for they are caught between the two. They are not actually members of the central staff, but are seen by some teachers' groups as "management" anyway. The principals found themselves with contractual obligations they didn't help decide, with policies to be implemented in which they had no say, and with losses of discretionary powers for which they had no opportunity to fight. It was apparent that they needed a voice for their unique position. Within the negotiation process now, there is usually a representative of the building administration to insure that their voice is heard. Also, these representatives sometimes act as liaison to both teacher and central staff groups.

The most common misconception is that there is a "negotiations season" that begins sometime before a contract expires. Closer to the truth is that good employee relations, group decision-making, active and fair grievance procedures, and free and open communication at all levels are ongoing components of a successful negotiations process.

See Also: ACADEMIC FREEDOM; ARBITRATION; COLLECTIVE BARGAINING; CONTRACTS; DEMANDS; EMPLOYEE RELATIONS; FACT FINDING; GRIEVANCES; IMPASSE; MEDIATION AND MEDIATOR; MEET AND CONFER; UNISERV.

NEW POLICY OR PROGRAM

See CHANGE STRATEGIES and NEEDS ASSESSMENT.

NEWS COVERAGE

Within any given school year, positive events occur in the school district which, in the opinion of those involved, should be shared with the general public. School boards, mindful that favorable public opinion helps pass budgets, often urge administrators to publicize the good things that are taking place in the school. Consequently, there may be a number of times when **news coverage** is desired.

Let something negative or violent happen in a school, and news media will come looking for the administrator. If the event is positive, however, administrators often find themselves frantically searching for some type of news media that will agree to cover it. In fairness to the news media, a photo of first graders presenting a play is not the type of front page material that sells newspapers. And, with hectic schedules and tight budgets, newspapers are highly selective in assigning reporters and photographers.

Administrators may wish to establish personal contact with the local news media. An established personal relationship can work wonders in getting press coverage. Often, it helps if the administrator offers to provide the press with written stories and developed photographs. Every school can find someone who is good with a camera and/or words. If a school event is written up and photographed within the school and then sent to the media, it stands a better chance of being published.

Administrators must be aware of the board's policy on granting interviews, having newspeople in the schools, and the extent and scope of their power to comment. The school has been held to be a public building. Consequently, the press has the right of access. This can be particularly troublesome during times of internal distress within the school.

See Also: COMMUNICATION; MEDIA; NEWSLETTER; NEWS RELEASES.

NEWSLETTER

A **newsletter** is an in-house publication containing items of interest or concern to the selective group it reaches.

There are many types of newsletters that may be used effectively in education. The community newsletter is intended for the taxpayers in the area served by the district. It aims at detailing positive information on the school system as a whole, as well as outlining the ways in which tax monies have been used with positive results. The *parental newsletter* is intended for the parents of children in one particular school, and it provides information on the activities in that school, the accomplishments of its students and faculty, and other public relations items. The *employee newsletter* is distributed to the faculty and staff of a school or school system. It details the accomplishments of individuals, gives news of upcoming events and explains and/or examines issues of interest to faculty and staff.

The content and style of a newsletter will vary depending on the audience for whom it is intended and the material covered. In general, the tone of a newsletter should be conversational and warm. A newsletter should not attempt to be a newspaper, but it must be viewed as a public relations vehicle that affords an opportunity to establish a positive attitude toward the school system.

A newsletter should be positive, detailing accomplishments, rather than dwelling on shortcomings or failures. It is important, however, that negative issues not be ignored. To do so would give the impression that the school system was unwilling to face up to facts. Rather, a newsletter can be used to acknowledge the unfavorable issue and then present the school's point of view in a clear, forthright manner.

The newsletter has proven value. Whether it consists of several mimeographed sheets or is professionally printed, the newsletter can be used to promote good feelings and disseminate information in a highly effective way.

See Also: BULLETIN; COMMUNICATION; EMPLOYEE RELATIONS; MEDIA; NEWS COVERAGE; NEWS RELEASES.

NEWS RELEASES

Schools constantly produce events that they wish to have publicized. Induction into the National Honor Society, a student-sponsored fund-raising activity for a worthy cause, a speaker, play or special assembly—these and more are all occasions for favorable public relations and positive press coverage. As outlined under NEWS COVERAGE, articles on these events that are prepared and written within the school, then forwarded to the press, stand a good chance of being published.

In writing a **news release,** one must remember to follow good journalistic practices. The first paragraph should contain the who, what, when, where, and possibly the why of the event. Hence, a lead paragraph might read, "Twelve juniors and seniors at Rock Township High School will be inducted into the National Honor Society during a ceremony to be held at 8 p.m. on May 14, at the High School Auditorium." Thereafter, subsequent paragraphs would mention details such as the names of those involved, the particulars of the event and any other pertinent information.

A news release sent to a newspaper must often be cut to fit available space, so it is wise to write the article in what is called the "inverted-pyramid" style. That is, the first paragraph contains the most important information, the second paragraph contains the next most important, and so on, down to the final paragraphs containing information that is not essential to the understanding of the article. The article may then be cut from the bottom and still retain its integrity.

The writer must also avoid editorializing. Personal opinion as to the merits or drawbacks of a situation has no place in a news release and is likely to be deleted by the newspaper. The facts must speak for themselves.

Many larger school districts employ the full-time services of a public relations officer who is the district's spokesman to the press. News media are often more inclined to deal with a single individual who will provide them with newsworthy events than with a number of people on a school-to-school basis.

See Also: COMMUNICATION; MEDIA; NEWS COVERAGE; NEWSLETTER.

NONFEASANCE

Three words are often used interchangeably, even though there are subtle differences. These are malpractice, malfeasance, and **nonfeasance.** Basically, they all deal with some non-performance of an action along a standardized, acceptable mode of conduct. While malpractice may be punishable by criminal action, malfeasance and nonfeasance generally involve civil suits.

In education, nonfeasance is the charge brought under the factor of "duty" in a negligence action.

See Also: NEGLIGENCE.

NON-PROFESSIONAL

See AIDES; AUXILIARY PERSONNEL; BUS AND BUS DRIVERS; CAFETERIA; CLERICAL SERVICES; CONSULTANTS; CUSTODIAL SERVICES; POLICE; P.T.A.; SECRETARY; STUDENT TEACHER; SUBSTITUTE TEACHER; VOLUNTEERS.

NON-PUBLIC SCHOOLS

See PRIVATE AND PAROCHIAL SCHOOLS.

NONRENEWAL OF CONTRACT

In sports, players find themselves out of a job when no one picks up their options for the next season. Teachers and staff members can also find themselves not rehired for the new year.

There is very little that the employee can do to combat **nonrenewal.** In most states, in fact, no reason or cause for nonrenewal need be given. Usually the procedures for due process protections used in the dismissal of personnel are the only means available to protest nonrenewal. Therefore, the board must be sure that the nonrenewal was not based on rumors, hearsay or false facts, that no violation of constitutional rights took place, that written policies and procedures existed and were accurately followed, that sufficient time was given to the person being discharged to prepare for a hearing, and that adequate notice was given to show the board's intent not to renew the contract.

The board may be asked to present concrete evidence for the nonrenewal. Generally, this is done through the observations and evaluations kept in the personnel file of the employee. Accompanying this data, there must also be evidence that adequate time and information was given to the employee to change in order to conform to the board's standards.

See Also: AUTHORITY, BOARD; DISMISSAL OF PERSONNEL; REDUCTION IN FORCE; SUPERVISION (STAFF).

NONRESIDENTS, ADMISSION OF

Admission of nonresidents refers to the attendance of a student in one school or district while living under the jurisdiction of another.

There is a wide variety within the states' statutes on the subject of the admission of nonresidents. Usually, the state education departments leave this decision to the discretion of local boards. The states do, however, require that local schools admit the nonresidents if these students need special equipment and/or facilities and none exist in their own districts. The local board accepting the nonresident may require a tuition payment.

In general practice, when parents wish to send a student to school outside the local school district, they must petition the board and *they* pay the tuition. If the local board uses the facilities of another system for the education of one or more of its students, the sending district pays the tuition. These fees may not be unreasonable and are usually based on the per-child costs to resident families.

Without state statutes, total discretion on the matter of both admission and tuition are left to the local district boards.

See Also: ADDRESS (RESIDENCE); RESIDENCE; SHARED-TIME; STUDENT INFORMATION; TRANSPORTATION.

NON-TENURED TEACHER

See PROBATIONARY TEACHER.

NURSE

The **nurse** is the health professional responsible for insuring the school's maintenance of health standards and protection.

The school nurse is one of the most important auxiliary personnel actively involved with the day-to-day operations of the school building. Qualifications for a school nurse may vary from state to state, but generally, they include at least a three-year certificate of nursing or even a B.A. degree in the field. Commonly, extra courses in Child Psychology, Education and Administration are also required for school nurses.

Their duties, functions and responsibilities are written as a part of the district's policy. The medical services they provide are under the direction of the board-appointed physician. The school nurse may also be a part of the child study team and work with the community on health-related projects.

See Also: AUXILIARY PERSONNEL; CHILD STUDY TEAM; DIAGNOSIS; FAMILY SERVICES; FIRST AID; HEALTH; IMMUNIZATIONS, INOCULATIONS AND VACCINATIONS; MEDICATION; MONTHLY REPORTS; YEAR-END REPORT.

O

OATHS

The U.S. Supreme Court has been wrestling with the problem of the legality of various types of **oaths** for over a hundred years. The teaching profession has generated numerous challenges to the requiring of loyalty oaths as prerequisites for teaching. As early as 1952, in the case of *Wieman v. Updegraff*, 344 U.S. 183 (1952), the Supreme Court ruled such oaths were unconstitutional. Still, the loyalty oath question arises periodically in various districts. When it does, there is a rule of thumb that may be used to protect the rights of prospective employees.

This rule stems from the Supreme Court decision in the case of *Cole v. Richardson*, 92 S.Ct. 1332 (1972), that stated that if the oath was aimed at defending the country and did not speak of past, present or future associations, then the 1st, 4th, 5th, and 14th amendment rights of the individual were upheld. It should be noted, however, that a close examination of current practices, as well as any shifts, clarifications or reversals at the Supreme Court level should be undertaken if loyalty oaths are considered in a district.

Aside from loyalty oaths, various positions, from President of the United States, to mayors, to school board members, require an oath of office. These brief statements generally state that the person will do whatever it is that they were elected or appointed to do. Again, no violation of constitutional rights takes place unless the oath infers, states or requires the loss of freedom of association, speech or access.

See Also: CIVIL RIGHTS; CONSTITUTIONAL RIGHTS; FIFTH AMENDMENT GUARANTEES; FIRST AMENDMENT GUARANTEES; FOURTEENTH AMENDMENT GUARANTEES; FOURTH AMENDMENT GUARANTEES; FREE SPEECH; PLEDGE OF ALLEGIANCE; POLITICS AND THE SCHOOL; ACTIVITY; PRIVACY; SELF-INCRIMINATION.

OBSERVATION (TEACHER EVALUATION)

Mention **observations** in the academic community and the reaction is similar to the red-flag-and-bull rumpus. Everyone thinks they should be done; nobody wants to do them; and nobody agrees with them after they are done. Everyone thinks they are a good technique of evaluation; no one can agree on how to evaluate. The arguments go on and on.

Two main points in the controversy should be understood. The first concerns the rights and protections of the teachers and administrators during the observation process. The second considers the validity of using them for evaluation.

First, the *procedure*—allowing for variations within the states, teachers are generally observed in their classrooms at least twice a year. According to the written policies of the particular district, a *notice* is given from the observer, usually the building principal or another supervisor, to the classroom teacher of an upcoming observation. The day, class and duration of the observation is given in that notice. The notice should be given far enough in advance to allow adequate preparation. Next, the teacher has the *option* of either agreeing to the time set or requesting an alternate class or time. The next step is the *actual observation period*. Each district has its protocol for the in-class behavior of the administrator. Some enter into the teaching environment, while oth-

ers remain carefully in the background. After (or in some cases, during) the observation, the administrator composes and signs an *observation sheet,* which states what was observed. Any praise, recommendations or criticisms are also added to the sheet. The sheet is then given to the teacher, and *a conference* is set for a discussion between the administrator and the teacher. At that conference, the teacher may address any point brought up that concerns the observation. At the close of this conference, the *teacher* signs his or her name to the sheet. If, at this time, the teacher disagrees with anything noted on the observation sheet, he or she may state this objection directly on the sheet before signing it. The sheet is then placed in the *personnel file* of the teacher. It should be remembered that the above procedures are general in nature and will vary greatly from district to district.

Second, there are arguments that center around the validity of observation as an evaluation tool. The contention is stated as follows: for an evaluation to be valid, it must be capable of being repeated by one or more people, at one or more different times, to insure equalness of data gathering; then a comparison must be made to show decline or growth. Under the usual guidelines of teacher observations, these criteria are impossible. The observer is subjective, and the reports call for subjective conclusions. Whatever thoughts, preconceptions and knowledge the observer brings into the classroom will naturally color what they see and hear. Such predispositions, then, eliminate any validity of the observation. Yet, if the observer uses any of the many forms of objective observation sheets, teachers claim that these leave no room for pupil-teacher interactions or other social aspects of teaching.

At present, research is being done to clarify the use, procedures and compilations of observations. Changes are undoubtedly going to be made to get the most from this educational practice.

See Also: ACADEMIC FREEDOM; EVALUATION; PERSONNEL FILES; SUPERVISION, STAFF.

OFFERS OF CONTRACTS AND RECRUITING

Today, the market in education favors the employer. There are sometimes twenty or more applicants for every position available. Even so, local boards must have policies and procedures to insure the best choice of prospective candidates.

There are several steps that must be followed before any hiring can be done. First, a *survey of personal movement* should be taken. How many members of the staff usually leave? How many are internally promoted? How many retire? How many short-term leaves are granted? How many return from leaves? These are just some of the questions for the survey. Second, *procedures for re-*

cruitment must be set. By what means will the system recruit? How much money has been allocated for recruiting activities (visitations, lectures, interviews, etc.)? How and by whom will the screening be done? Finally, decisions must be made on compliance procedures the board of education will follow regarding state and federal statutes for offering employment.

While practices may be slightly different throughout the country, all **offers of contracts** must fulfill the following requirements: First, the offer must be *genuine*. That is, there must be a real job available, and the board must have the authority to fill it. Second, the offers cannot be based on any criteria except *stated qualifications*. There can be no infringement upon the potential employee's civil or constitutional rights. Third, *full disclosure* of the starting date, the duration of the contract, and the compensation to be paid must all appear as part of the offer.

In many larger districts there is either a personnel department, or else a member of the central staff who has recruiting and hiring as a sole responsibility. In this situation, all administrators should express their needs throughout the department, rather than petitioning directly to the board.

No matter if the district is large or small, the search for the best qualified and competent future employees should be ongoing, not just at the end of an academic year. Planning ahead will ensure the district's getting the right person for the right job.

See Also: APPLICATION; AUTHORITY, BOARD; CONTRACTS; EQUAL EMPLOYMENT OPPORTUNITIES; INTERVIEW.

OPEN CLASSROOMS

Somewhere from the rigidness of the 40s and 50s and the permissiveness of the 60s, a more credible system of class management and instruction reached acceptance in the 70s. The philosophy of the first system might have been stated as, "The teacher is there to teach, and the students are there to learn whatever is being taught." The radical second system might have been stated as, "The child is only going to learn what he or she wants to; the teacher can only expose him to everything possible, and he will take what he needs." The compromise philosophy prevalent in today's classroom seems to state, "The student must adjust to society's standards, but he may do so at a pace and in a manner acceptable to both himself and the teacher."

In an **open classroom,** teachers act as initiators of units or lessons. Then, through instructional methods such as lectures, small group work, programmed materials, learning packets, learning centers, and independent study projects, they encourage the students to make their own learning schedules and discoveries. To ensure that a complete program is followed by both the teacher and student, the curriculum must incorporate multilevel instruction. The student "con-

tracts" for the work to be accomplished within a certain space of time.

Some of the stated goals of open classrooms are: the students should acquire habits and attitudes that will permit them to become responsible and contributing members of society; they should understand the need for wide use of human, natural and material resources; and, they should obtain optimum proficiencies in the basics. Because of these goals, there is much emphasis placed on both basic and creative skills. There is also a firm belief that individuals need to be both externally *and* internally disciplined.

There are some serious pros and cons of the open classroom. Those in favor of the practice claim that education has finally become relevant by teaching life skills. The students not only learn subjects but also how to work, schedule their time, work and share with others, and control their own environment. Those educators who oppose the concept of open classrooms grant that these objectives are laudable. Their objections are not with the intent but with the implementation. Teachers are asked to be structured and directing (intervening) during one instructional period, then flexible and nondirecting (non-intervening) in the next. This dichotomy is difficult for some teachers and impossible for others. The second issue the opponents raise is that of the maturity of the students. Some students react very well to an open classroom, while others are confused, frustrated and produce less than they would in a more traditional classroom.

Prior to starting an open classroom, administrators should work closely with curriculum supervisors, the faculty and parents to insure complete understanding of how the program will function. Also, it has been suggested that within the scheduling options, the administrator sets aside at least one classroom per grade for those students needing a more structured format. Finally, complete evaluation procedures should be decided upon beforehand, to be certain that the program is performing as expected.

See Also: ACADEMIC PROGRAM; CHILD-CENTERED; CLASS AND CLASS SIZE; CONTRACTED LEARNING; INDIVIDUALIZATION; INSTRUCTION; LEARNING CENTERS; PARENT CONFERENCES; SCHEDULE; STUDENT INFORMATION; SUPERVISION (STAFF); SUPERVISION (STUDENTS); UNGRADED; WORKSHOP AND INSERVICE.

OPEN COMMUNICATIONS

See COMMUNICATIONS.

OPEN HEARING

See HEARINGS.

OPEN HOUSE

An **Open House** is a public relations event in which parents and the general public are invited into the school to tour, observe and generally get acquainted with the facilities and personnel.

As the name implies, during an Open House, the school is opened to visitors from the community. Usually, the community is enthusiastic in accepting an open invitation to see the educational facilities that serve their children, and attendance is high. An Open House is a natural activity for special times such as during American Education Week.

The Open House has several advantages. It is an excellent way of sponsoring positive public relations and community support, especially if visitors can be provided with good experiences they can carry back to the community. It can help dispel unfavorable rumors about a school, as parents see for themselves what is taking place. It provides students and teachers with an opportunity to present to the public the fine things they have been doing. Finally, it provides a sense of openness, which assures the public that the schools are functioning well and have nothing to hide.

An Open House can have its drawbacks, however. Classes can be upset and disrupted, the flow of traffic in the halls can come to a standstill if groups of visitors block entrances, and a school can become rather tumultuous as students recognize parents and neighbors.

The key to avoiding these difficulties is planning. Teachers and staff should be given sufficient warning in order that preparations can be made. A system utilizing student guides to accompany parents on tours of the school should be implemented. Definite time limits should be established and adhered to. Finally, special events such as art shows and talent assemblies are excellent activities to schedule for the day.

When well-planned and executed, an "Open House" can be a success for everyone involved.

See Also: ACTIVITIES; AMERICAN EDUCATION WEEK; BACK-TO-SCHOOL NIGHT; BULLETIN; NEWS RELEASES; SCHEDULE.

OPENING PROCEDURES

Opening procedures are those practices and actions taken on or before the first day or week of a new school year.

The key word when dealing with this subject is *preparation*. The administrators and staffs who wait to initiate opening procedures until the first student enters the building, can safely assume that they are immediately two or three weeks *behind*. While each district may set its own policy, a consensus of several states and local districts had led to a reasonable checklist and time line of activities.

In the example to follow, "T" refers to opening day, "T − " refers to time before opening day, and "T + " refers to time after the year has started.

T − 3 weeks: Block scheduling should be completed. All teachers should be notified by mail of their classroom numbers, duty assignments and schedules. Final preparation of student schedules should be near completion. Staff assignments should be finished, and appropriate people in charge of departments and staffs should be notified.

T − 2 weeks: Students who are either moving from grade to grade, or from school to school, *but who have no special needs* should be notified by mail of their transportation schedules, class schedules (tentative to be sure, but at least with homeroom number and change of schedule procedures noted), school times, and calendar.

T − 1 week: Meetings with Special Services, Child Study Teams, Special Education coordinators, and Health professionals should be held to make all preparations for those students *with special needs* (major academic program changes, legal or religious forms needed, or mental or physical handicaps). As soon as these reports are completed, notification should be sent to the students involved. Also, often handled by separate facilitators or administrators, is the final preparation for kindergarten and new student/transfer registration. (Some districts handle this very close to opening day; others prefer even more time than is indicated in this checklist.) Final checks with custodial personnel, librarians and clerical staffs should be made to insure that all supplies needed for at least the first week of school are *on hand*. Also, calls to transportation coordinators and special auxiliary personnel are often made at this time as a final check on their preparations.

T − 2 days: All staff and faculty report to their respective buildings.

Meetings of the entire district's staff/ faculty, if possible, are held to ensure the communication of any changes in normal operating procedures. Meetings are also held within the individual buildings so that a complete understanding and cooperative effort can be made on opening day and throughout the first week. All class cards and schedules should be distributed to the appropriate faculty members. Orientation of new teachers and/ or staff to the district is conducted. Preparation time should be built into these days so that teachers can familiarize themselves with their classrooms.

T − 1 day: All staff and faculty should report to their respective buildings. Meetings are held within departments or grade levels, and with special members of the district's support personnel. Afternoon (or morning) entrance of students with special needs is facilitated. This is usually handled as a "walking tour orientation" and rarely takes more than a half-day. No actual classes are held, for the aim is merely to familiarize the students with the facilities, some of the staff members and the physical plant. Disbursal of all equipment and supplies to the classrooms is to be completed. Administrators should take note of any last-minute items needed before opening day.

T (Opening Day): Administrators and faculty should arrive several hours before the first pupil. This time is spent in checking such items as lockers and keys, the number of chairs in each room in relation to the number of students expected to arrive, etc. Students arrive and are directed to the rooms assigned. Administrators should stress that *no movement will take place until this "sorting" is completed.* Teachers are to check student lists to record who is or is not present, and physical items such as desks and locker keys. They are also to dispense student information packets (handbooks, schedules, etc.), and report to administrators the accomplishment of these tasks before the administrator allows for the movement of students to regular classes. Once control is complete and each teacher has reported to the main office, students may be issued books, change classes and begin following their schedules. At the end of Opening Day, meetings should be held with department heads or grade level coordinators to discuss and handle any problems.

T + 1 week: Emergency procedures should be checked. Holding at least one fire drill usually suffices at this point. Administrators should initiate the committees that will keep open the channels of communication within the building.

T + 2 weeks: The school should be running smoothly, and student activities can begin.

By following this checklist or a similar one, most administrators will survive this hectic time.

See Also: ASSIGNMENTS; CALENDAR; CLERICAL SERVICES; COMMUNICATION; STUDENT INFORMATION; SUPERVISION (STAFF); SUPERVISION (STUDENTS); SUPPLIES AND EQUIPMENT; TRANSPORTATION.

P

Parental Liability

Court cases have established the rule that parents/guardians are only liable for their own actions and not those of their children. The only exceptions to this refer to those actions covered by state, federal or municipal statutes. For example, if a child breaks a window, his parents/guardians could not be forced to accept liability unless a statute covering vandalism damages were part of the law. On the other hand, if a child does not attend school, the parent may be held liable because of the existence of Compulsory Education laws.

Most states now have some type of **parental liability** statute. As a *very* general rule, these statutes cover damages of between $200 and $2,000. When damages reach above $2,000, the parents cease to be liable, and liability then falls upon the child. However, persons under the age of majority cannot be sued and are considered "judgment proof." Therefore, any action done by a minor, and leading to a reward of damages of over $2,000, is usually settled by another source such as personal injury insurance.

See Also: AUTHORITY, PARENTAL; COMPULSORY EDUCATION; DAMAGES; LIABILITY; MAJORITY, AGE OF; NEGLIGENCE.

Parent Conferences

Parent conferences are face-to-face meetings between a child's parent or guardian and a member of the school community.

A functioning school system includes teachers, administrators, students, and even the local school board members. However, one other faction must be present if the student and the school itself can have any hope of success: the *parents*. Without their support and understanding of the academic program, the school has lost a valuable tool for helping its students. Therefore, it is essential that parent/school contact be worthwhile and positive experiences. Such a time is the parent conference.

There are some guidelines for effective parent conferences.

First, *have a purpose* for the conference. Whether the topic is academic, behavioral or social, the reason must be stated and understood by both parties.

Second, *relax* and make the atmosphere comfortable. Be conversational, not didactic. Treat the parent as a guest. Provide an area where privacy and cordiality are possible.

Third, *have all the needed materials present*. If the parent is there to discuss pupil progress, samples of work, class grades, or other items should be readily available. The parents, too, should have in hand any items they wish to discuss.

Fourth, *keep some kind of record of the conference*. Even if it is no more than jotted notes, most educators find that records make follow-up activities easier. Also, actions taken and/or information exchanged should be contained in any correspondence with the parent after the conference.

Fifth, if difficulties arise, *keep calm*. Arguments solve nothing. However, they do indicate a lack of communication. Try to determine what is not understood, and then deal with that particular topic first. If other personnel would help, get them; if more information is needed, get it. However, if nothing is being accomplished, end the conference before any progress is lost.

Finally, before the conference ends, *make plans for the next one*. Ongoing relationships have more credence than one-time encounters. Let the parents know that their help is going to be needed again.

If handled positively and enthusiastically, parental conferences can benefit everyone.

See Also: AUTHORITY, PARENTAL; AUTHORITY, TEACHER; COMMUNICATION; STUDENT INFORMATION.

PARKING

Sufficient **parking** space can be a real administrative problem, particularly in larger secondary schools in which a great percentage of students drive and add their cars to the number of spaces required for the faculty and staff. Moreover, some space must quite often be provided for school buses and visitors to the school. Therefore, in planning new schools, it is important that sufficient space be allocated for parking purposes.

When existing space becomes limited, many schools use a system of parking on school grounds by *permit only*. Faculty, staff and other essential personnel receive the first permits, with the remaining spaces given to students upon application and the availability of space allows. Evidence of such privilege is usually in the form of a decal or sticker that is affixed to a window or bumper. A fee may or may not be charged for this permit, according to individual policy and/or laws.

Moreover, a system of supervision should then be established, in order to insure that only authorized vehicles use the parking area; in addition, penalties should be assigned for abuses.

See Also: AUTOMOBILES; BUS AND BUS DRIVERS; DISMISSAL PROCEDURES (SCHOOL); GROUNDS; STUDENT INFORMATION; SUPERVISION (STUDENTS); TRANSPORTATION.

PARLIAMENTARY PROCEDURE

Meetings mean discussion, and discussions have a way of getting out of hand. Also, meetings are called to accomplish a purpose, and without some control, nothing will get done. In order to prevent any waste of time or energy, and to keep a centralized flow of communications, the administrator should be familiar with at least the rudiments of **parliamentary procedure.**

Robert's Rules of Order is the most common source of standardized practices for conducting any type of meeting. How to open the meeting, propose and follow an agenda, discuss issues, vote on proposals, form committees, adjourn a meeting, and a host of other topics are all covered in this volume. A copy of this book or a similar one would assist the administrator in using meeting times effectively and efficiently.

See Also: CHAIRPERSONS; COMMITTEE; DEPARTMENTAL MEETINGS; FACULTY MEETING; HEARINGS; QUORUM; STUDENT COUNCIL (STUDENT GOVERNMENT).

PASSES

In order to maintain discipline, prevent vandalism and curb practices such as the cutting of classes, many schools require that, while classes are in session, any student who is anywhere outside the classroom have a **pass** from a teacher granting permis-

---

Date: _____ Time: _____
Student's Name: _____
REASON FOR BEING EXCUSED (initial):
_____ **1. Main Office**
_____ **2. Nurse's Office**
_____ **3. Library**
_____ **4. Room #** _____
_____ **5. Lavatory**
_____ **6. Excused lateness by teacher**
_____ **7. Other (Explain)**
Teacher: _____ Room_____

sion to be there. A student who, for example, is roaming the halls may be asked to produce the pass; if none is produced, he or she may be referred to the main office. This is a method of control that aids in the smooth functioning of the school.

Many schools have printed passes that merely require a teacher to fill in a few blanks. Page 265 shows an example of such a pass:

A proper pass should contain the student's name, the date, the time out, the destination, the room to which the student must return, and the signature of the teacher issuing the pass.

See Also: STUDENT INFORMATION; SUPERVISION (STUDENTS).

PATERNITY LEAVE

Paternity leave refers to the leave of absence granted to a father, at or near the birth of his child.

In most school districts, there are provisions made for a female teacher to take time off to deliver, tend and care for her newborn child. The length of this leave is optional from district to district, but one academic year is the general length of the leave. However, very few districts set any policies concerning the father of the child. As stated in the case of *Danielson v. Board of Education of the City University of New York,* (4 Employment Practice's Decision 7773, U.S.D.C.S.D. [N.Y. 1972]), he, too, has the right to leave in order to be with his newborn. In not granting

leave to the father, the local school board would be liable to charges of discrimination.

The only exceptions allowed so far have been those in which stated board policies only grant women maternity leave for health reasons. Then, the father cannot claim the same reason, and is thus not eligible for leave. If no distinction is made as to why women are requesting and being granted leave, then men must be accorded equal treatment.

See Also: LEAVE OF ABSENCE.

PERCENTAGE OF PROMOTION

Percentage of promotion is the ratio, in a class of district, of the number of students enrolled and passed upward to the next grade; also, it is the number of employees in a firm or district who gain advanced positions within the firm or district.

In education, there has been a continuing call for accountability. One criteria often used to show the success of an academic program is the rate and percentage of students attaining the next step in growth and learning. If a sufficient number of students is not showing this steady progress, some modification of instructional methods, staff assignment changes or initiation of new programs is indicated. If the percentage is high and most of the enrollment is successful, by inference, so is the district's plan.

The argument against using percentage of promotion figures is that these figures are sometimes used for the wrong purposes. For example, if one particular teacher has a lower percentage than another, some failure on the teacher's part may be assumed. This may or may not be true, but using just the figures can be very misleading and simplistic. It does not take into account any other causative factors for the student's success or failure. Furthermore, a district, in order to show how well its academic program is working, may place pressure on its staff to promote a higher percentage of students than actual work accomplished would indicate.

A secondary concept is the use of percentage of promotion of staff figures to entice and keep employees within the district. If most administrative, department head, supervisory, coordinator, and support personnel positions are filled from the existing staff, new and prospective employees will try hard to excel and stay in the district. Some large districts actually use these figures as advertising incentives in recruiting.

There are several advantages to keeping these records, beyond the obvious one of getting good personnel. The longer a staff member stays in a district, the more interested he becomes in its success. Secondly, the district gains from the increased experience that the long-term employee accrues. Finally, a stationary work force allows for better staff and program planning. Being aware of the strength and weaknesses within a district, the school board can more confidently make needed adjustments.

Whatever the reason, as long as the purposes for recording percentages of promotions, either of students or staff, has a valid, educationally sound reason behind it, the administrator can find it an excellent evaluation tool.

See Also: OFFERS OF CONTRACTS AND RECRUITING; PROMOTION; RECORD KEEPING; STUDENT INFORMATION.

PER DIEM

Per diem is the payment for services on a daily basis.

Many employees of the school board are paid a *per diem* wage. The most common, such as bus drivers, crossing guards, aides, and substitute teachers, work directly within the educational process on a more or less steady rate. The major advantage to having these employees on *per diem* salaries instead of contractual ones is that they need not be given any additional benefits. Generally, there is no compensation for lost work days, health benefits or vacations that might otherwise be part of negotiated contracts. In fact, with few exceptions, these employees are not represented by any part of negotiation teams.

Some *per diem* wages are also paid to consultants and auxiliary personnel. These employees are usually more directly involved with operations rather than instruction. Also, they are more likely to be employed on a more infrequent basis. Here, too, no additional benefits are paid beyond that of the daily wage.

See Also: AUXILIARY PERSONNEL; HOME INSTRUCTION; SALARY.

PERMANENT RECORDS

When students register for the first day of school, the school fills out health and emergency cards for them. These cards are just the first in a series that will stretch over the next twelve or so years.

An analysis of **permanent records** could best be attempted by answering the questions most often asked about them.

What is in them? Permanent records contain a *student enrollment card* containing all personal data such as parents/guardians' names, their occupation and address, the age of the student, etc.; an *academic record card* containing comments and/or grades received by the student during each school year; *attendance cards* showing attendance records from year to year; *health cards* indicating both general health information such as inoculation records, childhood diseases, height and weight, etc., and specific information such as allergies, handicaps or serious diseases, prolonged illnesses, etc.; *test records* of all standardized test results; *special program information sheets* containing comments on instruction given and progress made; *social records* (some districts consider these optional) containing any behavioral difficulties the student has had, as well as any disciplinary actions taken; and, any other data deemed necessary by the local school board.

What purpose do they serve? To keep a continuity of program and progress with each student it instructs, the school uses the records to determine if the child is, indeed, advancing as hoped. Also, should students transfer out of a particular school, the new schools they attend will be able to insure the best matching of the student's needs to their programs.

By whom, where, and how are the records kept? Usually, the records are maintained in a file in the central staff office. Copies can also be maintained in individual buildings. Those who enter data will depend on the particular data being supplied. For example, nurses enter health data; teachers enter grade progress; and administrators enter attendance and disciplinary actions. The records can either be in actual file folders, on microfiche or on computer tapes.

Who has access to them? The need to protect a child's right to privacy must be balanced against the school's and the public's right to know. Several states have made stipulations as to what type of information can be gathered, who may see it, and under what conditions the information may be seen. Each school district should form a written policy as to how it views access rights. This will help minimize any abuses that might occur. Such abuses and resultant damages are the clear liability of the recording agency (generally, the school board, but this sometimes extends through the academic chain).

The parents/guardians are generally granted access to their own children's records. Here, too, there may be specific areas that the school feels the parent/guardian might misinterpret or abuse. However, under the *Family Educational Rights and Privacy Act of 1974* (PL 93-380, Title V), the school must supply such personnel as is necessary to clearly explain the material for the parent/guardian, or be prepared to show cause in court why the information was withheld.

If the school district does not permit reasonable access, or if it abuses its record keeping privilege, it is liable to forfeit its federal funds, as well as opening itself to libel charges by the students and/or their families. Records kept by professionals, acting within their prescribed duties, that are written in good faith, serve a myriad of beneficial purposes.

See Also: AUTHORITY, EXPRESS AND IMPLIED; CENTRALIZED FILING; COMPUTERS; LIBEL; PRIVILEGED COMMUNICATIONS; PUBLIC LAW 93-380; RECORD KEEPING; STUDENT INFORMATION.

PERMISSION SLIPS

During any school year, activities and situations arise that require the permission of the parents/guardians of a student in order for the student to participate. These are usually activities that lie outside the normal academics of a school such as field trips; sports, in which physical injury is possible; etc. The usual method of obtaining such parental consent is through use of the **permission slip.**

A permission slip is a form that details the activity in which the child intends to participate. It may include particulars of the time, place and nature of the activity, as well as any other items that the parents should know in order to make an informed choice as to whether or not they wish their child to participate. Usually, there is a section of the permission slip that is to be filled in and signed by the parent/guardian and returned to the school. This section states that the parent understands the nature of the

I HAVE READ THE DETAILS CONCERNING THE FIELD TRIP AS OUT-LINED ABOVE, AND I HEREBY GRANT PERMISSION FOR MY CHILD (Fill in complete name of child) _____
TO ATTEND, I HEREBY RELIEVE THE SCHOOL OF ALL RESPONSIBILITY BEYOND THAT OF NORMAL SUPERVISION. Signature (Parent/Guardian): _____
Date: _____

activity and grants permission for the child to participate. A typical permission slip to be returned to school might look like the one on page 269.

A permission slip should be kept in the school for a period of one year following the event or activity, in case difficulties should arise.

See Also: AUTHORITY, PARENTAL; GUARDIAN AND GUARDIANSHIP; IN-SURANCE; LIABILITY; PARENTAL LI-ABILITY; STUDENT INFORMATION.

PERSONNEL FILES

"My career in less than an inch," stated one teacher describing his **personnel file.** Indeed, the file is *the* record of a teacher within a district, from the first interview, through retirement or transfer.

Basically, the file is a *work record*. Such records are kept on all board employees, but principally on its instructional personnel. Beginning with the application, first interview data, letters of recommendation, educational transcripts, and certification papers gathered before actual employment is granted, the board starts keeping a file. Subsequently, additions are made. Performance valuations and observations sheets are placed there. Letters of commendation, from both inside sources and the public, are included. Any letters of reprimand are also kept there.

Sometimes in the same place, or nearby, is a permanent record file for teachers. Included in this are such data as how many years the teacher has been in the system, salary paid, seniority status, emergency information, health information, educational levels attained, leaves requested and/or granted, and accumulated or used sick leave.

Both these records are considered the property of the school district. Although teachers may add comments to any material placed in the file, they may neither alter, remove nor substantially amend with additional data anything in them. The files are considered *privileged* information. As such, access to them is governed by very strict guidelines. *Only* the employee, his/her representative or the appropriate administrative agent may review them. No public scrutiny is permitted.

It is recommended by teacher associations that employees review their own files at least once a year, and date and initial each new page found since the previous year. If they find anything that they feel needs clarification, they should request, in writing, a conference to discuss the specific information in question.

In some districts, personnel files are destroyed five years after the teacher has retired; in some, immediately upon retirement. Policies on retainment of files are written for each district, and each administrator and employee should be aware of them.

See Also: AUTHORITY, BOARD; AU-THORITY, EXPRESS AND IMPLIED; CENTRALIZED FILING; EVALUA-TION; PRIVACY; PRIVILEGED COM-

MUNICATIONS; RECORD KEEPING; SUPERVISION (STAFF).

PETITIONS

According to the First Amendment, each citizen is granted the right "...to **petition** (the Government) for a redress of grievances." (emphasis added) Since there have been numerous cases upholding the theory that no rights are surrendered by entering a school, all levels of the academic community have the right of petition.

The presentation of such petitions, however, can be made to conform with set policy. Such policies may include the following of approved grievance procedures, the maintenance of decorum and public safety, and the noninterference or interruption of the working capabilities of the school. *Restrictions may not be made on the content of the petitions, but, rather, only on its presentation.*

The right of petition also extends to students. Their grievance procedures, too, may be governed by board policy. Careful regard should be taken to insure that the regulations pertain only to the filing of such petitions and not to their content. The most common student petitioning body in the schools is the student council or student government. Any reasonable, sincere and earnest supplication must be accepted by this body, and, in turn, delivered to the school officials.

The *disposition* of petitions is another matter. What happens after the petition is properly presented is up to the petitioned authority. Commonly, the very fact that a petition has been filed is indicative of a need for more communication on both sides. Immediate meetings and discussions are recommended, in order to stop a further breakdown in understanding. The key points to remember, for both the students and the school authority, are that presentations and dispositions must be reasonable and prudent in nature, and that there should be a maintenance of the orderly functioning of the school.

See Also: ACADEMIC FREEDOM; CIVIL RIGHTS; CONSTITUTIONAL RIGHTS; DEMANDS; FIRST AMENDMENT GUARANTEES; GRIEVANCES; POLITICS AND THE SCHOOL; STUDENT COUNCIL (STUDENT GOVERNMENT); STUDENT INFORMATION.

PHYSICAL EDUCATION

Physical Education is a curriculum subject area or course of study that gives instruction in the exercise, care and hygiene of the human body.

Starting with kindergarten and progressing through each grade, the school maintains a continuous program of physical fitness for its students. Gymnasiums, tracks, swimming pools, ball fields, and other facilities accommodate this program. Physical Education instructors, often called Body Movement instructors in elementary schools, conduct classes in skills needed to participate in both organized and individual sports.

Also, "life skills" such as first aid, good nutrition, and "good exercise techniques" are explored.

In the lower elementary grades, stress is given to sensorimotor coordination, eye-hand coordination and sequential memory games and activities. In the middle and upper elementary grades, emphasis is placed on introducing athletic skills such as throwing, dribbling, kicking, and catching balls, and running drills.

In the past, it was generally at this point that the boys and girls were segregated into groups. With new anti-discrimination legislation, however, little, if any, division is made by gender. In the middle school and high school programs, most classes are now coeducational.

More choices are being offered within the school's Physical Education program. Both group and individual athletic skills are being taught. In some districts, this has come to mean small classes in tennis, golf, gymnastics, archery, soccer, and basketball, with more staff involvement, instead of larger classes that have only large-group activities to offer.

While participation in Physical Education is mandatory, cases have been brought concerning various violations of civil and constitutional rights of non-participating students. When the objections of the students and/or their parents/guardians are based on these grounds, the school may have no power to force the students to take part. The school would have to make "reasonable allowances" and not punish the students

through the withholding of grades of educational credit for such refusal (*Mitchell v. McCall,* 143 So. 2d 629 [AL 1962]). Also expenditures for sports, terms or classes cannot favor one sex over the other. (Educational Amendments, PL 92-318, 1972, Title IX and PL 96-374, Title V).

An adjunct to, but separate from, the Physical Education program is the school's sports program (see SPORTS).

See Also: ACADEMIC PROGRAM; ATHLETICS, SEX DISCRIMINATION IN; COURSE OF STUDY; EXTRACURRICULAR ACTIVITIES; FIRST AID; GRADUATION REQUIREMENTS; HANDICAPPED; SCHEDULE; SPORTS; SUPPLIES AND EQUIPMENT.

Playground

Left to their own devices, children would normally gather somewhere near the school for relaxation and fun. Schools, knowing this, have included **playgrounds** as an adjunct to their own grounds. Supervision is provided, and safe conditions are maintained.

The concepts of playground activities and recess time are generally peculiar to the elementary level. There are sound educational principles behind periods of unrestricted play, individual and group games, and the releasing of pent-up energy for younger children during a school day.

Practicality dictates that certain guidelines should be followed regarding both playground use and supervision. Each day, before students are permitted on the playground, it should be inspected to insure that there are no safety hazards. If more than one age group will be using the area at the same time, portions should be delineated for each. Adult supervision must be *actively* present during the entire time of the recess or activity. The most common supervision ratio of students to adults is twenty to one (dependent upon age level, activity and policy. Everyone should completely understand the limits of acceptable behavior, in order to prevent unwanted incidents.

In places where injunctions against corporal punishment exist, it should be remembered that keeping a child from recess as a punishment has been ruled to be corporal punishment. Moreover, it has been ruled that handicapped students may not be denied the use of the playground merely because it is inconvenient to give them such access.

See Also: GROUNDS; SAFE PLACE STATUTES; SAFETY; SAVE-HARMLESS STATUTES; SPORTS; STUDENT INFORMATION; SUPERVISION (STUDENTS); SUPPLIES AND EQUIPMENT.

PLEDGE OF ALLEGIANCE

Ever since the case of *West Virginia State Board of Education v. Barnette* (319 U.S. 624, 644) in 1943, American education has found itself grappling with two divergent concepts. On one hand, part of any academic program's aim is to produce good, well-rounded, informed citizens, capable of leading future generations of citizens. Toward this goal, the understanding of and pride in our country is fostered through courses of study and social experiences. On the other hand, education, like all public institutions, must protect the rights of the individual, and must, according to the cited case, "...make sure that no official ... prescribes what shall be orthodox (proper) in politics, nationalism, religion, or other matters of opinion...."

Even though the point at issue in the 1943 case was Communism and the matter of a teacher's protection, at various times since then, the **Pledge of Allegiance** or Flag Salute has come under fire from other groups or causes. In the past, various groups objected to the "...and Liberty and Justice for all..." clause, the "...one Nation under God ..." clause, and the very acts of standing and/or placing one's hand over one's heart. Whatever the reason for the objection, many districts have adopted policy statements clearly expressing their views on the saying of the Pledge of Allegiance. While the courts will show no tolerance towards the abridgement of a student's or teacher's right to refuse to lead or participate in this activity, they have held that school boards have the authority to require that "...respectful, non-demonstrative, and non-disruptive conduct..." be maintained by those not wishing to participate.

Each district's policy should be clearly stated and understood at all levels of the educational spectrum.

See Also: ACADEMIC FREEDOM; CIVIL RIGHTS; CONSTITUTIONAL RIGHTS; FIFTH AMENDMENT GUARANTEES; OATHS; STUDENT INFORMATION.

POLICE

There are several times and circumstances when the school and the **police** must work in conjunction. Since there may be overlapping responsibilities in these cases, a clear, understanding and open rapport should be established between the administrator and the local constabulary.

The police may be called upon to hold demonstration lessons, lectures and workshops for students and teachers on activities related to their particular expertise. While they are acting as "visiting teachers," the police must adhere to conduct becoming a teacher. For example, language is expected to be age-appropriate and the material presented should be educationally sound.

Police may also be called upon to assist with crowd control and safety precautions at special events offered by the school. Also, at opening and dismissal times, the police act as traffic safety and/or crossing personnel.

It is in the area of law enforcement, however, that school and police relations can become strained. Most schools are public institutions, and, as such, can be entered (with just cause) by any citizen or authority. However, the school does have the responsibility, under the theory of *in loco parentis,* to protect the rights of the students under their care. Strict procedures must be followed during any police interrogation, investigation or search. An administrator must be present, and a student must not only be informed of his or her rights but also must fully *understand* them. *A student may only be released to a parent or legal guardian, unless actually placed under arrest on a secured warrant.* Parents/guardians must be notified as soon as possible concerning the presence of the police if the police intend to involve their sons or daughters.

If it is the school that invites the police in to act, the administrator should state the reason for the request, without accusation or prejudice to any particular person, in order that the police may proceed legally. Again, if interrogations, investigations or searches stem from the call, all safeguards of civil and constitutional rights must be maintained.

See Also: AUTHORITY, EXPRESS AND IMPLIED; CIVIL RIGHTS; CONSTITUTIONAL RIGHTS; STUDENT INFORMATION; SUPERVISION (STUDENTS).

POLITICS AND THE SCHOOL

Politics and the school refers to the relationship between the instructional goals of education and the citizenship rights to engage in democratic activities by students, employees, educational officials, and outside agencies.

Voting booths in schools, teachers running for public office, student council elections, candidates for office lecturing at assembly programs, and campaign materials are just a few of the situations that keep administrators and school boards wondering about policy legalities.

Five points of law should be understood in order to aid in the analysis of the basic problems of politics and the school. First, *school personnel are public employees*. Therefore, care must be taken to avoid conflict of interest charges if they run for school-related offices. For example, teachers may run for the school board, but not of the district in which they are employed, since this would literally make them their own employers. Second, *educators may not be fired, demoted or harassed because of their affiliation* with or participation in political organizations *(Keyishian v. Board of Regents,* 385 U.S. 589, [1967]). Third, *the schools are purveyors of ideas,* and, as such, they may present, without abridgement, such information and activities as they deem appropriate for their students *(Albaum v. Carey,* 283 F. Supp. 3, 10-11, [U.S. Dist. Ct., N.Y. 1968]). Fourth, *elections, both school and non-school related, may be conducted in school buildings* because schools are public property. Requests for available space and access must be made in writing, by the requesting agent to the school board. Once the request has been granted, it is generally assumed to be valid henceforth (NJ Election Statute 19:8-2, 19:8-3, *et al.).* And, finally, students may engage in campaigns and elections for student representation. They may also participate in outside political activities *(Tinker v. DesMoines Independent Community School District,* 393 U.S. 503, 511, [1969]).

Certain restrictions are permitted on a state-by-state basis. Generally, mails and/or student carriers may not be used to disseminate political materials. No advertising material of a political nature sould be displayed or distributed in the school or on school grounds. At all forums, equal time must be given to all sides of any issue.

Most districts, with the aid of the board attorney, prepare carefully written policy statements to insure understanding of the rights and responsibilities of the students, employees and officials of that district concerning political activity.

See Also: AUTHORITY, EXPRESS AND IMPLIED; BUILDING; CIVIL RIGHTS; CONFLICT OF INTEREST; CONSTITUTIONAL RIGHTS; NEA-PAC; RIGHTS AND RESPONSIBILITIES; STUDENT COUNCIL (STUDENT GOVERNMENT); STUDENT INFORMATION; VOTING.

PRAYER

See RELIGION.

PREGNANT STUDENTS

Pregnant students are those students, married or single, who are expecting a child during the school year.

The marital status of a prospective mother is not relevant to her treatment by the school or her right to participate in educational activities, extracurricular activities or social events offered by the school *(Ordway v. Hargraves,* 323 F. Supp. 1155 [U.S. Dist. Ct. MA, 1971]).

A physician must authorize, in writing, the continuance of the pregnant student's attendance in school. This authorization must be on file in the school she attends. When advised that her actual attendance is detrimental to her health, the physician must so notify the school. At that point, the school must provide an alternate educational program of instruction to meet her special needs. This is usually accomplished through home instruction.

The general guidelines for the school's responsibility in aiding in the continuing education of pregnant students was stated by the National Council on Illegitimacy in 1968, and subsequently revised and updated. The guidelines call for the protection of all the pregnant student's rights, in order that she may reach her full educational potential and future career and social goals. Her home school district and any other agency may assist, enrich and facilitate her in her continued education.

See Also: FAMILY SERVICES; HEALTH; HOME INSTRUCTION; MARRIED STUDENTS; PRIVACY; SPECIAL SERVICES; STUDENT INFORMATION; SUPERVISION (STUDENTS); WELFARE.

PRINCIPAL

The **principal** is the chief administrative officer of an individual school, whether elementary or secondary, public or private.

The principal of a building has the right to establish and enforce reasonable rules for the governing and running of the school, providing that these rules are in accordance with board of education policy, local, state and federal laws. In a large school or school system, the principals may have one or more assistant or vice-principals to aid them with the tasks of administration, while in some smaller schools, the principals may carry a partial teaching load in addition to their administrative duties.

A principal functions as an employee of the school district and is not an officer of the school board as is the superintendent of schools who is usually the principal's immediate superior.

See Also: ADMINISTRATOR; AUTHORITY, EXPRESS AND IMPLIED; MINISTERIAL ACTS; MONTHLY REPORTS; PROFESSIONAL ASSOCIATIONS FOR SCHOOL ADMINISTRATORS; SUPERVISION (STAFF); SUPERVISION (STUDENTS); VICE-PRINCIPAL; YEAR-END REPORT.

PRIVACY

Privacy is the concept of the non-public, unopen and secure status of a person, group of persons, papers, or materials as granted by the Fourth Amendment of the United States Constitution.

One of the most crucial, compelling and essential rights of an American citizen is that of *personal sovereignty.* The courts have been asked to examine many cases pertaining to some conflict between the public's need to know and this personal security. In almost every case, the courts have found in favor of the individual. A general rule of thumb that has been held up to any questions on this matter is: "Are the person's rights being abridged by exposure of 'X?' If so, it will not be upheld."

Further, in recent years, citing the Fourteenth Amendment, the courts have extended the concept of "person" to those papers, activities, associations, and possessions for which a citizen has *legal* reason. For example, to dismiss a citizen from his job because of his/her sexual preference has been held to be an invasion of privacy.

Schools find themselves involved in many situations where their effective and efficient operation calls for the keeping of records, the gathering of data on students and staff, the evaluation of performances, and the setting of rules and policies aimed at general academic populations. Constant review of procedures by the board attorney, teacher association representatives and community groups can usually assure the administrators that they are doing everything possible to protect personal privacy. In those cases where special circum-

stances might call for some infringement, prior knowledge of when, how and by whom the rights of the individual may be in jeopardy will help protect the schools from liability.

See Also: ACADEMIC FREEDOM; AUTHORITY, BOARD; AUTHORITY, EXPRESS AND IMPLIED; AUTHORITY, TEACHER; CIVIL RIGHTS; CONSTITUTIONAL RIGHTS; FOURTEENTH AMENDMENT GUARANTEES; FOURTH AMENDMENT GUARANTEES; PRIVILEGED COMMUNICATIONS; RIGHTS AND RESPONSIBILITIES; SEARCH AND SEIZURE; STUDENT INFORMATION.

PRIVATE AND PAROCHIAL SCHOOLS

Private and parochial schools are those educational institutions owned and operated by private individuals, groups and/or religious affiliates.

The United States Supreme Court has been trying to decide issues concerning the roles of public educational institutions and their private and parochial counterparts for more than 50 years. With each new decision, new tests are applied to insure the protection of the separation of church and state. Entire volumes have been written to explain the Court's interpretations, but an attempt will be made here to give the relevant cases and their impact on the present educational scene. It should be understood that the challenges to these decisions are ongoing and care should be taken not to assume that what is stated here is the last word on the subject.

The First Amendment states that, "Congress shall make no law respecting an *establishment of religion* or prohibiting the *free exercise* thereof...." (emphasis added). These two clauses, the *"Establishment Clause"* and the *"Free Exercise Clause,"* have brought about all the other debates.

In 1923, in *Frothingham v. Mellon* (392 U.S. 83), the money that a taxpayer contributes to the national treasury was ruled to be not sufficient for him to challenge the constitutionality of a federal appropriation. This was immediately interpreted to mean that the government has a right to do what it feels is for the common good. In 1925, in *Pierce v. Society of Sisters* (268 U.S. 510), it was decided that although compulsory education laws were constitutional, parents did have a right to send their children to private or parochial schools for that education. In 1929, with the case of *Borden v. Louisiana State Board of Education* (123 So. 655) the Court ruled that states could issue secular textbooks free to *all* students, regardless of where they attend school. In this decision, the Courts introduced the Child Benefit Theory. That is, if state financial support was given to students and not to their schools, the assistance was constitutional. With the hallmark decision in the 1947 case of *Everson v. Board of Education* (330 U.S. 1, 15), the Court finally attempted to clarify the "Establishment Clause." The Everson Doctrine stated

that there must be "...a wall of separation between Church and State..." and that "no tax in any amount, large or small, can be levied to support any religious activities or institutions, whatever they may be called, or whatever form they may adopt to *teach* or practice religion. Neither a state nor the federal government can, openly or secretly, *participate in the affairs of* any religious organization or private group or vice versa." (Emphasis added.)

In 1948 *(McCallum v. Board of Education,* 333 U.S. 203), and in 1952 *(Zorach v. Clauson,* 343 U.S. 306), the Courts clarified the use of school time for religious instruction. If the instruction was held inside the school, it was unconstitutional; if outside, it was considered an accommodation and therefore legal. Bible reading and prayers in the school were declared unconstitutional in 1963 *(Abington School District v. Schemepp,* 374 U.S. 203, 222-223), as being in violation of the "Free Exercise Clause." The Warren Court heard the case of *Flast v. Cohen* (392 U.S. 83) in 1968. Here, in an almost complete reversal of the *Frothingham* case cited earlier, the Courts upheld that a taxpayer *could* challenge, as violations of both the "Establishment" and "Free Exercise" clauses, any grants to the states for the purchase of instructional materials for public and private schools, including those that are church-operated. Even with the restrictions that the Court placed on such challenges at that time, the *Flast* Decision has led to numerous test cases on public spending for private and parochial schools.

Finally, in 1971, in the case of *Lemon v. Kurtsman* (403 U.S. 602, 615), the Burger Court attempted to clarify the challenges to the constitutionality of state aid to *all* schools. This decision was basically a reaffirmation of the Child Benefit Theory.

Over the past decade, cases concerning the financing, establishing and accrediting of private and parochial schools have been presented to the Court. These have led to a series of tests that can be applied to any policies, to decide if they are in keeping with the Court's interpretation. First, will *students* benefit, rather than their places of instruction? Second, would the students be deprived of some right, service or instructional benefit *because* of their religious or private affiliation? Third, does the financing have any specific benefit or limitation to religious or private tenets as a *primary effect?* Fourth, is the legislation, statute or policy providing aid for *all* students; is it not directly granted to nonsecular school to give up its nonsecular tenets? If the answer to all of these questions is yes, the policy makers may assume that they are in compliance with the Constitution.

Private and parochial schools are permitted to set their own policies and standards of dress, conduct, curriculum, and evaluation. The common tests of due process, protection of civil and constitutional rights, and compliance with federal, state and local laws must be maintained.

See Also: BIBLE; CHURCH-STATE SEPARATION; FEDERAL AGENCIES, FEDERAL AID, FEDERAL PROGRAMS; FIRST AMENDMENT GUARANTEES; FUNDAMENTAL INTEREST THEORY; RELEASED TIME; SHARED-TIME; STATE AGENCIES, STATE AID, STATE PROGRAMS; TAXES; TEXTBOOKS; TRANSPORTATION; VOCATIONAL PROGRAMS; WORKSHOPS AND IN-SERVICE.

PRIVILEGED COMMUNICATIONS

The very nature of an educational system leads to questions of what constitutes **privileged communications** and what does not. Every day, a teacher hears comments about students or their home lives. Administrators gather evaluative information on students and staff. Child study teams, Special Services and family support personnel correspond with parents and each other on many aspects of a child's life. The central staff and the school's board of education discuss many sides of an issue before setting policy or making final decisions. Any of this information misused or improperly relayed to the public could constitute a breach of privacy and could place the communicator liable to a charge of defamation.

Therefore, knowing the legal status of various statements would be of great value to the educator. First, there is the *privileged* or *unconditionally secure* communication. An example of this occurs between a lawyer and his client. No authority can be exerted to make the lawyer divulge the client's statement. There is no public benefit that can supersede the client's right to privacy. The administrator is covered under this protection when compiling, storing and securing personnel files on the staff. The property has no value to anyone but the school, and thus it is protected from public scrutiny.

The second type of privilege is the qualified or *good faith* form that protects the educator who makes statements, *without malice,* in accordance with the duties, qualifications, and scope of his job. For example, an administrator petitions the board for the expulsion of a student. Providing that there is no animosity, the discussion during the debate is considered privileged because of the positions held by the parties. The board is given the right of decision-making discussion. Once the decision to proceed on the expulsion is made, however, only the privileges accorded to normal hearings are in effect. This type of communication does have limited public value, as far as the result, but not in terms of the communication itself. What happens because of the comments has more legal impact than the comments themselves. Once good faith has been established, no liability is present.

The last type is *moral privilege.* Some statutes will protect persons who do not divulge the origins of certain facts which, if circulated, could be detrimental to others. Also, part of the educator's code of ethics states that what children or parents "tell" will be treated as respected confidences, unless the educator has a valid reason to act upon it. Again, it should be noted that there may be no legal restrictions for divulging such statements, save the conscience of the individual educator.

Simple definitions placed in the policy book regarding the district's point of view on these types of privileged communications will greatly assist the administrators and staff in understanding their responsibilities and liabilities.

See Also: COMMUNICATIONS; HEARINGS; LIABILITY; PARENT CONFERENCES; PERMANENT RECORDS; PERSONNEL FILES; STUDENT INFORMATION.

PROBATIONARY TEACHER

A **probationary teacher** is a member of the instructional staff who does not have tenure.

When new teachers join the teaching staff of a district, they generally begin a three-year period of probationary review. The first contract that is signed covers only one academic year and has no renewal clause in it. Throughout this first year, administrators, curriculum supervisors and other chairpersons assist, monitor, guide, and evaluate the progress of the new employee. If this process is done with care, the probationary teachers can make those adjustments that will help them conform to the expectations present when they were hired. If any problems develop, quick handling usually solves them. This *"learning year"* should be taken as a growth experience only, unless such gross incompetence or negligence occurs that makes future employment unlikely. If, however, evaluations and observations show a steady progress and a willingness to perform the functions for which they were hired, the board usually offers probationary teachers a new contract. These contracts are generally for not less than one year, nor more than two, During this period, the new teachers are given more responsibility. Greater emphasis is placed on their performance, attitude and the results of their instructional duties and plans. If the district feels that the new employees have fulfilled their duties, it may offer them the standard contract of the district as negotiated. Once probationary teachers enter the classroom on the first day of the fourth year of their employment in a district, they are considered to have tenure.

The contractual differences between non-tenured or probationary teachers and tenured teachers may vary from state to state. Generally, the major difference is that the probationary teacher may be relieved from employment without cause, but at the discretion of the school board, at any time during the probationary period, particularly at the end of that "learning year." Another difference is in the granting of leaves, voting rights and negotiations representation. In most states, probationary teachers do not possess any of these guarantees.

As the job market gets tighter and each open position attracts more and more applicants, it behooves the administrator to not only interview and accept the best applicant, but also to assist, guide and keep those new staff members in order that they may become valuable additions to the district.

See Also: CONTRACTS; DIFFERENTIATED STAFFING; SUPERVISION (STAFF); TENURE.

PROFESSIONAL ASSOCIATIONS FOR SCHOOL ADMINISTRATORS

Professional associations for school administrators are those organized groups of educational personnel whose interests or concerns center in the area of school administration.

There are many professional associations for school administrators in the United States. Following is a list of fifteen of them:

American Federation of School
   Administrators
110 E. 42nd Street
New York, NY 10017

Association for the Gifted
3 Tyler Court
Guilderland, NY 12084

Association for Supervision and
   Curriculum Development
1701 K Street, N.W,
Suite 1100
Washington, DC 20006

Council of Administrators of
Special Education
6807 Park Heights Avenue
Baltimore, MD 21215

Council for Basic Education
725 15th Street, NW
Washington, DC 20005

Kappa Delta Pl
Box A
West Lafayette, IN 47906

National Association of
Administrators of State and
Federal Educational Programs
P.O. Box 1371
Ann Arbor, MI 48106

National Association of
Elementary School Principals
1801 N. Moore Street
Arlington, VA 22209

National Association of Pupil
Personnel Administrators
Upper Arlington City Schools
1950 N. Mallway
Columbus, OH 43221

National Association of Secondary
School Principals
1904 Association Drive
Reston, VA 22091

National Center for the
Development of Bilingual
Education
3700 Ross Avenue
Dallas, TX 75204

National Society of the Study of
Education
5835 Kimbark Avenue
Chicago, IL 60637

Phi Delta Kappa
8th & Union Streets
Bloomington, IN 47401

Pi Lambda Theta
4101 E. 3rd Street
P.O. Box A-850
Bloomington, IN 47402

Society for the Advancement of
Education
1860 Broadway
New York, NY 10023

See Also: AMERICAN ASSOCIATION
OF SCHOOL ADMINISTRATORS;
AMERICAN COUNCIL ON EDUCA-
TION; NATIONAL EDUCATION ASSO-
CIATION; WORLD CONFEDERATION
OF THE TEACHING PROFESSION.

PROFESSIONAL ASSOCIATIONS FOR TEACHERS

Professional associations for teachers are organized groups of professional educators who are interested in or concerned with the specific subject areas of teaching.

There are many professional associations for teachers in the United States. Following is a list of eleven such organizations:

Music Educators National
Conference
1902 Association Drive
Reston, VA 22091

National Alliance of Black School
Educators
Administration Building
1314 Ridge Street
Evanston, IL 60201

National Art Educators
Association
1916 Association Drive
Reston, VA 22091

National Association of Biology
Teachers
11250 Roger Bacon Drive
Reston, VA 22090

National Association for Sports
and Physical Education
1201 16th St., NW,
Suite 627
Washington, DC 20036

National Business Educators
Association
1906 Association Drive
Reston, VA 22091

National Council for Geographic
Educators
University of Houston
Houston, TX 77004

National Council of Teachers of
English
1111 Kenyon Road
Urbana, IL 61801

National Council of Teachers of
Math
1906 Association Drive
Reston, VA 22091

National Science Teachers
Association
1742 Connecticut Avenue, NW
Washington, DC 20009

World Educators Fellowship
43 Mist Lane
Westbury, NY 11590

See Also: AMERICAN FEDERATION OF
TEACHERS; AMERICAN COUNCIL ON
EDUCATION; NATIONAL EDUCATION
ASSOCIATION; WORLD CON-
FEDERATION OF THE TEACHING
PROFESSION.

PROFESSIONAL IMPROVEMENT PLAN

A **professional improvement plan** is an evaluation strategy using both overall district objectives and the personal goals of the employee. It may also be known as a profile sheet, PIP, personal evaluation form and a host of other names.

Each year, the entire professional staff of a district is observed and evaluated by various supervisory personnel. Usually, there is a set of criteria against which these evaluations are measured. The general, or master goals of the district are then either reached by the employee or not, according to the evaluation. The standardized criteria leaves no room for showing the personal, professional growth of individual staff members.

Because of this deficiency, various groups, including the American Association of School Administrators, began working toward an *individualized* style of evaluation, based not only on district goals but also on what the individual educator wanted to accomplish each year. Perhaps a district wanted the Reading scores to rise one percentage point above the year before, but Mr. Jones wanted to have his class reading more books and decided to expose his classes to as many new authors, styles and topics as he could to increase the scores. Further, he stated that he was going to have "quiet" reading periods as part of his instructional program. Finally, he was enrolled in two graduate courses on Reading, and planned to attend an English teachers' association convention, with the emphasis on learning other techniques of motivating his classes. At the end of the year, the district might find that the students' Reading scores did, indeed, go up one percentage point as planned, but the individual teacher has met his own goals as well, as *his* classes' scores had risen four percent.

Working with an evaluator, the teacher states each year's goal, spot checks progress throughout the year, and self-evaluates his or her success at the end of the year, and, in addition, projects into next year's goals.

The greatest advantages for districts that already employ this plan are the attitudinal changes in the staff. As they are asked to set their own professional expectations, they try to achieve more. The more the staff tries, the more actively involved they become with teaching again. The concentration again returns to results. Teacher frustration, also known as "burnout," appears to decline as personal professional growth is noticed by "the bosses" and does not just appear on standardized test results and promotion charts.

More and more states are recommending this evaluation strategy. Administrators, looking to increase staff impact on building, district and community goals, may find this method a viable alternative to their present system of staff evaluation.

See Also: ACCOUNTABILITY; CHANGE STRATEGIES; EVALUATION; GOALS AND OBJECTIVES; OBSERVATION; PERSONNEL FILES; SUPERVISION (STAFF).

PROM

One of the most popular school social functions is the **prom.** Held annually in most schools, the prom is usually a formal occasion held somewhere other than the school grounds and limited to the members of one class (generally seniors) and their invited guests. The prom is an excellent occasion for positive public relations for the school, and arrangements for media coverage should be made. Since proms are private affairs, they are not, technically, school-sponsored activities, and therefore have no restrictions as to the range of fees charged or paid by the students. Consequently, proms can often be expensive events for students as they rent formal attire, purchase evening wear and pay rather heavy fees for bids. Even so, proms remain extremely popular with students and their parents, who, perhaps remembering their own prom nights with fondness, find joy in watching their children prepare for their proms. The nature and extent of the school's prom will, of course, be determined by the socio-economic makeup of the school.

Administrators should see to it that there are sufficient chaperones and that the prom organizing committee has a faculty advisor. It is also advisable for the administrator to make a personal appearance with his or her spouse at the affair, as this will promote positive reactions from students and their parents.

See Also: ACTIVITIES; COMMITTEE; DANCE; FEES; MEDIA; STUDENT COUNCIL (STUDENT GOVERNMENT); STUDENT INFORMATION.

PROMOTION

Administrators are concerned with **promotion** in two different areas. The first applies to the *anticipated progression of students* from one grade to the next over a twelve- or thirteen-year period. Once a pupil has completed, learned, mastered or otherwise performed a prerequisite of material, the pupil is permitted *(promoted)* into the next grade level of instruction. The administrator, along with the curriculum coordinator, instructional supervisor, and other support personnel, sets the criteria for advancement. Promoting a student more than one step *(acceleration)* or holding a student at a previous step *(retention)* are administrative decisions. These decisions, however, must have concrete data behind them from classroom teachers, Child Study Teams, and other pupil personnel experts. The promotion is usually granted, with either a comment on last year's report card or in a standardized congratulatory letter. The others, acceleration and retention, should be announced in a parent conference, with full explanations to both the parents and the child.

The second area of promotions with which the administrator must deal is that of *personnel development*. Whenever an upper-level position opens, it is the administrator's duty to so publicize it, in order that one of the present staff may apply for it. Posting such notices on the staff bulletin board, sending a copy of the notice to the local teacher's association, and releasing the information informally at meetings or in conversations will show the administrator's concern for the advancement of others. The administrator usually instructs the school secretary to help facilitate all applications so that they may comply with deadlines or information requirements. Of course, the individual administrator may also apply for a position of advancement and should certainly do so.

See Also: ACCELERATION; APPLICATION; COMMUNICATION; EQUAL EMPLOYMENT OPPORTUNITIES; GRADES; OFFERS OF CONTRACT AND RECRUITING; PARENT CONFERENCES; QUALIFICATIONS; RECOMMENDATION; REPORT CARDS; RETENTION OF STUDENTS; SOCIAL PROMOTION.

PROTEST

See DEMANDS; DEMONSTRATION; PETITION.

PSYCHOLOGICAL STUDIES

Psychological studies are comprised of the testing, observations and evaluations of the motivational, mental and experiential makeup of a student, usually conducted by the school psychologist and/or child study team.

With the passage of Public Law 94-142, administrative codes were written and adopted by the states to insure the best application of services for the exceptional student. Regardless of the handicap, the public schools accepted the responsibility of developing an educational program for every student in order that they might reach their full potential.

In order for this program to be planned, a comprehensive battery of tests must be administered. Also, formal and informal studies are conducted by various members of the child study team along their particular lines of expertise. The school psychologist generally gives the *WISC Intelligence Test,* the *Bender-Gestalt* and the *Thematic Appreciation Test (TAT) for Emotional Analysis.* Most LDTC's administer the *Slossen Intelligence Tests, Berry's Integration Tests of Visual Motor Skills* and the *Wepman Auditory Discrimination Tests.* School nurses use *Audio-Metric Tests,* the *Snellen Chart for Vision,* the *Color Perception Tests,* and any results from outside physicians' testing. While this list is by no means complete, it represents the most common instruments available for the studies.

The procedures and policies for administering, evaluating and implementing these psychological studies are very strictly covered by legal guidelines. All testing must be agreed to *in writing* by the student's parent or legal guardian. If they refuse, a *hearing* may be called for by the local school district to appeal their refusal. The most common reason for the appeal is that some harm, to either the student or the general school population, would be possible if a true classification was not ascertained. No discussion of the results is permitted between those parties sanctioned by parental consent. Once a child study workup has been completed, the only notation permitted on a child's permanent record is that the workup was done, the *findings are not included.* Anyone wishing to know the findings must apply to the *parents/guardians for their written consent.* The only exception to this is the exchange between schools or special facilities in the *same* districts and/or schools within the *same* county or state sharing those facilities. There is also a "life span" of three years for the validity for these studies. After three years, the results are considered out of date and thus invalid. Some state codes call for the destruction of the results after the validity has expired; others require them to be kept for five years beyond the validity date. The actual testing and psychological study of students is free to the students and their parents. Such testing can also be granted to private and parochial school students under the Child Benefit Theory, if there are no adequate facilities for such testing in their schools.

The studies that assess the intellectual, social, adaptive, and emotional development of the student pinpoint both the classification and thus the educational program needed for the special student.

See Also: CHILD STUDY TEAM; DIAGNOSIS; EVALUATION; INTELLIGENCE TESTING; LEARNING DISABILITIES; NURSE; PERMANENT RECORDS; PRIVILEGED COMMUNICATIONS; SHARED-TIME; STUDENT INFORMATION.

P.T.A.

Regardless of what the organization is called, almost every school has some type of group that acts as a liaison between the school and the parents/community. National organizations such as the **P.T.A.** and the P.T.O. have very formal objectives, but as a rule, the local branches list rather specific goals and objectives aimed at *"their"* school.

The schools welcome this parent/community involvement, for it indicates interest in the youth whom the school is also trying to motivate. Administrators encourage their staffs to participate in these organizations and to call upon them to assist with the actual activities of the school. Elementary schools often encourage parent/community groups to act as room parents, volunteer tutors and aides; secondary schools actively involve them in fund-raising and the purchasing of items outside the budget such as sports equipment, band uniforms and/or instruments, instructional equipment for the library and media

center, and also in assisting decision-making by serving on advisory councils.

Many studies have shown that the more active and involved the P.T.A. is, the easier it is to motivate the students, the easier it is for both sides to see and help with the problems of the other, the more likely it is that budgets will be understood and approved, and the more likely it is that the entire educational program of the school will be successful.

Even without mandates such as the Educational Amendments of 1972, (PL92-318, Title I), schools are increasing the involvement of parent and community groups.

See Also: ADVISORY COUNCILS; AIDES; BULLETIN; COMMITTEE; COMMUNICATIONS; NEWSLETTER; SCHOLARSHIP; SPECIAL INTEREST GROUPS; SUPPLIES AND EQUIPMENT; VOLUNTEERS.

PUBLIC ADDRESS SYSTEM

A properly functioning **public address system** can be a real asset to a school. Important messages can be quickly transmitted to the entire building, which is an invaluable benefit in times of emergency, and it insures that everyone has heard the bulletin. It can also save time in contacting students and teachers or handling situations that may arise on the spur-of-the-moment. Moreover, many modern PA systems have the capacity to carry two-way conversations from individual classrooms to the main office where the system is usually housed, which is not only extremely useful in emergency situations, but also in conducting the normal business of the school.

PA systems can also have drawbacks. A teacher who is in the middle of a particularly heated lesson can become very upset when interrupted by an announcement about play practice. Also, when the PA system is used repeatedly, students and teachers tend to become so used to it that they "turn it off" and don't listen. Finally, since using the PA system is much easier than writing out notices, an office can become deluged by requests to use it, and the subsequent result is a seemingly endless chant of announcements, to which the school population pays less and less attention.

One way to avoid this is to set a policy for the system's use. For example, the policy may state that "The PA system may be used during Home Room period and at 2:15 in the afternoon, and at no other times except for emergency purposes." If this policy or a similar one is observed, students and teachers know precisely when the system is going to be used, can plan accordingly, and know that what they will hear will be important.

See Also: BULLETIN; COMMUNICATIONS; STUDENT INFORMATION.

PUBLICATION

Education is a "sharing" profession. As such, it generates a great deal of printed material, most of which is written by other educators. Therefore, many guidelines have been proposed to encourage administrators and their staffs to add to the body of professional knowledge.

Generally, there are no prior restrictions placed on material written and prepared *entirely on the educator's free time,* even if they developed their expertise while being employed. If they use material prepared *entirely or in part on school time,* using school equipment or facilities, however, they can be asked to submit a copy to their immediate supervisors for review. As a common practice, such review is seen as a courtesy and rarely denies **publication.** Sometimes, the district's policy will state the *percentage* of time and/or materials that may be taken and used outside the district without written permission. If the reviewed material exceeds this percentage, a written consent is usually needed prior to publication.

In the past few years, the "publish or perish" dictums have been challenged. If the writing of articles is clearly stated as part of the job description, the pressure of "publish or perish" has been upheld. While this is a problem mainly on the college level, there are some positions at other levels that consider writing and being published as imperative. While not being published cannot be used as the *single* cause for dismissal or demotion, it can be used as a hindrance to advancement.

Administrators should be encouraged, and so should encourage their staffs, to share any ideas they have with the general public and other educators.

One word about educators writing noneducational materials: while there can be no restrictions on what is written, there can be stipulations on professional conduct. For example, if a teacher wrote a racy, erotic work of fiction bordering on pornography, dismissal could result if it could be proved that such activity made it impossible for the teacher to control, teach or conduct class. Also, if the teacher were to write a scathing indictment of a fictionalized school system that could easily be identified as the district in which the teacher was employed, it is possible that libel charges might be forthcoming.

See Also: ACADEMIC FREEDOM; CENSORSHIP; CONFLICT OF INTEREST; FIRST AMENDMENT GURANTEES; FREE SPEECH.

PUBLIC LAW 93-380

Public Law 93-380 is also known as the Educational Amendments of 1974.

This law, enacted on August 21, 1974, was another in the series on legislative updates to the ESEA 1965. Each of these reviews and amendments, offered to and by Congress approximately every two years, has made major changes in the educational regulations affecting every school system.

Under the amendments of 1974, most of the original law was merely

clarified. There were some additional fundings allocated to the National Reading Improvement Program under Title VII, and to the Gifted and Talented and Career Education programs under Title IV. But it was Title V, Educational Administrative Protection of the Rights and Privacy of Parents and Students, that had the greatest immediate impact. Access by parents and students to permanent records, as well as parental authority over psychological testing and Child Study Team inquiries, caused several immediate court challenges. School boards saw this section of the law as detrimental to their record-gathering perrogatives. For a full review of this title, called the Family Educational Rights and Privacy Act of 1974, see the entry under PERMANENT RECORDS.

See Also: ELEMENTARY AND SECONDARY EDUCATION ACT OF 1965.

PUBLIC LAW 94-142

Public Law 94-142 is the law also known as the Education for All Handicapped Children Act of 1975.

This law, enacted on November 29, 1975, was originally proposed as an amendment to Public Law 93-380. However, so much new ground was to be covered that it was left for the new Congress to act on. Many of the deadlines that existed in the previous legislation were extended through this law.

Section 3 PL 94-142 showed the 94th Congress's intent to assist *all* children in seeking a "full, free and appropriate" education:

"The Purpose of the Act is to assure that all handicapped children have available to them a free, appropriate public education, which emphasizes special education and related services designed to meet their unique needs, to assure that the rights of handicapped children and their parents or guardians are protected, to assist states and localities to provide for the education of all handicapped children and to assess and assure the effectiveness of efforts to educate handicapped children."

The law went on to define "handicapped" and those services to which they were entitled.

It was *Section 6* that had the most immediate impact. Part A was listed as *"Amendments with Respect to Employment of Handicapped Individuals, Removal of Architectual Barriers, and Media Centers."* In Sections 606, 607 and 653, the act defined and allocated funds for this concept. Part B of section 6 gave all of the *allocations and eligibilities for the handicapped programs and state plans for compliance and reporting procedures,* as well as methodology for applying for allocations, and the rights of petition, review and administration of the act through Sections 611-617.

Even though the deadlines within the original act expanded into 1978 and beyond, almost immediate changes were seen in schools and public buildings such as ramps, free opening doors and other accommodations for handicapped individuals were installed. Individualized programs and accelerated responsibilities

for child study teams were also immediately in evidence. Since the original enactment, each successive Congress has extended this all-important piece of legislation.

See Also: CHILD STUDY TEAM; DIAGNOSIS; HANDICAPPED; LEARNING DISABILITIES; PUBLIC LAW 93-380; RETARDED CHILD; SPECIAL EDUCATION; TRANSPORTATION.

PUNISHMENT

See CORPORAL PUNISHMENT; DETENTION; DISCIPLINE; EXPULSION OF STUDENTS; IN-SCHOOL SUSPENSION; SUSPENSION.

PUPIL PERSONNEL SERVICES

See SPECIAL SERVICES.

PURCHASING

Purchasing is the buying of materials, goods, supplies, and equipment for a school system in accordance with state, municipal and district statutes and standards.

Each district sets its own policies and procedures concerning purchasing. However, there are some common practices that administrators have adopted to facilitate the spending of school funds.

First, *who in the district shall be the purchasing authority or agent?* Generally, unless the school board has a business administrator or manager, the purchasing agent is the superintendent of schools or an assistant, as designated in his or her job descriptions.

Second, *what amount can be expended without board authorization or by bid?* This usually ranges from $500. to $1500.

Third, *what must the purchasing agent do?* The purchasing agent must follow the district's policies on gathering, awarding and fulfilling bids and financial contracts. Written policies and procedures allow the administrator, board, community taxpayers, and potential sellers to fully understand what the purchaser can and cannot do, as well as who is ultimately responsible for the disbursal of funds.

Finally, *what are the accounting procedures?* These are usually available for review yearly by the board and any other interested parties.

While there may be individual differences in budgeting, bids and purchasing, all administrators dealing with school funds should know the rudiments of federal, state or municipal purchasing laws, as well as those of their own school district.

See Also: BIDS; BUDGET; EXPENSES; FUNDS, SCHOOL; SUPPLIES AND EQUIPMENT; VENDORS AND VENDING MACHINES.

Q

QUALIFICATIONS

In education, each position and level has its own list of **qualifications.** To understand each at a glance, these are listed below:

Board of Education President—(a) membership on a board of education for at least two terms; and (b) all the qualifications of a board member.

Board of Education Member—(a) United States citizen, (b) a validated voter in the school district, (c) capable of reading and writing English, (d) capable of fulfilling the duties of office.

Superintendent of Schools—(a) must possess at least a master's degree plus twelve graduate hours toward a doctorate, (b) a minimum of three successful years of teaching, (c) a minimum of four successful years in administrative posts, (d) proper certification in teaching, supervision and administration.

Principal—(a) master's degree with major in administration and/or supervision, (b) five successful years of teaching, with at least one year at the level of the school in question, (c) proper certification in teaching, supervision and administration.

Curriculum Coordinator—(a) a minimum of five successful years of teaching, (b) a master's degree, (c) proper certification in teaching and supervision.

Learning Disabilities Teacher-Consultant (LDTC)—(a) five successful years of teaching, (b) a master's degree, (c) proper teaching certification and LDTC certification.

School Psychologist—(a) a minimum of five years as a clinical psychologist, (b) minimum of a master's degree, (c) proper certification as a psychologist and state certification as a school psychologist.

Supervisor—(a) three successful

years of teaching, (b) master's degree, (c) proper certification in teaching and supervision.

Teacher—(a) state certificate in teaching, (b) Bachelor's degree.

Nurse—(a) certification as a registered nurse, (b) state certification as a school nurse.

There are general qualifications such as leadership abilities, successful performance of past positions, general ease in working with people, and good character, in addition to those characteristics listed above.

See Also: ADMINISTRATOR; BOARD OF EDUCATION; CENTRAL STAFF; CHILD STUDY TEAM; DIFFERENTIATED STAFFING; NURSE; PRINCIPAL; SPECIAL SERVICES; SUPERINTENDENT OF SCHOOLS; SUPERVISION (STAFF); UNIT COORDINATOR; VICE PRINCIPAL.

QUORUM

A **quorum** is the minimum number that needs to be present before a body or group of people can legally conduct business.

Unless otherwise specified by statute or bylaws, a quorum is generally a simple majority of the eligible voters or enactors. For example, in order for a seven-member school board to hire a new employee, at least four members of the board must be present.

All committees, councils and conventions should have stated policies concerning voting and quorums, in order that valuable time will not be wasted because of the inability to proceed.

See Also: PARLIAMENTARY PROCEDURE; VOTING.

R

RACE RELATIONS

Race relations refers to the ongoing drive in education to promote understanding and uniformity of treatment to all, regardless of national origin, language, skin color, or socioeconomic status.

There once was a premise in most American institutions, including education, that any differences had to be obliterated in order that the single "national American purity" could prevail. This meant that students learned English, and their subjects were taught in English; their religious preferences were accepted, but neither honored nor fostered; a general work-ethic established a middle-class value system that was impressed upon all; regardless of where a person was from, coming to America meant giving up the trappings of that previous culture. The whole of American society seemed to be based upon the concept, "when in America, act American."

Starting in the early 1950s, another viewpoint began to emerge. Namely, that each person or group had the right to exist, safely and securely in their rights of ethnicity, nationalism and universal opportunities. By the late 1960s and early 1970s, the pendulum had swung completely to this extreme. At that time, the national premise was that anything an individual or group wanted to do to keep its own ethnic, religious or national purity was to be accepted. No longer was *assimilation* the goal of American society; rather, *individualism* swept the land. And, to insure that no restrictions were placed upon the personal sovereignty of our citizenry, the government passed laws and provided legal precedents for the elimination of generalities in dealing with "stereotypical populations."

At the end of the 70s and the start of the 80s, the pendulum began to move again. While certainly not as conservative as the 50s nor as radical as the 60s, the premise in American education, and society at large at present, is that no government shall tell any group or individual how they must act *except* when the general good of the nation is involved. Because of this shift, mandates on busing, quotas, ethnic studies, etc., are being challenged. Wherever personal freedoms are being disallowed because of prejudice and discrimination, the fight for these rights will continue. But, and this is the new difference, where citizens have decided, through exercising their vote, that they do *not* desire some governmental imposition, here, too, their rights will be upheld.

This new view of race relations, like its predecessors, may take some time to understand, but educators must stand ready to help their students and their families adjust.

See Also: BILINGUAL EDUCATION; BUSING; CIVIL RIGHTS; CONSTITUTIONAL RIGHTS; CULTURE; DISCRIMINATION; ELEMENTARY AND SECONDARY EDUCATION ACT OF 1965; ETHNIC MINORITIES; SPECIAL INTEREST GROUPS; VOTING.

RATIFICATION

At the successful conclusion of negotiations, there is a *ratified* contract. There are two ways this **ratification** process can take place.

In the first, there is the *power to agree*. Here, both parties in the negotiations have received power from their constituents to approve the negotiated package. Once an agreement

has been reached, no further vote is needed. The contract becomes valid and ratified as soon as these empowered representatives sign it.

In the second form of ratification, there is *no power to agree* granted to the representatives. Instead, the parties negotiate in good faith, until a tentative contract is approved by both sides. Then they return to their respective constituents who must, in turn, vote on the proposed agreement. If they vote in favor of the proposal, it is thus ratified *on their side*. The agreement is not binding until *both* sides ratify or agree to the proposal.

Whichever type of ratification is used in the district, the administrator must be sure that all parties understand the full negotiations process.

See Also: ARBITRATION; COLLECTIVE BARGAINING; CONTRACTS; MEDIATION AND MEDIATOR; NEGOTIATIONS; REPRESENTATION; VOTING.

READINESS

No one believes that education begins at the point when a child first enters kindergarten. In point of fact, education has taken place from the moment of birth. What does begin in kindergarten are the formal procedures of instruction in learning experiences, which will give a basic body of understanding, attitudes and knowledge needed by the developing individual to gain intellectual curiosity, critical thinking, problem-solving ability, and esthetic appreciation. The curricular program to attain this basic knowledge includes written and spoken English, Math, Social Studies, Science, Music, Art, Health, and Physical Education.

All children have some smattering of knowledge in these subject areas before coming near a school building. Also, they have been exposed to and have mastered "life skills" such as personal hygiene, sharing, being around other children, and at least a modicum of behavioral control. The amount of proficiency in both of these "life skills" and subject areas, *prior to formal instruction,* comprises a student's *readiness level* (RL).

There are several methods of determining the RL of a child. For the pre-school youngster, *a parent conference* with both the classroom teacher and other student personnel is helpful at which a questionnaire is completed and/or a discussion is held about the child's background, skills, likes, dislikes, and attitudes. A typical questionnaire includes the parents' evaluation of their child's *personal abilities* (fastens his/her clothing: zippers, buttons, ties shoelaces or bows; feeds himself/herself; follows simple directions), *social attitudes* (takes turns with other children, finishes a game even when losing, bullies other children, is bullied by other children), *physical coordination skills* (jumps, hops on one foot, colors within the lines), *concrete development* (talks in sentences, says rhymes, names things like coins, parts of the body, animals and letters when they are pointed to),

environmental experiences (looks at books, watches TV; remembers riding in/on: a horse, train or airplane; remembers going to: a store, zoo, restaurant, movie, or museum), and any other general information about the child that the parent feels the school should know (This can be an essay type "My Child Is..." or a fill-in type "My Child Likes ... ; ... Gets Upset When ... ; Is Really Good At..."). Also, the parents should present the results of a recent physical checkup and an inoculation record.

The second step in reaching an accurate RL is the *administering of a series of standardized tests.* Some of these are given just prior to entry, soon after or during the first year. They are given by either the reading specialist, the child study team, or the kindergarten supervisor. They may include the *Metropolitan Achievement Pre-Test* in September/October, The *A B C Inventory* in the spring, and the *Metropolitan Achievement Post-Test* in May/June. There are also several kinds of physical tests given before and/or during the evaluation process. One such test was developed under Project ACTIVE (*ESEA Grant,* Titles III-IV C, 1974) and uses *Basic Motor Fitness Tests* (Hilsendager, Jack, Mann, 1968) to evaluate gross body coordination, balance-posture orientation, eye-hand coordination, and eye-hand accuracy.

The final method in determining RL's is the *assembling of anecdotal evaluations* from school personnel within the first two months of a child's attendance.

Once the RL has been accurately

established, the school can prepare an individualized academic program to aid the student in overcoming any deficiencies, maintaining steady progress and promoting demonstrated strengths. The process does not end when the child enters kindergarten, but rather, continues through the identical steps, whenever the child is faced with new subjects or freedoms, or when future schooling/career choices are to be made.

Federal programs and studies have placed great emphasis on raising the RL's of students who are physically, emotionally, financially, socially, or culturally deprived. Programs such as Operation Head-Start, Free Breakfasts and Lunches, and Reading Is Fundamental are but a few. National groups have also correlated geographical locations, home situations and other social factors with a low RL. Special interest groups have lobbied for more help in giving these children a better chance at success.

See Also: ABILITY LEVELS; ACHIEVEMENT; AGE LEVELS; APTITUDE; BASICS; CHILD STUDY TEAM; DIAGNOSIS; EARLY CHILDHOOD PROGRAMS; KINDERGARTEN; PARENT CONFERENCES; STUDENT INFORMATION.

READING

In order to function in any civilization, one must be able to communicate with others. In modern society, this communication is set down and recorded. A person does not have to be physically present to gain information from another; past knowledge is available to the present and the future. Almost every piece of information conveyed to the people involves some type of **reading.** Therefore, nothing takes a higher priority in a school's curriculum than that of its Reading program. Beginning with kindergarten and the introduction of decoding skills, progressing through the middle grades, with exposure to styles and experiences, and finally at the secondary level, with the growth of appreciation for well-written books, plays and articles, the school tries to shape its students into educated and adept readers.

Throughout this process, teachers act as guides and facilitators, not as purveyors of information. The child is not so much taught to read as he/she is taught to overcome obstacles to reading. The skills or tools of reading are taught so that these can be used by the students to decipher whatever they wish. Because of this very fundamental difference between Reading and any other subject, it has been said that all good Reading programs should be basically diagnostic.

There are many aspects of testing done by Reading specialists, LDTCs and child study teams, but no screening tests for early detection of visual and audial blocks to reading readiness have been proven to be more reliable than *parental and teacher observations*. Parent conferences can give clues to many problems. Teachers using experience, plus materials such as *Teacher's Guide to Vision Problems* (American Optometric Association, 1967), can aid in the early diagnosis of difficulties. Some tests have been questioned recently as to their validity. For example, the *Snellen Letter Test* measures accurately a child's vision at twenty feet, but it does not indicate the visual ability at the fusion point of a reading distance of 18 inches or less. The student cannot read what he cannot see. Further, poor or lost hearing has a severe impact on reading ability, since the student has trouble with auditory discrimination and cannot use sound in order to aid with word recognition.

But the single most persistent obstacle to reading is *societal*. No matter who does the study, where the study is conducted or when the data is compiled, the correlation between environmental deprivation and poor reading ability remains inescapable. A background that places no value upon reading ability, gives little or no practice for reading skills, or provides poor reading readiness levels, definitely and directly adversely affect reading performance. Also, should this effect be complicated or compounded by language barriers, perceptual problems, minimal brain dysfunction, poor nutrition, or mental and/or physical handicaps, the difficulty may be insurmountable. Consequently, the schools place great emphasis on Remedial, Supplemental, and Compensatory Education programs, as well as social assistances such as bilingual education and food programs.

The modern administrator, when dealing with this foundation "R" of education, must be familiar with every aspect of the problem, the methods of helping to overcome disabilities, and the choices of solutions that various members of the staff have available to them. Further, the administrator and staff can be invaluable in their public relations role in fostering good attitudes toward reading in the community.

See Also: ACADEMIC PROGRAM; BASICS; COMPETENCY-BASED PROGRAMS; DIAGNOSIS; INSTRUCTION; LANGUAGE; LANGUAGE ARTS; READINESS; STUDENT INFORMATION.

REASONABLE AND PRUDENT

Reasonable and prudent refers to the rational, sensible care taken during the exercising of one's judgment; it is the cautious performance of duties.

The courts call for the assignment of expertise to professionals in the discharging of their services. Simply stated, this means that once a person or group of persons is understood to be an expert in some field, the level of care and responsibility expected from them is raised appropriately. They are expected to be reasonable and prudent in their actions. Malpractice, nonfeasance and/or incompetence charges stem from these increased expectations.

There are many implications of this educational theory. It behooves all educators to be aware of their status as professionals in their dealings with the community, parents, students, and fellow colleagues.

See Also: FORESEEABILITY; LIABILITY; NONFEASANCE; SUPERVISION (STUDENTS).

RECESS

See PLAYGROUND.

RECOMMENDATION

Administrators are called upon to recommend many different things in the course of performing their duties. Sometimes it is a student who wishes to be proposed for a job or a college entrance, or a staff member who wants to advance to a new position, or a new program, textbook or service that needs approval by the local school board. In all cases, administrators add their opinions in the hope of a *favorable outcome*.

The way in which administrators are asked to give a recommendation allows them to decide how to proceed. A verbal or written, "Will you recommend..." from a staff member, parent's group or superior generally permits them to say, "Yes..." if they are in favor of the proposal or, "No..." as diplomatically as possible if they are not. It is here that a **recommendation** differs from a reference. In the former, there is *always* the belief in what is being proposed; in the latter, an opinion is being asked for, the use or results of which may or

may not show a desire for a successful outcome.

Good understanding of an entire situation is the only conscientious way that administrators can execute recommendations. Once the facts are in hand and the administrators believe in the outcome, a clear, concise, and well-written letter or report should be presented to the party or parties having final control over the issue.

See Also: COMMUNICATIONS; REFERENCES.

RECORD KEEPING

When one person reports to another, and the second party writes a memo to a third, who sends it to a fourth with the admonition to "file and record this," and the sequence is repeated twenty times a day, hundreds of times a week and thousands of times a year, the paperwork generated can be staggering. Still, valuable information must be stored and understood if the school system is to function properly. The key to the problem is good **record keeping.**

Each school system has its own procedures for the management of data, but certain general practices have been adopted for overall success throughout the nation. The first point for an administrator to remember is that record keeping is a four-step process.

First, is the *gathering* of data. A common mistake in this step is to gather more than one item or factor per record. For example, if the record consists of the number of students in individual grade levels, then IQ breakdowns, bus schedules or aptitude/achievement test scores are unnecessary data. Separate record sheets might be generated for each of the factors.

The second step is *correlation*. Here, the relationship between various records can be compiled. With the involvement of computers in record keeping, it has become easier for many kinds of data to be gathered separately, but filed with several "keys." Then, on any "run" or "call," any series of information can be culled. Therefore, a record of boys and girls per class, a record of expenditures for girls' and boys' physical education programs, and a record of budget proposals for the next fiscal year can be correlated to determine the cost per female pupil taking physical education in the coming year.

The third step involves *analyzing* the records. Once the data has been correlated, decisions can be made about it. Sometimes this may lead to the discovery that not enough is known. In that case, the process must be started again at step one. At other times, with sufficient data, whole programs can be changed because of new understandings gleaned from the data.

The fourth step is the *passing on, reporting* and *storing* of the records. This all-important step is the basic reason for the whole process. Some purpose must be served by the data, or else it is nothing but a waste of time, money, space, and energy. There are many reports that must be filed, on either a monthly or yearly basis. Each report needs certain data, and knowing which information is needed for what report, calls for a good reporting and storing system.

It is this system that is the second major point of record keeping over which administrators must keep control. Accuracy and clarity are essential. *The closer to classroom responsibility, the less actual reporting and record keeping time available.* Therefore, reporting from *classroom staff* should be of the checklist type, or at the most, one- or two-sentence fill-ins. The *supervisory personnel* should be asked for sentences and paragraphs only if necessary. *Building administrators* may be asked to report in paragraph form and occasionally in a short, one- or two-page format. *Central staff and board* reports are usually of the one-to-three page variety, with some longer. Any lengthier reporting at the various levels can lead to sloppy and inaccurate data because of the low priority given to the task.

The last aspect of record keeping that administrators must coordinate are the various duties of the *clerical staff.* The larger the district, the larger the staff, and thus the more responsibility that can be delegated to one or more of the secretaries. Assigning various reports to each, making sure that data is accessible to those staff members who require it, knowing when deadlines are for the different reports, and knowing to whom they are to be returned are just some of the tasks for which the clerical staff and the administrator are responsible. All this requires a well-run record keeping structure.

Periodic checks into the record keeping operation will insure that it is running smoothly. If, however, any problems should develop, the administrator can initiate change strategies to get vital information flowing again.

See Also: CENTRALIZED FILING; CLERICAL SERVICES; COMPUTERS; DIFFERENTIATED STAFFING; MONTHLY REPORTS; PERMANENT RECORDS; PERSONNEL FILES; SECRETARY; STUDENT INFORMATION; YEAR-END REPORTS.

REDUCTION IN FORCE

Reduction in force refers to the nonrenewal of contracts due to declining enrollment.

Education is very susceptible to population shifts. In today's mobile society, school populations fluctuate up or down as the economic base of the community rises or falls, and people move in or out of the district. Also, because of concepts like "Zero Population Growth" and "consolidation," student populations have been steadily declining nationwide. Finally, programs that require specific staff members may be suspended because of budget cuts. Consequently, from time to time, school boards may find themselves having to make the painful decision of reducing the instructional staff. Having determined that such a step is necessary, the board

usually turns to the administrator to decide who will have to be released.

Reduction in force (RIF) has never been a pleasant process, either for the RIFfing agent or the staff member being RIFfed. However, because the process has become so frequent, policies and procedures must be adopted to insure fairness and impartiality in the dismissals.

For example, let us say that ten positions must be RIFfed in a district. The first reductions would come to those personnel not holding full state certification, providing that fully-certified personnel could replace and perform all the duties of the RIFfed staff. If that were not possible, some other measures must be found. The next place to look is to the fully-certified staff members who have exhibited questionable performance, as *proven* by poor evaluations of building principals and/or supervisors. The third step lies in areas of expertise. If all staff members are equally certified, those who are proficient in more than one grade level or subject area, or who possess expertise in a wide variety of curricular materials, might be switched in order to keep those teachers with the most expertise. Finally, if further cuts are still required, then staff members with the least number of years of continuous service to the district will be RIFfed. Since this "last-hired-first-fired" approach is the most repugnant to most districts, it is always kept as a last resort.

Should administrators not want to propose a staff member for RIFfing, or feel that *any* RIFfing would be detrimental to the instructional level of the district, they may protest the board's decision to reduce the force. Also, teachers can protest, who feel that some adverse effect would be brought about to education if their positions were terminated. In both cases, if the school board does not relent, the parties may ask the courts for a *writ of mandamus* to review, and, if necessary, to reinstate any terminated personnel or programs.

See Also: DISMISSAL OF PERSONNEL; NONRENEWAL OF CONTRACT; UN-EMPLOYMENT.

REFERENCES

Because of their professional positions, administrators and teachers are often asked to act as **references.** It may be a student, action committee or program chairman who makes the request, but for whatever reason, expert opinion is being sought, and, once asked for, it should be given.

Sometimes the process is informal, as when one asks, "What do you think of...." More frequently, however, the rendering of an opinion is formalized, both in the request and the execution. Reference forms are issued by some occupations, colleges and services. In these instances, the administrator may merely be asked to fill in a checklist or write a short paragraph. Committees and boards usually call for written documentation accompanying the opinion.

There is quite a difference between a reference and a recommendation. When the administrator gives a reference, there is no *connotation of approval or disapproval of the final outcome.* For instance, a senior has asked his principal to be his reference on a college application. The principal cannot refuse, even if he feels that the student will probably not succeed in his chosen school. Since the principal knows the performance of the student and has the authority and position to judge that performance, he has an obligation to discharge the reference. However, if the same student asked for a recommendation, the principal might, as gently as possible, tell him his doubts about his eventual success. Because a recommendation states and infers approval, it can be withheld.

See Also: COMMUNICATION; RECOMMENDATION.

REINSTATEMENT

If staff members of administrators are removed from their positions, they may seek to have the decision reversed. If they are successful in their appeal, they are reinstated. While the procedure seems clear enough, the actual disposition of the **reinstatement** can be quite complicated.

The first condition of a reinstatment concerns *what* will be restored. For example, if a teacher were improperly dismissed, the *position* of "teacher" is what will be returned. Nothing is implied in a reinstatement that a teacher will be returned to *exactly* the position as before. The teacher must be permitted a class and all the rights and privileges of teaching, but that class can be in another building, at the same or similar grade level and within the same instructional area if not the same course title.

Another factor of reinstatement is the *condition* of employment. During the entry on reduction in force, it was noted that the courts could be asked to review the reduction and decide if it should stand or be reversed *(writ of mandamus)*. If the courts rule against the reduction, the program or personnel involved must be reinstated. Here, precise instructions are given as to the reinstitution of the interrupted employment or service. As an example, if the school has been offering an independent study program for gifted and talented children, and the board has RIFfed the teacher in charge and subsequently the program has been discontinued, reinstating the program would mean that the teacher must also be reinstated, since the condition of employment (i.e., the program) was now available.

Finally, reinstatement is not dependent upon the tenure, rank or certification of the person being restored. Rather, it is a policy, supported by statute, to which the school board adheres. In fact, sometimes it is even written into the contracts between the teacher association and board.

Clear understanding of the rights of the staff member who is dismissed,

nonrenewed or RIFfed, by both the administrator and the board, as well as any liability for damages, can alleviate much confusion should reinstatement be called for in the future.

See Also: DISMISSAL OF PERSONNEL; NONRENEWAL OF CONTRACT; REDUCTION IN FORCE.

RELEASED TIME

Released time is the authorized hour(s) spent by a student outside of school while classes are still in session.

Released time is not a new concept in education, having been around ever since students were allowed to leave early or come in late during planting and harvesting seasons. Schools have always been concerned with the total child and, therefore, have tried to make accommodations for outside obligations. Nowadays, released time has come under scrutiny because of its multifaceted nature. It can be for religious, curricular, extracurricular, economic, or social purposes. Each type has its own attendant policies, and school boards must decide which type they will permit and how they will structure them.

First, there is released time for *religious* purposes. This is permitted provided that certain criteria are met. Students must leave school grounds in order to participate in religious instruction/observation. They must be properly enrolled in such instruction and must present copies of proof of such registration and attendance as the board may require. The actual time away from class should be *no more than one hour per week*. If more is needed, the child's parents must petition the board and show cause why their child must be out of class for an extra amount of time.

The second type of released time is for *curricular* purposes. If the school conducts an independent study program or a work-study program, students may be permitted to arrange their class schedules in such a way as to leave the school grounds in order to attend either other classes or jobs. This is sometimes called the "open campus" method. Usually, course credits are arranged for these outside activities, and some proof of attendance is required by the board.

In the case of *extracurricular* released time, board policies are generally very carefully structured. Students participating in debates, musical performances or sports activities are permitted to leave the school only if very strict eligibility requirements are met. High grade averages and approval of the classroom teachers are common criteria.

With drop-out rates skyrocketing in some areas, some schools have been trying a type of *economic* released time as an incentive for staying in school. While not actually a work-study arrangement, students who are gainfully employed are permitted to arrange their class schedules on a more open basis. The board usually requires documentation of the employment, the need for the student to work and his or her attendance record, both in class and on the job. The percentage of time spent both in and out of school is generally individually arranged between the school, community support services and the parents. In the systems trying this approach, great care is taken to insure that education is the primary goal, rather than the job.

The last type of released time is fairly new. It is called *social integration* released time. It has been gaining support among school districts dealing with "disaffected" students. These are juvenile offenders who have been in prison or reform school, who are involved with drug or alcohol rehabilitation centers, and/or who are in need of counseling on a steady basis. The school, working through the child study team and outside agencies, coordinates a schedule of class attendance and released time to allow the student the opportunity of a structured re-entry into "normal" education.

Whatever the purpose for the released time, there should never be a sacrifice of the basic reason for students being in school: namely, instruction. If the children are not getting enough of this instruction to meet their educational needs, then it is the released time that must be curtailed, not the class time.

See Also: CHURCH-STATE SEPARATION; COUNSELING; EXTRACURRICULAR ACTIVITIES; MIGRANTS; SCHEDULE; STUDENT INFORMATION; WORK-STUDY PROGRAM.

RELIGION

See BIBLE; CHRISTIAN SCIENTISTS; CHURCH-STATE SEPARATION; FIRST AMENDMENT GUARANTEES; FUNDAMENTAL INTEREST THEORY; JEHOVAH'S WITNESSES; PRIVATE AND PAROCHIAL SCHOOLS; RELEASED TIME; SHARED TIME.

REMEDIAL INSTRUCTION

Mention **remedial** classes to any member of the academic community and the sparks immediately begin to fly. Parents wonder why *their* child is in them; kids would rather be horse-whipped than attend them; teachers see them as either a godsend or play-pens; administrators advocate them to insure educational success, but see little concrete results; and school boards find them a large drain on the budget, often with little to show for the cash spent.

The focal points in the discussion revolve around four basic questions concerning remedial instruction. Looking at each, perception might be the real key to understanding. Remember, it has been said that reality is not what matters as much as our *perception* of reality. Therefore, let us look at some of the questions concerning remedial instruction, as well as the various perceptions they have engendered.

First, *who should get remedial instruction?* If the belief is that every child who enters school deserves to reach his full potential, then *every* child could be placed in some type of remedial class at some point. Because that is impossible, each state and/or local board has set some guidelines for entrance. As with any kind of guidelines, however, there are always cases that hover around the edges. What to do with these borderline cases can cause enough discontent to destroy the whole program.

Second, *how will those enrolled be chosen?* Standardized tests, teacher observation recommendation and parental requests are all methods that have been used for selection. But what of the child who *can't*, as opposed to the one who *won't?* This quandry, too, can ruin a program.

The third question begins to set a focus to the program. *How long should a student receive remedial instruction?* If the student *can't* perform, then it would seem he would stay in the program until he can. But, if the student *won't*, should he be kept in the program until he will? Also, if they *can't*, is remedial instruction the answer?

Which leads to the last question. *What should remedial instruction accomplish?* In some districts, the aim of the remedial instruction program is to help students over minor difficulties so that they do not become major obstacles to learning, and then return these students to mainstream classes as soon as they are ready. In others, the program is a permanent adjunct to the academic structure. If ability groups are sometimes called "airplanes," "cars," and "boats," then remedial instruction is for "slow boats." But even with this method, some districts differ on the program's aim. Some see this slower tract as a way to allow underachievers to gain success at their own pace, so that at some future point, perhaps next term or next year, they can be placed in regular classes. Others see it as a "holding action" against further skill deterioration that will be maintained *ad infinitum*.

According to some states, classified or learning disabled students must be given assisted learning programs *above* the remedial level. In fact, including a classified student in remedial classes is *against* the codes and statutes in some states. Yet written into the administrative codes of other states is the dictum that remedial instruction's purpose is to assist *just* these students. Imagine the difficulties of an administrator who is faced with an irate parent who has just moved into the state and is confused by the placing of her child in a remedial class under the new district's policy. The administrator is put in the position of saying that the child either got better instruction in the old district or that the old district "cheated" the child.

What is being called for by administrative groups and school boards is a national policy on remedial instruction. Further, individualized programs are being adopted so that once a child moves, the program continues, regardless of the instructional title into which the child's program falls. Finally, the more the students, parents, teachers, and the community in general know about the various instructional levels that are used in the district, including remedial, the less confusion, distrust and hostility there will be towards programs whose only true function is to allow students to reach their full potential.

See Also: ABILITY GROUPING; ABILITY LEVELS; COMPETENCY-BASED PROGRAMS; COMPENSATORY EDUCATION; GOALS AND OBJECTIVES; INSTRUCTION; LEARNING DISABILITIES; STUDENT INFORMATION; UNDERACHIEVERS.

RENEWAL OF CONTRACT

School boards and their employees enter into yearly contracts. Therefore, notification of the rehiring of staff and their intent to continue service must be exchanged each year. Each district must have clear and unambiguous methods for this exchange. Every staff member must know (and in some cases have in their possession) the exact methodology used in his district. The reason for the precision is to insure that no staff member receives a contract to which he or she is not entitled, nor is any employee denied a contract that is due.

The most common practice for **renewal** is for the board to send *"letters of intent"* to its employees sometime during the last two months of school. The employees then reply that they either will or will not be back for another year. The board is bound by its letter; that is, a contract exists that they are offering to the employees. The employees, however, are free to change their minds. That is, they do not have to finally accept the contract. Often the letters are sent and replied to, regardless of how negotiations for any new contracts are going. In fact, the letters usually contain a clause worded "...pursuant to the new contract...."

Whatever the administrative structure used, the person up for renewal must be notified in sufficient time to prepare either for other employment or to continue in the present district.

See Also: ACCEPTANCE OF CONTRACTS; CONTRACTS; OFFER OF CONTRACTS AND RECRUITING.

REPORT CARDS

Administrators can tell when **report cards** are about to go out without ever having to look at a calendar. Nothing seems to cause as much tension in a school as this seemingly innocent information delivery system. There are many reasons for this apprehension, and educators have always struggled with the causes. As part of a quick analysis, a brief look into what report cards convey and how they are used might be helpful.

Generally, report cards are small, two- or four-sided forms, containing the subjects and activities in which the student participates. Beside each entry, there are spaces for numerical or alphabetical evaluations of the student's achievement during the marking period. In some districts, there is also space provided for symbols concerning study habits, conduct and personality development. At the bottom, there may also be space to show attendance figures for the period. In addition, there is a place for the parents/guardians to sign and make their own comments.

The very nature of reports cards often inspires many questions about them. What do those marks mean? How is that particular child's mark decided? Was there a criterion against which the child was measured? If so, how were the criteria compiled? Some schools have made concerted efforts to reduce this confusion by holding parent group conferences, spending counseling time with entire classes to discuss the marking system, and publicizing through newsletters, lectures and workshops *exactly* what the school means to convey by its report card.

The second point about report cards concerns *how they are used*. Are they, as one second grader sadly stated, "...just another thing to stop me from getting my bicycle for Christmas," or do they indeed serve some positive educational purpose for everyone? Most educators agree that some reporting system is vital. A record must be kept of what the student has accomplished, and that record must be shared with the home. The reasoning is simple. the school requires certain information to be learned, the children must learn it, and any help the home can provide will assist them in learning it. Under this reasoning there can be neither "good" nor "bad" report cards. Rather, there are statements implied such as "Reading seemed harder for Johnny this period than last," or "Mary is finally grasping long division." When comments on study habits or conduct are added, students and their parents can see which areas help or hinder learning. For example, if the grade in Social Studies indicates that a problem is developing and the behavioral grade also shows some slippage, but the student knows that the material was not too difficult, more concentration on conduct is obviously advantageous. This is, of course, the ideal usage, and it quite often differs in practice. An attempt should, however, be made to use them to the best educational advantage possible.

Constant review of the methodology of grading, along with community and student understanding of the validity of report cards, and open and fair discussions of student evaluations will assist administrators and their staffs in taking some of the panic out of this vital educational tool.

See Also: COMMUNICATIONS; EVALUATION; GRADES; PARENT CONFERENCES; PERMANENT RECORDS; STUDENT INFORMATION; UNGRADED.

REPRESENTATION

Educators and school boards enter into contract negotiations with each other. They also form liaison committees, both with themselves and with the community at large. Since practicality prohibits every member of both parties to speak to every issue, selected members take part as representatives of the larger constituency.

There is no statute, code or policy that can stipulate who shall be this representative. That decision *always* rests with the person or group that seeks **representation.** while it is customary for two or three teachers to be the representatives in negotiations on the teacher's side, it is not mandatory. They could select an attorney, a trusted retired colleague, or anyone else they want. Also, the board could be represented by anyone who could speak for them.

The question of who shall represent a group can cause considerable turmoil if not handled sensibly and calmly. Teacher's groups rival each other to be representatives at national, state, and local levels. Sometimes the "hawks" (liberals) and "doves" (conservatives) in a district argue about who should work on and how negotiations should be carried on for a new contract. By following two main premises, much disruption can be avoided. First, when an issue is in doubt, it should be presented to the larger group, and they should be allowed to vote upon it by *secret ballot*. Second, once the decision has been made as to which faction shall represent the whole, efforts should be made to form an immediate liaison to the defeated or disenfranchised minority.

See Also: ADVISORY COUNCILS; AGENT; LIAISON; MEDIATION AND MEDIATOR; RATIFICATION; VOTING.

RESERVED POWERS

Reserved powers are those rights, duties and privileges of the states not expressly shared or relinquished to the national government by the United States Constitution.

The Constitution is often called a "living document," and nothing seems to keep it more lively than the constantly recurring conflict of *"state's rights"* (as stated in the 10th Amendment) and *"national supremacy"* (according to Article VI). The Founding Fathers must have had clear ideas about what each of those concepts meant, but the distance of over 200 years, innumerable judicial interpretations, and changing politics and situations have so clouded them that precise, practical applications are all but impossible.

At the present time, education has become the new battlefield for the conflict of these two policies in American government. In all discussions of policy and power in this area or any other, the basic question remains, "Who has the power to do what, for whom and to whom?"

There are three types of Constitutional powers. First, there are *exclusive rights.* Succinctly stated, these are the powers of the Congress to govern the nation for the good of all. Herein lies its right to coin money, raise and maintain a navy, declare war, raise taxes, and pass laws. Rarely are these powers challenged. The second type are the *reserved powers* of the states. According to the Tenth Amendment, these are "The powers not delegated to the United States by the Constitution, nor prohibited by it to the States, (and) are *reserved to the States* respectively, or to the people." (emphasis added) Strictly interpreted, these would cover any areas of activity *not expressly mentioned* in the Constitution. Purists on constitutional law feel that such matters as education, safety, health, and welfare, since there is no mention of them in the Constitution, are the sole province of the states and the people (voters). It is the third type of power which exists within the Constitution that is the most explosive and divisive. These are the *concurrent powers.* Simply, these exist where both the state *and* the national government have jurisdiction. This includes areas that are not expressly provided for by the Constitution, or by judicial interpretation exclusively, to either the national government or the states. Here, the states are permitted to act, but *only* if the action is consented to by Congress. This final "right of review," sometimes called "national supremacy," takes its authority from Article VI of the Constitution: "This Constitution ... shall be the supreme Law of the Land; and the Judges in every State shall be bound thereby, *any Thing in the Constitution or Laws of any State to the contrary notwithstanding ...* and all executive and judicial Officers, *both of the United States and the States, shall be bound to support this Constitution...."* (emphasis added). Under this authority, Congress may exercise its full power and the states may not interfere with the national government as it pursues constitutional activity. It is this power that has permitted Congress its regulatory systems, as well as its power to make laws concerning such diverse areas as trucking, food subsidies and energy.

While few people would argue with the national government's right to handle national security, many do challenge its "interference" with individual desires and goals. Such demands as revenue sharing, state autonomy in education and welfare and state referendums for divergent taxation codes are but a few points in the conflict. The national mood seems to be shifting toward the "states' rights" approach. Indeed, the election of Ronald Reagan, in 1980, was seen as a renewal of demands for return to the states of the full use of their reserved powers.

See Also: CONSTITUTIONAL RIGHTS; FEDERAL AGENCIES, FEDERAL AID, FEDERAL PROGRAMS; STATE AGENCIES, STATE AID, STATE PROGRAMS; TAXES.

RESIGNATION

There are circumstances which occur that preclude board members, administrators or staff members from completing their duties. At that point, they may wish to resign. The procedure for tendering a **resignation** may differ from place to place, but, in substance, they all call for a written statement to be sent to the controlling body expressing the individual's intent to resign.

The *reasons given by board members* may be health, change of residence to outside of the district, or anything of such a compelling nature that it could distract them from the performance of their duties. No prescribed length of time is required for a board member's notification of intent, but courtesy usually calls for 30 days.

Reasons stated by administrators from central staff to building level, may include health and the impossibility of performance. Because contracts are involved, the time of notification is generally a part of board policy. Commonly, it is 60-90 days prior to the new term starting. If the resignation must occur during a school year, notification should be given as soon as possible to the controlling body.

The *teaching staff,* too, may give the same reasons for resigning and is generally bound by the same time periods for notification.

This is all assuming that the resignation was voluntary, albeit regretted. However, should board members, administrators or staff members be convicted of a felony or engage in such conduct as to make the carrying out of their duties impossible, they may be given the option of "resigning" rather than being summarily dismissed. As long as this decision is reached *without pressure* being placed upon the "resigner," there is nothing illegal about the practice. But, should an employee be *forced to resign* without due process and under great duress, there is recourse *after the fact* through a writ of mandamus. If the courts can find that there was illegal pressure, the resignation can be withdrawn and the employee reinstated.

See Also: MENTAL DISTRESS; PERSONNEL FILES; REINSTATEMENT.

RETARDED CHILD

A **retarded child** is one possessing an intellectual capacity below the average range of intelligence and having deficits in adaptive behavior that adversely affect educational performance and social functioning.

This entry specifically deals with those children who are *mentally retarded,* and not those who are physically or culturally handicapped, even though they may also have these deficiencies.

Precise definitions are difficult, but school administrative codes and public laws have given educators guidelines for both identifying and arranging for the instructional environment of retarded children. In the figure on page 312, derived from the U.S. President's Panel on Mental Retardation, the four most common types of retardation and their characteristics are noted.

Specialists have further defined and proposed optimum environments for these children.

Educable—a level of retardation that is characterized by intellectual capacity, as measured by a clinical test of intelligence, within a range encompassing approximately 1½ to 3 standard deviations below the mean, and a low level of ability to think abstractly; the optimum environment is 15 pupils, in a self-contained classroom, with one instructor.

Trainable is a level of retardation that is characterized by intellectual capacity, as measured by a clinical test of intelligence, which falls 3 standard deviations below the mean, shows an inability to use symbols in the solution of problems of even low complexity, and demonstrates an inability to function socially without direct and close supervision; the optimum environment consists of 10 pupils, in a self-contained classroom, with one instructor.

Both of these educational programs can be and usually are available within the school and/or district in which the child resides. This may not be the case for the next two classifications.

Eligible for Day Training is a level of retardation characterized by an inability to give evidence to a child study team of understanding and responding, in a positive manner, to simple basic wants or needs; the optimum environment consists of 9 children, in a self-contained classroom, with a pupil/staff ratio of 3 to 1.

Residential children who need day training may have to, and gener-

TYPE	CHARACTERISTICS FROM BIRTH TO ADULTHOOD		
	Birth Through Age Five	**Six Through Twenty**	**Twenty-One And Over**
Mild: **EDUCABLE**	Often not noticed as retarded by casual observer but is slower to walk, feed himself and talk than most children.	Can acquire practical skills and reading and arithmetic to a third to sixth grade level with special education. Can be guided toward social conformity.	Can usually achieve social and vocational skills adequate to self-maintenance, may need occasional guidance and support when under unusual social or economic stress.
Moderate: **TRAINABLE**	Noticeable delays in motor development, especially in speech; responds to training in various self-help activities.	Can learn simple communication, elementary health and safety habits, and simple manual skills; does not progress in functional reading or arithmetic.	Can perform simple tasks under sheltered conditions; participates in simple recreation; travels alone in familiar places; usually incapable of self-maintenance.
Severe: **ELIGIBLE FOR DAY TRAINING**	Marked delay in motor development; little or no communication skill; may respond to training in elementary self-help, for example, self-feeding.	Usually walks barring specific disability; has some understanding of speech and can make some response; can profit from systematic habit training.	Can conform to daily routines and repetitive activities; needs continuing direction and supervision in a protective environment.
Profound: **RESIDENTIAL**	Gross retardation; minimal capacity for functioning in sensorimotor areas; needs nursing care.	Obvious delays in all areas of development; shows basic emotional responses; may respond to skillful training in use of legs, hands and jaws; needs close supervision.	May walk, needs nursing care, has primitive speech; usually benefits from regular physical activity; incapable of self-maintenance.

ally do, go outside their district to centers that have the facilities and staff to care for them, but they return to their homes for most of the day. However, residential students live at the centers.

Once the classification of the student has been made, an Individualized Education Program (IEP) must be written by the child study team. The IEP must include a statement explaining the rationale for the type of educational program and placement is the least restrictive environment appropriate for the pupil, and a description of the extent to which the pupil will participate in regular educational programs (mainstream) if appropriate. The local board of education is responsible for the cost of placing educationally handicapped pupils. The board shall not be responsible for residential costs when the reason is home condition or parental choice. They are responsible for the cost of non-medical care, and room and board that is necessary to provide special education and related services to an eligible, handicapped pupil placed in a residential program.

See Also: CHILD STUDY TEAM; DIAGNOSIS; HANDICAPPED; INTELLIGENCE TESTING; LEARNING DISABILITIES; MAINSTREAMING; PSYCHOLOGICAL STUDIES; PUBLIC LAW 94-142; REMEDIAL INSTRUCTION; SPEECH THERAPY; SPECIAL EDUCATION; STUDENT INFORMATION; TRANSPORTATION.

RETENTION OF STUDENTS

Nothing seems sounder educationally, yet more abhorrent socially than **retention.** Words like, "left back," "failure," "dummy" and worse are common epithets used to characterize those students who are retained. Educators more often use concepts such as "reinforcement," "increased confidence through success," "giving a little more time to mature," and "caring for the child rather than the calendar" as the true reasons behind retention.

There is no built-in clock inside a child that mechanically says Reading will be mastered by 6.5 years of age or the last day of first grade, whichever comes first. Such subject-area skills as telling time and rudimentary math, and sociability skills such as following directions, working independently and sharing materials are equally not automatically conquered in set time limits. Therefore, school districts have adopted procedures that allow for flexibility, especially in the lower grades of elementary school, to compensate for these individual differences.

Retention is considered when a child is in grades K-3, or, on rare occasions, in grades 4-8, when the child is achieving significantly below ability or grade levels, when it will not cause undue social and/or emotional hardship, and when it has a reasonable chance of benefiting the total growth and success of the child.

Notification of the intent to retain

should be given to the parents/guardians as soon as possible. Teachers and administrators can usually decide that retention is a viable educational plan after the child has been in their class for at least one full semester. Consultations with supervisors and/or support personnel before forming the opinion is also a sound practice. But, as soon as all the facts are in hand, the teachers must be ready to discuss retention and its ramifications with the parents/guardians.

Overcoming the negativism of retention can be very difficult. So difficult in fact, that some systems have adopted open scheduling or "continuous progress" programs so that there are no absolute steps, advances or "promotions" at all, until at least the fourth or fifth grade. Rather, the students learn new things as they master the old *at their own pace*. One other advantage to this program is that rarely does a child have difficulty with all aspects of learning. Consequently, Spelling and Writing might be on level, Math a few steps ahead, and Reading a few steps late. Under retention programs, all subjects would have to be taught at the lowest level of progress, with no consideration for those skills the child has already mastered.

If administrators discover great opposition to retention, a re-education of the community, in order that it may understand retention's benefits, would have to become a major priority. If there were still adverse feelings about retention, then perhaps the school system should consider using another educational program to aid those students who would benefit from a second chance at success.

See Also: CHILD-CENTERED; INDIVIDUALIZATION; PARENT CONFERENCES; PERMANENT RECORDS; READINESS; SOCIAL PROMOTION; STUDENT INFORMATION; SUPERVISION (STAFF); SUPERVISION (STUDENTS); UNDERACHIEVERS; UNGRADED.

RETIREMENT

Several municipal, state and federal positions have not only maximum age limits, but also length of service requirements for employees to be eligible for **retirement.** While there is no consensus, the most common age limit is 65-70, with at least twenty years on the job. It has been held unconstitutional that a person be required to retire at a certain age, but there is nothing to say that the same person must retire after serving twenty years.

The process for retirement involves notification to the controlling body of the employee's intent to retire. The controlling body then reviews the employee's record to assure itself that the requirements have been met. If all is in order, the retirement will be accepted. In education, the usual time for retirement is the end of the school year, although there is nothing to prevent the employee from leaving at any time during the year, providing that adequate notice has been given.

The central staff office performs several services for the retiree to facilitate any compensations due. Pension and/or annuity fund accounts must be put in order and financial matters concluded *before* the employee actually leaves service.

Since administrators and staff members who retire have contributed much to the community, school and profession they have served, it is common for dinners, parties or other testimonials to be given to honor them. Often simple gifts are also presented as tokens of appreciation.

See Also: ACKNOWLEDGEMENT; ADDRESSES (SPEECHES); APPRECIATION, LETTER OF; GIFTS; INSURANCE; NEWS RELEASES; PERSONNEL FILES.

RIGHTS AND RESPONSIBILITIES

Rights and responsibilities are those duties and protections maintained by educational professionals while actively engaged in teaching, administrating and dealing with the academic community.

A separation between the professional staff of a school district and the students, parents and/or community has been made here for clarity. This entry will only deal with the former.

Much has been said about the constitutional protections given to educators as pertains to their personal conduct or beliefs. However, with the single exception of a nationally established "Code of Ethics" by teacher associations, little has been mentioned about the rights and responsibilities of educators as they deal with the actual performance of duties. Since the mid-1960s, more and more has been written about what the schools can and cannot do, should or should not try to accomplish, and will or will not be held accountable for. During this change, educators are finding themselves seemingly stripped of much of their "powers," while being held liable for everything from increased violence and lack of discipline in the schools to lower Reading scores.

The courts are writing the new educators rights and responsibilities views by handing down case-by-case decisions, which immediately become precedents for more cases. One of the main reasons for this "judge-made law" has been the feeling that education is everybody's business, not just the professionals'. No matter what is done, everyone has the right to challenge it. Since everyone contributes to the operation of the schools, each should be given an opportunity to decide how they should be run. This has left the professional educator somewhat adrift.

With so much controversy surrounding an educator's rights and responsibilities, state boards of education have been trying to establish written policies on many aspects of education that were heretofore "assumed." Some, like job descriptions and professional ethics are fairly straightforward, but others, like the scope of record keeping responsibilities, instructional freedoms and fiscal responsibilities are being fashioned to enable all those involved in the schools to work from the same point of understanding. Usually, with the announcement of the policy, any court challenges can be made and decided upon before the educator becomes involved.

In the future, it is hoped by teachers, administrators and board associations that education will once again be accorded the status of a profession capable of setting its own regulations while safeguarding the academic, behavioral and social activities of the students it serves.

See Also: ACADEMIC FREEDOM; ACCOUNTABILITY; AUTHORITY, TEACHER; CHIEF STATE SCHOOL OFFICIAL; CIVIL RIGHTS; CODE OF ETHICS; CONSTITUTIONAL RIGHTS; INSTRUCTION; LIABILITY; POLITICS AND THE SCHOOL; PROFESSIONAL ASSOCIATIONS FOR SCHOOL ADMINISTRATORS; PROFESSIONAL ASSOCIATIONS FOR TEACHERS; SUPERVISION (STAFF); SUPERVISION (STUDENTS); TAXES; UNIONS.

S

SABBATICAL LEAVE

Sabbatical leave is a leave of absence, with full or partial financial compensation, granted to an educator for the purpose of self-improvement.

A teacher may apply for a sabbatical leave usually only following a designated number of consecutive years of service within a school district. This number may vary depending upon the district, but the minimum number is usually six years.

During the leave, the recipient is expected to furnish evidence of self-improvement within his professional field. For example, a sabbatical might be granted for a teacher to earn a Master's Degree in Guidance or Administration and Supervision. Evidence of the accomplishment of this objective might be the degree itself or a transcript of courses taken. Leave might be denied, however, if the educator sought a degree in Business Administration in order to open his own business.

When the sabbatical leave is terminated, it is expected that the teacher granted such leave will return to the school district that has granted the sabbatical and will serve there for a specified time.

In general, teachers must apply to administrative authorities, and only a limited number of sabbatical leaves are granted each year. Determination of who shall be granted such leave must rest upon criteria established by individual school boards.

See Also: LEAVE OF ABSENCE; PERSONNEL FILES; PROFESSIONAL IMPROVEMENT PLAN.

SAFE PLACE STATUTES

Safe place statutes are laws requiring that buildings and areas used by the public be maintained in a safe and secure manner.

In order to protect people using public buildings, areas and conveyances, laws were passed to insure that these "public" places would be safe. This leads to the secure assump-

317

tion, under law, that the public places will not have broken steps, lightless corridors, faulty wiring, etc. Therefore, people taking responsible precautions for their own safety can then expect that nothing will harm them.

Schools, being public buildings, fall under these statutes. Students, their parents, employees, and members of the community have the right to assume that the school buildings and grounds are free from hazard. The school may require visitors, students and employees to act in a safe, reasonable and prudent manner, but it must still be ultimately responsible for maintaining a safe and secure area.

See Also: AUTHORITY, EXPRESS AND IMPLIED; BUILDINGS; CAPACITY; GROUNDS; HABITABLE; IMPUTED NEGLIGENCE; LIABILITY; NEGLIGENCE; SAFETY; SUPERVISION (STUDENTS); TRANSPORTATION.

SAFETY

Safety is the freedom from danger, injury or damages; it includes any device, service or prevention of accident.

Under the Fourteenth Amendment and its interpretations, one of the top priorities of the state is "the protection of public health, safety and morals." Schools, which are actually agents of the state, will and must promote these same goals.

Safety is a wide category, and it is generally divided into three major areas of interest. These are *protection and security, prevention through in-*

struction and prevention through supervision.

When a school is made safe, one of the first items checked is its overall environment of *protection* and *security*. Often, if the neighborhood presents a major safety hazard to those using the facility, the school system may consider the possibility of consolidating and moving out of the area entirely. If this alternative is not possible, outside agencies or internal security personnel may be hired to insure safety. Also, locked doors with a limited number of keys offer protection to equipment, buildings and grounds.

Prevention through instruction is the area of curricular studies and outside programs that deals with safety precautions and procedures. Age and/or grade-appropriate classes in traffic, bicycle and pedestrian safety, driver education, fire prevention drills, emergency procedures, and first aid courses are all part of this prevention method. Frequently, the school, through liaison officers, works closely with local police, fire and first aid groups to help make students and staff aware of good safety procedures.

It is the last major thrust of the safety practices, *prevention through supervision,* of which the school is most aware. Assigning proper personnel to hazardous areas like playgrounds and street crossings helps the school maintain high safety profiles. Careful supervision in laboratory Science classes, Shop or Industrial Arts courses, and Physical Education and sports activities can eliminate unsafe conditions. The school boards, too, help maintain close supervision of compliance with safety regulations through regular plant inspections, driver and vehicle inspections, fire inspections, traffic safety, and emergency evacuation procedures.

Safety regulations should always be posted and observed in all public buildings, but because of the age and concentration of their occupants, schools must be especially aware of them.

See Also: AUTHORITY, EXPRESS AND IMPLIED; BUILDINGS; FORE-SEEABILITY; FOURTEENTH AMENDMENT GUARANTEES; GROUNDS; HABITABLE; INSURANCE; KEYS; NEGLIGENCE; SAFE PLACE STATUTES; SPORTS; SUPERVISION (STAFF); SUPERVISION (STUDENTS); TRANSPORTATION.

SALARY

Salary guides or schedules are present in virtually all contracts between teachers and their respective boards.

There are many types of increases and deductions negotiated and allowed in the basic salary of a beginning teacher. Without getting into a discussion of merit pay, the most common increases are steps or increments, generally given to an employee after each completed year in the district. There may also be seniority increases or increments given after the employee has been in the district for five, ten or twenty years. Salaries are also reflective of furthered education, and increases are

generally given at Bachelors + 10, BA + 30, Masters, MA + 10, MA + 30, and the Doctorate. The salary deductions are also clarified in the contract. Generally, these include federal or state taxes, insurance plans, pension/annuity funds, and association/union dues.

There is very little consensus on the "proper" salary for the various levels of responsibility in education. What does appear to hold is that starting building principals make about twice the amount of a starting teacher, assistant superintendents and support personnel (psychologists, curriculum coordinators, supervisors) make about three times the amount, and superintendents about four times that salary.

Salaries were perhaps the first major area teachers were permitted to negotiate. Therefore, it is difficult to say which entered the public's mind first: teacher pay or teacher accountability. Whichever it was, salaries are more often becoming points of contention between the community and educators. Teacher, citing increased difficulties in teaching, poor comparison with outside employment, and their monumental responsibilities, are demanding higher salaries. Taxpayers, citing the poor performance of some school functions along with rising taxes and high inflation, and "short" days and "180-day" years, demand that the "product," the educated child, must improve before any more salaries are increased.

The best that administrators can do, both for themselves and their staffs, is to increase the community's awareness of just what is happening in the schools, including not only the achievements but also the problems. Only when the public fully understands what is being done will it feel a vested interest in the outcome, including a decently paid academic staff.

See Also: ACADEMIC FREEDOM; BUDGET; CONTRACTS; DIFFERENTIATED STAFFING; INCREMENTS; MEDIATION AND MEDIATOR; MERIT PAY; NEGOTIATIONS; WITHHOLDING.

SANCTIONS (PERMISSIONS)

Sanctions (Permissions) refers to the giving of authorization to carry out a plan, idea or action; it includes sharing responsibility for the outcome.

In every academic community there is a chain of command that is used to filter decisions down and push information up. Each link in the chain has its own sphere of responsibility. If a person wished to skip one or more steps, he would have to discuss the reason with each link in the chain of command before the final decision could be made. The decision to allow the skipping of the step would constitute a sanction at that level.

For example, suppose some teachers wanted to propose a demand directly to the superintendent, or a superintendent wished to submit a proposal directly to teachers. The link between the two is the building principal. If either party wished to skip that link in the command structure, it would require the permission or sanction of the building principal in order for it to be justified within the setup of the district. Diagrammed, it looks like this:

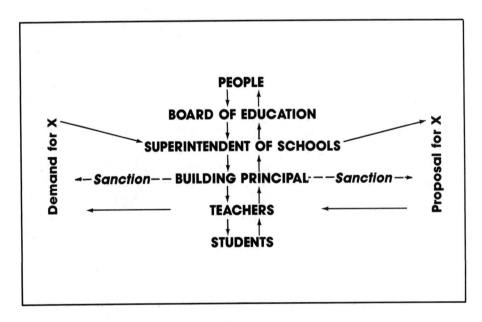

The chain becomes a bit more difficult to follow when the district is run under decentralization. Building principals are encouraged to handle many more items internally. Still, these administrators are ultimately responsible to their central staff. Since it was considered unlikely that the central staff would be constantly aware of each local principal's problems, local advisory councils (LAC) were formed. The LAC's were given the permission of the board of education to act as liaisons in the chain. They are also given the right of sanctioning the flow of information.

Under the decentralized plan, the same situation we diagrammed earlier would look like this:

decision; second, they provide for careful preparation and study before submission, which prevents poorly-conceived actions; and, finally, with each step being consulted, the administrators and their personnel remain on firm ground. They can then move with complete authority.

See Also: ADMINISTRATOR; ADVISORY COUNCILS; AGENT; AUTHORITY, BOARD; AUTHORITY, TEACHER; BOARD OF EDUCATION; CENTRAL STAFF; CHANGE STRATEGIES; DECENTRALIZATION; DIFFERENTIATED STAFFING; FACULTY; MEDIATION AND MEDIATOR; RATIFICATION; SUPERINTENDENT OF SCHOOLS.

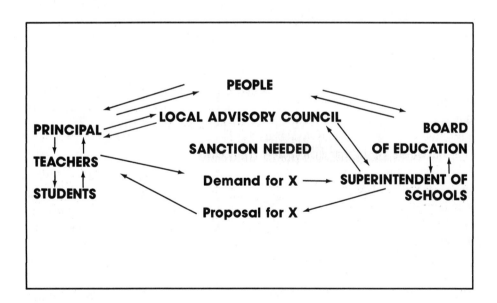

Sanctions serve three main purposes for educational organizations: first, they assure support from those who share responsibility for the final

SAVE-HARMLESS STATUTES

See IMPUTED NEGLIGENCE.

SCHEDULE

Building administrators go through a yearly struggle to ensure the maximum use of all human and physical plant resources, the most effective handling of all guidance and support programs, and the ultimate accomplishment of the goals and objectives of the school. The way this is managed is through the **scheduling** of students, teachers and classes.

Every level of the academic community has input into this basically administrative function. Teachers are concerned about what classes they are going to teach, the number of students in them, and the number of preparations needed to institute instruction.

Individual differences among the staff can cause administrators their first set of scheduling headaches. Some teachers want one preparation per day. This means that each of their classes must be in the same subject and level. These teachers claim that this allows for greater individualization, but others claim that this leads to decreased enthusiasm as the same material is repeated class after class. Another group of teachers, rare but equally adament, prefer one preparation per class, because they feel it puts a high level of freshness into their instruction. Also, these teachers seem to prefer to have cross-level or cross-grade classes. Their opponents contend that there is too much valuable time spent on paper work and lesson plans to warrant the slight gain in teacher "morale." Generally, the staff is most content with two preparations at one level or two preparations at two levels.

Problems also come from *the courses* needed to progress from grade to grade and eventually to graduate from the system. Certain courses, such as English, Math and Social Studies, the *"requireds,"* must be taught every day and each child must receive a set number of hours of instruction in them. There are also *"special"* courses such as Art, Music and Industrial Arts that are offered as part of the curriculum. Finally, there are *electives, mini-courses, and independent study programs* that may also be included. Each of these three segments are vital parts of the school's academic program and must be scheduled.

But it is the actual placement of students that takes the most time for the administrator. Many decisions must be made before the first student enters the first classroom. These decisions are based upon a series of questions:

What level is the school, elementary or secondary? If it is elementary, the classes are usually self-contained with a couple of "specials." Scheduling here is done without student input and is done daily by the teachers within the class and yearly within the school. If the level is secondary, the students will select their courses, and the overall planning of the schedule may be done by quarter, semester or year.

How will the courses be presented pursuant to movement pat-

terns? In lower elementary levels, students stay in one room while teachers come in to them; in upper elementary and some levels of middle schools, students go to teachers who stay in the rooms with their instructional materials; in secondary schools, both students and teachers move to areas that best suit the class which is being presented.

How many periods, of how long a duration, will how many students attend? Excluding self-contained classrooms where time spent on tasks can vary throughout the day, items like *class length* (optimum: 45-50 minutes), *length of day* (generally six or seven periods), and *class size* (average: 30-35 pupils per instructor) will determine how students can be scheduled. Class size can be particularly difficult, since more students can be placed in lecture situations than in labs or other specialized instruction; more can fit into some "specials" than into supplemental instruction programs.

What method of scheduling is best suited to student, staff and community needs? There are three distinct methods of placing students. The first is the *Group (Block) Method*. Its characteristics include very little or no student selection of courses and an academic program weighted toward "requireds," with just a few "specials," and almost no electives. Control rests solely with the administrator. Once class size is decided, students are distributed, with a certain number taking certain courses with specific teachers. Little conflict is apparent because of the lack of possible variables. If "specials" or electives are available, these are assigned in the same one or two periods of the day only. A typical group master schedule is shown below.

If the end of the day is not optimum for the school, any periods can be selected for "specials." By adding sections (more than one class of the same subject), the above grid could contain any number of students.

The second method is the *Individualized (Mosaic) Method*. Here, students select those courses they want and decide when they want to take them. The program is weighted toward "total education," with "requireds," "specials" and "electives/mini-courses" all being considered important. While control rests ultimately with the administrator, it is also the province of the students, their parents and the school's guidance per-

Periods	1	2	3	4	5	6	or	1	2	3	4	5	6	7
	A	B	C	D	E	"S"		A	B	C	D	E	"S"	"S"
	B	C	D	E	A	"S"		B	C	D	E	A	"S"	"S"
	C	D	E	A	B	"S"		C	D	E	A	B	"S"	"S"
	D	E	A	B	C	"S"		D	E	A	B	C	"S"	"S"
	E	A	B	C	D	"S"		E	A	B	C	D	"S"	"S"

sonnel. Since this method is the most commonly used in middle and secondary schools, its procedures warrant a closer scrutiny.

During the last two weeks of April or the beginning of May, students fill out a *preliminary registration form*. These are correlated into how many students want which subjects. Then, the administrator constructs a *conflict sheet* that shows how many combinations of subject sessions can be scheduled within a certain number of periods, including homerooms, lunches, and study halls. Either two weeks before, or during the first week of the new term, students fill in their own schedules against this *Individualized Master Schedule*. Administratively, senior classes and students taking those subjects meeting in only one time slot per week are given first choice; each successive class is then permitted to complete its schedules. The selection process is monitored by Guidance personnel to avoid conflicts.

Another method, the *Variable Modular Schedule*, came into favor in the late 1960s and early 1970s. It allowed for variations in both class size and length. It brough the college concept of "open campus planning" to high schools and even some middle schools. Within this scheduling system, there were great blocks of "open time" that could be used for labs, studio work, work-study programs, off-campus courses, and for auditing classes. However, it has come under fire as the competency/control/college entrance/career planning demands rose as public priorities.

See Also: ACADEMIC PROGRAM; CAPACITY; CLASS AND CLASS SIZE; ELEMENTARY SCHOOL; GUIDANCE; HIGH SCHOOLS; INSTRUCTION; MIDDLE SCHOOLS; RECORD KEEPING; STUDENT INFORMATION.

SCHOLARSHIP

The belief that only the rich may attend college is repugnant to the ideals of American education. From the time of the first English colonists, there has been a tradition of granting opportunities for better education to those who might otherwise not be financially able to reach their full potential.

There are many different types of **scholarships** awarded each year. Some are for academic accomplishments only, while others are for excellence in athletics, citizenship or other fields of endeavor. Special awards are granted on behalf of curricular departments, service organizations, foundations, business and unions, and individuals.

While the scholarships have cash value, they are rarely redeemable by anything other than actual college attendance. Further, the awards are rarely for full tuition and support. Consequently, some scholarships may be accompanied by work-study opportunities and/or other supplementary assistance programs. Even so, these less-than-full scholarships present hardships for those families who are econmically unable to even partially support a child in college. There is a continuing gap between those who wish to attend college and have worked hard at being qualified to do so, and those who can afford to do so. The available scholarships have proven inadequate to fill this chasm.

One of the ways that the gap is being closed is through low-interest deferred-payment loans. Here, too, competition and qualification requirements are very high, but they do represent some other viable alternatives to low income families.

The school, through its support personnel, should assist any child who sincerely wishes to attend college and is adequately qualified. Guidance departments should have material available on the entrance criteria and availability of scholarships for a wide variety of colleges and universities that students may wish to attend. Review by the administrators can insure that scholarships are being awarded fairly throughout the system and are being offered to those students who might best benefit from them.

See Also: COUNSELING; GUIDANCE; QUALIFICATIONS; RECOMMEND-ATIONS; SPECIAL INTEREST GROUPS; SPORTS; STUDENT INFORMATION.

SEARCH AND SEIZURE

Search and seizure is the stopping, questioning, looking for, and confiscating of personal property by an authority acting in the public interest.

Somewhere between citizen's rights, as accorded by the Fourth Amendment to be "secure in their persons, houses, papers and effects" and the school's obligation "to maintain a safe, secure and healthy" environment for students and staff, stands a Constitutional tightrope that administrators must walk.

Federal, state, and local laws, statutes and codes carefully, and in great detail, state what is permitted by the administrators in relation to search and seizure as they endeavor to operate their schools. School boards, too, prepare and present multiple policy statements on what is required of them and the procedures they must follow. But front-line administrators cannot always be expected to carry these dictums in their heads when confronted with day-to-day, "right now" decisions.

Therefore, some very succinct guidelines have been suggested concerning search and seizure for those needing practical help. First, when danger is present, *handle the danger first*. If the administrators need assistance from an outside authority, they should call for it immediately. Second, if the contraband is in sight, even partially, it should be confiscated, and, once in hand, the matter can be further investigated. Third, if a *reliable* person states that contraband has been *seen* that constitutes a clear and present danger to the school environment, the administrator should go to, search and confiscate the material, then instigate further proceedings. If the suspected contraband is not of a lethal nature, questioning of the student can take place first. Finally, when dealing with the students and staff, protection of the *entire* population is the prime responsibility. After all, the rights of one individual must be weighed against the rights of others to a safe and secure environment.

Wherever possible, courteous, calm, and fair investigation will protect most rights.

See Also: CIVIL RIGHTS; FOURTH AMENDMENT GUARANTEES; HALL DUTY; LOCKERS; POLICE; PRIVACY; REASONABLE AND PRUDENT; SAFE PLACE STATUTES; SAFETY; SELF-DEFENSE; SMOKING; STUDENT INFORMATION; SUPERVISION (STUDENTS).

SECRETARY

The school **secretary** holds an extremely responsible position, performing such duties as preparing and duplicating materials, seeing to their distribution, handling correspondence and telephone contacts, keeping accurate records and files, possibly calling for substitute teachers, and a host of other duties as assigned. Obviously, while the duties may vary from school to school, it is apparent that the school secretary is a very busy person.

Moreover, the secretary often acts as an intermediary between the principal and the public. A secretary is often the first adult encountered by a parent or other visitor who enters a school, and the first impression may well formulate a continued opinion of the school. Consequently, school secretaries should be trained in this public relations role as a representative of the school system.

It must be remembered that a school secretary is employed for the performance of nonacademic duties. A secretary should not be permitted to cover classes or perform any professional instructional duty without proper certification and commensurate re-imbursement.

See Also: CLERICAL SERVICES; EQUAL EMPLOYMENT OPPORTUNITIES.

SECRETARY OF EDUCATION, U.S.

The **U.S. Secretary of Education** administers the Department of Education, represents education in the Cabinet, and serves as the President's principal adviser on federal education policy.

The department was established on May 4, 1980. President Jimmy Carter appointed Shirley M. Hufstedler, a former federal judge, to serve as the first U.S. Secretary of Education, a position she held until the Carter Administration left office on January 20, 1981.

Nominated by then President-elect Ronald Reagan and confirmed by the Senate, Terrel H. Bell became Secretary on January 23, 1981. Dr. Bell had previously served as U.S. Commissioner of Education under the Nixon and Ford Administrations. He has had broad experience in education, in positions ranging from teacher of science to Higher Education Commissioner of the State of Utah. Bell was an early supporter of separating education from the then

Department of Health, Education, and Welfare. Although he never endorsed a Cabinet-level status for a separate education agency, he believes that "Education ought to be placed in a structure where the needs of Education can be heard."

In commenting on Dr. Bell's appointment as Secretary, then NEA Executive Director Terry Herndon called him "a distinguished educator (who) understands the problems and issues of public education, and its importance for the nation."

See Also: U.S. DEPARTMENT OF EDUCATION.

SELF-CONTAINED CLASSROOM

A **self-contained classroom** is an educational management system based upon the placement of one group of students under the primary instruction of one teacher.

So basic is the concept of the self-contained classroom, that other concepts such as multilevel learning, "changing" classes and continuous progress seem radical innovations. Actually, from the time of the one-room schoolhouse, these latter ideas have been a part of American education. The feeling that the best method of instruction consisted of one teacher with one class was a logical evolution caused by the availability of more teachers and more students wishing an education. Even today, this picture is virtually unchanged at the elementary school level.

As a management system, self-contained classrooms have several distinctive features. First, for control of socialization and behavioral needs, the all but autonomous teachers have a limited territory with absolute authority. Students operate under their classroom control; most punishments and rewards are meted out internally by them. Second, the teachers are in closest contact and familiarity with the needs and wants of those the school is most anxious to serve, namely the students and their parents. Consequently, the teachers are natural liaisons who soften administrative dictums and relay instructional and community demands. The advocacy is heightened by the small size of the constituency in a self-contained environment. Finally, the instructional programs become highly individualized and adaptable within this system. Teachers become very involved with their students' progress, and, whether stated or implied, adjust their teaching methods to include *all* of them in the learning process. The individual strengths and weakness of the student, as well as the personality of the instructor, make each classroom a different environment for learning.

Which leads to the greatest difficulty inherent in self-contained classrooms. Because of the autonomous nature of the teaching, students develop behavioral patterns to suit that particular environment. If, during the next year, the personality and expectations are different, the children must adjust to them or find themselves out of step with their new situation. But, the question comes, is the adjustment beneficial or detrimental to the child's development?

Let's use a drastic example to illustrate. Andrew enters Miss J.'s first grade class as an intelligent, eager, and rather rambunctious and independent child. Miss J. is relaxed and competent, and works with Andrew to develop his self-control. Andrew has no difficulty and progresses nicely under her guidance. Next year, Andrew is placed with Mr. S. However, he is very easy with his class and uses very light restraint. Andrew, without a guiding hand, loses any control gained during first grade, and the year produces no new social behavioral growth. In third grade, Andrew goes to Mrs. W's class, and she works patiently to establish in all her students, including Andrew, a good self-image and self-control. Andrew adapts well, and he succeeds in having a fine year. Fourth grade finds Andrew with Mrs. M., who is very authoritarian and does not permit any deviation from her explicit demands. Andrew's new-found confidence and progress in self-learning are almost destroyed. However, he somehow manages to make it through the year, albeit with plunging grades and many reprimands. When the next year comes, Andrew's parents wonder why their child doesn't want to go to school, is getting such poor grades, and is being held in the principal's office so much.

While certainly no school is this destructive, most districts do lack a consistent program for behavioral or "life skill" development. One of the reasons cited is the self-contained classroom teacher. Each has his or her own way of doing things, and district-wide changes are difficult. The single most imperative job of the elementary supervisor and administrator is to keep the staff's attention focused on the open goal of the whole academic program: a child with good self-esteem, self-control and learning habits, as well as being educated in the basic subject areas.

See Also: ACADEMIC FREEDOM; ASSIGNMENTS; AUTHORITY, TEACHER; CLASS AND CLASS SIZE; DISCIPLINE; ELEMENTARY SCHOOLS; INSTRUCTION; SUPERVISION (STAFF); SUPERVISION (STUDENTS); WORKSHOPS AND IN-SERVICE.

SELF-DEFENSE

Self-defense is the protection, by force, of one's personal property from an attempted injury by another person.

Teachers and administrators are increasingly becoming the targets of violence in schools. All the legal privileges accorded any citizen are also available to educators who find themselves faced with a potential battery. They may defend themselves through any means appropriate. The key word here is *"appropriate,"* for if a student slaps a teacher, the response may not be to place the student in jeopardy of grievous bodily harm. The term acceptable to the courts is *"equal force and intent."* Self-defense in a non life-threatening situation would also have to be non life-threatening. However, the courts have ruled that educators may, indeed, defend themselves and do not have less rights to protect themselves because of their profession or the age of their assailant.

The courts have also reviewed cases dealing with the *"duty"* or self-defense and have ruled that it applies to professional educators. While there is usually no duty to come to the defense of another person, certain special relationships impose such a duty. The police, fire and medical professions all share this type of responsibility and would be negligent if they did not defend others. Since, under state administrative codes, educators have the express duty to protect the "health, safety, welfare of the students, and the school from any destruction in its orderly operation," they must assist in those instances where danger of injury is possible.

The common points of intervention under this "duty" are when two or more students might injure one another, when a student could injure himself/herself, when a student could endanger lives or property necessary to the safe operation of the school, and, of course, when the student tries to injure a member of the teaching staff. There are common sense provisions that alleviate responsibility to act alone, but the duty to give aid or seek assistance is present, and educators must be aware of it.

See Also: AUTHORITY, EXPRESS AND IMPLIED; AUTHORITY, TEACHER; BATTERY; CHILD ABUSE; CONSTITUTIONAL RIGHTS; FOURTEENTH AMENDMENT GUARANTEES; FOURTH AMENDMENT GUARANTEES; IMPUTED NEGLIGENCE; LIABILITY; REASONABLE AND PRUDENT; SAFETY; SUPERVISION (STUDENTS); VIOLENCE.

SELF-INCRIMINATION

Self-incrimination means to imply or impute culpability to oneself for a criminal action.

The protection against self-incrimination is granted under the Fifth Amendment of the Constitution. It was designed to place the burden of proof that the accused committed a criminal act on the *prosecutor,* who must base the case on evidence rather than the statements of the accused, specifically those statements obtained through duress.

Nowadays, while threats of physical violence are virtually unknown, fear of public censure, imprisonment or fines are still enough to cause some defendants to "take the Fifth."

Not every defendant or witness is accorded this constitutional privilege, however. A person may not refuse to answer a proper question that could incriminate another person but not himself. Nor can a defendant refuse to answer questions in a case concerning a civil, but not a criminal, breech of law. Finally, if the court has granted an "immunity against prosecution" in order that the witness may testify without fear of future suit, the witness may not refuse to answer, for there is no jeopardy involved.

Perhaps the most widely-held feeling about "taking the Fifth" as a protection against self-incrimination is the perception that only those with something to hide use the tactic. This is not only a false impression, but a dangerous one, because it negates a person's freedom to defend himself from unfair prosecution. Great care must be taken to guard this freedom and keep the citizenry as secure as they were originally intended to be.

See Also: BURDEN OF PROOF; CIVIL RIGHTS; CONSTITUTIONAL RIGHTS; FIFTH AMENDMENT GUARANTEES.

SEX EDUCATION

The latest change in education's modern curricular responsibilities has been the addition of courses in **Sex Education.** This came about because of increased evidence of venereal disease, the rise in teenage pregnancy, and a rising involvement in sexual activity at a younger and younger age. Also, there was a perception that part of the problem was a gross lack of information and understanding of sexual matters coming from either the home, the various churches or the medical community to the students, whereas this had formerly been the primary source of such information. Citing its basic responsibility to produce well-informed, educated and capable graduates, the schools began to fill the apparent vacuum of needed information.

The public reaction was swift, divided and adamant. The proponents were delighted and expressed a willingness to support increased expenditures to enlarge this new curricular program. Introductions in kindergarten to the "easy" questions (Where did I come from?), through the middle school (What's a "wet dream"?), and up to the hard facts (What is the best form of birth control?), were hailed as appropriate and vital material for classroom discussion. The opponents were equally aroused by the new programs, but they were incensed at the intrusion into areas they considered no business of the schools. They claimed that if parents wanted their children to be exposed to such explicit material, they would and should do it themselves. Further, they claimed that the usurpation by the school of this "parental responsibility" violated the authority of parents and the community, and invaded their privacy and right to freedom from control over their private lives.

The courts, administrative codes and state board policies have finally agreed upon some universally acceptable guidelines for school-mainstreamed classes in sex education, in order that both factions may be satisfied.

First, *on the material itself,* an advisory committee consisting of representatives of the school, parent's groups, and community will review all the materials before they are presented. Further, the material as well as the program will be periodically reviewed by this committee, in order to insure both high standards and appropriate instruction.

Second, *concerning the program,* the school will provide the most qualified instructor available to teach the course. Generally, this person is a health professional, but any staff member who has taken courses in Sex Education Psychology, who has worked with the materials to be used, who has a good mental outlook on the subject, and who has a good working rapport with the students can be assigned to it.

Finally, *parents must be given the option of not having their child attend the class.* This must be allowed without loss of credit or grade, and without any duress. Students not taking the course must be permitted some other educational experience, instead of, for example, merely being placed in a study hall. In order to insure that those attending are there with parental consent, permission of parents/guardians should be obtained in writing and kept on file, either with the instructor or in the main office.

In-service training for administrators and teachers, joint workshops with parents and community representatives, and good communications and rapport can ensure that this new program serves its students well.

See Also: ACADEMIC FREEDOM; ACADEMIC PROGRAM; COURSE; INSTRUCTION; WORKSHOPS AND INSERVICES.

SEXISM

With the societal impact of Title VII of the Civil Rights Act of 1964 (PL88-352), a group of new words and concepts entered the American consciousness. Phrases such as "male chauvanist pig," "sexist," and "affirmative action" showed a rising resentment to stereotypical thinking based upon preconceived abilities, expectations and potentials of one sex over another.

Education, not just as a place of employment but as a purveyor of ideas, was also affected by Title IX of the Educational Amendments of 1972 (PL92-318) and 1980 (PL96-374). Administrators and staff members became conscious of role-models, equalized expenditures and programs, and elimination of sexist classrooms.

Schools can and do reflect society and its values. As society in general became aware of sexism in job opportunities, salaries and advancements, the schools began to examine themselves to see if they might be practicing *sexism,* too. Review upon review showed that they were. Some teachers were still lining up boys separately from girls, and, of course, permitting the girl's line to go first. Boys cleaned blackboard erasers and opened and closed windows; girls watered plants and passed out paper. Boys played football, basketball and other sports in organized inter- and intramural programs; girls received most of their sports in regular Physical Education classes.

Education, to steal a phrase, has come "a long way, baby," in eradicating the insidious evil of implied weakness to one gender or automatic expectations to another. Administrators should be ever alert that such practices do not creep into their schools. Children are now, and should continue to be, encouraged to reach their own true potentials without encountering roadblocks.

See Also: AFFIRMATIVE ACTION; ATHLETICS, SEX DISCRIMINATION IN; CIVIL RIGHTS; DISCRIMINATION; ELEMENTARY AND SECONDARY EDUCATION ACT OF 1965; EQUAL EMPLOYMENT OPPORTUNITIES; VOCATIONAL PROGRAMS; WORK-STUDY PROGRAMS.

SHARED-TIME

Shared-time is an arrangement whereby students avail themselves of facilities and services not found in their own buildings, but which are operated for common educational usage by all the students in a system, district or county.

Not every class has the money to purchase a gymnasium or hire a nurse. Instead, the school constructs or hires that equipment and personnel "for the common good." All classes use the services thus available. This, in miniature, is the concept of shared-time. Services and facilities are jointly used by schools and districts that could not otherwise provide those opportunities to their students.

The most common shared-time facilities are the district or county vocational schools. Under one roof are housed expensive courses and materials in "career skills." These places have become so expensive that only one or two may be present in any given area. Therefore, all the schools in that area send the students who want this educational opportunity to the shared-time facility.

But it is not vocational training, shared specialists or special education classes that have caused the most problems for the shared-time concept. Rather, it is the imperative that these facilities are open to *all* the students in an area, including those coming from private and parochial schools. Under the edict of ESEA, 1965 (PL89-10) Title I, funds could be and were to be used for joint public-private services under shared-time principles.

While public school instructors could not go into private or parochial schools to teach, arrangements could be made to have students from those schools participate in public school programs not available in their own buildings or systems *(Fisher v. Clackamas County School District,* 507 P.2d 839, [OR, 1973]). Further, while still citing the 1929 case of *Borden v. Louisiana State Board of Education* (123 So. 655), the opening of shared-time facilities and services to non-public school students had been held by the courts to fall under the Child Benefit Theory and is not express aid to the non-public schools.

With rising building costs and greater movement toward consolidating special services, schools are using more and more shared-time facilities. Careful checks on state law requirements, true community needs and budgetary responsibilities can immeasurably aid the administrator in using these facilities wisely.

See Also: CHURCH-STATE SEPARATION; CONSOLIDATION; ELEMENTARY AND SECONDARY EDUCATION ACT OF 1965; FUNDAMENTAL INTEREST THEORY; PRIVATE AND PAROCHIAL SCHOOLS; SPECIAL EDUATION; SPECIAL SERVICES; SUMMER SCHOOL; SUPPLIES AND EQUIPMENT; TEXTBOOKS; VOCATIONAL PROGRAMS; WORKSHOPS AND INSERVICE; WORK-STUDY PROGRAMS.

SICK LEAVE

See ABSENCE.

SIGN-IN SHEETS

Virtually every district has some system of recording the attendance of teachers at school. In some schools this is accomplished by the use of a time clock and cards that teachers use to "punch in" and "punch out." It is more common, however, to find a sign-in sheet in the main office, which lists the names of faculty members. Next to the names are columns of spaces with each column dated to represent a school day in a particular month. Next to their names and in the space for the correct date, faculty

members indicate their arrivals and departures each day.

Sign-in sheets serve a variety of purposes. They can tell an administrator at a glance just who is and is not present on a given day. This is invaluable in mornings when a teacher might be delayed and administrators must ascertain which classes have to be covered, or in afternoons when a teacher receives a phone call and the secretary can easily check to see if the teacher has left the building. They also present a clear record of teacher absences over a continued period of time.

Some systems require teachers to record the times of arrival and departure, while others merely require a check mark in the appropriate space. This is strictly a matter of individual policy and could possibly be an item for negotiation between a board of education and a local teacher's association.

See Also: ABSENCE; ATTENDANCE; AUTHORITY, EXPRESS AND IMPLIED; FACULTY; PERSONNEL FILES; RECORD KEEPING; SUBSTITUTE TEACHER.

SMOKING

Despite the reports of the Surgeon General, a considerable mass-media anti-smoking campaign and warnings clearly printed on every cigarette package, students **smoking** in school remains a problem. Indeed, the idea of "sneaking a cigarette in the lavatory" has become all but a cliché in our literature. Yet cigarettes *are* considered a danger to health and are classified as part of the universal contraband for schools.

Consequently, school boards should establish a clear policy on smoking in the school, and administrators should see to it that the entire school population is familiar with the regulations, including the penalties assigned for violation. These may vary from school to school, but they generally range from a day's detention to several days of out-of-school suspension. Moreover, teachers on hall duty should be instructed to check appropriate lavatories on an irregular schedule to discourage the practice. Also, Physical Education and Science teachers should be encouraged to include units in their curriculums on the effects of smoking.

Even with these precautions, some systems have found the problem extensive enough that they have established "Smoking Areas" on school grounds where students may legitimately smoke. While this is a decision for the individual district, such a proposal usually finds great resistance in the community, and many districts find that students continue to smoke in unauthorized areas anyway.

Among the adults in a school, the issue of smoking may often prove divisive, as smoking and non-smoking members of the faculty and staff complain about the violations of their rights by the other group. Therefore many administrators establish a specific place in the school where adults may smoke and ban the prac-

tice in all other areas. The area is usually the faculty lounge or a specific part of it.

While the number of people who smoke is dropping nationwide, it is likely that smoking on school grounds will continue to present a problem for some time to come.

See Also: DISCIPLINE; STUDENT INFORMATION.

SOCIAL PROMOTION

Social promotion is advancement without proper qualifications, but as a result of some recognized need.

The retention of students can be a traumatic experience. So traumatic, in fact, that its negative aspects of slowed behavioral growth, decreased self-esteem and increased peer abuse seem to far outweigh the educational benefits intended by the retention. In these cases social promotion, or the placement of students into the next grade level, even if they are not actually academically achieving at that level, is the best decision. Usually, provisions are made for some remedial or supplemental help to be given at the new level until the student can catch up.

These are the proper considerations given to social promotion. In practice, however, sometimes the high purposes become clouded. When students are passed on because they are discipline problems, or are needed on an athletic squad, or because there is a sense that "they'll-never-get-this-stuff-anyway-so-why-not," the social promotion is injurious. The individual student is being denied a chance of reaching the goal of a good education. The unfortunate result of this uncaring attitude is that functional illiterates are being graduated from some schools. All aspects of education suffer from the public's righteous indignation, even if only a very small percentage of students are so affected. Therefore, administrators should maintain extreme supervision over promotions and retentions to insure that all of the students are being granted the best opportunity available to them in the school's program.

See Also: ACCOUNTABILITY; RETENTION OF STUDENTS; SUPERVISION (STAFF); UNDERACHIEVERS.

SPEECH THERAPY

Speech therapy is that remedial assistance given to individuals who have a disorder that interferes with communication at the verbal level that calls attention to itself, and that causes its possessor to be maladjusted.

Under Public Law 94-142, Section 6:28-1.2, students possessing the above handicap are termed either *"communications handicapped"* (cannot use oral native language to communicate) or *"eligible for speech correction services"* (can speak, but with some impediment).

The first type of handicap may be handled by an outside agency or support system, but, under the law, the speech therapist of the school may work with the student to reinforce and/or prescribe speech therapy. Individual educational programs (IEP) are often for one-to-one sessions.

The second type of speech handicap is characterized by the presence of defective and incorrect sounds, including substitutions, omissions, additions, distortions of the speech sounds, and other speech abnormalities. Here, the speech therapists work to *improve* speech. The IEP can be for one-to-one or small-group sessions. Indeed, in a self-contained structure, the law permits eight pupils per instructor/therapist.

Classifications are made by the child study team. The speech correctionist must be fully certified by the state. Also, all students who are classified as needing speech therapy must be kept on their IEP until their particular handicap is corrected. That is, there is no time limit placed upon the program. Finally, clear distinctions must be made concerning those students who have difficulties with oral communication because of the above-defined handicaps, and those whose difficulties stem from a lack of familiarity with the language or from cultural deprivation. The latter might need a program such as bilingual education, but would not qualify for speech therapy.

See Also: CHILD STUDY TEAM; CONSULTANTS; DIAGNOSIS; HANDICAPPED; LEARNING DISABILITIES; PUBLIC LAW 94-142; SHARED-TIME;

SPECIAL EDUCATION; STUDENT INFORMATION.

SPECIAL EDUCATION

Special Education consists of individually designed, free instructional services that meet the unique needs of handicapped pupils as required by law.

The classification of students as handicapped, whether emotionally, mentally or physically, places upon the schools the burden of preparing and administering a specific program of educational instruction that will best suit them. Merely discovering and/or naming the handicapped is not enough. The schools, operating under the premise that every citizen is to be afforded *a free and appropriate education,* must ensure the opportunity for all students to reach their full educational potential. And, it is added, this is to be done in the least restrictive environment possible.

Historically, education placed handicapped children in "Special Ed" classes. Multiple handicaps were placed apart, in one or two rooms of the school, and kept there with an instructor whose sole purpose appeared to be "let the poor children do what they can." The classes were aimed at socialization skills, and only the most rudimentary academic work was attempted. By the mid 1960s, greater attention was being paid to the individual differences in handicapped children. Also, additional courses and degrees were being offered to those

teaching the handicapped. Then, with the passage of the Education For All Handicapped Children Act of 1975 (PL 94-142), standardized classifications, definitions, environments, and programs were developed.

The classifications and their definitions that require special education programs, along with their maximum self-contained environments, are shown on the following three pages.

Proper certification is needed for teaching in each classification. Teacher aides are extensively used throughout the program. With increased training and understanding, administrators are developing a wider range of educational opportunities for their handicapped students. Special Education today means a springboard that helps students to reach their full potential, instead of putting them into a box and packing them away.

See Also: ACADEMIC PROGRAM; CHILD STUDY TEAM; DIAGNOSIS; HANDICAPPED; INDIVIDUALIZATION; LEARNING DISABILITIES; MAINSTREAMING; PSYCHOLOGICAL STUDIES; PUBLIC LAW 94-142; RETARDED CHILD; SHARED-TIME; SPEECH THERAPY; SPECIAL SERVICES; TRANSPORTATION.

SPECIAL INTEREST GROUPS

School administrators are constantly approached by outside agents who represent companies or organizations that wish to participate in the school's policy or programs. Some, like the American Red Cross and

CLASSIFICATION	DEFINITION	ENVIRONMENT
Auditorily Handicapped	Inability to hear properly.	8 per instructor
a. Deaf	Severe loss of hearing with or without amplification	8 per instructor
b. Hard of Hearing	Permanent or fluctuating loss of hearing, but not as severe as deafness.	8 per instructor
Chronically Ill	Temporary or permanent illness that prevents steady classroom attendance	15 per instructor (not necessarily all at the same time)
a. Chronically Ill	A chronic condition that makes steady school attendance impractical	15 per instructor (not necessarily all at the same time)
b. Eligible for Home Instruction	A temporary condition requiring short instructional assistance	15 cases per instructor, but done in the home
Communications Handicapped	Impaired spoken native speech that hampers development	8 per speech therapist
a. Communications Handicapped	Severe interference with spoken native language	8 per speech therapist
b. Eligible for Speech Correction Services	Incorrect use of sounds and speech in spoken native language, but not as severe	8 per speech therapist

CLASSIFICATION	DEFINITION	ENVIRONMENT
Emotionally Disturbed	Behavioral disorders that affect performance	8 per instructor
Mentally Retarded	Intellectual capacity below the standard range	varies
a. Educable	1-3 degrees below standard mean intellect	15 per instructor
b. Trainable	3 degrees below standard mean intellect	10 per instructor
c. Eligible for Day Training	Inability to respond in a positive manner to simple tests	9 students, with a ratio of 3 children per staff member
Multiple Handicapped	Two or more handicapping conditions which, in combination, present a severe condition for single handicap programs	8 per instructor
Neurologically or Perceptually Impaired	Inability to process information	varies
a. Neurologically Impaired	Severe specific impairment of the central or peripheral nervous system	8 per instructor
b. Perceptually Impaired	Exhibition of a specific learning disability due to a disorder in one or more of the basic psychological processes of understanding and learning	12 per instructor

CLASSIFICATION	DEFINITION	ENVIRONMENT
Orthopedically Handicapped	The loss of function of bones, muscles or tissues that require special facilities, equipment or services	10 is the maximum, but not this many if merely for the school's convenience
Socially Malajusted	A pattern of social interactions that are characterized by conflicts which severely interfere with the well-being of others but are not due to emotional disturbance	12 per instructor
Visually Handicapped	Inability to see within normal limits	8 per instructor
a. Blind	Visual acumen of $20/200$ or less, and needs special services or devices to aid learning	8 per instructor
b. Partially Sighted	Visual acumen of $10/70$ or less, and needs more than regular classroom assistance	8 per instructor

certain book companies, have been involved in education for so long that it is difficult to find a school that does not have contact with them. Even so, the idea of using a school and its student body to raise money, buy products or distribute material is a very sensitive area. School boards must also be concerned with the running of contests, the granting of scholarships, and the holding of meetings and/or demonstrations by outside groups. There can even be legal difficulties with some of these practices.

Determining guidelines that delineate the difference between outside help and outside interference can be very difficult. Several considerations should be studied before any final decisions are made. First, does the material or practice conform with the academic program of the district? If it does not, why bring it in? Second, who is the ultimate beneficiary of the school's acceptance? If the school stands to gain nothing either educationally, monetarily or publicly, why do it? And, finally, does the activity accurately reflect the concerns, needs or desires of the community? If it only involves a very small part of the total community, or if it is contrary to the majority interests in the community, will the school's participation antagonize or disrupt the good rapport that the school so vitally needs?

Once a review of the total situation is made, the school or school system can decide the policies for controlling **special interest group** participation. Open communication with all groups in the community will assist the schools in fully utilizing the beneficial aspects of these groups while minimizing any possible negative or disruptive influences.

See Also: ACCEPTANCE OF DONATIONS; ACTIVITIES; AUDIO-VISUAL MATERIALS; CHURCH-STATE SEPARATION; CLUBS; DEMONSTRATIONS; LEASE OF SCHOOL PROPERTY; PETITIONS; POLITICS AND THE SCHOOL; P.T.A.; SANCTIONS; VENDORS OR VENDING MACHINGS.

SPECIAL SERVICES

Special Services is an organizational division of a district's central staff devoted to those support personnel responsible for student development.

The administrators in charge of Special Services have supervisory responsibility over a myriad of functions carried out by the schools. Each of the functions or services has its own personnel and purpose.

One of these services is Guidance. The administrator, through the Guidance director, coordinates and supervises the Guidance counselors in the district. Further, the placement of students in various schools and classes, availing them of career/college opportunities, and assisting with other guidance-related duties must be coordinated through their office.

Another field of jurisdiction for them is the Health Services provided by the district. Working with the school physician and school head nurse, all school health professionals, health rooms and their equipment, physicals for participation in various activities, accident reports, etc., must be supervised by Special Services.

Attendance information, present and/or projected enrollments and insuring full compliance with state compulsory education statutes is another task the Special Services administrators perform. Working with the Attendance Officer (Truant Officer) and community support personnel, they maintain records on and help students with any attendance/absenteeism problems.

Perhaps their most exacting duty is also their most vital. The administrators of Special Services are the people who are responsible for all the child study teams and support services that are available to the students, their parents and the community at large. The mandate of "a free and appropriate education for all" falls on their shoulders. Through active participation with school psychologists, special education supervisors and teachers, speech therapists, and family service coordinators, these Special Services administrators facilitate any individualized instructions needed by the students. They also organize and coordinate any shared-time relationships with outside agencies and schools. Further, they maintain, administrate and supervise programs for handicapped, mentally retarded or other classified students. Finally, they assist and arrange home or out-of-school instruction.

The Special Services administrators must be extremely well-qualified

because of their great responsibilities. Generally, those individuals holding such positions have several academic degrees and have experience at several levels.

See Also: CENTRAL STAFF; CHILD STUDY TEAM; COUNSELING; DIAGNOSIS; DIFFERENTIATED STAFFING; FAMILY SERVICES; FIRST AID; GUIDANCE; HANDICAPPED; HEALTH; HOME INSTRUCTION; LEARNING DISABILITIES; MIGRANTS; MONTHLY REPORTS; NURSE; PSYCHOLOGICAL STUDIES; PUBLIC LAW 93-380; PUBLIC LAW 94-142; REMEDIAL INSTRUCTION; RETARDED CHILD; SHARED-TIME; SPEECH THERAPY; SPECIAL EDUCATION; STUDENT INFORMATION; SUPERVISION (STAFF).

SPORTS

Separate from, but closely allied to, a school's Physical Education curriculum is its **sports** program. This program, generally under the supervision of the school's Athletic Director, contains the various competitive activities the school offers to the teams and individuals.

The sports program of a district consists of both *intramural* and *interscholastic* competitions. The intramural activities are more closely connected to the Physical Education program and are more likely to be found in the elementary school. When the Physical Education program is concentrating on basketball, for example, intramural squads from different classes, sections, home rooms, or some random selection process may play each other to determine the "best squad in the school." Generally, a great many more students participate in this level of competition than at the interscholastic level. Middle schools usually have an equal amount of intramural and interscholastic activities in their programs, while high school sports are almost entirely interscholastic. At the interscholastic level, standards for participation can be very high; therefore, fewer students participate.

Disproportional expenditures of time, money, facilities, and attention to interscholastic sports have caused much concern among educators. When a school's entire academic program appears to be judged by the success or failure of its varsity football team, priorities seem confused. Sadly, however, this has been the case, even at the middle school level. Further, when faced with budgetary deficits and proposed cutbacks, some school planners have found the community prepared to reduce career programs, teaching staffs and even instructional services without a whimper, but become irate if one of the instructors to be fired is the "winning" coach.

Money, both generated and dispersed, has always been a problem to schools with large sports programs. If the school produces a successful sports program, the revenue from ticket sales and booster campaigns can be sizeable. In most cases, this money is put back into the program, and the school can then afford more equipment, which improves the chances for another successful season that will generate more money, and so on. But controversies develop when the money is not being distributed fairly such as when the girls' sports activities get limited funds and support, while the boys' programs get expensive equipment or more coaches. While an absolute, equal split of funds may be too optimistic to hope for, the disparity of 90 percent for the boys' program and 10 percent for the girls' is not only unfair, it is illegal under Title IX of the Educational Amendments of 1972, (PL 92-318) and 1980 (PL 96-374) which prohibit sex discrimination in athletics.

Finally, administrators, staff members, students, and community members should keep in mind why the sports programs exist in the school. They are *opportunities for the students' extracurricular enjoyment.* Sports are intended to help students grow physically and intellectually, through steady exercise and self-discipline. The life skills such as sharing goals, dedication and good sportsmanship are also taught through the program. However, when everyone is aware that Number 19 is on the hockey team, but few know his name, or when teachers allow a "star" special consideration on tests, or when the *winning* by a few has become more important than the *playing* by the many, a sharp look should be taken to see if the sports program really is part of the school's true academic program.

See Also: ACADEMIC PROGRAM; AFFIRMATIVE ACTION; ATHLETICS, SEX DISCRIMINATION IN; EXTRACURRICULAR ACTIVITIES; INSURANCE; NEWS COVERAGE; PHYSICAL EDUCATION; SUPPLIES AND EQUIPMENT; TRANSPORTATION.

STATE AGENCIES, STATE AID, STATE PROGRAMS

Each state and commonwealth in the United States has individual structures for handling public services, tax expenditures and programs. Education departments in each of the states oversee the programs, fiscal planning and services used at the local school levels through an organizational structure headed by the state superintendent of schools or the chief state school official.

Although there are several state educational grant programs, information services, and scholarship and loan programs operated by individual states, most of the funds available are from the federal government, and these are *passed through* the state government.

These "passed through" programs come by way of *categorical grants*. In these, the federal government decides how, for what and by whom the funds will be used. The state merely takes the money as it comes, acknowledges the allocations

through reports, and dispenses it to the local districts whom the federal government has listed as qualified. The state departments have almost no input into these allocations and can neither change nor redirect any of the programs or aid. Each federal program, its fiscal allocation and the state dispersal plan for categorical grants is listed in the *Catalog of Federal Domestic Assistance*. For the exact federal programs available in a particular state, *federal outlays in* (name of state) is published each year. Both these publications are available, either in the local library or through the state department of education.

With the rising call for more state and local impact on and control over federal funds, which actually are generated from the taxpayers in specific areas, Congress passed the *State and Local Fiscal Assistance Act of 1972* (Public Law 95-512). Extended twice, this legislation is also known as General Revenue Sharing (GRS). Under this, the federal government allocated funds to the state, according to need, based upon a population formula. This was conceived by the Department of the Treasury, which manages GRS. It called for a single dispersement or "block" of funds to be given to the states. The states could then take these *formula block grants* and dispense them to the local districts as they needed them. Originally, there were many restrictions on what this money could be used for within the states, but with each congressional extention, these restrictions have loosened. Consequently, state control over the funds has become almost complete. Certain amounts are used for educational programs, for aiding school districts with matching funds, and for plant improvement. With more state control, however, competition has increased and local districts have found the need to hire full- or at least part-time grantsmen, to supervise the proposals and applications for the available funds. A listing of all the block grants and the state disbursement structure for them can be found in the *U.S. Code Service, Codes of Federal Regulations,* or in publications available through the state department of education.

The auditing system for these programs and fiscal expenditures requires very careful record keeping and detailed reports from the local systems and the states. Administrators, under whose purview this falls, must allow sufficient time to collect, correlate and then compose accurate annual accountings. Not only is this important for the past year, but it can spell success or failure in receiving state assistance in the coming year.

See Also: ATTENDANCE; BONDS; BUDGET; CHIEF STATE SCHOOL OFFICIAL; COMPETENCY-BASED PROGRAMS; COMPENSATORY EDUCATION; COMPULSORY EDUCATION; COUNTY SUPERINTENDENT OF SCHOOLS; EDUCATION COMMISSION OF THE STATES; ELEMENTARY AND SECONDARY EDUCATION ACT OF 1965; ENROLLMENT; FEDERAL AGENCIES, FEDERAL AID, FEDERAL PROGRAMS; PUBLIC LAW 93-380; PUBLIC LAW 94-142; RESERVED POWERS; TAXES; TEXTBOOKS; VOCATIONAL PROGRAMS; WORKSHOPS AND IN-SERVICE; YEAR-END REPORT.

STRIKES

The intent of any **strike** is to get the employer to grant the demands of the employees. These demands may concern wages and hours, or terms and conditions of employment. Whatever the demands, the real cause of a strike is the breakdown of communications and obstinacy on the part of one or both sides.

In education, any interruption in the learning process should be avoided if at all possible. However, when teachers or other employees feel they have no other recourse, a strike can develop.

Public employee strikes are handled differently in each state. Some state statutes have very severe penalties, while others are more lenient. Before a strike is contemplated by an employee association, careful study should be made of the laws, statutes, codes, and board policies concerning the right to strike, injunction procedures and penalties, the use of substitute workers, and insurance liability.

Strikes hurt; nobody wins one. Even if all of the demands are met, the striking association has lost the smooth working rapport with its board, the parents and the community that it desperately needs to facilitate educational progress. The boards lose too, because cooperation is vital to initiating new programs and services with its staff and community, and it will be hard to renew. Resentment between those who supported the strike and those who opposed it, even within the two sides, can fester for years.

Correctly used, fairly administrated and up-to-date grievance procedures, competent negotiators and mediators, and free, open and ongoing channels of communication can do much to avoid this negative and divisive barrier to good employee relations.

See Also: COMMUNICATION; DEMANDS; DEMONSTRATIONS; EMPLOYEE RELATIONS; GRIEVANCES; IMPASSE; INJUNCTION; JOB ACTION; LIAISON; NEGOTIATIONS; PETITIONS; UNISERV.

STUDENT COUNCIL (STUDENT GOVERNMENT)

The **Student Council (Student Government)** is a district-chartered agency, composed of students who have been elected democratically on a representative basis, having one or more faculty advisors, that deals with matters of concern to the students in the school.

The structure and tasks of a student council will vary drastically from school to school. Usually, one or two student-representatives are freely elected from each grade level or "homeroom" in the school. This body meets and either elects its own officers or proposes members for executive positions who are then voted upon by the student body. This is commonly done under the supervision of a faculty member who acts as an advisor.

The functions of a student council may vary, but generally they are concerned with extracurricular activities such as dances, student recreational activities, student welfare funds, fund raisers, and the like. They can also become involved with school conduct and discipline, making suggestions for the adoption or deletion of certain school rules, along with setting penalties for infractions, holding Student Court, etc.

In order to prevent dissention and misunderstanding about the rights, responsibilities and role of the student council, periodic reviews of the charter should be undertaken by representatives of the board, the administration and students. A clear intent as to what the student council should, can and will accomplish should be recorded as policy and kept on file. If the true feeling of the district is that students should have no power over anything, so be it. Giving lip service to student control over student activities, but not allowing them to exercise any decision-making, is a major cause of turmoil. Whatever the guidelines, make them clear. If, after review, changes are necessary or desirable, they should be well-publicized.

Student councils are used effectively in both elementary and secondary schools, as well as on college campuses.

STUDENT INFORMATION

Student information is that material, either written or oral, which is obtained from, gathered about, or given to the student population of a school.

The largest single factor of concern in any school district is the student population enrolled in it. They are reason for the entire academic program. Courses of study, special instructional programs, support services, and recreational activities are arranged for their health, safety and well-being. Therefore, communicating of information to, from, and about them is vital to a system.

There are three main aspects of student information. First, there is the information *obtained from* students and their parents/guardians. Even before children enter kindergarten, health histories, parent conferences and readiness information must be gotten. Children or their parents/guardians tell the school whom to notify in case of emergency, and explain the pertinent facts about their home situations. Over the years, changes in their families' health or residential status are noted in their Permanent Records.

Second, information on students is *gathered, correlated and evaluated* throughout their school lives. Standardized achievement, aptitude and intelligence tests are administered to them. Steady progress reports, in the form of report cards, grades and parent conferences are evaluated and maintained by their teachers. If special difficulties arise, the Special Service's support personal gather and interpret data to determine the most effective way to assist them. Constant communication between the administrators, the children and their parents/guardians keeps the school up-to-date on many facets of the children's growth and development.

Finally, there is the material that the school *gives to* the student, which it categorizes as their "need to know" information. Most of the school's policies concerning students fall under this heading. The major piece of material distributed by the district to each of its students is the *student handbook*. In the elementary schools, this generally contains a few simple rules of conduct, along with clear instructions concerning fire, street and playground safety. The "handbook," at this level, is often one or two sheets of paper, either given to the students or sent directly to their parents/guardians. At the middle school level, the handbook is a little more formal and is often larger. It now contains items such as regulations for conduct, schedules of extracurricular events and emergency procedures. There may even be a few actual board policy statements on major issues as definitions of contraband, descriptions of disciplinary procedures, and lists of eligibility requirements for various activities. It is not until the high school level that the student handbook becomes the primary source of student information. In some schools, the High School handbook is a large, bound paperback, containing policy statements on every aspect of student activity within the system. Board policy on conduct and dress, student publications and censorship, grades and graduation requirements, students rights and responsibilities, and many other items are spelled out clearly. In other schools, the student handbook is a loose-leaf-type book that is housed in either the main office of the main guidance office in each building. Students wishing to know board policy go there to read a particular item. In still other schools, simple policy statements, schedules and rules are given to each student, and the board policies are contained in a handbook that is kept in the central staff office of the district.

As an additional method of giving information to its student body, the building and/or central staff administrators may issue student information bulletins, which alert students to decisions affecting them. Compliance then becomes a clear and workable possibility. Also, any changes that affect students are immediately understood and noted.

In all, open communications is the key. Administrators, students, parents/guardians, and the community at large must be aware of the goals and objectives of the school. This can be accomplished with good student information.

See Also: ACHIEVEMENT; APTITUDE; ATHLETICS, SEX DISCRIMINATION IN; ATTENDANCE; AUTOMOBILES; CALENDAR; CHILD STUDY TEAM; CLOSE OF SCHOOL; CLUBS; DISCIPLINE; DISMISSAL PROCEDURES (SCHOOL); DRESS CODES; DRINKING OF ALCOHOLIC BEVERAGES; DRUGS; DUE PROCESS; EVALUATION; EXAMINATIONS; EXPULSION OF STUDENTS; EXTRACURRICULAR ACTIVITIES; FAMILY SERVICES; GRADES: GRADUATION REQUIREMENTS; GRIEVANCES; GUARDIAN AND GUARDIANSHIP; GUIDANCE; HEALTH; IMMUNIZATION, INOCULATION AND VACCINATION; INTELLIGENCE TESTING; KINDERGARTEN; LOCKERS; MARRIED STUDENTS; MIGRANTS; PARENT CONFERENCES; PERMANENT RECORDS; PREGNANT STUDENTS; PROM; PSYCHOLOGICAL STUDIES; PUBLIC LAW 93-380; PUBLIC LAW 94-142; READINESS; RECORD KEEPING; REPORT CARDS; RETARDED CHILD; RETENTION OF STUDENTS; SCHEDULE; SCHOLARSHIP; SMOKING; SPORTS; STUDENT COUNCIL (STUDENT GOVERNMENT); SUPERVISION (STUDENTS); TARDINESS; TRANSFERS; TRANSPORTATION; TRUANCY; WORKING PAPERS.

STUDENT TEACHER

College students who are preparing for a career in education are required by law to participate in *practice teaching and internship*, in a recognized school, as a prerequisite to obtaining state teacher certification. Coordination of this effort between the college and the district is usually arranged through a member of the central staff, most often an assistant superintendent. The **student teacher** is assigned to a fully-certified *"cooperating teacher"* in a school, stays with that teacher for a period from six to ten weeks, observes, learns by doing, and finally takes over that teacher's classes. In this way, it is hoped that the student will gain practical experience in the process of teaching. Indeed, the period of student teaching is often referred to as a *"practicum."*

This practicum usually takes place during the student's senior year of college. Many colleges, however, also require the student to serve a limited internship during the junior year, whereby the student goes to a school, observes various teaching styles, and generally gets acquainted with the "mechanics" of teaching and school life. It is hoped that this experience will better prepare the student for the practicum of the senior year.

The "cooperating teacher" has a number of responsibilities relative to the student teacher. The teacher is expected to exercise supervision over the student teacher, and is required to prepare and submit periodic reports on his or her progress and fitness. The student's college mentor/advisor/supervisor observes periodically and discusses progress with the cooperating teacher. The teacher prepares a final report on the student teacher, from which a final grade for the practicum is determined. For his or her efforts, the cooperating teacher usually receives an "honorarium" from the student teacher's college.

Great care should be taken by the administrator to see to it that the student teacher is placed with an *experienced* teacher. The student-teaching period can be invaluable for the college student, and placement with a cooperating teacher who understands the nature of the practicum, and who will take the time to advise and guide the student through this period, will facilitate a growth-producing learning experience that will ultimately benefit the would-be teacher and his or her future classes.

See Also: CERTIFICATION; EVALUATION; OBSERVATION; RECOMMENDATION; REFERENCES; SUPERVISION (STAFF).

SUBSTITUTE TEACHER

"Oh, good morning, Mrs. Smith; I understand that you're Mr. Jones today." This should be a laughable beginning to a comedy skit, but it is, instead, a commonly heard remark in any school on any given day. Mrs. Smith is a **substitute teacher.**

School districts can be hard-pressed to continue functioning without an adequate, qualified and readily available pool of substitutes. Consequently, schools maintain long lists of possible candidates for future needs. On a day-to-day basis, approximately 10 percent of the total staff will be absent and/or need to have classes covered by a substitute. Should a flu epidemic hit the staff, however, or very inclement weather prevent many teachers from coming in, the need will rise proportionally.

The qualifications for substitute teaching have risen steadily over the past several years. A state-approved teaching certificate is now generally required. Often, the class, course, or grade level that the substitute is most qualified for will be the only one they will be permitted to enter, except in cases of extreme emergency. On those occasions when a support staff member such as a nurse, Special Education instructor, or speech therapist is absent, only those *equally* qualified may replace them. If no qualified substitute can be found by the district, those services must either be suspended or be filled with outside professionals.

Administrators are responsible for the integration of substitutes into their buildings. They may require each of the staff members to prepare *emergency lesson plans* to be kept on file in the main office in case of their absence, as well as seating charts and pertinent emergency information about their classes. This material, along with any other information the administrator deems necessary, should be presented to the substitute upon his or her arrival in the building. Periodic checkups and observations can insure the quality of the substitutes on which the administrator must rely.

The certified substitute teacher is accorded the same rights and is under the same restrictions of law as the regularly-employed staff member even though the substitute may be employed on a part-time or *per diem* basis. Liability is the same, as are the protections of the school's insurance, provided the substitute conducts him or herself in a reasonable and prudent manner. Inclusion of the substitutes in workshops and in-servicing, orientation seminars and social functions can help instill a feeling of personal worth and professional value in this much-needed support person.

See Also: ASSIGNMENTS; AUTHORITY, EXPRESS AND IMPLIED; AUXILIARY PERSONNEL; CERTIFICATION; LESSON PLANS; LIABILITY; *PER DIEM;* SECRETARY; SIGN-IN SHEETS; SUPERVISION (STAFF).

SUMMER SCHOOL

Summer school is a program in which the plant facilities and professional instructors are made available to students during off-school months.

Throughout many parts of the country, the concept of summer school classes has become an increasingly important facet of the school's overall academic program. While the traditional time period for it has been four- to ten-week courses, taught between the fourth of July and the opening of school in September, many schools have added "block vacations" or "intersessions" (often in January, February or March) in order to hold these short courses.

There are three types of summer school programs. The first is the *Remedial-Only Program*. Here, students are given concentrated instructional assistance in mastering skills they have not conquered during regular class hours. The courses primarily include math and reading, but other curricular subjects might be offered.

The second type is the *Remedial, Makeup and Enrichment Program*. This is the most common summer school program. Students are given opportunities to get remedial instruction if they need it, to makeup courses they have either failed or received a lower grade than they needed for future career or for college entrance, or to take enrichment courses that will broaden their experiences. Often, students who normally carry heavy class loads, who are involved with the school extracurricular program or who are seeking early entrance into college will take regular courses in the summer to lighten their class load during the regular term.

The third form of summer school is the *Independent Program*. Generally school and/or community sponsored, this type focuses on enrichment programs and opportunities. The students, often away from the school itself, engage in in-depth studies. It is this type of program that spawns the four-week "intercessions."

Some programs are free to all students in the township or municipality, regardless of whether they attend common, private or parochial schools under the principle of shared-time. Others charge a nominal tuition fee to non-system students. Still others charge a fee to all who attend. Charging fees is permissible because summer schools are considered over and above the normal state requirements of a free education. If fees are charged, however, very clear and concise policies must be written concerning the save-harmless protections of the instructors, the liabilities of the school, and the rights, responsibilities and requirements of the students.

See Also: ACADEMIC PROGRAM; CALENDAR; COMMON SCHOOLS; CURRICULUM DEVELOPMENT; ENRICHMENT; IMPUTED NEGLIGENCE; PRIVATE AND PAROCHIAL SCHOOLS; REMEDIAL INSTRUCTION; SHARED-TIME; STUDENT INFORMATION; TRANSPORTATION; YEAR-ROUND SCHOOLS.

SUPERINTENDENT OF SCHOOLS

The **Superintendent of Schools** is the educational administrative officer and chief member of the central staff within a system or district.

The superintendent has a wide and varied field of responsibility. Serving directly under (and at the pleasure of) the local board of education, these administrators must control every aspect of the system, including instructional and operational (in some districts, the operational duties are shared by the business administrator). Working with assistant superintendents or supervisors of Curriculum, Personnel, and Special Services, they must carry out board policies. Further, they must provide an example of leadership for all levels of the system.

Some of their other duties include evaluating the effectiveness of the entire academic program, planning for both current and long-range programs and improvements, reporting and making recommendations to the board on all personnel, acting as chief public relations officer, forming advisory committees, providing for educational programs for the staff, meeting frequently with the board in order to inform them and to receive from them any new policies, and, finally, acting as liaison officer from the district to all outside agencies.

Because of the immensity of their responsibilities, superintendents of schools must be highly qualified. Each state superintendent or chief state school official sets the requirements for the local superintendent's credentials. These usually include a Master's or higher degree, with at least a Master's plus twelve credits if not a Doctorate; graduate study in School Administration, Curriculum and Supervision; and, a strong educational background with a minimum of three years teaching and four years in administration.

See Also: ADMINISTRATION; CENTRAL STAFF; CHIEF STATE SCHOOL OFFICIAL; COUNTY SUPERINTENDENT; MONTHLY REPORTS; YEAR-END REPORTS.

SUPERVISION (STAFF)

Staff supervision is the program of steady support, evaluation and instruction leading to the improvement of instructional expertise, employee relations, in-service training, and curriculum development.

Supervisory personnel must perform their duties precariously balancing their roles as administrators and their duties as resources for the instructional staff. On one hand, they must interpret and carry out the superintendent's academic program design. The assistant superintendents provide the curricular guidelines, the staff tries to implement the curriculum, and the parents and community wait for the results. On the other hand, students are the primary concern. The parents and community want well-educated, reasonably happy and productive children, the staff needs help and support in meeting the student's needs, and the central staff must be made aware of any needed expansions or changes in the academic program. Keeping these two communications chains working smoothly is the role of the supervisor.

Supervisors approach their duties from one of three perspectives or alternate supervisory strategies. The first is called the *school-oriented strategy.* Here, the supervisors aid the teachers in developing instructional objectives in the classroom along the guidelines of the goals and objectives of the school's educational program. The supervisor acts as an interpreter of the school.

The second perspective is the *teacher-oriented strategy.* The teacher expresses an instructional goal, and the supervisor observes, comments and acts as a resource person to the teacher. Unspoken, but still present, is the supervisor's responsibility to the school's program. In this strategy, however, the guidance to follow it is subtle and undemanding, and the supervisor interprets for the teacher.

The third, *coordinated* or *multi-level strategy,* is by far the most difficult for the supervisory personnel to maintain. In it, the supervisors act as interpreters for both sides by defining each side's needs and goals and by acting as liaison between them. In this strategy, there is constant feedback from one to the other as to how each side's needs and objectives are being met. The supervisors act as resource personnel to them both.

Each system must decide not only the role the supervisors will play, but also the organizational position they will hold. In some systems, the supervisors are collectively under an assistant superintendent of schools in charge of curriculum; in others, there is a head supervisor, with other supervisors at various grade of unit levels. These act as curriculum or unit coordinators in whichever strategy is chosen. Their administrative tasks may include observation and evaluation of personnel, curriculum development, and coordination and arrangement of workshops and in-service training.

Qualifications for supervisors include a minimum of three to five years teaching experience, a Master's degree, and proper certification in both teaching and supervision.

See Also: ADVISORY COUNCILS; CENTRAL STAFF; CHANGE STRATEGIES; CONSULTANTS; CURRICULUM DEVELOPMENT; DIFFERENTIATED STAFFING; EMPLOYEE RELATIONS; EVALUATION; GOALS AND OBJECTIVES; INSTRUCTION; LIAISON; NEEDS ASSESSMENT; OBSERVATION; PROFESSIONAL IMPROVEMENT PLAN; RECOMMENDATIONS; REFERENCES; SPECIAL WORKSHOPS AND IN-SERVICE.

SUPERVISION (STUDENTS)

Supervision of students refers to the overseeing of children while on, coming to, or leaving school property.

With state compulsory education laws come the full responsibility of the schools for the "health, safety and well-being" of the children who attend those schools. Under such dictums as "safe place statutes" and "habitable codes," the physical plants are to be safely maintained. But the major thrust of the supervisory duties of the school is toward the students themselves, and it is assigned to the administrators and staff, both professional and nonprofessional, who are in direct contact with them.

The schools, when defining the duties of their staffs in policy statements, always include the phrase "active, reasonable and prudent supervision." Each word of this phrase has its own legal ramifications. *Active* denotes involved movement. Teachers standing in one part of the playground during recess are not providing proper supervision; they must move through and mingle with the students. *Reasonable* has been taken to mean "according to professional expertise." Teachers and administrators receive a high degree of training and are thus expected to show a higher degree of care than the lay person. Finally, *prudent* has been understood to mean the responsibility to foresee possible dangers. Again, this idea is based upon the enhanced knowledge of the professional.

The supervision of students falls into two divisions, *classes* and *assigned duties*. While with their classes, the teachers are responsible for any activity in which the students are involved. During the assigned duties, they are generally responsible for certain areas and have overlapping supervision with other professionals. In this latter circumstance, the administrator has the overall supervisory responsibility. Therefore, if aides, noncertified volunteers, or other non-professionals are used for these duties, the administrator is culpable as well as the nonprofessional.

Supervision is also the duty of bus drivers, cafeteria personnel, custodial and maintenance staff members, and certain auxiliary personnel, but their responsibility is limited to their particular area of expertise. For example, the bus drivers must maintain and operate safe vehicles, but they may not be held responsible for actions taken by the students on their buses.

The need for proper supervision is ongoing. Periodic checkups and evaluations will insure that all students in the building and the system are as well protected as they possibly can be.

See Also: ACCOUNTABILITY; AGENT; AIDES; ASSIGNMENTS; AUTHORITY, EXPRESS AND IMPLIED; COMPARATIVE NEGLIGENCE; CONTRIBUTORY NEGLIGENCE; FORESEEABILITY; HABITABLE; HALL DUTY; IMPUTED NEGLIGENCE; LIABILITY; MINISTERIAL ACTS; PLAYGROUND; REASONABLE AND PRUDENT; SAFE PLACE STATUTES; SAFETY.

SUPPLIES AND EQUIPMENT

Supplies are the consummable materials in regular school use. **Equipment** is the physical property other than land, buildings, or improvements, sometimes called capital outlay.

One of the most time-consuming but necessary tasks performed by administrators is the management of supplies and equipment. Between the requisitioning, warehousing, distributing, inspecting, and budgeting of these items, the school spends an enormous amount of time, money and energy. Administrators, despite their great educational expertise, find themselves in the role of "Supply Sergeants."

The management system most commonly used is the *"central supply method."* The district allocates a certain amount of its budget for supplies and a separate amount for equipment. A standardized supply requisition form is drawn up, dividing them into various categories such as Library supplies, Industrial Arts supplies, janitorial supplies, classroom supplies, etc. These forms are passed to the classroom teachers, custodians and others who need them. The forms are filled out and returned to the administrators who correlate them and pass them on to the purchasing agent. The same procedure is followed for equipment requisition forms. The needed items are then purchased and kept in a central location in the district. Building administrators or their surrogates then draw upon this "central supply" for their building's needs. Once in the building, a "central supply room" holds the materials until they are needed by individual staff members.

While other systems may be used, the ideas are basically the same. The group needing the supplies and equipment tells the group who purchases the items what they need; it is bought, then dispensed. The amount of control and restraint required by administrators and purchasing agents is considerable. With inflated costs

and limited budgets, meeting supply and equipment demands can be next to impossible. However, with careful planning and a great deal of understanding by both administrators and staff, the task is not insurmountable.

See Also: AUDIO-VISUAL MATERIALS; BIDS; BUDGET; CLERICAL SERVICES; CUSTODIAL SERVICES; EXPENSES; FUNDS, SCHOOL; LIBRARY AND MEDIA CENTER; MONTHLY REPORTS; MORATORIUM; PURCHASING; RECORD KEEPING; SPORTS; YEAR-END REPORT.

SUSPENSION

Somewhere between compulsory education laws, which require a student to be in school, and the school's rights and responsibilities to keep and maintain a "healthy, safe and secure" environment, stands the problem of out-of-school **suspensions** and expulsions. The questions, "When?" "For what reason?" and, "For how long?" are at the heart of the dilemma.

Suspension is a short-term disciplinary action taken *only* when the school's environment must be immediately protected. This interpretation has become the most common guideline for administrators using this option. The fact that a student must be removed from the educational process is so serious that suspension should only be used in emergency situations. When a rule has been broken which, while a serious disobedience to recognized authority, is not dangerous to the school's population, the student is generally isolated *within* the building in an in-school suspension.

The infractions for which suspensions may be given will vary from district to district. However, a hierarchy of offenses must be established, from *detention* (for minor infractions: handled by classroom teacher), *in-school suspension* (for minor infractions, but including constant and disruptive behavior: initiated by either the teacher or administrator), *suspension* (for major and dangerous infractions: controlled by the administrator), and *expulsion* (for major and dangerous infractions that threaten life: initiated by the administrator, but enacted by the board). Once established, the administrator, the students, and their parents/guardians should be made aware of the hierarchy and the procedures that will follow. Some states require a hearing on all out-of-school disciplinary actions, while others place this stipulation only on expulsion and leave suspension an administrative perogative.

The length of suspension may also vary from district to district. Some have set lengths for various infractions of from one to ten days; others, believing that suspension is only a method of removing danger, have indefinite but short periods that give the school sufficient time to contact and meet with parents/guardians, support personnel and teachers to decide the best course of action.

Whatever the view of suspension, the administrator should treat this procedure as the serious matter that it is.

See Also: ASP (ALTERNATE SCHOOL PROGRAM); AUTHORITY, EXPRESS AND IMPLIED; CORPORAL PUNISHMENT; DETENTION; DISCIPLINE; EXPULSION OF STUDENTS; IN-SCHOOL SUSPENSION; PARENT CONFERENCE; STUDENT INFORMATION.

T

TALENTED CHILD

See GIFTED STUDENTS.

TARDINESS

Few things are as annoying to a teacher as starting a class only to have it interrupted by a tardy student, particularly when the class is working and the late arrival doesn't know what is going on or what to do. Obviously, common sense must prevail, and when students are tardy *upon occasion,* it presents no more than a minor annoyance. When, however, a student or group of students is tardy *on a continuing basis,* then it may be assumed that a problem exists that requires attention.

Whether **tardiness** involves lateness to school in general or to a particular class or classes, it is to the benefit of all involved that the root causes of the tardiness be exposed. It may be as innocent as the fact that the path from one classroom to another covers a considerable distance against the flow of hall traffic. It may also be as devious as stopping in a lavatory or storeroom to take drugs. Whatever the cause, once it is known, it is up to the administrator, working with the teacher and student and often the parent, to achieve an amicable solution and see to it that the student gets to school or class on time.

Toward this goal, it is helpful if the school has established a clear policy on tardiness and disseminates that information to everyone. These policies often vary from district to district, and can range from a certain number of unexcused latenesses equalling a detention, to continued tardiness equalling loss of course credit, to placing tardiness entirely within the province of the individual teacher's judgment. Whatever the case, the policy should be clearly stated and, whenever possible, derived from the efforts of all levels of the system involved.

If, however, educators look for the cause of tardiness and make an effort to deal with these causes in getting the chronically tardy student to school and class on time, then the student as well as the school will benefit.

See Also: AUTHORITY, TEACHER; DISCIPLINE; HALL DUTY; STUDENT INFORMATION.

TAXES

Taxes are the compulsory payment of a percentage of income, property value, sales price of a home, etc., for the purpose of supporting a government and its functions.

It has been said that taxation is the method of securing collectively what could not be secured individually. Schools, as governmental agencies, could not function without the revenue generated by the people. While this may seem simple, the problem of schools running on taxpayer's money has become monumental.

Historically, when all the community had to support was a one-room schoolhouse with a single teacher, there was no hardship for anyone. Today, with sophisticated physical plants, expensive educational materials and elaborate instructional programs, as well as numerous and better-paid teachers, communities often find it difficult to keep pace with the costs. The standard formula for financing schools is one half from federal and state revenues and one half from the local community.

Ninety-eight percent of the community's half is generated through local property taxes.

Inevitably, inequities arise when poorer districts cannot support the same kinds of educational systems as the richer districts. This inequity has led to certain landmark court cases such as *Serrano v. Priest,* (487 P.2d 1241 [CA 1971]), *San Antonio Independent School District v. Rodrigues* (93 S.Ct. 1278 [1973]), *Everson v. Board of Education* (330 U.S. 1,15,18 [1947]), and *Abington School District v. Schempp* (374 U.S. 203 [1963]). The decisions in these cases were aimed at trying to achieve educational equity across all socio-economic and religious lines.

Also, if taxpayers do not have children in the school, have no knowledge of how the school is working, do not believe in the values being taught, nor see the necessity for expenditures for the school, there is a feeling of "taxation without representation." Let this feeling hang around long enough, and a taxpayers' revolt is likely.

The failure of tax referendums and bond issues are symptoms of the taxpayer's displeasure. A prime example of this was the *Jarvis-Gann Amendment to the California State Constitution,* better known as "Proposition 13," which was passed in 1978.

Better school/community relations and improved communications can help overcome and ease some of the frustrations and misunderstandings of the taxpayer.

See Also: BUDGET; COMMON SCHOOLS; FEDERAL AGENCIES, FEDERAL AID, FEDERAL PROGRAMS; POLITICS AND THE SCHOOL; PRIVATE AND PAROCHIAL SCHOOLS; STATE AGENCIES, STATE AID, STATE PROGRAMS; VOTING.

TEAM-TEACHING

See INTERDISCIPLINARY APPROACHES.

TELEPHONE

The **telephone** is very much a part of the modern school. Many schools find it necessary to have three, four or even more telephone lines into the building. The telephone is often the chief instrument for contacting parents, conducting business with outside agencies, and for interagency communications within the school system.

Problems often arise concerning the unauthorized use of telephones. Various individuals may attempt to make personal calls using the school's telephones. Often these may be toll calls, and even a small number of unauthorized toll calls can add substantially to the bill that must be paid by the district.

Consequently, many school systems have established a policy that all calls or at least all toll calls be logged, and that anyone using the telephone is required to fill out a form or enter information on a master sheet relative to the user's name, the number called, the purpose of the call, and the time and charges (which may be obtained upon request from the operator). Thereafter, everyone using the phone for something other than school business is expected to pay for his or her calls.

Invariably, students find many valid reasons for using the telephone during the school day. Many schools, in order to keep phones free for school business, have installed pay telephones for student use, usually located near or in the main office where their use and possible abuse can be monitored.

If there are handicapped students in a school, it would be wise to have at least one pay telephone placed lower on the wall where it may be conveniently used by someone in a wheelchair, for example.

See Also: CLERICAL SERVICES; COMMUNICATION; RECORD KEEPING; SECRETARY.

TENURE

Tenure is the holding of a position; in education, it is the automatic renewal of a contract, provided a probationary period has been served and performance has been consistent with state laws and local requirements.

Tenure has been alternately seen as vital to educators, as a monetary and legal millstone around the necks of local boards of education, and by the public as a "free ride for teachers." The reason for the wide disparity of views is a lack of understanding about what tenure can and cannot do, along with the purposes it was meant to serve.

As early as 1909, when New Jersey passed the first state teacher-tenure legislation, it was clear that education should be *free and unrestricted.* Teachers had to be protected from political interference, capricious employment and dismissal practices, and public censure for teaching certain materials or using certain methods if the concept of academic freedom was to survive. Subsequently, most states have adopted these tenure laws, along with more-or-less standardized certification, dismissal and due process procedures.

The exact wording, elements and descriptions of tenure laws vary from state to state. Some states leave tenure up to the local districts; others have called for mandatory tenure in *large districts only;* others *specify the cities or counties* in which the laws are to apply; and still others call for mandatory tenure *across the board. Extension of the laws has also been made to include administrators at all levels.*

Because of societal factors, population decreases and tight budgetary restraints, tenure has been going through some subtle changes. Updated tenure laws are using a kind of *seniority system,* much like the Civil Service, for some of their provisions. Also, *"self-terminating contracts,"* without benefit or need of tenure, are helping school districts cope with changing tax bases and fluctuating populations. These contracts are made for a specified length of time and amount of money. If further funded, they are continued (extended) for another set period; if not, they are allowed to expire. The staff personnel who take contracts on this basis know that their programs will remain only "at the pleasure of" the board and local community.

Tenure does not protect against the termination of contracts as a result of the ending of a service or program (See REDUCTION IN FORCE), because of a reduction in salary or status (See DEMOTIONS), or due to reassignment among institutions (See TRANSFERS). Nor does it protect educators from dismissal for certain cited violations (See DISMISSAL OF PERSONNEL).

The building administrators have the responsibility to judge whether or not a teacher should receive tenure. There is ample time for them to observe, evaluate and work with probationary teachers to insure that only those worthy of tenure receive it.

See Also: ACADEMIC FREEDOM; ACCOUNTABILITY; AUTHORITY, BOARD; CERTIFICATION; CONTRACTS; EVALUATION; MERIT PAY; OBSERVATION; PERSONNEL FILES; PROBATIONARY TEACHER; RENEWAL OF CONTRACT; SUPERVISION (STAFF).

TEXTBOOKS

Textbooks occupy 75 percent of student's classroom time and 90 percent of their homework time. Some curricular programs are generated and implemented based upon available and currently printed textbooks. Over 50 percent of a school's budget is spent on instruction, and a sizeable proportion of that percentage goes to textbooks.

The *selection of textbooks* is generally made by committee. Teachers and supervisors review those that are available, analyzing them for content, reading levels, and age-appropriate material. Recommendations are then made for purchasing those selected. Administrators then pass on these recommendations to the board, which either approves or rejects the selection.

The *dispersal of textbooks* is based upon two concepts. First, textbooks are considered part of a "free and appropriate" education. Therefore, one-child, one textbook is the general rule in most schools. The textbooks are distributed at the beginning of the year and returned at the end. They are generally maintained as part of the school's property, and are replaced regularly as needed, without charge to the students. The only exceptions are if the students lose, destroy or wish to keep the books for their own personal use.

Second, is the concept that textbooks are deemed necessary to education. Therefore, the economic status, place of residence or school attended by the student is of no consequence. Under both the Child Benefit Theory and the Fundamental Interest Theory, secular textbooks may be given to any child who needs them. Cases such as *Board of Education v. Allen (392 U.S. 236 [1968])* and *Serrano v. Priest (487 P.2d 1241—[CA, 1971])* have further clarified that each child shall be given whatever materials are generally available, without exception.

See Also: ADVISORY COUNCILS; AGE LEVELS; BUDGET; CHURCH-STATE SEPARATION; COPYRIGHT; CURRICULUM DEVELOPMENT; FEES; FUNDAMENTAL INTEREST THEORY; INSTRUCTION; PRIVATE AND PAROCHIAL SCHOOLS; PURCHASING; SUPPLIES AND EQUIPMENT.

THEFT

Theft can be a problem in any school. It may involve the taking of students' property or money left in desks or lockers, or personal property may be stolen from faculty and staff members. In some cases, it may even involve a mugging or assault upon students or teachers in the hope of quick gain. Whatever the case, the culprit is usually long gone before the theft is realized and/or reported, and the chances of retrieving the stolen property are slim.

Therefore, clear policy should be established for everyone concerning the bringing of valuables to school. For example, students may be urged to bring nothing worth more than ten dollars to school, to carry only as much money as they require for the school day, and to make certain that locker keys/combinations are not widely circulated in the school. Teachers may be instructed never to leave handbags or personal property in the classroom either attended or unattended, to make certain that classroom doors are locked when not in use, and to take precautions that extreme valuables are not brought in to school except under close supervision. These policies should be put in writing and should be a part of student information and the faculty handbook or policy book.

In some cases, teachers and students may be required to leave all valuables and all but a nominal amount of money in the school safe at the start of each school day, to be picked up before leaving the building. While this is not a common practice, it can prove valuable in school settings where there may be a history of violence, since it removes the incentive of getting "quick cash" by attacking a student or teacher. If this policy is to be implemented, it should be widely publicized in order that potential muggers will know that there will be no profit from their actions. The school safe should be available in any school, however, for those students or faculty members who wish to temporarily store valuables for safe-keeping.

Removing the incentive for theft, as well as taking common-sense precautions for theft prevention, will go a long way toward ameliorating the problem.

See Also: BURGLARY; CASH; POLICE; STUDENT INFORMATION; VIOLENCE.

TRAINABLE CHILD

See RETARDED CHILD.

TRANSFERS

Transfers involve the moving of a staff member from one place or position within a district to another within the district; it also concerns facilitating the moving, through paperwork and/or personal contact, of a pupil from one district's jurisdiction to that of another.

Staff movements are quite common. The increased need for personnel in one particular building, the special expertise or qualifications called for by a certain department, or even the personal request for a change of environment can all be reasons for shift of personnel. Staff transfers are considered the board's perogative, and as sighted in the case of *State ex rel Withers v. Board of Education of Mason County* (172 S.E.2d 796, 803—[WV 1970]), they do not automatically denote punitive action. Tenure cannot be used as an impediment to being moved unless there is also a demotion involved; this may require a hearing.

Students also go from place to place in the course of their school lives. Some, as in the case of children of military personnel or migrant workers, move frequently in and out of states, as well as districts. Others, through being advanced in grade levels or being enrolled in special programs, may move within the district or county. Whichever is the case, these transfers must be carefully coordinated in order that no vital information on the student or their educational programs will be lost or interrupted. *Within counties or districts,* the school's support personnel such as guidance counselors handle the exiting of students, the moving of their documents, and their entrance into the new building. The out-of-state transfers are often coordinated through "transfer systems." One such system, operated for the children of migrant workers, is called the Migrant Student Record Transfer System (MSRTS). These systems are generally used at the state and county levels. There may or may not be fees assessed for the transfer of documents according to the policies of the boards involved.

See Also: ADDRESS (RESIDENCE); ASSIGNMENTS; AUTHORITY, BOARD; AUTHORITY, PARENTAL; CHIEF STATE SCHOOL OFFICIAL; CONSOLIDATION; GUIDANCE; MIGRANTS; NONRESIDENTS, ADMISSION OF; PERMANENT RECORDS; STUDENT INFORMATION; TENURE.

TRANSPORTATION

Transportation is the mechanical conveyance system used by a school district to insure the safety, attendance opportunity and movement of its students.

Schools were once, and in some cases still are, located within acceptable walking distance (1-2 miles) from a student's home. But as districts became geographically larger and pulled students from increasing distances, transportation became a concern. How the students were to get to their assigned buildings and then return safely to their homes began getting more and more complicated. Also, the more students involved, the more vehicles and personnel needed to convey them. Add to this the enormous increase in field trips, class outings, extracurricular activities, along with handicapped students with special needs, and the problems seemed to get rapidly out of hand.

There were several general solutions used to handle this administrative Gordian knot. First, for economic purposes, bus routes were arranged so that the fewest number of buses would be needed to transport the most students. Along with this, school opening and closing times were staggered, in order that buses might be used several times during the day for multi-age-level students.

Second, a group of separate but coordinated management structures were established to operate the district's transportation system efficiently. Each of these structures is commonly under a separate director who answers to the district's transportation director, who in turn is responsible to either the superintendent or the business administrator.

These structures are the *general student conveyance system* (GSC), which is responsible for the daily movement of the main student population. The assigning of buses and bus drivers to various routes, schools and time schedules according to the district's needs, the training and supervision of general transportation personnel, and the maintenance of the vehicles is covered under this system.

Another structure is the *special service* or *handicapped transportation service* (HTS). Under this, specially-equipped vehicles and trained operators assist handicapped students in reaching district and non-district facilities. This service has several vehicles on constant call throughout the day.

Finally, there is the *emergency transportation service* (ETS). Every district has some sort of contingency system, regardless of the name used, that will go into effect should an emergency requiring a mass movement of students arise. There is much careful planning needed to insure that there will be sufficient buses and drivers available. Generally, districts maintain a fleet of "standby" vehicles throughout the school day for just such a possibility.

Transportation is considered a shared-time service. Because of this, it is permissible for public school buses to pick up, convey and deposit non-public school children at their schools *(Everson v. Board of Education,* 330 U.S. 1, 18 [1947]).

Whether the district owns or rents its vehicles, the board of education is ultimately responsible for maintaining an adequate, safe and economic transportation system.

See Also: AUXILIARY PERSONNEL; AUXILIARY SERVICES; BUS AND BUS DRIVERS; CLOSE OF SCHOOL; DISMISSAL PROCEDURES (SCHOOL); FIELD TRIPS; HANDICAPPED; PUBLIC LAW 94-142; SHARED-TIME; TRIPS.

TRESPASSER

Schools are public property. As such, the public has an implicit right to access to them. However, this does not mean that *anyone* may enter a school building at *any* time, for *any* purpose. Indeed, it has been upheld that the school has the right to make reasonable rules limiting public access to the building.

Unfortunately, these rules are often necessitated by instances of outside intruders who have entered schools and perpetrated heinous crimes. These have included pushing drugs, assaulting students and school personnel, and, in one horrendous instance, raping an elementary school teacher in front of her startled and frightened class.

Consequently, many schools take measures to prevent would-be **trespassers** from entering school grounds. While all doors in a public building must open from the *inside,* the doors may be locked in such a manner that entrance to a school from the *outside is through one door only.* Members of the faculty and staff may be assigned to *hall duty,* with instructions to report unfamiliar or suspicious individuals. Security guards may be hired in some instances to perform similar functions. A *workable system of communications* and check-ins for faculty members may be established. Finally, *all visitors* to the school, regardless of whom they may be, *may be required to check in* at the main office before going elsewhere inside the school. Any trespasser on the school grounds may be legitimately reported to the police and/or be asked to leave, and if compliance is not forthcoming, the police may escort the trespasser off the premises or arrest the offender.

Many would agree that this is a sad commentary upon the state of society, but whatever the feeling, schools *are* charged with protecting the "health, safety and well-being" of the students and the faculty and staff. Consequently, many schools find it necessary to take the actions outlined above, in order to protect the school population from the dangers of trespassers.

See Also: BUILDINGS; GROUNDS; JUVENILE DELINQUENCY; MALICIOUS MISCHIEF; PASSES; POLICE; REASONABLE AND PRUDENT; SAFE PLACE STATUTES; SAFETY; SELF-DEFENSE; SUPERVISION (STUDENTS); VIOLENCE.

TRIPS

It is necessary to make a distinction between **trips** and field trips, for they are not the same. In a field trip. students are taken to a place or event *directly related to the curriculum*. It is a learning experience for the students. For example, students may go to a nature preserve to look for fossils as an adjunct to their Science classes, or to a museum with a display of medieval armor to supplement their studies in History. The primary purpose of a trip, on the other hand, is to entertain. A trip to an amusement park or to a circus will certainly amuse the students, but one would be hard-pressed to relate it to the curriculum.

Traditionally, trips have been used as rewards. A student safety patrol, for instance, might be taken to a baseball game toward the end of the school year as a reward for their work during the year. Some similar reward used for the members of any club, class or extracurricular activity.

When trips are paid for by the participating members of the group and are taken after school hours, there usually is no problem. Difficulty may arise, however, when a trip is taken during school time and/or is partially or totally subsidized by the district. A budget-conscious community may well raise objections to spending educational funds and/or time for something basically noneducational in nature. Not only the community, but also the educators may have strong feelings on the subject.

When moratoriums are placed on spending within a district, trips planned in the budget are usually the first things to go.

See Also: ACTIVITIES; CLUBS; CULTURE; EXTRACURRICULAR ACTIVITIES; FEES; FIELD TRIPS; INSURANCE; MORATORIUM; TRANSPORTATION; VOLUNTEERS.

TRUANCY

Truancy is a continued un-authorized absence from school by a student under the age of majority (state age limit).

Truant behavior can manifest it-self in many ways. However, since there is a characteristic common to them all, the only difference is one of degree. Actions such as faking a stomach ache to either stay home or get out of school or class early, the occasional cutting of classes that be-comes more frequent, the playing of "hookey" occasionally that develops into staying out of school for days, weeks or even dropping out entirely, all show the same disregard for or lack of interest in the activities taking place in school.

From the first sign of indifferent attendance patterns, the school should become actively involved. This can be done in many ways, either through the district's attendance officer (truant of-ficer) or through Special Services. Sometimes these support personnel also work with and through the state's department of youth and family serv-ices in the area. Some even coordinate their efforts to assist students by working with the juvenile division of the local police dpeartment or through the juvenile court system. No matter what kind of support personnel is used, the thrust must be toward rein-teresting the child in and giving value to his or her education.

In some states, truancy is han-dled as a juvenile crime with stiff penalties. In some districts, too, the punishments are quite severe. They can range from 3 to 10 days of out-of-school suspension to expulsion for continuous violations. Punishing the act does nothing to solve the problem, however. In fact, this can aggravate it by further alienating the child from school.

See Also: ABSENCE; ABSENTEEISM; ASP (ALTERNATE SCHOOL PRO-GRAM); COMPULSORY EDUCATION; CUTTING; JUVENILE DELINQUENCY; PARENT CONFERENCES; SPECIAL SERVICES; STUDENT INFORMATION; SUPERVISION (STUDENTS).

TUITION

See NONRESIDENTS, ADMISSION OF.

U

UNDERACHIEVERS

When speaking of the **underachiever,** care should be taken to see to it that this student is not confused with the child who *cannot* do the work. This latter student often has some sort of learning difficulty and may even be classified. Teachers usually have unbounded patience when working with this kind of student. Rather, an underachiever is a child who has the recognizable ability to perform in a satisfactory manner yet over a period of time has consistently and on a steady basis achieved considerably below that potential.

This student is quite often a frustration to educators who must deal with him. In spite of any extra help and special attention the teacher may give, the child fails to respond. Often, it seems as if this student does only the minimum amount necessary to pass and not one thing more. The student's grades reflect this fact.

Teachers with such a student should be encouraged to seek the assistance of Guidance counselors, teaching supervisors and similar support personnel in working toward a solution to the problem. Often, a system of positive communications between the school and the home can go a long way toward getting the underachiever to produce. In fact, a liaison between the teacher and the home is often the only way with an underachiever to see to it that homework, study and projects are forthcoming.

With the help of a plan jointly devised by the teacher, the supervisor or support personnel member and the parents, which is geared to the individual child, everyone can work toward getting the underachiever back on track toward the achievable goal of academic success.

See Also: ACHIEVEMENT; APTITUDE; COUNSELING; GUIDANCE; INTELLIGENCE TESTING; PARENT CONFERENCES; REPORT CARDS; STUDENT INFORMATION; SUPERVISION (STAFF); SUPERVISION (STUDENTS).

UNEMPLOYMENT COMPENSATION

Unemployment compensation is payment of a certain amount of money at a fixed rate, for a specific length of time, resulting from the loss of employment.

The granting of unemployment compensation to teachers is a fairly recent development in education. While employment insurance has always been part of the withholding from employee's paychecks, very few positions were actually eligible. When decreased enrollments and consolidations began to reduce the number of teachers needed in the district, however, more teachers began to receive such benefits.

Even considering state-by-state differences, employees are generally eligible for unemployment compensation if they are "RIFfed" (See REDUCTION IN FORCE), are released because of the nonrenewal of a "self-terminating" contract (See TENURE), or are employed under a special grant that ends before a school year is concluded such as compensatory education or CETA. The length of the benefit period or the amount given is up to the discretion of the local unemployment bureau.

In most cases, a letter from the employer (board of education) is necessary to show their intent to rehire the employee, should the position ever become eligible again. This letter is not necessarily binding on either party in the future, but merely shows "good relations" at the time of the termination of employment.

Should a tenured teacher be fired, unemployment compensation may not be automatically collected. Instead, depending on state law and local statutes or policies, hearings must be held to determine eligibility.

See Also: NONRENEWAL OF CONTRACT; WITHHOLDING.

UNGRADED

Ungraded refers to an educational, organizational and instructional method that allows for student-centered advancement; it is sometimes referred to as continuous progress programs.

The saying that "the more things change, the more they remain the same" was never truer than when applied to education. Educational innovations have been cyclical, with good ideas rising in importance then falling away only to reappear as some "new" ideas, promising to improve the whole thrust of instruction. This is not to say that change is not necessary. Often, however, the concepts and philosophies that were of real merit are still sound and still produce good results, regardless of the "cosmetic modernization" they have undergone in the name of change.

A primary case in point is the ungraded method that has returned to favor. The concept of ungraded systems is a two-pronged affair. First, there is the belief that all students do not learn the same material at the same rate or in the same manner. Second, there is the view that over-all or classwide reporting systems do not accurately reflect the learning done by the individual child. Some schools rely on both parts of this concept, while others choose one or the other.

In practice, the first prong of the approach is often called *continuous progress programs, schedules or classes*. This means that students who are chronologically in the first, second or third grades might be taught not at these arbitrary levels, but at their own levels. For example, Mary (a chronological second grader) might be reading on a fifth grade level, doing Math at a second grade level, and working in Social Studies or Science at a third grade level. Her classes might be in different rooms or areas, because her teachers would be giving instruction at the level of the students and not at the fixed grade level. Mr. Jones would not be teaching second grade Math, for example, but he would be teaching Math of a "second grade concept/mastering/performance level," and all the students in his class would be at that level regardless of their chronological ages. Because this happens in all subjects and there is so much movement within the year's program, students quickly lose any sense of being "behind" or "accelerated" —they are just going to school.

The second aspect of the concept of "ungraded" is particularly adaptable to a self-contained classroom. When materials are mastered and the students are given some acknowledgement of *their* mastery, *reporting systems* become just that: reports. For instance, on Friday (March 3rd) John mastered compound verbs, on Tuesday (March 7th) he mastered compound subjects, but it took him two more weeks to master adverbs. His report would look like this:

Compound Verbs—$3/3$
Compound Subjects—$3/7$
Adverbs—$3/22$

It is assumed by the teachers, supervisors or curriculum coordinators that various masteries will take certain amounts of time. The student's progress is then supervised to ensure that he is given any help he needs.

If any part of the ungraded concept sounds familiar, it is not suprising. At the beginnings of American education, in the one-room schoolhouse, the teacher taught subjects to *groups* of students rather than grades of students.

See Also: ABILITY GROUPING; ABILITY LEVELS; CHILD-CENTERED; CONTRACTED LEARNING; GOALS AND OBJECTIVES; INDIVIDUALIZATION; INTERDISCIPLINARY APPROACHES; LEARNING CENTERS; OPEN CLASSROOMS; RECORD KEEPING; REPORT CARDS; SCHEDULE; SELF-CONTAINED CLASSROOM; SUPERVISION (STAFF); SUPERVISION (STUDENTS).

UNIONS

Relative to public education, the school administrator must often deal with **unions.** Many of the auxiliary services required by the modern school involve workers who belong to various unions. While their function is not educational in nature, they contribute to the effective operation of the school. Disputes between a board of education and these unions may often have a paralyzing and devastating effect upon a school system.

In regard to the professional staff, the courts have held that First Amendment guarantees allow teachers to join and participate in unions. When using the term "teacher's union," however, it should be noted that, by definition, a teacher's union is an association that is affiliated with organized labor as opposed to a local, state or national education association, which is not. Consequently, the American Federation of Teachers, which is affiliated with the AFL-CIO, may be classified as a teacher's union, while the National Education Association may not.

See Also: ACADEMIC FREEDOM; AMERICAN FEDERATION OF TEACHERS; CONTRACTS; JOB ACTION; NEGOTIATIONS; REPRESENTATION; STRIKES.

Unit Coordinator

See SUPERVISION (STAFF).

UniServ

UniServ is a function of the NEA that provides a unification of services (hence, its name) designed to coordinate the service programs at all levels of the association and its affiliates.

Started in 1970, there are presently UniServ offices in over 1,200 locations throughout the United States and Puerto Rico, serving educators both overseas and from its headquarters in Washington, DC.

The UniServ office acts as a single unit providing a myriad of services. Basically, there are eight areas of service. These are coordination of state and national resources including professional development, instructional improvement and human relations; negotiation services; contract, administration and grievance adjudication; local members' consultations and individual services; public relations and publicity; legislation and political activity; leadership development skills, and organizational business management and membership projects.

The officers who staff UniServ units are experts in educational law, business management and contracts, as well as the profession itself.

See Also: CONSULTANTS; MEDIATION AND MEDIATOR; NATIONAL EDUCATION ASSOCIATION; NEGOTIATIONS; POLITICS AND THE SCHOOL; REPRESENTATION; SPECIAL INTEREST GROUPS.

Unwed Mothers

Society's views on sexual activity and pregnancy have changed a greal deal in the last two decades. As has been shown in the entry on PREGNANT STUDENTS, the schools have reflected this changed attitude by the extention of both services and support to the students.

The legal protections of the female employee have also been extended. No longer can a teacher be terminated *solely* because of her pregnancy. Instead, the operative reasons must be her "failure to carry out professional duties" or "unfitness to teach." If the students in her classroom are not adversely affected by her presence, if education is not being disturbed or disrupted, and if she is not proselytizing or using her pregnancy as an endorsement to sexual promiscuity, the board may be hard-pressed to fire **an unwed mother.** It should be understood, however, that the perogative to dismiss is the board's, but it must accord her all the due process procedures to which she is entitled.

See Also: AUTHORITY, BOARD; DISMISSAL OF PERSONNEL; DUE PROCESS; FIRST AMENDMENT GUARANTEES; FOURTH AMENDMENT GUARANTEES; HEARINGS; MATERNITY LEAVE; NONRENEWAL OF CONTRACT; PREGNANT STUDENTS; PRIVACY.

U. S. DEPARTMENT OF EDUCATION

The **U.S. Department of Education** is the 13th cabinet-level department of the federal executive branch.

With the urging of various educational organizations such as the NEA, President Jimmy Carter worked to establish a cabinet-level department of Education. This was accomplished when he signed Public Law 96-88 on October 17, 1979. The Department became operational on May 4, 1980. Shirley M. Hufstedler, a former federal judge, was appointed to serve as the first U.S. Secretary of Education.

Under the Department of Education Organization Act (PL 96-88), the Department of Health, Education and Welfare (now the Department of Health and Human Services) transferred to the Department of Education the programs of its Education division. Most of these programs were in the division's Office of Education and comprised the bulk of the Department of Education's programs.

Also from HEW came programs that fund rehabilitative services for handicapped persons. A few education-related programs were transferred from the National Science Foundation and from the Departments of Labor, Justice, and Housing and Urban development.

The legislation authorized offices headed by Assistant Secretaries for Elementary and Secondary Education, Postsecondary Education, Vocational and Adult Education, Special Education and Rehabilitative Services, Educational Research and Improvement, and Civil Rights. A general counsel and an inspector general were also authorized.

In addition, the Department operates offices to administer bilingual programs, to represent nonpublic education, and to serve in the areas of planning, budget, management, legislation, and public affairs.

The Act also established the Intergovernmental Advisory Council on Education. Representing educators, parents, students, and the public, the Council advises the Secretary of Education and the President on the impact of federal policies on state and local education agencies and institutions.

The federal Interagency Committee on Education, a long-active group, was reauthorized under the Act. As in the past, its purpose is to assure effective coordination of policies and administrative practices among all Executive Branch agencies that have education-related programs.

With the inauguration of President Ronald Reagan, concern was expressed in some educational circles that there might be a dismantling of the new Department of Education. This concern was somewhat alleviated by the appointment of Dr. Terrel H. Bell as the second U.S. Secretary of Education. While never an advocate of a cabinet-level status for federal education, he was an early supporter of separating Education from the then Department of Health, Education and Welfare, and he has been hailed as a "distinguished educator" who understands the "problems and issues of public education."

While the future of the Department is debatable, and while many believe that the Reagan Administration is moving toward establishing an independent federal agency of non-cabinet status, it seems unlikely that federal education programs will ever return to the diversity of placement and command that prompted the establishment of the U.S. Department of Education in the first place.

See Also: FEDERAL AGENCIES, FEDERAL AID, FEDERAL PROGRAMS; SECRETARY OF EDUCATION, U.S.

V

VANDALISM

The increased instances of violence in society have been reflected in the school. According to an interview with one researcher in the field, the actual number of instances of **vandalism** and other related antisocial acts may run as high as a million cases a year, carrying a pricetag of over half a *billion* dollars.

The effects of vandalism on a single district can range from the annoying (the painting of graffiti on exterior walls) to the devastating (a ransacking spree after hours). Even so, there is always a cost factor involved in fixing the broken window, repainting surfaces, replacing lavatory equipment or whatever has been damaged. That money, which should be spent as part of the instructional budget, is instead allocated to the maintenance department.

The local board sets policy on how the particular district will handle the problem. While there is no na-

tional consensus, some common practices are used. First, administrators should stress to their faculties, staffs, students, and parents/community just how the board feels about vandalism, what penalties will be leveled for the offense, and what rights will be exercised concerning calling police, signing criminal complaints, pressing for court-assessed damages, etc.

Next, precautions should be taken to protect the school buildings and grounds. This may be done as casually as having aides, staff members and students "keep an eye out for anything suspicious" during school hours with police and school neighbors doing the same at night, or as formally as hiring security guards to patrol twenty-four hours a day. Here, each system must assess its own problems and act accordingly.

Another practice taken against vandalism is the analysis of the "vandalism quotient" of the school. Administrators usually set up advisory councils, consisting of elements from all educational levels, to determine how the students feel about the school, its staff, the facilities and programs, and the many other items that make up a student's school experience. Then, usually in the form of a needs-assessment questionnaire, the students express their extreme displeasure, satisfaction or approval of each item. The results are then analyzed, hearing in mind that the steps toward vandalism are seen as a downward spiral. First, there is hostility, followed by anger, followed by vandalism or violence if nothing is done to end the problem that caused the initial hostility. Those items that have caused significant anger or displeased responses can be attended to through some change strategies in order to defuse the potential for vandalism.

Finally, several programs have been developed that use students to fight vandalism under the premise that people do not destroy what they own. Under supervision, student groups become responsible for various areas of the building where vandalism is most likely to strike.

Any one of these techniques or all of them in combination can assist the administrator in reducing this single, most costly drain on educational time and money—vandalism.

See Also: ADVISORY COUNCILS; GRAFFITI; JUVENILE DELIN-QUENCY; PARENTAL LIABILITY; PO-LICE; TRESPASSER; VIOLENCE.

VENDORS AND VENDING MACHINES

Nowadays, almost every school has at least one beverage or candy machine in it somewhere. Some schools also have various food **vending machines** that dispense cold sandwiches, yogurt, fruit, and a variety of other items. In a few cases, there are even amusement machines in high school lounges.

Whatever type machines are in the school, the policies concerning them are determined by the local board of education. Since the machines may usually be used by both adults and students, separate guidelines for each group are given. Further, the age level of the students involved is also a factor in the policy.

Vending machines available in faculty rooms or lounges are for the use of the staff. Use of these machines by students is generally prohibited. The funds collected from these machines is taken directly by the **vendor.** Sometimes a contract may be drawn in which the vendor guarantees that a certain percentage of the proceeds will be returned to the school for "teacher/lounge funds," but this is not mandated.

Machines may be placed in student access areas in and around the school. Student access times may be set to avoid disruption of educational time. Money accrued from these machines often goes into "student activity funds." The contracts with vendors whose machines are used by students are held by the school. That is, the school leases or rents the machines and services, and the profits go directly back into the school.

The replacement of the contents of the machines, their repair, money collection, and other maintenance and operational duties are strictly the responsibility of the vendor. These operations and the machines as well may not interfere with the school's operation in any way, and if they do, the machines may be removed. The board, after a review of the problem, may relocate, remove or discontinue use of any machines, at any time, without being liable for "breach of contract" suits because of its primary responsibility, which is to the education of the students.

See Also: AUTHORITY, BOARD; BIDS; CASH; STUDENT INFORMATION.

VICE PRINCIPAL

A **vice principal** is a member of a school building administration who functions as an assistant to the principal and carries out duties and responsibilities as delegated by the principal.

A vice principal is sometimes known as an assistant principal. He or she is an employee of the board of education and reports directly to the principal, who is the vice principal's immediate superior.

The duties of the vice principal will vary, often drastically, from school to school. Generally, the vice principal is placed in charge of specific areas such as attendance or school discipline. The limit and scope of the vice principal's authority in these and other areas is often defined by the principal's wishes as well as board policy. For example, a principal may wish to personally handle all discipline cases that require suspension and may dictate that all these cases be personally reviewed by him or her prior to the actual suspension. Other principals may delegate this authority to the vice principal, wishing to be notified only in the most serious of cases such as those in which expulsion is a possibility.

Generally speaking, a vice principal has more student contact than the principal. He or she also acts as a screening agent for the principal, handling those matters of daily routine that save the principal's time for other administrative, supervisory and operational considerations.

See Also: ADMINISTRATOR; AUTHORITY, EXPRESS AND IMPLIED; EMPLOYEE RELATIONS; MINISTERIAL ACTS; MONTHLY REPORTS; PROFESSIONAL ASSOCIATIONS FOR SCHOOL ADMINISTRATORS; RIGHTS AND RESPONSIBILITIES; SUPERVISION (STUDENTS); YEAR-END REPORT.

VIOLENCE

Within a single year, there were 115,000 attacks upon educators, teachers *and* administrators, and over 15,000 of these required serious medical attention and involved long periods of recovery and/or the loss of a career. In some cases, the result was death.

There are few people, either inside or outside of education, who do not decry this abominable situation. Indeed, the very idea of **violence** is so foreign to the ideals of education that its presence in a school is devastating. Educators and politicians make speeches about it, various agencies condemn it soundly, everyone says it must be stopped, yet it continues to plague our schools. Of course it is not a problem in every school, and most schools, even the majority of schools, are safe places, but the figures mentioned above speak for themselves.

What can be done about it? Various authorities have various solutions. Part of the answer might be to make the schools more secure from intruders (*See* TRESPASSER). Another solution might be to treat juvenile offenders as offenders rather than juveniles (*See* JUVENILE DELINQUENCY). Or, committees might be formed to look for the root causes of violence, with the aim of dealing with these causes in order to alleviate the greater problem. (*See* VANDALISM)

When an administrator is faced with dealing with someone who is engaged in violent behavior (beating another student, destroying property in a room, attacking a teacher or student with a weapon, etc.) the primary course of action is to *isolate the offender*. Constitutional and civil rights notwithstanding, the administrator's first duty is to stop the vio-

lence and keep the violent person away from others. Then, authorities may be notified and board policy followed.

Boards of education should write clear policy, including penalties, about violence in the schools. Thereafter, this information should be widely disseminated and adhered to vigorously. Violence in the schools is a drastic situation that requires drastic measures to deal with it.

See Also: ADVISORY COUNCILS; ASSAULT; AUTHORITY, EXPRESS AND IMPLIED; BATTERY; JUVENILE DELINQUENCY; MALICIOUS MISCHIEF; POLICE; SAFE PLACE STATUTES; SAFETY; SELF-DEFENSE; STUDENT INFORMATION.

VOCATIONAL PROGRAMS

A **vocational program** is the curriculum design that includes the pre-entrance level training of students in various fields and career options.

Schools do not operate only for the college-bound student. Instead, it is a basic belief of education that students should be able to choose, prepare for, and succeed at whatever "life program" best suits them. This has meant that while courses are offered in traditional academic curricular designs, there has been an increased call for vocational education as well. Indeed, schools have recognized that if the school follows only one path, then those not wishing to follow that path will rebel, leave or drop out.

Actually, the emphasis in education has changed considerably over the years. Originally, the schools were interested in producing students who could "make their way" in the world. At that time, this meant learning a skill or trade. It was only a small percentage of students in the school who were given the college preparatory classes. Then, the pendulum shifted, and education went through a period where it was felt that *everyone* should go to college, and only the few who "couldn't or wouldn't" make it were grudgingly given "Shop" and Business courses. After these two extremes, education seems to have returned to a more realistic approach. Students now *choose,* with the help of guidance and career counselors, those courses they will need for *their* chosen career.

In order to provide for vocational programs, districts budget for courses in Career Education, Consumer Education, such fields of endeavor as are indicated by community needs, student desires and staff expertise. Also budgeted for are counseling and placement services, and all supplies and equipment needed.

Vocational programs can be housed either in single *district units* or in *county coordinated unites* that service several districts. These buildings and programs are available to *all* students wishing to attend, whether they are actively enrolled in the district's common schools, enrolled in private or parochial schools, engaged in adult education programs, or are interested

members of the community. Payment for courses taken at vocational schools is dependent upon pupil status and state statutes.

See Also: ACADEMIC PROGRAM; ADULT EDUCATION; CAREER EDUCATION; COUNSELING; FEDERAL AGENCIES, FEDERAL AID, FEDERAL PROGRAMS; NONRESIDENTS, ADMISSION OF; SHARED-TIME; STATE AGENCIES; STATE AID; STATE PROGRAMS.

VOLUNTEERS

A **volunteer** is a person who works for an institution or cause without pay, giving freely of his or her time and efforts.

Volunteer workers can be an invaluable adjunct to any school. Parents and other community members regularly volunteer to serve as chaperones, class mothers, part-time teacher's aides, and a host of other positions that make school life a great deal easier and smooth-flowing for everyone. Consequently, volunteers should be encouraged by the school.

Volunteers may be solicited through the school's PTA, through flyers mailed or sent home to parents via students, or even by means of ads in local newspapers. Volunteers should be given explicit information on what the job entails, and if necessary, they should get specific training. It should be remembered, however, that without proper certification, volunteers may not be asked to assume professional duties. Moreover, a system of informal supervision of volunteers should be established in order that the efforts of individuals and the entire program may be evaluated.

A functioning volunteer program is extremely effective in the area of public relations, as volunteers from the area bring back to the community positive news and views about the school. Administrators, therefore, should see to it that the efforts of volunteers are properly acknowledged and that proper appreciation is shown.

See Also: ACKNOWLEDGEMENT; AIDES; EMPLOYEE RELATIONS; NEWS LETTERS; P.T.A. SUPERVISION (STAFF).

VOTING

See POLITICS AND THE SCHOOL.

WELFARE

See FAMILY SERVICES.

WITHHOLDING

Withholding refers to the recognized deductions paid by employees through their paychecks.

The difference between the employee's gross income and his net or actual take-home income is the withholding tax. The deductions may vary slightly because of positions held, state statutes or local board contracts, but generally, they consist of the following items. First, there are deductions for state (if applicable) and federal *income taxes*. Once the employee has filed with the district the number of dependents he or she is claiming, the proper amount is withheld. At the end of the year, the district issues a W-2 form to indicate the year's deductions. Second, *Social Security taxes* and *Unemployment In-*

surance are withheld in the appropriate amounts according to a prorated scale, based on gross income.

With the state and federal taxes taken care of, the district's withholdings are then deducted. According to the district's contract, items such as hospitalization, pension and annuity funds, and dues for various associations may be withheld.

Finally, *the employees themselves may request* certain withholdings. If any *additional coverage* is offered to hospitalization or dental plans, they may take this coverage and deduct the difference in the premiums directly from their paychecks. Undoubtedly, the most common employee-requested withholding is the *summer payment plan*. Offered in almost every district, this allows the employees to spread their ten-month paycheck schedule over a twelve-month period by deducting one-tenth of each month's salary. Teachers then receive the accrued amount during the two months of non-payment. This is done entirely at the employee's discretion, and is often handled through the local credit union. Similarly, *private retirements funds* or *savings bonds* may be withheld through these facilities.

All withholdings must be clearly stated on the paycheck stub issued to the employee. Any questions about any withholdings should be immediately directed to the superintendent, business administrator or the assistant superintendent in charge of payroll.

See Also: CREDIT UNION; FINANCE; HOSPITALIZATION; INSURANCE; SALARY; TAXES; UNEMPLOYMENT COMPENSATION.

WORKING PAPERS

Working papers are the permits obtained by students under the age of majority (between 12 and 18) to enable them to seek and gain employment.

Two bills, enacted by Congress, have set the basis for child employment in this country. The first, *The Walsh-Healey Act of 1936* (c. 881, 49 Stat. 2036 [U.S.Code of 1976, Title 41 §§35-45]), established the minimum working wage and the 40-hour work week. It also placed restrictions on the use of child labor. The scope of the Act, however, was only for such employment held in connection with government contracts or any form of government work. When the second bill, *The Fair Labor Standards Act of 1938* (c. 676, 52 Stat. 1060 [U.S.

Code of 1976, Title 29 §201 *et seq.*]), was passed, the stipulations of *Walsh-Healey* were accepted into the private sector. Further, both Titles 29 and 41 show that there can be no sex-discrimination or bias in conditions of employment, equality of wages for equal work and responsibility, or rights of promotion.

The fact that a student wishes to work is of no concern, nor should it be, to the school. Rather, only the *conditions* of that employment are of concern because of the school's overall responsibility to protect the "health, safety and well-being" of its students. Therefore, under the dictums of the state departments of education and labor and industry (names may vary in certain areas), local schools generally require the filing of working papers.

There are several forms, each serving a specific purpose. First, there is the *School Record*. This verifies that the child is a student in a particular grade, and is within the jurisdiction of a certain building and district. This is signed by the student's building administrator. The second is the *Promise of Employment*. This is a blank that the prospective employer fills out and signs. Accompanying this form (sometimes actually attached to or part of it) is the *Parental Permission Statement*. The parents sign and attest to both their knowledge of and agreement to their child's employment. They may stipulate the number of hours or type of work they will allow their child to do. Next, there must be a *Physician's Certifi-*

cate of Physical Fitness, completed and signed by the child's own doctor. Finally, there is the *Vacation Employment Certificate.* This vital piece of data verifies the child's age, any school information needed, and a copy (photostats are permitted) of the child's birth certificate. Further, it must state *in plain English* (or other languages if appropriate) the precise regulations regarding child employment in the state or commonwealth. Three copies are made of this, with one each going to the employer and the state offices, and one kept on file in the district. Another form is required if the students are to be working in agriculture. This is the *Special Agriculture Permit,* which is similar in all major respects to the Vacation Employment Certificate. This form has two copies required, with the blue going to the state office of labor and the yellow one staying in the district.

Student employment is to take place *only* after school, on weekends and during vacations. Any other periods of employment must be approved by and accredited under a work-study program and state statutes. Also, periodic checks are made by all levels of government and the district's support personnel to insure the propriety of the child's employment.

See Also: AUTHORITY, PARENTAL; MIGRANTS; STUDENT INFORMATION; WORK-STUDY PROGRAM.

WORKSHOPS AND IN-SERVICE

Workshops and in-service are the methods of professional education used to explore needs, review and update goals and objectives, evaluate programs and policies, and share ideas and strategies.

Education does not exist in a vacuum. Instead, many factors effect how curriculums will be taught, what materials will be used, and how problems may best be solved. Teachers and administrators are constantly communicating to each other what they have learned. One of the best and most consistently effective of these communication methods is the professional workshop or in-service training session.

The types of workshops and the various ways of handling professional education are as diverse as can possibly be imagined. From short, after-class sessions, with an in-house/district staff member acting as the resource person, to a year-long change strategy being adopted one step at a time through steady weekly faculty sessions, or from single grade or level meetings with textbook designers to full-scale research projects conducted under the auspices of a nearby college or university, the possibilities for in-service training are endless.

Whatever the methodology, the purpose is always the same: to learn, to share and to grow professionally.

See Also: ACADEMIC FREEDOM; CHANGE STRATEGIES; CURRICU-

LUM DEVELOPMENT; DEPARTMEN-
TAL MEETINGS; DIFFERENTIATED
STAFFING; FACULTY MEETINGS;
NEEDS ASSESSMENT; PARLIAMEN-
TARY PROCEDURE; SUPERVISION
(STAFF).

WORK-STUDY PROGRAM

A **work-study program** is the
academic and nonacademic structure
that facilitates a student's entry into
the work force.

Under the mandate of the *Vocational Education Act of 1963* (PL
88-210) and updated in the *Educational Amendments of 1976* (PL
94-482, Title 2), the schools became
actively involved in presenting on-site
job training to their students. While
vocational schools were maintaining
purely job-oriented education, it was
proposed that students in the *regular
academic program* be given similar
career opportunities simultaneously
with their class work. The methodology for intermixing these programs
became known as work-study programs or vocational opportunities
programs.

Once students who want these
opportunities have applied for and
received their working papers, they
have three main types of programs to
follow. First, there is the *co-operative
education program* for students who,
through written training agreements
between the school and the employers, engage in supervised, part-time
employment and receive related class

instruction. The employment is coordinated, and the related classes are
taught by a school-appointed teacher-
coordinator. This teacher-coordinator
must be a fully-certified teacher who
has taken courses in the field of vocational guidance, and who has been
gainfully employed in a business,
skill or trade for at least two years.
The students, through their guidance
counselors, schedule all their state
and local board-mandated required
courses as well as their job-related
class during the *first half of the school
day*. They report to their job for the
last half. They must work at least 15
hours per week and receive credit as
well as fair compensation for that
work. The funding for this is through
state and federal funding, with the
school providing only the personnel.

Second, the *work-study program*
is a non-credit financial support program designed to help needy vocational students remain in school by
providing them with a job outside
school hours. To be eligible, the
pupils must be *needy* (determined by
the funding criteria, either economically, socially or both), must be *enrolled in an acceptable vocational
program* (taking either a full-year
course in career training or a sequence
of skill courses), and must be a student *between the ages of 15 and 20*.
Funding is through a 50-50 matchup
with the local board and the state or
federal program.

The last is the *summer work-
study program*. The guidelines are
generally the same as for the work-

study program, except that the students may *work more hours* (up to 30 hours per week) and the thrust of the program is aimed at *younger students* (14-15 years of age) who cannot compete in the job market. The funding is the same as for work-study.

Strict supervision of working conditions, pay schedules and the academic side of the program by all agencies involved ensures the protection of the student worker.

See Also: CAREER EDUCATION; COUNSELING; COURSE OF STUDY; FEDERAL AGENCIES, FEDERAL AID, FEDERAL PROGRAMS; GUIDANCE; MAJORITY, AGE OF; STATE AGENCIES; STATE AID; STATE PROGRAMS; STUDENT INFORMATION; VOCATIONAL PROGRAMS; WORKING PAPERS.

WORLD CONFEDERATION OF THE TEACHING PROFESSION

The **World Confederation of the Teaching Profession** is an international organization of professional educators.

This organization encompasses 116 National Organizations in 76 countries, covering over five million educators. Its stated goals are to promote, through education, international understanding and good will; to defend the rights of the teaching profession; and to maintain and promote closer relationships between educators in different countries.

The organization holds a biennial convention, always in July or August. For further information contact:

World Confederation of the
    Teaching Profession
5 Aveneu Du Moulin
CH-1110 Morges, Switzerland

See Also: PROFESSIONAL ASSOCIATIONS FOR SCHOOL ADMINISTRATORS; PROFESSIONAL ASSOCIATIONS FOR TEACHERS.

X, THE LETTER

Within the day-to-day operation of the public schools, it is often necessary to have documents signed by parents or guardians for a variety of legal or quasi-legal reasons. Usually, this presents no problem. Difficulty ˙may arise, however, on the rare occasion when the parent or guardian is illiterate and therefore unable to write his or her name. In this case, the "signature" would be in the form of a mark, usually the letter **"X."**

In order for this mark to be a legal signature, certain procedures must be followed. The document in question must be read aloud to the individual in the presence of witnesses. Then, if the person agrees to "sign," the individual's name is written in the proper place, leaving a space between the first and last name. The words "his (or her) mark" are placed above and below the space, and the individual then places an "X" in the space. The signature looks like this:

his
John (X) Smith
mark

After the mark has been made, the witnesses also sign the document.

While the chances of encountering someone who cannot write his or her own name are slim, today's educator should be prepared for such situations.

See Also: ADULT EDUCATION; FIELD TRIPS; GUARDIAN AND GUARDIANSHIP; PERMISSION SLIPS; REPORT CARDS.

X-RAY REPORT

Schools periodically test students and staff for indications of tuberculosis and other communicable diseases. This is vital because the health and well-being of the school population might be in jeopardy if an undetected case were present in the school. Usually, this is accomplished by the use of a non-x-ray type of test such as the Mantoux or a similar procedure.

Should the results of any of these tests prove positive, however, the school may require that the individual be further tested by means of a chest **x-ray.** This is a very serious business, since a person with evidence of a communicable disease may be legitimately banned from attending school at all. Consequently, the school is within its rights to require that the x-ray report be sent to school officials.

Usually, the individual is sent to a doctor or medical agency under special contract with the school district. The chest x-ray is done at no cost to the individual, and the results are sent directly to the proper authorities within the school district.

While these procedures may vary slightly from district to district, requiring an x-ray report is fairly standard. If the results are negative, nothing further is done. If, however, there are positive indications of illness, appropriate action would be taken to make sure that the individual is directed toward proper treatment while the health and safety of the remaining school population is fully protected.

See Also: AUTHORITY, BOARD; HEALTH; PERSONNEL FILES.

Y

YEARBOOK

Yearbooks mean memories, or so claim the ads for their sale that are often found posted in schools. However, many people do cherish and retain their school yearbooks throughout their adult lives. Yearbooks, therefore, are not a subject to be taken lightly by a school administrator.

While the production of the yearbook is assigned to the students working on it, that production is usually under the guidance of a faculty member who serves as an "advisor" to the student work crew. The actual printing and production of the book has been greatly simplified by yearbook publishing companies who usually provide advisors with production "kits" specifying directions and deadlines for each stage of production. Even so, the advisor must direct the students with great care to see that deadlines are met, that fees are collected and accounted for, and that assigned work such as photographs

and the like are forthcoming. It is not an easy task.

Although yearbooks are generally associated with colleges and high schools, one sees them with increasing regularity at lower grade levels. Many junior high and middle schools regularly produce yearbooks, and even elementary schools put out yearbook-like products ranging from professionally printed to the home-grown variety, utilizing the school's copying and mimeograph machines.

Yearbooks often play a major role in effective public relations. Therefore, every effort should be made to see to it that the yearbook portrays a true picture of the school. This is often a matter of focus, as one can always find the silly and frivolous, just as one can always find the serious and meaningful. Of course, the rules about censorship apply, but while it may be difficult to achieve, a careful balance that accurately reflects the vital nature of the educational institution should be the goal of every administrator and yearbook advisor.

See Also: APPRECIATION, LETTER OF; CENSORSHIP; CLUBS; EXTRACUR-RICULAR ACTIVITIES; EXTRACUR-RICULAR DUTIES; STUDENT INFORMATION.

Year-End Report

A **year-end report** is a compilation of materials generated on a yearly basis within individual buildings and facilities of a school district, for use by the central staff, local school boards, or state or federal authorities.

At the end of each year, administrators must reflect on, review and report what has been accomplished. This is done by first gathering the monthly reports and synopses that have come into the office. Then, through careful study, administrators further encapsulate the material and determine what information must be sent where.

There are many categories of reports (names will vary from state to state). *The annual state funding report* contains figures on attendance and/or enrollment along with other statistical data needed to receive an appropriate state allotment. The *accreditation report* contains such data as the district's name, enrollment, number of students in each grade or class, lists of courses, facilities available, and present and past student college expectations and successes. The *health report* contains immunization records, communicable disease incidents, and the number of students with special needs. The *inventory* contains the amount and condition of present supplies and equipment in the building or district. Finally, the *federal reports* are each designed for the particular program used in the school. These reports all have very clear-cut reporting and/or evaluation systems, and require great care in compilation.

A well-trained clerical staff, plus an accurate and efficient record keeping system are the all-year, on-going developmental projects that culminate in clear, concise and well-organized year-end reports.

See Also: ACCREDITATION; ATTEND-ANCE; CLERICAL SERVICES; EN-ROLLMENT; FEDERAL AGENCIES, FEDERAL AID, FEDERAL PRO-GRAMS; MONTHLY REPORTS; REC-ORD KEEPING; SECRETARY; STATE AGENCIES, STATE AID, STATE PRO-GRAMS; SUPPLIES AND EQUIPMENT.

Year-Round Schools

Year-round schools refers to an organizational, instructional and operational structure that utilizes the facilities of a school building or district on an all-year or continuous basis.

While it is impossible to totally cover such a complex subject as year-round schools in a few brief paragraphs, it is both feasible and necessary to clarify the term in regard to what year-round schools are and what they are not.

There are many different year-round structures that have been tried. The *Hayward Four Quarter Plan*

(CA) calls for four ten-week instructional periods, interspersed with four three-week recesses, exemplifying the single-stream continuous learning year. The *Valley View 45-15 Four-Stream Calendar* (IL) calls for 45 days of continuous instruction followed by 15 days recess. Its variation, the *La Mesa Plan* (CA), adjusts the cycle to 43 or 47 days and includes a one-week vacation at Christmas and a five-week recess between June and September.

Each structure was intended to get the most out of the school's facilities, teachers and programs. Teachers, it was felt, would get salaries commensurate with their *true* work. Students would benefit because there would no longer be the need for "start-up reviews" after such long lay-offs. Also, it was felt that students would progress further because of short, steady instructional periods rather than long, traditional ones due to their need for change and variety.

Whatever the structure and purpose, however, public outcries and professional skepticism exist. The public may see the year-round school as an oppressive monetary burden because of perceptions (both real and imagined) of "air-conditioned class-rooms," year-round energy bills, "over-scheduled tots with no time to play," and increased staff and support personnel needed to work the extra time. Educational skeptics point to the tremendous organizational and operational changes needed within a district to make the needed adjustment from 10- to 12-month school years. Also, they point out, there have been no statistically significant increases in the productivity of the year-round schools to balance the overwhelming loss in public relations. Without public support, they quickly add, no school can function while alienating the entire community because of "possible" growth.

While year-round schools as a concept have been around for over 40 years, there are still many arguments concerning them that have yet to be resolved. Reading widely, attending workshops and attaining a good understanding of the students, staff and community are the best tools for the success of an administrator contemplating this approach.

See Also: ACADEMIC PROGRAM; CALENDAR; CURRICULUM DEVELOPMENT; HEARINGS; SCHEDULE; SUMMER SCHOOLS.

Z

ZONING

Zoning is the act of dividing an area, city, township, or the like into sections reserved for different purposes.

Most areas served by a school system, such as a municipality or township, are zoned according to purpose. Hence, there may be residential zones, light industry zones, business zones, and the like. The school, however, is under the directive to educate *all* the children within its purview, whatever the zone in which they live.

Historically, this posed no apparent problem. A school was erected, designated as serving the children of such and such zones or areas that surrounded it, and went into operation. This was often called the concept of the "neighborhood school."

However, when national attention began to focus on the Civil Rights Movement, it was often discovered that this practice had led to *de facto* segregation. This was because a school serving an area zoned for a particular type of housing, for instance, might receive more children of one race, while a school across town serving an area zoned for a different type of housing might receive children from another race. Subsequently, the courts upheld that busing was a legitimate tool for fighting this situation, and in order to achieve integrated school systems, children were often bused out of their zones or districts to other zones, in order to achieve racial balance and end the *de facto* segregation that existed.

This practice encountered a great deal of resistance on the part of many parents and educators. Quite often, this resistance was vocal and frightening. Still, busing has been and continues to be used. Recently, there has been a movement to do away with busing in all cases, except those in which the establishment of *de facto* segregated schools was *intentional* in nature. It is likely that this will take a number of years to fully resolve.

It is also likely that arguments over which zones shall be incorporated into what sending districts for which schools will remain a heated issue for some time to come.

See Also: ADDRESS (RESIDENCE); BUSING; DISCRIMINATION; TAXES; ZONING BOARD.

ZONING BOARD

A **zoning board,** sometimes called a zoning commission, is a board authorized by a local government to prepare and propagate zoning rules and regulations, and to affect changes in them according to statutory requirements.

Zoning regulations apply to the use of both lands and buildings. There are regulations whereby land use is restricted to specific purposes and building construction is controlled as to the type, size and physical proximity to other structures. Any school board or board of education, therefore, contemplating a change in the physical plant, acquisition or new use of lands, or new or additional construction would do well to clear these activities through the local zoning board.

Should the new construction violate existing zoning rules or regulations, the school would be required to obtain a *variance* from the local zoning board before construction could begin. This can sometimes be a lengthy process, as there are set rules and procedures that must be followed, and everyone who might be affected by the new construction has a right to be heard. Consequently, if a board of education must seek a variance, it is usually handled by the board attorney.

See Also: ACCESS RIGHTS; ADDRESS (RESIDENCE); AUTHORITY, BOARD; BUILDINGS; TAXES; ZONING.

APPENDIX A

TOPIC LOCATOR
BY
EDUCATIONAL
SUBJECT AREAS

APPENDIX A

TOPIC LOCATOR
BY
EDUCATIONAL SUBJECT AREAS

AREA ONE: *Administrative Agencies*

Accreditation
Administrator
Adult Education
Advisory Councils
Affirmative Action
Agent
American Association of School
    Administrators
American Council on Education
American Federation of Teachers
Arbitration
Auxiliary Services

Board of Education

Central Staff
Chief State School Official
Code of Ethics
Collective Bargaining
Convention
County Superintendent

Differentiated Staffing

Education Commission of the
States

Federal Agencies
Federal Aid
Federal Programs

National Assessment
National Education Association
NEA-PAC

Politics and the School
Principal
Professional Associations for School
    Administrators
Professional Associations for Teachers
Pupil Personnel Services

Secretary of Education, U.S.
State Agencies
State Aid
State Programs
Superintendent of Schools

Unions
UniServ
U.S. Department of Education

Vice-Principal

Welfare
World Confederation of the Teaching
    Profession

Zoning Board

AREA TWO: *Curriculum Areas*

Ability Groupings
Ability Levels
Academically Talented
Academic Program
Acceleration
Accountability
Achievement
Activities
Adult Education
Age Levels
Aides
Aptitude
Art
ASP (Alternate School Program)
Audio-Visual Materials

Bilingual Education
Books

Career Education
Change Strategies
Child-Centered
Competency-Based Programs
Compensatory Education
Contracted Learning
Course
Course of Study
Curriculum Development

Departments
Diploma

Electives
Elementary Schools
Enrichment
Examinations

Federal Programs
Foreseeability

Gifted Students
Goals and Objectives
Grades
Graduation
Graduation Requirements
Groupings

Heterogeneous Grouping
High Schools
Home Economics
Home Instruction
Homework
Homogeneous Grouping
Honor Roll

Individualization
Industrial Arts
Instruction
Interdisciplinary Approaches
Intermediate Schools

Kindergarten

Language
Language Arts
Learning Centers

Mainstreaming
Mathematics
Media
Metrics
Mini-Courses
Movies
Music

National Honor Society
Needs Assessment

Physical Education

Professional Improvement Plan

Readiness
Reading
Remedial Instruction
Report Cards
Retarded Child

Scholarship
Self-Contained Classroom
Sex Education
Social Promotion

Summer School
Supervision (Staff)

Underachievers
Ungraded
Unit Coordination

Vocational Programs

Workshops and In-Service
Work-Study Program

AREA THREE: *Educational Law*

Absence
Absenteeism
Academically Talented
Academic Freedom
Acceptance of Contract
Acceptance of Donations
Accessory
Access Rights
Accidents
Accountability
Accreditation
Administrator
Addresses (Residence)
Adult Education
Affirmative Action
Agent
Arbitration
Assault
Assignments
Athletics, Sex Discrimination in
Attendance
Authority, Board
Authority, Express and Implied
Authority, Parental

Authority, Teacher
Automobiles

Basics
Battery
Bible
Bilingual Education
Breach of Contract
Burden of Proof
Burglary
Busing

Calendar
Capacity
Censorship
Certification
Child Abuse
Child Benefit Theory
Christian Scientists
Church-State Separation
Civil Rights
Class and Class Size
Collective Bargaining
Common Schools

Comparative Negligence
Conflict of Interest
Constitutional Rights
Contracts
Contributory Negligence
Corporal Punishment
Copyright

Damages
Decentralization
Decertification
Defamation
Demonstrations
Demotion
Departmental Meetings
Differentiated Staffing
Discipline
Discrimination
Dismissal of Personnel
Dismissal Procedures (School)
Dress Codes
Due Process

Early Childhood Programs
Easement
Elementary and Secondary Education Act of 1965
Enrollment
Equal Employment Opportunities
Ex Post Facto
Expulsion of Students

Fact Finding
False Imprisonment
Federal Agencies
Federal Aid
Federal Programs
Field Trips
Fifth Amendment Guarantees
Foreseeability
Fourteenth Amendment Guarantees
Fourth Amendment Guarantees

Free Speech
Fundamental Interest Theory

Gambling
Gifted Students
Gifts
Grievances
Guardian and Guardianship

Hall Duty
Handicapped
Hearings
Hearsay
Hiring Practices
Homosexuals

Immunization, Inoculation and Vaccination
Impasse
Imputed Negligence
Incompetence
Increments
Injunction
In Loco Parentis
Intelligence Testing

Jehovah's Witnesses
Job Action
Jurisdiction
Just Compensation

Leave of Absence
Liability
Libel
Lockers
Loyalty Oath

Majority, Age of
Malpractice
Malice
Malicious Mischief
Mandatory Education

Married Students
Mediation and Mediator
Meet and Confer
Military Leave
Ministerial Acts
Minor
Minorities
Moral Turpitude
Moratorium

NEA-PAC
Negligence
Negotiations
Nonfeasance
Nonresidents, Admission of
Non-Tenured Teacher

Oaths
Observation
Open Hearings

Parental Liability
Parliamentary Procedure
Paternity Leave
Permanent Records
Personnel Files
Petitions
Pledge of Allegiance
Police
Pregnant Students
Privacy
Private and Parochial Schools
Privileged Communications
Protest
Public Law 93-380
Public Law 94-142
Pupil Personnel Services

Qualifications
Quorum

Race Relations

Reasonable and Prudent
Record Keeping
Reduction in Force
Religion
Renewal of Contract
Representation
Reserved Powers
Retention of Students
Rights and Responsibilities

Safe Place Statutes
Safety
Sanctions
Save-Harmless Statutes
Search and Seizure
Self-Defense
Self-Incrimination
Sexism
State Agencies
State Aid
State Programs
Strikes
Student Teacher
Substitute Teacher
Supervision (Students)
Suspension

Talented Child
Tenure
Theft
Trespasser
Trips
Truancy

Unemployment Compensation
Unions
UniServ
Unwed Mothers

Vandalism
Violence
Vocational Programs

Voting   X, the Letter

Welfare   Zoning

AREA FOUR: *Extracurricular Duties and Activities*

Access Rights   Field Trips
Accidents
Achievement   Lease of School Property
Activities   Liability
Age Levels
Art   Movies
Assembly Program   Music
Athletics
Athletics, Sex Discrimination in   National Honor Society
Automobiles   Needs Assessment

Back-To-School Night   Prom
Band
                                               Safety
Calendar   Special Interest Groups
Capacity   Sports
Censorship   Student Council (Student Govern-
Change Strategies   ment)
Clubs   Supervision (Students)

Dance   Trips

Equipment   Yearbook
Extracurricular Activities
Extracurricular Duties

AREA FIVE: *Public Relations*

Acceptance of Donations
Access Rights
Accountability
Achievement
Acknowledgment
Activities
Addresses (Speeches)
Administrator
Adult Education
American Education Week
Appreciation, Letter of
Arbitration
Assembly Program
Athletics
Authority, Parental

Back-To-School Night
Bilingual Education
Board of Education
Bulletin
Busing

Calendar
Censorship
Change Strategies
Close of School
Commencement
Committees
Communication
Culture

Demonstrations
Drugs

Field Trips

Graduation

Honor Roll

Lease of School Property

Media

News Coverage
Newsletter
News Releases

Open Communications
Open Hearings
Open House

Parent Conferences
Police
Protest
P.T.A.
Publication

Scholarship
Secretary
Special Interest Groups
Strikes
Student Council (Student Government)
Summer School

Work-Study Program

Yearbook

AREA SIX: *Pupil Personnel Services*

Ability Levels
Absence
Absenteeism
Academically Talented
Acceleration
Accountability
Achievement
Administrator
Age Levels
Aides
Aptitude
ASP (Alternate School Program)
Auxiliary Services
Audio-Visual Materials

Bilingual Education

Cafeteria
Career Education
Child Abuse
Child Benefit Theory
Child-Centered
Child Study Team
Civil Rights
Competency-Based Programs
Compensatory Education
Consultants
Counseling
Culture

Diagnosis
Drop-Outs
Due Process

Early Childhood Programs
Electives
Elementary Schools
Enrichment
Enrollment

Exceptional Students
Expulsion of Students

Family Services
Federal Programs
Field Trips
First Aid
Fundamental Interest Theory

Gifted Students
Groupings
Guidance

Handicapped
Health
Hearings
High Schools
Home Instruction

Immunization, Inoculation and
   Vaccination
Individualization
Intelligence Testing
Intermediate Schools

Juvenile Authorities

Learning Centers
Learning Disabilities

Mainstreaming
Married Students
Medical Services
Medication
Mental Examinations
Migrants

National Honor Society
Nurse

Permanent Records
Pregnant Students
Promotion
Psychological Studies
Public Law 93-380
Public Law 94-142
Pupil Personnel Services

Readiness
Record Keeping
Remedial Instruction
Retarded Child

Speech Therapy
Special Education

Special Services
Student Information
Summer School

Talented Child
Trainable Child
Transfers
Truancy

Underachievers
Unwed Mothers

Working Papers
Work-Study Program

AREA SEVEN: *School Finance*

Acceptance of Contracts
Acceptance of Donations
Accidents
Arbitration
Athletics
Attendance
Authority, Express and Implied
Automobiles
Auxiliary Services

Bank Accounts
Bids
Bill of Lading
Bonds
Books
Budget
Buildings
Bus and Bus Drivers

Cafeteria
Calendar
Cash
Collective Bargaining
Contracts
Credit Union

Debts
Demands

Easement
Enrollment
Estimates
Expenses

Federal Agencies
Federal Aid
Federal Programs

Fees
Field Trips
Foreseeability
Funds, School

Graffiti

Home Instruction
Hospitalization

Illness
Increments
Insurance

Job Action
Just Compensation

Liability

Merit Pay
Moratorium

Offers of Contract and Recruiting

Per Diem
Purchasing

Reduction in Force

Salary
Sanctions
Scholarship
Sick Leave
State Agencies
State Aid
State Programs
Summer School
Supplies and Equipment

Taxes
Textbooks
Transportation
Tuition

Unemployment Compensation

Vandalism
Vendors and Vending Machines

Withholding

Year-End Report

Zoning Board

AREA EIGHT: *School Organization*

Academic Program
Access Rights
Accidents
Administrator
Address (Residence)
Adult Education
Aides

Application
Assembly Program
Automobiles
Auxiliary Personnel
Auxiliary Services
Audio-Visual Materials

Back-To-School Night
Bids
Bill of Lading
Books
Buildings
Burglary
Bus and Bus Drivers

Cafeteria
Calendar
Capacity
Centralized Filing
Chairpersons
Class and Class Size
Clerical Services
Consultants
Commencement
Comparative Negligence
Consolidation
Contracts
Contributory Negligence
Computers
Copying Services
Corporal Punishment
Custodial Services

Decentralization
Differentiated Staffing

Early Childhood Programs
Easement
Elementary Schools
Energy Legislation
Enrollment

Field Trips
Fire Drills

Grounds

Habitable
High Schools

House System

Intermediate Schools

Junior High School

Keys
Kindergarten

Lavatories
Library and Media Center

Mail
Middle School
Monthly Reports

Non-Public Schools
Non-Tenured Teacher

Open Classrooms

Parking
Physical Education
Playground
Principal
Probationary Teacher
Promotion
Protest
Public Address System
Pupil Personnel Services

Recess

Safe Place Statutes
Safety
Schedule
Secretary
Self-Contained Classroom
Shared-Time
Sign-In Sheets
Student Teacher
Substitute Teacher

Summer School
Supervision (Staff)
Supervision (Students)
Supplies and Equipment

Team Teaching
Telephone
Transfers
Transportation
Truancy

Ungraded

Vandalism
Vice-Principal
Vocational Programs
Volunteers

Work-Study Program

Year-End Report
Year-Round Schools

Zoning

AREA NINE: *School Rules and Class Management*

Absence
Absenteeism
Administrator
Age Levels
ASP (Alternate School Program)
Assault
Assembly Program
Authority, Express and Implied
Authority, Teacher
Automobile

Bible
Bus and Bus Drivers

Cafeteria
Child-Centered
Civil Rights
Close of School
Code of Ethics
Contracted Learning
Corporal Punishment
Cutting

Demonstrations
Detention
Discipline
Discrimination
Dress Codes
Drinking of Alcoholic Beverages
Due Process

Elementary Schools
Expulsion of Students

Fire Drills

Gambling
Gifts
Graffiti

High Schools
Homework

Immunization, Inoculation, and
    Vaccination

In-School Suspension
Insubordination
Intermediate Schools

Juvenile Delinquency

Language
Learning Centers
Lockers

Needs Assessment
New Policy or Program

Opening Procedures

Passes
Permission Slips
Petitions
Playground

Promotion
Protest
Punishment

Recess
Record Keeping

Safety
Self-Defense
Smoking
Summer School
Supervision (Students)
Suspension

Tardiness
Truancy

Vandalism
Violence

AREA TEN: *Teacher Relations and Evaluation*

Academic Freedom
Academic Program
Accountability
Accreditation
Achievement
Administrator
Affirmative Action
Application
Appreciation, Letter of
Arbitration
Assignments
Authority, Teacher

Board of Education
Books

Breach of Contract

Censorship
Certification
Chairpersons
Change Strategies
Child-Centered
Civil Rights
Class and Class Size
Code of Ethics
Collective Bargaining
Committees
Contracts

Decentralization

Representation
Resignation
Retention of Students
Retirement

Sabbatical Leave
Salary
Sanctions
Schedule
Self-Defense
Sick Leave
Sign-In Sheets
Social Promotion
Special Interest Groups
Strikes
Student Teacher
Substitute Teacher
Supervision (Staff)
Supervision (Students)

Team-Teaching
Telephone
Tenure
Textbooks

Unemployment Compensation
Ungraded
Unions
UniServ
Unit Coordination

Vice-Principal
Voting

Workshops and In-Service

X-Ray Report

Year-End Report

APPENDIX B

A
SELECTED
BIBLIOGRAPHY

APPENDIX B
A SELECT BIBLIOGRAPHY

Arnold, L. Eugene, *Helping Parents Help Their Children*. New York, NY: Brunner-Mazel, Inc., 1978.

Bean, Reynold, and Harris Clemes, *Elementary Principal's Handbook: New Approaches to Administrative Action*. West Nyack, NY: Parker Publishing Co., Inc., 1978.

Brembeck, C., *Social Foundations of Education*. New York, NY: John Wiley and Sons, Inc., 1966.

Caldwell, Bruce G., *Differentiated Staffing—The Key to Effective School Organization*. New York, NY: The Center for Applied Research in Education, Inc., 1973.

Carlson, Thorsten R., ed., *Administrators and Reading*. New York, NY: Harcourt, Brace, Jovanovich, Inc., 1972.

Chaplin, Dora, *The Privilege of Teaching*. New York, NY: Morehouse-Barlow Co., 1964.

Clifford, Geraldine Joncich, *The Shape of American Education*. Englewood Cliffs, NJ: Prentice-Hall, Inc., 1975.

Code of Federal Regulations. Washington, DC: Office of Federal Regulations, National Archives and Records Service, General Services Administration, published as needed.

Cressey, Donald R., and David A. Ward, *Delinquency, Crime, and Social Process*. New York, NY: Harper and Row, Publishers, 1969.

Dickinson, William E., ed., *Educational Policies Reference Manual, 3rd Edition*. Evanston, IL: The Educational Policies Service of the National School Boards Association, 1975.

Digest of Education Statistics. Washington, DC: National Center for Education Statistics, 1980.

Fuller, Edgar, and James B. Pearson, eds., *Education in the States: Nationwide Developments Since 1900*. Washington, DC: NEA, 1969.

Gatti, Richard, and Daniel J. Gatti, *Encyclopedic Dictionary of School Law*. West Nyack, NY: Parker Publishing Co., Inc., 1975.

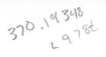

Gittell, M., and Hevesi, A., *The Politics of Urban Education*. New York, NY: Frederick A. Praeger, Publisher, 1969. 370.19 349 6447p

Goldhammer, Robert L., *Clinical Supervision: Special Methods for the Supervision of Teachers*. New York, NY: Holt, Rinehart & Winston, 1969.

Good, Carter V., ed., *Dictionary of Education, 3rd Edition*. New York, NY: McGraw-Hill Book Co., 1973.

Greene, Harry A., Albert N. Jorgensen, and J. Raymond Gerberich, *Measurement and Evaluation in the Secondary School*. New York, NY: Longmans, Green & Co., 1954.

Hall, Gene E., and Howard L. Jones, *Competency-Based Education*. Englewood Cliffs, NJ: Prentice-Hall, Inc., 1976.

Hamachek, Don E., *Human Dynamics in Psychology and Education*. Boston, MA: Allyn and Bacon, Inc., 1968.

Hamilton, K. Norman, *New Techniques for Effective School Administration*. West Nyack, NY: Parker Publishing Co., Inc., 1975.

Harris, Ben, *Supervisory Behavior in Education, 2nd Edition*. Englewood Cliffs, NJ: Prentice-Hall, Inc., 1975.

Jacobson, Paul B., James D. Logsdon, and Robert R. Wiegman, *The Principalship: New Perspectives*. Englewood Cliffs, NJ: Prentice-Hall, Inc., 1973.

Jarvis, Oscar T., and Lutian R. Wootton, *The Transitional Elementary School and Its Curriculum*. Dubuque, IA: William C. Brown Company, Publishers, 1966.

Johnston, Edgar G., Mildred Peters, and William Evraiff, *The Role of the Teacher in Guidance*. Englewood Cliffs, NJ: Prentice-Hall, Inc., 1959.

Johns, Roe L., and Alexander Kern, eds., *Alternative Programs for Financing Education*. Gainesville, FL: National Eduational Finance Project, 1972.

Johns, Roe L., and Edgar L. Morphet, *The Economics and Financing of Education*. Englewood Cliffs, NJ: Prentice-Hall, Inc., 1969.

Kindred, Leslie W., Don Bagin, and Donald R. Gallagher, *The School and Community Relations*. Englewood Cliffs, NJ: Prentice-Hall, Inc., 1976.

Mamchak, P. Susan, and Steven R. Mamchak, *Encyclopedia of School Letters*. West Nyack, NY: Parker Publishing Co., Inc., 1979.

Mamchak, P. Susan, and Steven R. Mamchak, *Handbook of Discovery Techniques in Elementary School Teaching*. West Nyack, NY: Parker Publishing Co., Inc., 1977.

Mamchak, P. Susan, and Steven R. Mamchak, *101 Pupil/Parent/Teacher Situations and How to Handle Them*. West Nyack, NY: Parker Publishing Co., Inc., 1980.

Mamchak, P. Susan, and Steven R. Mamchak, *The New Psychology of Classroom Discipline and Control*. West Nyack, NY: Parker Publishing Co., Inc., 1981.

Mamchak, P. Susan, and Steven R. Mamchak, *Personalized Behavioral Modification: Practical Techniques for Elementary Educators*. West Nyack, NY: Parker Publishing Co., Inc., 1976.

Meyer, William J., *Readings in the Psychology of Childhood and Adolescence*. Waltham, MA: Giner-Blaisdell, 1967.

Minuchin, Patricia, et al., *The Psychological Impact of School Experience*. New York, NY: Basic Books, Inc., 1969.

Morphet, Edgar L., Roe L. Johns, and Theodore L. Reller, *Educational Organization: Administration Concepts, Practices, and Issues*. Englewood Cliffs, NJ: Prentice-Hall, Inc., 1974.

Neagley, Ross L., and N. Dean Evans, *Handbook for Effective Supervision of Instruction, 3rd Edition*. Englewood Cliffs, NJ: Prentice-Hall, Inc., 1980.

NEA Handbook. Washington, DC: NEA, 1979-80.

Otto, Wayne, and Richard J. Smith, *Administering the School Reading Program*. Boston, MA: Houghton Mifflin Co., 1970.

Peltason, Jack Walter, and James MacGregor Burns, *Government by the People, 7th Edition*. Englewood Cliffs, NJ: Prentice-Hall, Inc., 1969.

Richards, Martin, *The Integration of a Child Into a Social World*. New York, NY: Cambridge University Press, 1974.

Richardson, E., *The Environment of Learning*. New York, NY: Weybright & Talley, 1967.

Robbins, Stephen P., *The Administrative Process, 2nd Edition*. Englewood Cliffs, NJ: Prentice-Hall, Inc., 1980.

Sergiovanni, Thomas J., Martin Burlingame, Fred Coombs, and Paul W. Thurston, *Educational Governance and Administration*. Englewood Cliffs, NJ: Prentice-Hall, Inc. 1980.

Sergiovanni, Thomas J., and Robert J. Starratt, *Emerging Patterns of Supervision: Human Perspective.* New York, NY: McGraw-Hill, 1971.

Shepard's Acts and Cases by Popular Names: Federal-State, Colorado Springs, CO: Shepard's, Inc., 1979.

Steenhauer, Paul D., and Quentin Rae-Grant, *Psychological Problems of the Child and His Family.* Toronto, Canada: MacMillan Co. of Canada, Ltd., 1977.

Stein, Herman D., and Richard A. Cloward, *Social Perspectives on Behavior.* New York, NY: The Free Press, 1965.

Stephens, John M., *The Psychology of Classroom Learning.* New York, NY: Holt, Rinehart and Winston, Inc., 1965.

Stradley, William E., *Administrator's Guide to an Individualized Performance Results Curriculum.* West Nyack, NY: The Center for Applied Research in Education, 1973.

Stradley, William E., and Richard D. Aspinall, *Discipline in the Junior High/ Middle School: A Handbook for Teachers, Counselors, and Administrators.* West Nyack, NY: The Center for Applied Research in Education, 1975.

Thomas, George Isiah, *Administrator's Guide to the Year-Round School.* West Nyack, NY: Parker Publishing Co., Inc., 1973.

Thompson, John Thomas, *Policymaking in American Public Education.* Englewood Cliffs, NJ: Prentice-Hall, Inc., 1976.

Thorndike, Robert L., and Elizabeth Hagen, *Measurement and Evaluation in Psychology and Education.* New York, NY: John Wiley & Sons, Inc., 1962.

U.S. Code Congressional and Administrative News. St. Paul, MN: West Publishers, published per session of Congress.

Wiles, Kimball, and John T. Lovell, *Supervision for Better Schools,* 4th Edition. Englewood Cliffs, NJ: Prentice-Hall, Inc., 1975.

Wilson, L. Craig, *School Leadership Today: Strategies for the Educator.* Boston, MA: Allyn & Bacon, Inc., 1978.